THE CRISIS OF INDIAN UNITY
1917–1940

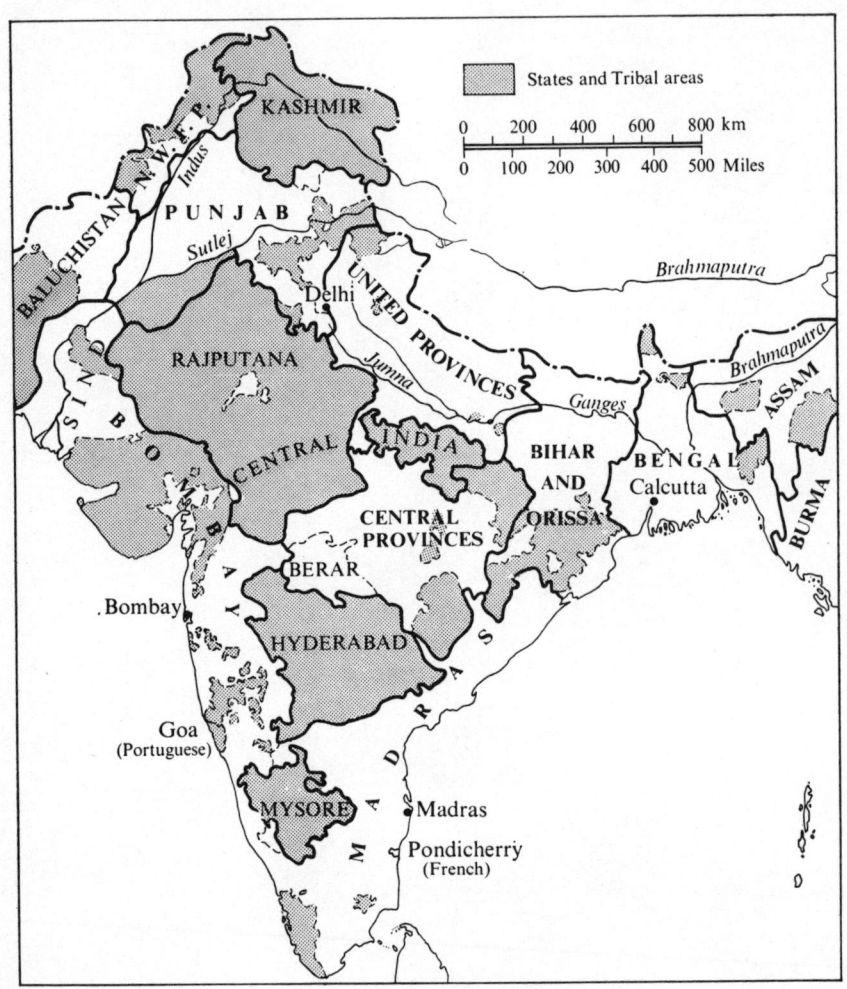

The Indian Provinces and States in 1935

THE CRISIS OF INDIAN UNITY
1917–1940

BY

R. J. MOORE

CLARENDON PRESS · OXFORD
1974

Oxford University Press, Ely House, London W. 1
GLASGOW NEW YORK TORONTO MELBOURNE WELLINGTON
CAPE TOWN IBADAN NAIROBI DAR ES SALAAM LUSAKA ADDIS ABABA
DELHI BOMBAY CALCUTTA MADRAS KARACHI LAHORE DACCA
KUALA LUMPUR SINGAPORE HONG KONG TOKYO

ISBN 0 19 821560 6

© OXFORD UNIVERSITY PRESS 1974

PRINTED IN GREAT BRITAIN BY
WILLIAM CLOWES & SONS, LIMITED, LONDON, BECCLES AND COLCHESTER

You can not achieve unity through any Conference. But we can through fighting for common causes . . .

M. K. GANDHI, 3 March 1930

If we are animated by anything, it is by the conception of India herself —India a unity . . .

RAMSAY MACDONALD, 19 January 1931

Preface

INDIA's transition from imperial subjection to freedom created the world's largest parliamentary democracy and the largest Muslim state. It brought the centuries-old dynasties of the ruling princes to an abrupt end. It presaged the liquidation of the greatest empire of modern times. Yet scholars have neglected the process of transition as a whole. In consequence of its culminating in the partition of British India and the mediatization of the princely states, they have concentrated upon the final demission of empire. The first volume of the British Government's published documents on the transfer of power begins with the Cripps mission of 1942.[1] A Chatham House essay on the achievement of independence focuses on the end-game of empire.[2] A project that the School of Oriental and African Studies organized on the partition is concerned essentially with the 1935–47 period.[3] A substantial recent analysis of independence and partition is devoted almost exclusively to the last viceroy, Lord Mountbatten.[4] No comparable works have yet appeared on the earlier phases of the transition.

Yet the reconciliation of the principles of freedom and unity was not a problem posed suddenly in the 1940s. It appeared the moment that Edwin Montagu promised India freedom in his revolutionary declaration of 1917. Montagu and Chelmsford hoped that as power was devolved by stages Muslim apartness and princely aloofness would diminish sufficiently to enable India to become a single self-governing unit. Instead, the devolution of power by stages, which was hardly avoidable in view of the complex relationship between Britain and India, steadily pushed the Indian parties apart. The very process of devolution demanded the co-operation of Indian collaborators, whose entrenchment at one stage restricted the choices open to British policy-makers at the next. The advantage of studying the earlier stages of the transition is that the ultimate partition of India is

[1] P. N. S. Mansergh and E. W. R. Lumby (eds.), *Constitutional Relations between Britain and India: Documents on the Transfer of Power, 1942–7*, vol. 1 (1970).
[2] H. R. Tinker, *Experiment with Freedom: India and Pakistan, 1947* (1967).
[3] C. H. Philips and M. D. Wainwright (eds.), *The Partition of India* (1970).
[4] H. V. Hodson, *The Great Divide: Britain—India—Pakistan* (1969).

placed in its true historical perspective: as the final resolution of the crisis of unity that was coincident with the devolutionary process.

The present study is concerned with the Indian problem at the stage when the Montagu–Chelmsford constitution was generally considered to be inadequate and all parties were devising new schemes. Its nucleus is the remarkable experiments in freedom and unity that Lord Irwin and the British Labour Government on the one side, and Gandhi and the Indian National Congress on the other, carried out between 1930 and 1932. The Round Table Conference experiment began as an attempt to make an Indian constitution at a free conference. It failed because the Congress refused to negotiate with the Raj except on a basis of guaranteed equality; because the Hindus and the Muslims could not agree over safeguards for the Muslims in a revised constitution; because the princes could not agree among themselves or with Britain about the terms upon which they would enter into a political relationship with British India; and because in 1931 it fell into the hands of a British government more concerned with British interests in India than with Indian freedom. The civil disobedience experiment was Gandhi's attempt to secure a mandate from the masses, classes, and communities that would prove the right of the Congress to rule India. It failed largely because the Muslims stood apart, and partly because in 1931 the Raj became alarmed at the danger of a *de facto* parallel administration and indulged in vigorous repression.

The analysis of the experiments affords insight into the irreducible constitutional demands of the various British and Indian parties in the comparatively fluid context of 1930–1. It suggests that the failure of the experiments was portentous. It points to the conclusion that the dualities of Indian politics—the existence of Hindu and Muslim majority areas, of British India and the princely states, and of the Congress claiming parity of status with the Raj as a parallel government—made the reconciliation of freedom and unity less likely than is usually supposed. It also reveals that the constitution to which the discussions of the early thirties gave rise, the federal constitution of 1935, exacerbated rather than mitigated the elements of intractability that bedevilled the Indian problem.

Constitutional history is unfashionable. Most historians of

modern South Asia are now concerned with analyses of the relationships between social change and political development. Probably scholarly publications will soon identify the social bases of the freedom movements during the last phase of empire. The author regards the constitutional and the socio-political as equally necessary approaches to the study of history. The opportunities offered by constitutions, as well as the interests of local societies, may contribute to organization for political ends. Max Weber observed pithily: 'Not ideas, but material and ideal interests, directly govern men's conduct. Yet very frequently the "world images" that have been created by "ideas" have, like switchmen, determined the tracks along which action has been pushed by the dynamic of interest.'[1] During the devolution of power in India the 'switchmen' were 'images' of constitutions.

Here, then, is a history of high politics to set against the histories 'from below'; a study of the politics of unity to put beside the many studies of the politics of partition.

I owe a special debt to the School of Oriental and African Studies, London, for giving me the study leave and financial support to visit India from December 1969 to April 1970. The Flinders University of South Australia and the Australian Research Grants Committee have extended substantial support to the project. I have benefited from conversations with Professor Anthony Low, and from his generosity with copies of documents. Professor L. F. Rushbrook Williams helpfully recalled events to which he was witness. Lieutenant B. B. Moonje kindly allowed me to consult his late father's papers. Among numerous considerate librarians in India and England, Miss D. G. Keswani and Dr. Richard Bingle are remembered with particular gratitude.

R. J. M.

The Flinders University of South Australia,
December 1972.

---

[1] H. H. Gerth and C. Wright Mills (eds.), *From Max Weber: Essays in Sociology* (1948), p. 280.

Contents

MAP OF INDIA IN 1935	*frontispiece*

1. **THE STRAINS OF DEVOLUTION: AUGUST 1917 – DECEMBER 1928** 1
   - I. The Raj 1
   - II. Nationalist politics 11
   - III. Muslim politics 19
   - IV. Princely politics 25
   - V. The political spectrum 33

2. **THE PROMISE OF PARTNERSHIP: DECEMBER 1928 – DECEMBER 1929** 41
   - I. The Round Table Conference initiative 41
   - II. The Dominion Status initiative 51
   - III. The campaign to prevent the declaration 59
   - IV. The debates over dominionhood 80
   - V. The Indian response 94

3. **THE FORMULA FOR ALL-INDIA FEDERATION: JANUARY 1930 – JANUARY 1931** 103
   - I. Overtures to the conference 103
   - II. The conference delegations 117
   - III. Schemes for federation 132
   - IV. Federation: consensus or chameleon? 154

4. **THE WAY OF *SATYAGRAHA*: JANUARY 1930 – AUGUST 1931** 165
   - I. 'Swaraj' and solidarity 165
   - II. The negotiation of a truce 175
   - III. The pursuit of unity and parity 186
   - IV. Gandhi's dilemma 204

5. **THE FAILURE OF CONSULTATION: JANUARY – DECEMBER 1931** 208
   - I. The ascendancy of imperialism 208

	II.	The communal impasse	218
	III.	The recoil of the princes	223
	IV.	The retreat towards 'Simonism'	232
	V.	The end of the truce	239

6. THE RESURGENCE OF REACTION:
   JANUARY 1932 – JANUARY 1933   250
   I. The reluctance to confer   250
   II. The play for sectional support   261
   III. The diplomacy of drift   270
   IV. The vestigial conference   284
   V. Unrepentant repression   288

7. THE PROBLEM OF FREEDOM
   WITH UNITY:
   JANUARY 1933 – MARCH 1940   292
   I. The failure of civil disobedience   292
   II. The failure of the Round Table Conference   296
   III. Congress unitarianism   305
   IV. Muslim separatism   309
   V. Experiment, devolution, and partition   312

BIBLIOGRAPHY   318

GLOSSARY   324

INDEX   327

CHAPTER 1

The Strains of Devolution: August 1917—December 1928

The policy of His Majesty's Government, with which the Government of India are in complete accord, is that of the increasing association of Indians in every branch of the administration and the gradual development of self-governing institutions with a view to the progressive realization of responsible government in India as an integral part of the British Empire.

EDWIN MONTAGU, 20 August 1917

I. THE RAJ

AMONG British statesmen and administrators the full significance of the Montagu declaration was slow to be generally realized and slower to be generally accepted. The declaration was something of a compromise and something of a mistake. The original draft of the announcement, prepared by Lord Chelmsford's government in 1916, provided only for 'the largest measure of Self-Government compatible with the maintenance of the supremacy of British rule'.[1] At the India Office this passage was altered, and it was presented to the Cabinet by successive secretaries of state, Austen Chamberlain (1915-17) and Edwin Montagu (1917-22), in the form: 'His Majesty's Government and the Government of India have in view the gradual development of free institutions in India with a view to ultimate self-government within the Empire.'[2] The deletion of 'compatible with the maintenance of the supremacy of British rule' made the India Office draft a much more positive avowal and cut policy away from the traditional burden of doubt about India ever being fit for self-government. However, the draft still fell far short of Montagu's eventual promise of the 'progressive realization of *responsible* government in India as an integral part of the British Empire'. To a constitutional lawyer

[1] R. Danzig, 'The Announcement of August 20th, 1917', *Journal of Asian Studies*, xxviii (1968), 20.
[2] Ibid., p. 21.

'responsible government' could only mean the responsibility of the executive to the legislative branch of government. The Montagu declaration therefore promised the Westminster model of parliamentary government to India, whereas a promise of self-government would have meant simply that Indians should govern themselves under whatever system was found suitable to Indian conditions. The declaration swept away doubts about the eventual fitness of India to receive British institutions of government.

Ironically, the draftsman of this extreme form of words was the arch-imperialist, Lord Curzon, who seems to have believed that 'responsible government' connoted the responsibility of the legislature to the electorate. His intention was to avoid the devolution of power upon lawyer legislators and to secure the eventual passing of control to the 'real India', the India of the toiling millions. The education of a mass electorate would be the task of generations. Promising the long path to responsible legislatures would forestall demands by the precocious but unrepresentative lawyer politicians for a short cut to self-government. The franchise under which the reformed legislatures operated was indeed vastly enlarged. Whereas the elected members of the old Morley–Minto legislatures had been returned by indirect election or, in the case of the Muslim and landholders' representatives, by handfuls of voters, the Government of India Act of 1919 increased the enfranchised to over five millions. This did help parties other than the largely high-caste lawyer Indian National Congress to achieve success at the 1920 elections, the prime example being the Justice or Non-Brahman party in Madras. Certainly, too, Curzon's reasoning was followed by the bureaucracy of Bengal, which saw large electorates as the means of breaking the legislative predominance of the Hindu *bhadralok* (respectable classes) of the Congress. The emergence of mass politics in Bengal enabled the more backward Muslim majority community to achieve ascendancy by the mid-twenties.

Curzon's weapon soon proved to be a two-edged sword. Montagu exploited the phrase 'responsible government' ruthlessly in order to demand that the new constitution should acknowledge the principle of executive responsibility in the provinces, whose powers should be enhanced by a large measure of decentralization. To Curzon's chagrin, the system of provincial 'dyarchy' placed the 'nation-building' departments of state in the hands of Indian ministers drawn from the legislatures. Other departments were left to British official members of the governors' councils. Certainly, the Indian ministers were selected and appointed by the governor and they were not removable by the legislature, but the pressures of popular politics induced the government to choose men who would command the confidence of a majority of the elected members. Though provincial ministers were not removable in the Westminster manner, their need for majority approval of bills ensured that they would feel responsible not only to their constituents but also to their legislatures.

Like the Montagu declaration itself the Montagu–Chelmsford scheme of devolution through decentralization, which was embodied in the Act of 1919, meant different things to different policy-makers. During the war the heads of provinces had felt that the central government was overloaded with work. The Government of India's disastrous mismanagement of the Mesopotamian expedition in 1915, over which Chamberlain, accepting ultimate responsibility, resigned, suggested that the central administration was overburdened. Administrative devolution was a cry for which a reforming secretary of state could secure universal assent from the provincial governors, however their attitudes towards Indian politicians diverged. Highly conservative provincial heads, such as Lord Pentland (Madras), Sir Michael O'Dwyer (Punjab), and Sir George Lloyd (Bombay), supported decentralization enthusiastically. A liberal reformer like Lord Willingdon (governor of Bombay, 1913–18, and later of Madras, 1919–24) welcomed it as a means of providing Indians with a fair field for their political talents. While the conservatives were prepared to accept dyarchy in order to acquire a large measure of provincial autonomy it was not to be expected that they would work it in the liberal spirit that Montagu intended.

The local variations in the operation of dyarchy were substantial. In Bengal, it enabled the governor to break the power of the Hindu nationalists and to consolidate an Anglo–Muslim raj. In Madras, Willingdon used it to push Indian responsibility to the limits of the 1919 Act. In Bombay and the United Provinces leading Indian Liberal ministers resigned in 1923 because of the persistence of official influence over the departments that had been assigned to them. In 1924 the Indian members of a committee of inquiry into the working of the Act complained that the ministers had not enjoyed real responsibility, that except in Madras the governors had not encouraged collective ministerial responsibility, and that in several provinces the two halves of the government had not met in joint session. Of course, the narrow and illiberal interpretation of the reforms by many governors was not the sole cause of the disappointing results of dyarchy. Initially, the boycott of the 'Montford' councils by the Congress and the Khilafatists, and later, the Swarajists' non-co-operation from within the councils, inhibited the effective devolution of power upon responsible Indians.

To many nationalists it seemed that the hollowness of the Montagu declaration and the illusory liberalism of the reforms were betrayed by the continuing repressiveness of the authorities in India. In 1919 and 1920 Congressmen and Khilafatists had more regard for the evidence of imperial mistrust and bad faith than for that of liberal intentions. The Rowlatt Bills (1919), which extended the wartime restrictions on individual rights, the brutal massacre at Amritsar, the widespread British sympathy for General Dyer, and Britain's failure to observe earlier promises to deal generously with the temporal possessions of the Khalifa, all these acts of imperial arrogance were deemed incompatible with a sincere concern to make India self-governing.

In fact, from 1917 the Raj was reappraising its policies towards nationalist agitation. It was moving away, though by fits and starts, from reliance upon reform and repression, the twin strands of the Morley–Minto policy, towards nationalist moderates and militants. In view of the declaration on the object of British rule it was prepared to extend the limits of tolerable dissent. In conflicts with nationalism it would play pragmatically for the high ground of moral advantage and win over those who could be coaxed or conciliated into the ways of constitutionalism. The beginnings of the new policy have been traced to the treatment of Mrs. Annie Besant between 1916 and 1918. In 1916 she was prohibited from entering Bombay because of her Home Rule agitation and 'hints of violence', and in June 1917 she was interned by the Madras government. Both actions were approved by the Government of India. After the inauguration of the age of devolution she was released, and, to the alarm of the governors of the Punjab and Madras, Chelmsford was prepared to give her an interview. Even an extremist agitator might be conciliated.[1]

The Government of India in fact rode out the non-co-operation campaign of 1920–2 by pursuing a policy of studied forbearance.[2] Gandhi was left at liberty throughout the campaign, despite the vigorous protestations of the advocates of the old policy of repression, notably Sir Reginald Craddock, once Home Member of the Government of India (1912–17) and now governor of Burma, and the governors of Bengal, Madras, Bombay, and the United Provinces. Successive viceroys, Chelmsford (1917–21) and Lord Reading (1921–6), persisted in the views to which their Home Member, Sir William Vincent, gave succinct expression in October 1920 when he replied to Craddock's demand for suppressing the non-co-operation movement and locking up the conspirators:

We are fully alive to the dangerous situation created by the acute racial feeling that prevails but we doubt whether it would be improved by repressive action on the lines you suggest. . . . I hope you will also realize our difficulties, recognizing that the gradual change from Autocratic to responsible Government cannot be effected without taking risk . . . and that they are not to be remedied by drastic repressive action alone.[3]

In January 1921 the Government of India told local governments that 'any extensive interference with the freedom of speech and liberty of the Press is inconsistent with, and would be likely to prejudice, the working of the new constitution'.[4] However, in November the non-co-operation movement degenerated into serious rioting in Bombay, Calcutta, and towns in northern India. The Government of India at once informed local governments that it was prepared to sanction their use of the Seditious Meetings Act (1907) and the Criminal Law Amendment Act (1908) to combat picketing and intimidation. The Congress leaders, C. R. Das, Motilal Nehru, and Lajpat Rai, were soon imprisoned. This was stern, but the Government of India explicitly shrank from governing 'by force naked and

---

[1] I owe the argument of this paragraph to Dr. Peter Robb.
[2] D. A. Low, 'The Government of India and the First Non-Cooperation Movement, 1920–1922', *J.A.S.* xxv (1966), 241–59.
[3] Ibid., p. 244.   [4] Ibid., p. 245.

undisguised'.[1] When the moderate supporters of the government became uneasy at the new turn of events Reading responded to an overture by the veteran Congressman, Madan Mohan Malaviya, by agreeing to meet Gandhi and other nationalist leaders at a round table conference, provided that non-co-operation was called off. Several of the provincial governors were horrified. Lloyd construed the offer as revealing that Reading was 'little short of panic stricken'.[2] There is good reason to suppose that Reading was prepared for a round table conference to consider the replacement of dyarchy by full responsible government in the provinces. A Cabinet committee composed of Montagu, Chamberlain, Curzon, Churchill, Worthington-Evans, and H. A. L. Fisher was shocked. It disregarded Montagu's sympathy for the proposed conference and demanded that Montagu instruct Reading that it would be 'impossible to recommend to Parliament, after one short year's trial, to extend the Government of India Act, 1919'.[3] The conference never took place, not because of the Cabinet committee's instructions, which arrived too late to influence the situation, but because Gandhi sought to impose conditions that the moderates as well as the government considered unacceptable. However, the incident does illustrate the extreme difficulty of the government holding to the agreed pace of devolution and pursuing policies towards agitation that would be accepted as consistent with the goal of self-government. To recover the moral advantage lost by mild repression in November 1921 the Government of India was prepared to pursue a policy of consultation and constitutional concession.

Similarly, in 1922 Reading and Montagu felt that the only adequate response to the Muslim accusation of a breach of faith in the treatment of the Khilafat was to publish the Government of India's request for the reconsideration by His Majesty's Government of its policy towards the Treaty of Sèvres.

The implications of the Montagu declaration were nowhere scrutinized more closely than in the realm of imperial relations. The declaration betokened a new status for India in the long

[1] Ibid., p. 248.
[2] I owe this quotation (Lloyd to Austen Chamberlain, 24 March 1922) to a seminar paper by Professor J. A. Gallagher.
[3] Viceroy to Sec. of State, 18 December 1921, and Sec. of State to Viceroy, 20 December 1921, in Cabinet Conclusions, 93 (21) App. II, Annexures I–II.

run and suggested the need for interim preparatory arrangements. From 1917 India was accorded membership of imperial conferences with the self-governing dominions. In 1919 she enjoyed separate representation at the Paris Peace Conference. She became a founder member of the League of Nations. In 1920 she obtained diplomatic recognition in London through the appointment of a high commissioner.

In recognition of her future national status, in 1919 India was freed of subservience to the trading interests of Britain through the grant of autonomous control over her fiscal policy. However, her currency remained securely tied to sterling. In 1926 the exchange rate was fixed at 1s. 6d. to the rupee, despite vigorous protests that India's interests demanded a lower sterling value in order to boost the rupee earnings of agricultural exports and stimulate the demand for Indian goods manufactured for the Indian market. The interests of the Indian peasant and industrialist alike were held to be postponed to those of British capital. British manufactures could enter India at a rate that stimulated demand for them, while the rupee earnings of British operations in India were exchangeable into sterling on highly favourable terms.

The Montagu declaration had promised the increasing association of Indians with the administration. The senior civil administration—the all-India services, and the élite Indian Civil Service in particular—were still overwhelmingly British in 1919. It was recruited by the secretary of state and it enjoyed terms and conditions of service laid down by Act of Parliament. The logical concomitants of self-government in India must be the Indianization of the civil administration and its effective subordination to government in India. Furthermore, a change in the function of the British element in the senior administration was implied: the role of imperial guardians must be shed and that of educators of popular representatives assumed. The point was not lost on Britons. In the early twenties resignations and premature retirements from the all-India services abounded and recruitment became difficult. Reading asked pertinently: '... for the Englishman who has to envisage Dominion Status for India ... are we quite sure that there is any real future ... out here?'[1]

[1] Marquess of Reading, *Rufus Isaacs, First Marquess of Reading*, London, 1945, p. 209.

Montagu seems to have regretted, and not without good reason, that he and Chelmsford had not provided for comprehensive administrative changes. In 1921 he wrote to Reading that 'we have got to go in for Indianization. We have got to realize that self-government does not merely mean political reform, but the substitution of an indigenous administration for a foreign administration.'[1] Reading agreed that it was useless to declare an intention to give India 'full Dominion Status [sic] and yet at the same time to hesitate to put her in the position to manage her affairs'.[2] Montagu believed that 'the work which Lord Chelmsford and I accomplished . . . is incomplete [without the] . . . subordination of the Services to the Governments in India rather than to the Secretary of State . . . [and] the general alteration of the Services from a governing caste to an executive agency'.[3] However, in 1922, when the Government of India consulted provincial governments about the question, its circular letter was leaked to the press and a storm of indignation broke. The result was Lloyd George's famous speech in defence of the great traditions and continuing relevance of the imperial services: the I.C.S. and the all-India services were the 'steel frame' of the structure of the Raj; the Montford reforms were experimental and it was impossible to foresee a time when India could dispense with the British element in the administration. Thus would Lloyd George reassure the now predominant Tory element in his coalition. In 1924, when a royal commission reported on Indianization, it recommended that recruitment should be adjusted so that the I.C.S. would be half Indian within fifteen years and the Indian police half Indian within twenty-five years. The all-India services remained the responsibility of the secretary of state. The threat to the British element was hardly immediate.

The rate of Indianizing the army was slower still. Reading expressed with vigour the relevance of the question to political advance:

I have never myself been able to understand the views of those who comfort themselves by the thought that, supposing . . . full Dominion

---

[1] Montagu to Reading, 21 July 1921, ibid.

[2] Reading to Montagu, n.d. (reply to preceding), ibid.

[3] Montagu to Sastri, 5 March 1923, in T. N. Jagadisan (ed.), *Letters of V. S. Srinivasa Sastri*, London, 1963, p. 112.

Status was given to Indians the British Army would still remain in India, controlled by India and not by the War Office at home. Who can possibly expect that such a state of things will happen? . . . I am absolutely convinced that it never could happen. Consequently, steps must be taken to enable Indians to take the high command and to direct their own Army. . . .[1]

In 1917 there were no fully commissioned Indian officers. In 1918 Indians were made eligible for the King's commission and ten places were reserved for them at Sandhurst. In 1921 the Government of India rejected a resolution of the Legislative Assembly for the accelerated Indianization of the army. In 1922 the British Government rejected a proposal of the Government of India's for complete Indianization by 1955. In 1923 it was decided to Indianize the command of a mere eight units. The next year, the commander-in-chief, Lord Rawlinson, alluded to the 'supreme difficulty' of Indianizing the army at a rate commensurate with the advance towards self-government:

In five years' time from now, instead of having eighty Indian officers with King's commissions, as we have at present, we shall have, under the most favourable circumstances, probably not more than two hundred to three hundred. If the Indian army is to be completely Indianized, we want over two thousand, and it is more than doubtful whether a sufficient number of the right type of Indian will ever come forward to supply the military requirements of the army. . . .[2]

In 1926 the Skeen (Indian Sandhurst) committee proposed that a 'substantial and progressive scheme for the Indianization of the Indian Army be adopted without delay': an increase in the Indian places at Sandhurst from ten to twenty in 1928 and the addition of four further places each year until 1933, when an Indian Sandhurst would be established with a capacity to accept thirty-three cadets a year. The army would be half-Indianized by 1952![3]

As for the Political Service, very slender provision was made for Indianization. This service, recruited from the I.C.S. and the army, was responsible for relations between the Government

[1] Reading to Montagu, 18 August 1921, Reading, op. cit., p. 334.
[2] C. H. Philips (ed.), *The Evolution of India and Pakistan, 1858–1947: Select Documents*, London, 1962, p. 530.
[3] Ibid., pp. 531–2.

of India and the princely states. Its fate must depend upon an imperial decision as to the relationship between British India and the states in a self-governing India. Here policy was most obscure. On the one hand, Montagu and Chelmsford followed Lord Minto's dictum of *laissez-faire* in relation to the constitutional development of the states. On the other, Reading as viceroy and Lord Birkenhead as secretary of state (1924–8) were to assert the Raj's unlimited 'paramountcy' over the states' internal affairs. Relations between British India and the states were thus frozen. The princes would be neither pushed into constitutional reforms that would make their states suitable partners of democratic provinces in some future all-India self-governing structure, nor given the full internal sovereignty that British India must enjoy in due course. (The obverse of this policy—the relaxation of paramountcy in return for the princes' advance towards constitutional government—would have been constructive but it was never pursued.) Policy not only dismayed the princes but mystified the nationalists, who, noting the attachment of northern Ireland to the United Kingdom under the Irish Treaty of 1921, feared the retention of princely Ulsters in a future Indian dominion.

The whole complex process of restructuring the Raj after 1917 was bound to produce apparent inconsistencies. The declaration, the reforms, and the consequential amendment of policies and practices were the work of many minds and hands. The hierarchy of empire was no monolith. There were differences in the government at home: between the elements of Lloyd George's coalition, and between the coalition's successors, the minority Labour administration of Ramsay MacDonald (1924) and Baldwin's Conservative ministry (1924–9). The latter, with Lord Birkenhead at the India Office, seemed to slide back towards the pre-Montagu era of racialism, reaction, and repression. In 1924 Birkenhead wrote to Reading: '[This Cabinet] is in my analysis under the influence of a considerable reaction from the Montagu reforms. It has a general impression that under the Coalition, and since, too much has been given away . . . through the general malaise which succeeded the War, in India, Ireland and Egypt.'[1] There were also differences between the Govern-

[1] Birkenhead to Reading, 20 November 1924, H. M. Hyde, *Lord Reading*, London, 1967, p. 382.

ment of India and the home government: in 1921 and 1922 contrasts were apparent over the Indianization of the I.C.S. and the army, and Reading was more prepared than even Montagu for a round table conference and constitutional concessions. When Montagu allowed Reading to publish the Government of India's objection to the Treaty of Sèvres there occurred a clear conflict between the senior policy-makers of the Raj and the statesmen at the helm of the empire at large. There were also differences between the central and provincial authorities, notably over the question of a round table conference in 1921–2 and the suitable treatment of non-co-operation. It is scarcely surprising that to nationalists the Raj often acquired the aspect of Janus or Machiavelli. There were diversities, inconsistencies and omissions enough to give Indians reason to wonder whether the objective avowed in 1917 remained the purpose of the Raj.

II. NATIONALIST POLITICS

During the decade following the Montagu declaration the main question facing Indian politicians was whether or not to co-operate in the working of the reforms.

The debate among the nationalists produced four main answers to the question, and politicians grouped themselves into parties adopting the various answers as the essence of their policies. A main effect of the devolutionary process was, therefore, to precipitate a series of fissures within the body politic. While the precise nature of the divisions in terms of community, caste, class, region, and political ideology is obscure, the broad lines of the fragmentation are clear.

The first casualty of the policy of the reforms was the shortlived unity of those old feuding factions, the Congress moderates and extremists. The extremists, expelled in 1907 because of their unwillingness to accept that *swaraj* (self-rule) should be pursued only by constitutional means, had returned to capture the Congress in 1916. Within a few months of the Montagu declaration the moderates were contemplating the formation of a separate party, and in June 1918, a month before the appearance of the Montford Report, a National Liberal League was set up in Bengal under the presidentship of the moderate leader, Surendranath Banerjea. While Congress condemned the Report as 'disappointing and unsatisfactory', in November 1918 the first All-India Moderates' Conference expressed its 'cordial welcome' for a 'real and substantial step' towards responsible government.[1] In December 1919, at the second Moderates' Conference, which adopted the name 'National Liberal Federation of India', Banerjea declared that under the 1919 Act 'India was at last free'. In 1920 the Liberals went to the polls for the provincial and central elections. It was largely because of them that the Raj was able to launch the reformed constitution and keep it working in spite of the non-co-operation movement. Mostly Hindus, though with some Parsis in their ranks, they were never impressive numerically. However, they included men of immense talent and practical experience: Sir C. P. Ramaswami Aiyer, Sir P. S. Sivaswamy Aiyer, and V. S. Srinivasa Sastri from Madras; Sir Chimanlal Setalvad and the Parsi Sir Cowasji Jehangir from Bombay; Sir Surendranath Banerjea from Bengal; and C. Y. Chintamani and Sir Tej Bahadur Sapru from the United Provinces.

Even before the Liberals' defection from the Congress, and while the reforms were still over the horizon, a non-Congress Hindu party appeared in south India. The extremists' creation of Home Rule Leagues in 1916 had brought fears of a Brahman political take-over in south India, and by the end of the year, a non-Brahman organization, the South Indian Liberal Federation, soon to be known as the Justice Party, appeared. Like the N.L.F. the Justice Party contested the elections in 1920, and it succeeded in dominating the Madras Legislative Council until 1926.

Though in 1918 the Congress pressed for the immediate grant of full self-government for the provinces, and in 1919 condemned the Reform Act as 'inadequate', it was nevertheless disposed to co-operate 'so as to secure an early establishment of full Responsible Government'.[2] Only in September 1920 was the policy of responsive co-operation set aside in favour of non-co-operation. The change was the result largely of the accumulating evidence of breaches of trust by Britain. The publication of the Treaty of Sèvres in May 1920 revealed the allies' intention to dismember

---

[1] S. R. Mehrotra, *India and the Commonwealth, 1885–1929*, London, 1965, pp. 151–2.
[2] Ibid., p. 110.

the Khilafat, despite pledges by Lloyd George in 1918 that Turkey should retain Constantinople, Asia Minor, and Thrace. The Hunter Committee Report (1920) on the massacre at Amritsar in 1919 appeared to whitewash the culprits, while the debates in parliament and British press commentaries had revealed substantial sympathy for General Dyer. While Gandhi was doubtless sincere in his condemnation of British policies and attitudes at this time, he recognized that they provided him with a unique opportunity to assail the Raj from high moral ground, flanked by substantial national support, both Hindu and Muslim.

During 1920 Gandhi sought to reconstruct the Congress as a truly national and revolutionary organization, a sort of alternative national government parallel to the Raj. The goal of the Congress was to be 'the attainment of *Swaraj*', which was not defined and could mean freedom either in association with or apart from Britain: 'partnership at will'.[1] The method that he advanced for the organization comprehended 'all peaceful and legitimate means'. Congress might pursue or it might reject the constitutional avenues opened by the Raj. From August 1920, when Gandhi inaugurated non-co-operation, until February 1922 when he called off the campaign, the chosen method was '*satyagraha*'. The word was coined by Gandhi and means truth-force, or soul-force, or non-violent non-co-operation, employed to convince an adversary of the truth, or consonance with the highest law of being, of one's cause. Between 1920 and 1922 Gandhi's campaign involved the boycott of British goods and institutions, chiefly councils, courts, and colleges. Gandhi announced, but then postponed, and finally cancelled, its extension to include civil disobedience, or the disobedience of laws, in particular the refusal to pay land revenue due under the land laws.

Gandhi gave to Congress a 'constitution whose working is in itself calculated to lead to Swaraj', 'a system of voluntary government'.[2] It provided for executives at central, provincial, and local government levels, a parliament, and a cabinet. India was divided on a linguistic basis into twenty-one provinces, which

[1] Ibid., pp. 114–15, 126.
[2] *Young India*, 30 March and 29 June 1921, cited in D. Rothermund, 'Constitutional Reforms versus National Agitation in India, 1900–1950', *J.A.S.* xxi (1961–2), 511 n. 34

were subdivided into units of local government from district to village level. The executives at the lowest levels were elected by primary members of Congress (persons over twenty-one years who accepted the Congress goal and method and paid four annas annual subscription). By a system of indirect election, the executives at each level elected the executive of the level above. The Provincial Congress Committees elected the three hundred members of the highest executive body, the All-India Congress Committee. The A.I.C.C. conducted the business between the annual sessions of the Congress, to which delegates were returned in the ratio of one for every 50,000 people. The A.I.C.C. appointed the Congress cabinet, the Congress Working Committee, consisting of the president, three general secretaries, two treasurers, and nine others. In Gandhi's words: 'The Working Committee is to the Congress what a Cabinet is to Parliament.'[1] Gandhi repudiated the suggestion that Congress was a political party: 'I do not consider Congress as a party organization, even as the British Parliament though it contains all parties and has one party or other dominating it, from time to time, is not a party organization.'[2] However, the majority party should control the C.W.C.: 'It cannot have two policies or two or three parties within itself.'[3] Here was a model of centralized responsible government. Gandhi was to describe the Congress as a 'parallel Government' to the Raj.[4]

In effect, Gandhi viewed the Congress as the Indian nation. Its citizens subscribed to the goal of Indian freedom and to the pursuit of peaceful and legitimate methods. But within those limits it could contain a diversity of parties. As if to emphasize the representative character of the Congress, in 1921 the C.W.C. resolved that the A.I.C.C. should reflect the communal composition of the nation. The Hindu percentage of the population was 68 and the Muslim 21. In 1920 the Hindus accounted for 82 per cent and the Muslims for 13 per cent of the A.I.C.C. By 1922 the respective figures were 71 per cent and 25 per cent.

[1] *Young India*, 29 June 1921, cited in Gopal Krishna, 'The Development of the Indian National Congress as a Mass Organization, 1918–1923', *J.A.S.* xxv (1965–6), 415.

[2] *Young India*, 28 April 1920, ibid., p. 428.

[3] *Young India*, 29 June 1921, ibid., p. 415.

[4] *Indian Round Table Conference (Second Session)*, *7 September 1931—1 December 1931*, *Proceedings*, Cd. 3997, 1932, p. 390.

During the non-co-operation movement the Congress succeeded in mobilizing widespread support. The year 1921 saw spectacular growth, and the Hindu urban dominance of the pre-Gandhi era gave way to a massive increase in the number of rural and Muslim delegates. Between 1919 and 1921 the percentage of Muslim delegates rose from 4·5 to 10·9. Between 1919 and 1922 the district as against the town membership of the A.I.C.C. changed from 41:59 to 61:39. However, despite the growth of the Congress, the government was able to win sufficient support in the provinces and at the centre to keep the new constitution working. Its success owed much to its ability to hold the moral ascendancy over the Congress. The Liberals in Bengal, the Justice Party in Madras, landlords in the U.P., and Muslims in the Punjab were impressed not only by the advantage to themselves of working the constitution but also by the reasonable and moderate strategy with which the Government of India confronted the agitation. Gandhi was left at liberty and non-interference with freedom of speech and association was maintained except in clear cases of sedition. On the other hand, towards the end of 1921 Congress demonstrations became unruly and violent.

By the end of 1921 Gandhi was no longer able to maintain the unity of his movement. In December, two former Congress presidents, Malaviya and Mrs. Besant, sought to act as intermediaries between Gandhi and the government. They found that Reading was prepared to release political prisoners and meet Gandhi at a conference, if only he would call off non-co-operation. C. R. Das, the Bengal Congress leader, and M. R. Jayakar, the Hindu communalist barrister from Bombay, favoured accepting the offer. However, Gandhi insisted on the release of Shaukat and Muhammad Ali, the Khilafat party leaders, who had been arrested for declaring that Muslims must withdraw from the British army. Gandhi was doubtless acting in the interests of Hindu–Muslim solidarity but he was censured by erstwhile followers for failing to reap the rewards of a long campaign. He lost further support when he declared his intention to inaugurate a no-tax campaign in the Bardoli taluk of Surat district, Bombay. The murmurings of discontent late in 1921 and early in 1922 portended an early return by some Congressmen to constitutionalism once the campaign was over.

The dissidents' opportunity soon came. In February 1922 a violent incident at Chauri Chaura in the U.P. persuaded Gandhi that his experiment had failed and he suspended it.

While the *satyagraha* prisoners were still in Alipore gaol during the second quarter of 1922 a sharp division was already developing over future strategy. Whereas some favoured adherence to the Gandhian boycott of the councils, others wanted to seek election and then overthrow the Montford constitution by non-co-operation from within the councils. The 'pro-changers' would refuse to accept official office, attempt to carry resolutions demanding swaraj, and vote down government measures, especially finance bills. With Gandhi serving a six-year gaol sentence, in December 1922 the pro-change leaders, Das and Motilal Nehru, proposed that the Congress adopt a policy of 'council entry'. They were defeated but on 1 January 1923 they formed the Congress–Khilafat Swaraj Party. Its goal was swaraj and its immediate object was to secure the right to frame a dominion constitution.

The formation of the Swaraj Party by such eminent Congressmen as Das in Bengal, Motilal in the U.P., and Vithalbhai Patel and N. C. Kelkar (editor of Tilak's *Kesari* and *Mahratta*) in Bombay, marked the second cleavage in the ranks of the nationalists during the post-declaration decade. However, the comprehensive national structure that Gandhi had given to the Congress enabled the Swarajists to operate from within the Congress, even though a large body of members remained opposed to council entry. The Swaraj Party developed its own constitution and held its own separate conferences. A special Congress session in September 1923 accepted that Congressmen might enter the councils, though it disclaimed that Congress was responsible for their activities. In May 1924, when Gandhi was released from gaol for health reasons, he met the Swaraj leaders. He made clear his objection to council entry as inconsistent with non-co-operation, but at the same time he accepted that the Swarajists would remain members of Congress.

The Swarajists enjoyed remarkable success in the central and provincial elections of 1923. They formed the largest party in Bengal (under Das), the Central Provinces, and in the legislative assembly (under Motilal), while they occupied an impressive number of seats in most other provinces. However, their activities during the term of the 1923–6 councils were ineffective. They were unable to bring government to a standstill by defeating money bills because the Act gave the governor-general and the governors overriding powers of certification.

Appeals were of no more use than obstruction. At the centre the Swarajists formed an alliance with the Independent Party, led by M. A. Jinnah, and in February 1924 Motilal introduced a motion embodying the 'National Demand': the revision of the 1919 Act with a view to establishing full responsible government; a representative round table conference to frame a constitution; the presentation of the new constitution to a newly elected legislature and its subsequent presentation to parliament for enactment. The demand was not full responsible government 'in a bundle' but recognition of India's right to self-determination and a round table conference to revise the constitution. The official response was the appointment of a committee to inquire into the working of the Act. The results were disappointing. In March 1925 Das offered to co-operate with government if a promise was given that swaraj would follow automatically in due course. Both these appeals fell far short of Gandhi's demand in 1920 for immediate swaraj. But both fell on deaf ears. After Das's death in June 1925 Motilal became more moderate still. In September 1925 he reiterated the National Demand but was ready to accept a representative constitutional commission in lieu of a round table conference. He also accepted that foreign affairs, defence, and relations with the princely states should remain the Raj's responsibility. On 8 March 1926, towards the end of the councils' life, an utterly frustrated Motilal staged a walk-out from the legislative assembly.

The ineffectiveness of the Swarajists' non-co-operation from within the councils prepared the way for the third split in the body politic. By the mid-twenties many high-caste Hindus were becoming alarmed at the steady accession to political power of rival groups: in Madras of the Non-Brahman Justice Party, and in the Punjab and more recently in Bengal of the Muslims. While Congress had non-co-operated, rival groups had consolidated themselves in office. In 1924 orthodox Hindu opinion had been aghast at the price in terms of political guarantees that Das had been prepared to pay for an anti-government alliance with the Muslims of Bengal. There was also evidence of a high price being asked by Muslims generally for participating in the nationalist movement. In 1924 the old Punjabi Congressman and Arya Samajist, Lajpat Rai, was provoked to extremities by the Muslim ministers' policies in his own province and by Muslim schemes for establishing their strength in Muslim majority provinces. In a series of newspaper articles he sketched a plan for the partition of the Punjab and the creation of a Muslim India and a non-Muslim India. Hindu communalism was becoming resurgent.

In December 1924 the rapidly growing Hindu Mahasabha, under the presidentship of Malaviya, appointed a committee to 'ascertain and formulate Hindu opinion on the subject of Hindu–Muslim problems in their relation to the question of further constitutional reforms'.[1] Lajpat Rai was the committee's chairman and the members included Raja Narendra Nath, C. Y. Chintamani, B. S. Moonje, M. S. Aney, N. C. Kelkar, and several others. For the first time the Mahasabha had acquired a political orientation. The organization of provincial Hindu Sabhas soon followed, and it is notable that M. R. Jayakar was recruited as president of the Bombay Sabha. In 1926 Lajpat Rai, who was also deputy leader of the Swaraj Party, defeated a move by Malaviya for the Mahasabha to contest the coming council elections. However, though the Mahasabha refrained from becoming an explicitly political organization, in 1925–6 its leaders formed a breakaway movement from the Swaraj Party.

The beginning of a movement towards a policy of Responsive Co-operation in lieu of Swarajist non-co-operation occurred in the legislatures of Bengal and the Central Provinces in July and August 1925. In October S. B. Tambe, leader of the Swarajists in the C.P., infringed Swarajist policy by accepting membership of the Executive Council. B. S. Moonje, also a C.P. Swarajist, declared that while he was still against accepting office he regarded Responsive Co-operation as the only viable alternative to Gandhian non-co-operation. Jayakar, the Bombay Swarajist leader, soon declared that if the Swarajist policy had failed the time was ripe for office acceptance. In October the Berar Swarajist Party executive pronounced for Responsive Co-operation.

[1] Quoted in Indra Prakash, *Hindu Mahasabha, Its Contribution to India's Politics*, New Delhi, 1966, p. 23.

Immediately, Kelkar wrote a letter to the press, in favour of office acceptance and against obstructionism. In November he and Jayakar resigned from the Swaraj Party. In December 1925 and January 1926 the Responsive Co-operation movement, with Malaviya, Moonje, Kelkar, and Jayakar as its leaders, gathered substantial support from Swarajists in the legislatures of Bombay and the U.P. At the 1926 elections the Swarajists lost ground almost everywhere. In Bombay and the C.P. the Responsivist Party stood against Swarajists. Elsewhere Swarajist discipline was weak and nominal Swarajists proved to be Responsivists or Hindu communalists at heart. In northern India an Independent Congress Party under Lajpat Rai and Malaviya advocated responsive co-operation. In the legislative assembly many Hindus gathered behind them and Jayakar. The Congressmen in the councils of India were arrayed in sad confusion.

By the middle of 1927 nationalist politics had plunged to a nadir. The failure of the Congress to respond to the policy of devolution by stages had resulted in a series of fissures. Groups not entirely satisfied with the strategy or leadership of the Congress had formed one by one to take advantage of the new opportunities, while satyagraha and the Swarajist techniques had proved equally unsuccessful. The devolutionary process was attended by divisions that the Congress must repair if it were to substantiate its claim to comprehend the Indian nation.

III. MUSLIM POLITICS

The process of devolution also imposed strains upon Muslim solidarity and upon Hindu–Muslim unity.

In 1916, before the advent of the Montagu declaration, Muslim politicians of many shades gathered at Lucknow under the umbrella of the All-India Muslim League and reached agreement with the Congress. The Congress–League Scheme, or Lucknow Pact, gave Muslims separate electorates in all provincial legislatures. Substantial weightage was accorded to Muslims in the Hindu majority provinces, so that in the U.P. 30 per cent of the Indian seats would be filled by separately elected Muslims, whereas Muslims accounted for only 14·3 per cent of the population. In the other minority provinces similar weightage obtained: in Bihar and Orissa 25 per cent of seats for 10·9 per cent of the population; in C.P. 15 per cent for 4·4 per cent; in Madras 15 per cent for 6·7 per cent; in Bombay 33·3 per cent for 19·8 per cent. However, in the Muslim-majority provinces of Punjab and Bengal, weightage was effectively given to the non-Muslims. In the Punjab the Muslims were 54·8 per cent of the population but secured only 50 per cent of the Indian seats, while in Bengal the 52·7 per cent Muslim population obtained only 40 per cent of the Indian seats. In the central legislature the Muslims would have one third of the elected seats though they accounted for only 24 per cent of the British Indian population. The scheme also provided other safeguards. No bill affecting a community could be passed by a legislature if three-quarters of the community's representatives opposed it. Furthermore, the scheme envisaged central and provincial governments whose members would be appointed for five years and up to one half of whom might be non-Indians. An irremovable or non-responsible executive government was therefore assumed, which, together with the European strength in the government, gave the Muslims substantial safeguards against Hindu-dominated legislatures.

The Montford reforms implemented in substance the Congress–League scheme of representation, though the proposal for a communal veto on legislation was rejected, and, of course, the principle of responsibility was adumbrated in the provinces. In 1918 the League failed to calculate at once the implications of provincial self-government for the Muslims. In its reaction to the Montford constitution it marched in step with the Congress, calling in 1918 for full self-government immediately, and agreeing in 1919 to work dyarchy in order to achieve early self-government. Caught up in the anti-British euphoria, in 1920 the League resolved that swaraj should be achieved by all legitimate and peaceful means. While the League as a body maintained its alliance with Congress during the non-co-operation movement, it became subordinate to the Khilafat Committee as the driving force in Muslim politics. Its support for the Congress–Khilafat satyagraha lost it the adherence of two of the greatest Muslim politicians of the century: Muhammad Ali Jinnah of Bombay and Mian Fazl-i-Husain of the Punjab. In Bengal, where the Muslim Leaguers led by Fazlul Huq had been excoriated by their co-religionists for selling out the community's interests in the Lucknow Pact, the League had already lost some of its following by 1920. Many Bengali Muslims preferred to cooperate with the government and the Hindu Liberals in the working of the Montford reforms. In India at large, some of the more far-sighted Muslims soon began to develop constitutional schemes at variance with those of the Congress.

In the early twenties Muslims became increasingly aware of the strengths and weaknesses of their position under the new constitution. The League's strategies, first at Lucknow and secondly in response to the reforms, had each been based upon an extreme and unreal assumption: the first, upon the continuation of representative government without responsibility, of a political order in which executive authority could be checked by a communal veto and tempered by British arbiters; the second, upon a leap to swaraj at once and India's inheritance of the constitutional structure of the Raj essentially intact. The Montford approach was different: the decentralization of the structure and the steady devolution of power upon responsible Indians in the provinces. The first step, dyarchy, gave Indian ministers the realities of power and patronage in important departments of state. In their majority provinces the Muslims soon enjoyed the fruits of devolution. With an assured 50 per cent of the elective seats in the Punjab, and with some Hindu and Sikh support, Fazl-i-Husain developed a Unionist Party of formidable strength. His success in the new politics of the Montford councils gave him a secure base from which to influence Muslim policies throughout India. More slowly, Fazlul Huq came to realize the strength that their 40 per cent of the elective seats gave to the Bengali Muslims. Decentralization, devolution, and the rights of numbers brought power to Muslim politicians in majority provinces. The lesson was clear: Muslims should press for further Muslim-majority provinces being carved out of British India, and for the steady devolution of central authority upon autonomous provinces. The corollary of the proposition was a federation of free states, rather than the perpetuation under swaraj of unitary government.

While the new Muslim strategy flowed logically from constitutional realities it was hastened and confirmed by the erosion of Hindu–Muslim agitational unity during the Congress–Khilafat non-co-operation movement. Even in 1921, the peak year of unity, the divergence of Congress and Khilafat aims and methods was already apparent from the Ali brothers' attempts to subvert the army and their insistence upon complete independence. In August the bloody rising of Muslim peasants (the Moplahs) on the Malabar coast against their Hindu landlords brought latent communal animosities to the surface all over India. When Gandhi called off non-co-operation his Muslim supporters felt deserted. Soon afterwards, the publication of Reading's plea for the revision of the treaty of Sèvres convinced many Muslims of the wisdom of switching their allegiance from Congress to the government. The defeat of the Sultan of Turkey by Ataturk in September 1922 lent an air of unreality to the Khilafat cause, which was virtually destroyed two years later when Ataturk abolished the Khilafat. From 1922 it was clear that the main result of the exacerbation of religious feelings during the non-co-operation movement was the revival of communalism. The failure of the movement bred communal rioting and rivalry. In 1923 Muslims accounted for only 3·6 per cent of the delegates to the Congress. Mass politics became characterized by movements to reconvert those who had turned from their original faith. Claims to legislative representation based upon numbers intensified attempts to fortify the faith of waverers. The alleged disbursement of patronage on communal lines in the Punjab encouraged the activities of bodies such as the Arya Samaj and the proliferation of Hindu Sabhas.

As early as December 1921 the Khilafatist president of the Muslim League, Hasrat Mohani, advocated the creation of a federation of free Indian states:

for, while the Mussalmans as a whole are in a minority in India yet nature has provided a compensation; the Mussalmans are not in a minority in all the provinces. In some provinces such as Kashmere, the Punjab, Sind, Bengal and Assam, the Mussalmans are more numerous than the Hindus. In the United States of India the Hindu majority in Madras, Bombay and the United Provinces will not be allowed to overstep the limits of moderation against the Mussalmans.[1]

This policy gained adherents steadily as attempts at Hindu–Muslim co-operation faltered. At the 1923 council elections there were many Muslims willing to stand on the Swarajist

---

[1] Cited in Mehrotra, op. cit., p. 198.

ticket, and in Bengal Das achieved an electoral alliance by promising Muslims separate electorates on the basis of population and a generous allocation of public appointments. However, Das's deal, the so-called 'Bengal Pact', failed to receive endorsement from the annual session of the Congress. The Mahasabha attacked it bitterly. During the term of the 1923–6 councils Fazlul Huq taught the Muslims of Bengal to stand on their own feet, in co-operation with the government and against the Hindus. At the centre, Jinnah led a predominantly Muslim Independent Party, which, though it supported the Swarajists' 'National Demand', always pursued a policy of responsive co-operation rather than non-co-operation from within.

In December 1924 the Muslim League met as a body separate from the Congress for the first time since 1920. At Fazl-i-Husain's invitation it assembled at Lahore. Jinnah presided. The resolutions reveal the adoption of a new strategy, born of the experience of dyarchy in Muslim-majority provinces and of growing estrangement between the communities:

(a) The existing provinces of India shall all be united under a common Government on a federal basis so that each province shall have full and complete provincial autonomy, the functions of the Central Government being confined to such matters only as are of general and common concern.
(b) Any territorial redistribution that might at any time become necessary shall not in any way affect the Muslim majority in the Punjab, Bengal and N.W.F.P.
(c) The mode of representation in the legislature and in all other elected bodies shall guarantee adequate and effective representation to minorities in every province subject, however, to the essential provision that no majority shall be reduced to a minority or even to an equality.
(d) Full religious liberty, i.e. liberty of belief, worship, observance, propaganda, association, and education shall be guaranteed to all communities.
(e) The idea of joint electorates with a specified number of seats being unacceptable to Indian Muslims on the ground of its being a fruitful source of discord, to achieve the object of effective representation of various communal groups, the representation of the latter shall continue to be by means of separate electorates as at present, provided that it shall be open to any community, at any time to abandon its separate electorates in favour of joint electorates.

(f) No bill or resolution or any part thereof affecting any community, which question is to be determined by the members of that community in the elected body concerned, shall be passed in any legislature or in any other elected body, if three-fourths of the members of that community in that particular body oppose such a bill or resolution or part thereof.[1]

In 1925 the League reiterated the strategy of federation, provincial autonomy, and separate electorates at a session that was representative of most shades of Muslim opinion: British loyalist (Sir Muhammad Shafi), nationalist (Jinnah), Khilafatist (the Ali brothers), and Muslim-majority province communalist (Sir Abdur Rahim of Bengal). The burden of the resolutions and of Rahim's presidential speech was that further constitutional advance was impossible unless the Muslim safeguard demands were met. John Coatman, the Director of Public Information in the Government of India, commented: 'It cannot be denied that the proceedings of this session of the Muslim League clearly showed the existence of basic differences between influential Muslim opinion and that of leading Hindus.... It was, in effect, a clear call to Muslims to look to their own communal interests....'[2] The following year brought the worst communal rioting of the decade. A massacre at Calcutta shocked leaders of all parties. The League met in December 1926 in the wake of the murder by a Muslim fanatic of Swami Shradhanand, a leader of the movement for the reconversion of Hindus who had become Muslims or Christians. The session paid lip-service to the need for Hindu–Muslim unity though it was unconciliatory over the question of separate electorates. However, a Muslim overture was made on 20 March 1927 at Delhi, when Jinnah presided over a meeting of Muslim members of the central legislature that offered to abandon separate electorates in favour of joint electorates if: Sind were separated from Bombay and given provincial status; the North-West Frontier Province and Baluchistan were given full provincial status; seats in provincial legislatures were reserved to communities on the basis of population, with minorities receiving weightage on a basis agreed with the Hindus; and Muslims were conceded one third of the seats at the centre. Here was an attempt to develop the federal

[1] Cited in A. Husain, *Fazl-i-Husain*, Bombay, 1946, pp. 244–5.
[2] *India in 1925–26*, Calcutta, 1926, p. 80.

and provincial autonomy strategy by expanding the number of Muslim provinces to five in return for accepting joint electorates. However, it was at once disavowed by Fazl-i-Husain and the Punjab Provincial Muslim League and by the Muslim press throughout India. In July twenty-seven members of the Punjab council signed a declaration in favour of maintaining separate electorates until Hindus and Muslims abandoned them by common consent. Moreover, the Hindu members of the central legislature responded to the Delhi proposals by demanding joint electorates throughout India while refusing to discuss the rearrangement of provinces. Their stand was endorsed by the Mahasabha and the Hindu press.

At the December 1926 elections there were few Muslims who would stand on the Swaraj ticket. In Bengal, the Punjab, and the U.P. Muslims stood first and foremost as communal representatives, and in the latter two provinces they were opposed by Hindu communalist candidates. In Bengal and the Punjab Muslim ministries were formed. Coatman describes the scene in the central assembly as members took their places early in 1927:

... nearly all the Hindu elected members of the Assembly who did not belong to the Swaraj party formed themselves into a 'Nationalist' party under the leadership of Pandit Madan Mohan Malaviya, Mr. Jayakar and Lala Lajpat Rai.... Two Hindu members and a few Mohammadans sat on the benches behind Mr. Jinnah.... The majority of Mohammadan members sat aloof in an un-organized group.... The grouping of the Legislative Assembly illustrates faithfully ... the communal antagonism which at present cuts across all other lines of political division.[1]

In the decade since the Lucknow Pact the process of devolution had taken heavy toll of Hindu–Muslim unity.

IV. PRINCELY POLITICS

Perhaps the most outstanding effect of the inauguration of the age of devolution was to emphasize the contrast between the British-administered provinces and the princely states. The Montford Report was explicit in viewing the new age as a break with the 'durbar politics' of the past and the beginning of the

[1] *India in 1926–27*, Calcutta, 1928, p. 47.

politics of popular control. Lord Minto had resolved the tension inherent in extending the principle of representation in British India, while encouraging the princes to rule according to their own traditions, by casting the reforms of 1909 in the mould of 'constitutional autocracy'. In the councils of British India the governors were then under a constitutional obligation to consult Indian advisers but not to accept the advice. In the states the princes were constrained not by law but by custom. The distinction was one of codification rather than of principle, and by 1917 several states in fact enjoyed a formal right of representation. When the Montford constitution conferred the germ of responsibility upon the provinces there appeared a clear distinction between the principles upon which the two Indias were to be governed. Moreover, as the Montagu declaration promised ultimate responsible government to India, not British India alone, there was an explicit contrast of principles between the traditional form of princely government and the form to which India was now encouraged to aspire.

Montagu and Chelmsford were clear about the implications for the states of responsible government. In the first place, the matters of common concern to the states and British India were legion. As long as the control of all-India matters (e.g. communications, customs, defence, etc.) was exercised by the Raj, the princes had little reason to complain that their interests were prejudiced by the activities of the central authority. But once British India was given a say in such matters the princes would naturally claim a similar right of consultation. Secondly, and of even greater importance, the Montford concessions to the demands of the nationalists could only encourage the spread of national and democratic sentiments, and it was natural to expect that 'hopes and aspirations may overleap frontier lines like sparks across a street'.[1] Montagu and Chelmsford dealt realistically with the first implication by accepting the demand of a group of the more advanced princes for a council or chamber in which they might meet to concert policies on matters of concern to the states as a whole, and which might represent the states' interests to the Government of India. However, Montagu and Chelmsford were virtually silent on the constitutional development of the states: 'Our business ... is to observe our treaty obligations and to

[1] *Report on Indian Constitutional Reforms*, Cd. 9109, 1918, para. 157.

refrain from interference and to protect the States from it.'[1] This was scarcely an inducement for the states to reform themselves. Rather, it encouraged the princes to retain their autocracies unsullied and place their trust in British protection against democratic infiltration. This inconsistency in the joint authors is doubtless to be explained in part by British gratitude for the princes' loyal support during the German war. With the wisdom of hindsight it is clear that the princes would have been better served by vigorous and authoritative British advice about placing their governments upon a broad basis of popular support. In 1920 the Congress was serving the princes better than the Raj, by calling upon them to share their powers with their subjects. Britain wasted her substantial leverage: the support and defence of the princes might have been made contingent upon gradual but adequate constitutional change.[2]

In the absence of firm official 'advice' about their future in a self-governing India the princes entered the age of devolution convinced of the validity of a false analogy: that if Britain were to confer free institutions upon the provinces of British India then she must liberate the states from the interference of the Crown in their internal affairs. Though originally the rights and obligations of individual princes were variously defined by treaties with the Crown, the Political Department of the Government of India had developed a policy of 'reading all treaties together'. A treaty authorizing official interference on certain grounds in one state was made the justification for similar interference in others, even where their treaties were less permissive. Usage and sufferance combined to produce the unlimited paramountcy of the Crown, which claimed to enjoy its supremacy by dint of conquest and to be the source from which the princes derived their sovereignty. However, the princes of substance regarded themselves as allies of the Crown, who, with sovereign status, had entered into treaties ceding specific powers in return for certain rights and privileges. Some forty princes had treaties with the Crown, and in general they claimed sovereign status in their internal affairs except where the treaties provided for

[1] Ibid.
[2] This point has been made by Sir Conrad Corfield, 'Some thoughts on British Policy and the Indian States, 1935–47', in C. H. Philips and M. D. Wainwright (eds.), *The Partition of India*, London, 1970, pp. 527–34, see p. 534.

the cession of specific powers. From the outset, many of the princes viewed their new chamber not only as the body that should define and protect their common interests in all-Indian affairs but also as the medium through which their demands for the limitation of paramountcy should be codified and secured.

In February 1921 the Chamber of Princes was established by royal proclamation as a consultative assembly of 120 members. It was presided over by the viceroy. It met annually in Delhi to advise the viceroy on matters of concern to the empire or to the states at large. In the viceroy's absence, a chancellor elected annually by the members presided. In practice, the chancellor acquired large powers over the convening of Chamber meetings and he headed the Standing Committee, a body of seven princes elected annually to act as the Chamber's executive. The chancellorship, the Standing Committee, and the Chamber itself were dominated by a few of the medium-sized states: Patiala (pop. 1·5m.) in the Punjab; Bikaner (·6m.), Alwar (·7m.), and Dholpur (·23m.) in Rajputana; Bhopal (·7m.) in Central India; and Kutch (·48m.) and Nawanagar (·34m.) in Western India. The Maharaja of Bikaner was chancellor from 1921 until 1926, and the Maharaja of Patiala from 1926 until 1930. Of the seventy appointments to the Standing Committee during its first decade, fifty-five were accounted for by the seven dominant states. Yet those states accounted for only 4·8m. of the 70m. states' peoples. Though they were represented in the Chamber, the medium-sized states of Bengal, Bihar, Orissa, Assam, the U.P., and Baluchistan played little part in its proceedings. Most of the great states of India—in the south Hyderabad (pop. 12·5m.), Mysore (6m.), Cochin (1m.), and Travancore (4m.), in the west Baroda (2m.) and Kolhapur (·8m.), in Rajputana Jaipur (2·3m.), Jodhpur (1·8m.), and Udaipur (1·4m.)—played no part, or only an insignificant part, in the Chamber's affairs. To the great princes parity of representation with lesser luminaries in a common assembly had few attractions. Their negotiations with the Crown could be conducted on the more dignified basis of individual relationships. Moreover, some 327 rulers of tiny states, with an aggregate population of under one million, had no representation in the Chamber, while the 127 states next largest in size (aggregate pop. 8m.) had to be content with electing twelve of their

The Strains of Devolution 29

number to sit with the 108 princes who enjoyed individual representation.

If the princes expected that their grievances against the interference of the paramount power would be dealt with expeditiously in consequence of the Montford constitutional changes then they were bound to be disappointed. In 1919 a conference of princes drew up a list of twenty-three matters of internal administration in which the British Government had interfered. The Political Department was loath to yield to pressure for the codification of its practice, and the Chamber proved to be a cumbersome body through which to co-ordinate an approach to the problem of paramountcy. In the second half of 1921 some princes, led by Bikaner, became apprehensive of the threat of nationalist agitation, and early the next year the Chamber petitioned Reading to confer with a representative gathering of all princes about their rights and obligations *vis-à-vis* the Government of India. Unless the question was settled during the transition from British to Indian control in British India, 'the position of the Princes and States will be an unenviable one and in many respects probably even worse than that of the loyalists in Ireland'.[1] Reading rejected the appeal as born of panic. With the defeat of non-co-operation in 1922 the Government of India could feel confident of its supremacy. It did, however, concede the desirability of legislation in British India to prevent the dissemination of printed matter calculated to incite disaffection against the princes. When the moderate legislative assembly opposed a bill for this purpose the viceroy certified its necessity.

The question of the princes' relationship with the Crown, which was subsumed under the concept of paramountcy, was brought to a head by Reading's treatment of the claims of the greatest of the princes, the Nizam of Hyderabad. The Nizam's treaty with the Crown (1800) guaranteed him protection against the aggression of any state or power in return for the payment of certain sums for the maintenance of troops. In 1853, when the payments were in substantial arrears, Lord Dalhousie attached the Berar areas of the Nizam's dominions to British India. The Nizam's debts were recovered from the land revenues of Berar, which was administered as part of the Central Provinces. From

[1] Bikaner's confidential note to Reading in 1922, in K. M. Panikkar, *His Highness the Maharaja of Bikaner*, London, 1937, p. 243.

time to time the Nizam petitioned the viceroy for the restitution of Berar, but always without success. The 1924 appeal was prepared with consummate care but Reading saw no reason to reverse the decisions of his predecessors. He was impressed by the reluctance of the Hindus of Berar to be placed under a Muslim dynasty: '... at least 90 per cent of the population is Hindu ... and in these days more particularly, the Hindu does not wish to place himself under the sovereignty of a Mahommadan.'[1] The timing of the Nizam's appeal was inopportune, for it coincided with the growth of communal tension in India at large. However, from the Nizam's point of view, the trend of politics in the C.P. gave a new urgency to the old grievance. The C.P. was the scene of the Swarajists' greatest electoral success in 1923. It was also a Mahasabha stronghold and was to spearhead the Responsive Co-operation movement in 1925. The Hinduization and democratization of the C.P. threatened to alienate Berar permanently from the Nizam. Indeed, Berar might provide a launching pad for aggression on the Nizam's dominions.

Reading's refusal to restore Berar provoked the Nizam to challenge the supremacy of the Crown over the administration of any of his territories. The question of restoring Berar became a test case for the interpretation of paramountcy. The Nizam claimed that as regards the internal administration of his territories he enjoyed the same status as did the Raj in the internal administration of British India, and he restricted the application of paramountcy to the realm of external affairs:

Save and except matters relating to foreign powers and policies, the Nizams of Hyderabad have been independent in the internal affairs of their State just as much as the British Government in British India. With the reservation mentioned by me, the two parties have on all occasions acted with complete freedom and independence in all inter-Governmental questions that naturally arise from time to time between neighbours. Now, the Berar question is not and cannot be covered by that reservation. No foreign power or policy is concerned or involved in its examination, and thus the subject comes to be a controversy between the two Governments that stand on the same plane without any limitations or subordination of one to the other.[2]

[1] Reading, op. cit., p. 317.
[2] In *Report of the Indian States (Butler) Committee, 1928–29*, Cd. 3302, 1929, p. 56.

The Nizam called for the submission of the Berar question to an independent commission of inquiry, such as might be appointed to arbitrate on the competing claims of two sovereign national authorities. Reading, a former Lord Chief Justice, corresponded with the secretary of state, Lord Birkenhead, a former Lord Chancellor. The Nizam could have encountered no more formidable legal adversaries than were provided by this extraordinary conjunction of juristic talents. Reading was taken aback by the 'claim to absolute equality with the British government except in foreign affairs', which Birkenhead believed 'demands immediate refutation'.[1] In reply to the Nizam, Reading produced and Birkenhead approved a definitive statement of the doctrine of paramountcy. When it was issued it became Reading's last major official action as viceroy:

> The Sovereignty of the British Crown is supreme in India, and therefore no Ruler of an Indian State can justifiably claim to negotiate with the British Government on an equal footing. Its supremacy is not based only upon treaties and engagements, but exists independently of them and, quite apart from its prerogative in matters relating to foreign powers and policies, it is the right and duty of the British Government, while scrupulously respecting all treaties and engagements with the Indian States, to preserve peace and good order throughout India. . . . The right of the British Government to intervene in the internal affairs of Indian States is [an] instance of the consequences necessarily involved in the supremacy of the British Crown. . . . The internal, no less than the external, security which the Ruling Princes enjoy is due ultimately to the protecting power of the British Government. . . .

As for the Nizam's request for an independent inquiry into Berar, Reading ruled:

> It is the right and privilege of the Paramount Power to decide all disputes that may arise between States, or between one of the States and itself, and even though a Court of Arbitration may be appointed in certain cases, its function is merely to offer independent advice to the Government of India, with whom the decision rests.[2]

Though the viceroy might, if he chose, appoint tribunals on states' cases, he was neither obliged to do so nor to accept any

[1] Reading, op. cit., pp. 318–19.   [2] *Butler Report*, pp. 56–7.

advice that they might proffer. It would be difficult to imagine a more absolute rebuttal of the Nizam's claim or a stronger declaration of the absolutism of the paramount power.

Reading's statement on paramountcy alarmed the princes at large. They found Reading's successor, Lord Irwin (April 1926 —April 1931), more receptive, and he agreed to meet a representative group of princes informally in May 1927. The princes prepared an *aide-mémoire* in which they expressed anxiety, first, at the paramount power's encroachments, under cover of 'political practice', upon their individual treaty rights; and secondly, at the uncertainty regarding their future relations with a self-governing British India. The two issues were related, for the unlimited exercise of paramountcy by the Political Department conjured up the spectre of a future in which the states would fall before the bureaucratic domination of a democratic British India. The princes 'asked for the appointment of a special committee to examine the relationship existing between themselves and the paramount power and to suggest means for securing effective consultation and co-operation between British India and the Indian States, and for the settlement of differences'.[1] In December 1927 the Indian States Committee was set up under the chairmanship of Sir Harcourt Butler. The Standing Committee established a Special Organization to prepare a case for submission to the Butler Committee and briefed Sir Leslie Scott, K.C. (for a fee of Rs. 1,500,000). Some three-quarters of the states individually represented in the Chamber associated themselves with the operations of the Special Organization, of which Colonel K. N. Haksar, K. M. Panikkar, and Professor L. F. Rushbrook Williams were leading members. However, the great states—Hyderabad, Mysore, Baroda, and Travancore—and Cochin, Rampur, Junagadh, and some of the Kathiawar states placed their cases before the Committee independently. Scott and four other British constitutional lawyers produced an opinion that Reading's doctrine of unlimited paramountcy was false: the proper relations between Britain and the states were governed by contracts in the form of treaties, which specified precisely the powers ceded to the Crown by sovereign princes. Counsel also argued that powers ceded to the Crown could not be transferred to any body that was not under Crown control.

[1] Ibid., p. 5.

Thus, in 1928 the Standing Committee princes sought shelter against the awesome implications of devolution in British India by appealing to a contractual interpretation of paramountcy. If their case were accepted they would at once secure immunity against the Political Department's interference in the present, and against the interference of a self-governing British India in the future. Paramountcy would become defined and non-transferable, while the obligations of the Crown to protect their Highnesses would be confirmed. Not surprisingly, five of the seven Standing Committee princes travelled to London in summer 1928 to attend Scott's presentation of their case. They waited anxiously during the following months while the Butler Committee deliberated. During that interim the politicians of British India were to foregather at an All-Parties Conference to enunciate their views of the future relations between the two Indias. Nor did the threat to the princes come only from beyond their frontiers. The appointment of the Butler Committee brought forth a demand from the All-India States' Peoples Conference, which first met at Bombay in December 1927, for 'responsible government for the people in the Indian States through representative institutions under the aegis of their Rulers'.[1] The movement was to receive impetus from the interest of some of the leading politicians of British India, among them C. Y. Chintamani and N. C. Kelkar.

V. THE POLITICAL SPECTRUM

On 8 November 1927 the secretary of state announced the appointment pursuant to the Act of 1919 of a commission to review the Montford constitution. For many Indian politicians the membership of the commission was proof positive of imperial insincerity. The Montagu declaration had made an unequivocal promise of the progressive Indianization of the administration and government of India, and during the twenties Indians had been appointed to the committees and commissions that investigated the working of dyarchy and recruitment to the civil and military services. Yet the Statutory Commission was to consist solely of seven representatives of the British parties in parliament. Whereas the Congress at once resolved to boycott the Commission, many of the Indians who had worked the reforms

[1] Cited in R. Coupland, *The Indian Problem, 1833–1935*, Oxford, 1942, p. 91.

now chose to collaborate with it. The secretary of state's announcement was to sound the depths of the cleavages caused by the strains of a decade of devolution.

The announcement had the effect of healing the divisions that had developed within the Congress since the collapse of the non-co-operation movement. No-changers, Swarajists, Responsive Co-operators, and members of the Independent Congress Party were at one in their readiness to join in the boycott. Though a section of the Mahasabha favoured collaboration, the main political leaders, Jayakar, Malaviya, and Moonje, lined up with the Congress. When many of the Bombay and U.P. members of the National Liberal Federation also joined in the boycott Hindu nationalist solidarity seemed impressive. However, divisions along caste lines remained. The Non-Brahman or Justice Party of Madras decided to co-operate with the Commission. So too did the Untouchables, who took their decision at an All-India Depressed Classes Conference in February 1928.

It seemed for a time that the appointment of the Commission might bring the Congress and the Muslim League together again on a common platform. Jinnah condemned the Commission and in December 1927 led a section of the League towards *rapprochement* with the Congress. The League held its annual session at Calcutta, the venue of the Congress session. The Congress, meeting from 26 December, resolved in favour of joint electorates with reservation of seats on a population basis in each province, provided that each community made reciprocal provisions for weightage to minorities. It agreed to the elevation of Baluchistan and the N.W.F.P. to the full status of governors' provinces and the creation of linguistic provinces, including Sind. It also accepted the 'three-fourths safeguard'. The League, meeting from 30 December, resolved to boycott the Commission. It urged the recognition of Baluchistan, the N.W.F.P., and Sind as full provinces. If that were conceded then Jinnah's League would accept joint electorates with reservation of seats on a population basis. At the centre, Muslims must have one third of the seats. However, concurrently with Jinnah's meetings, a section of the League gathered behind Shafi at Lahore to vote for co-operation with the Commission. Its position was essentially that of the Muslims of the majority provinces, Bengal and Punjab. It passed resolutions in favour of separate electorates and the recognition of the claims of Baluchistan, the N.W.F.P., and Sind. Early in 1928, as Hindu Liberal and Mahasabhite opinion in favour of the boycott grew stronger, the balance of Muslim opinion swung steadily towards co-operation. Hindu communal criticism of the Calcutta Congress resolutions confirmed the swing. There was little prospect that any but the few Muslim Congressmen and some of Jinnah's followers would reach an agreement with the Hindu boycotters.

In general, those who collaborated with the Commission were the religious minorities, who were anxious about their future in a free India, and those who had co-operated to work the Montford reforms since 1920. The former included the Muslims, the Non-Brahmans, the Untouchables, the Sikhs, the Anglo-Indians, and the Indian Christians. The latter included the majority of members in the legislatures of all provinces except the C.P.

During February and March 1928 the boycotters, styling themselves an All-Parties Conference, convened a series of meetings with the object of designing a constitution for an Indian dominion. The Conference was the nationalists' answer to a taunt of Birkenhead's that Indians were incapable of devising a constitution for themselves. It was attended by representatives of the Congress, the Responsive Co-operation, the Independent Congress, and the Liberal parties among the Hindus, and of the Congress, the Jinnah League, and the Khilafatists among the Muslims. It broke up at the end of March without having resolved the major communal questions. Though some solution to the problem of representation might have been found by reserving seats, the Mahasabha firmly opposed the Sind, Baluchistan, and N.W.F.P. demands. Electoral arrangements and the separation of Sind were referred to sub-committees. In May, when the Conference was reconvened under the chairmanship of the Muslim Congressman, Dr. M. A. Ansari, the electoral sub-committee was found to have failed in its task while the Sind sub-committee had still to report. The Conference appointed a small sub-committee to determine the principles of a constitution for a free Indian dominion and to report by August.

The All-Parties Conference Committee Report was chiefly the work of Motilal Nehru and Sapru. Commonly called the Nehru Report, it is highly significant as the first attempt of Indians to draft a constitution for a free India. It was essentially a plan by nationalist Hindus for Indians to inherit a united centralized Raj, embracing the princely states as well as the British Indian provinces. It alienated not only Jinnah's League but also the princes. Its proposals on the communal question were such as virtually to ensure that no non-Congress Muslims would subscribe to them. There were to be joint electorates everywhere and reservation of seats to Muslims only at the centre and in Muslim-minority provinces. While the Report conceded that the N.W.F.P., Sind, and Baluchistan should become full provinces the concession was vigorously opposed by the Mahasabha, and it was effectively negated by the unitary nature of the constitution. Though the Report spoke of an Indian federation it was, as Professor Coupland writes, 'dominated by the tradition of unitary government established by British rule. . . . The constitution could hardly be called federal.'[1] Decentralization of central powers was to be extended no further than in the Montford constitution, while residual powers were to remain with the centre. Furthermore, the new Indian commonwealth was to stand in the same relation to the Indian states as did the Raj. Paramountcy was, in effect, to be transferred from the Raj to the Hindu democrats of British India. The princes' devolutionary nightmare had acquired embodiment as a nationalist policy.

The Nehru Report was considered by the All-Parties Conference from 28 August at Lucknow. The Conference resolved that India should have a responsible government, 'that is to say a government in which the executive should be responsible to a popularly elected legislature', and a status no lower than that of any self-governing dominion.[2] The Conference accepted the separation of Sind with two provisos: that after inquiry the new province was found to be financially viable, and that the Hindu minority obtained the same weightage that Muslims enjoyed in Hindu-majority provinces. Furthermore, the separation was to be specifically dependent upon the establishment of the Indian dominion. The Conference also accepted the Baluchistan and N.W.F.P. demands and the principle of general electorates without reservation of seats in the Punjab. There was an immediate Muslim reaction. Shaukat Ali demanded the reservation of seats to Muslims in the Punjab and Bengal, while Muhammad Yakub —the president of the Jinnah League in 1927—complained of

[1] Ibid., p. 94.   [2] *India in 1928–29*, Calcutta, 1930, p. 31.

the treatment of Muslim claims. The Conference met again from 22 December at Calcutta, where the Jinnah League was also in session. The Jinnah League delegates did not attend the Conference until shortly before the proceedings concluded. Jinnah claimed one third of the centre seats, reservation in the Punjab and Bengal, the vesting of residual powers in the provinces, and that the separation of Sind should not depend upon the achievement of dominionhood. He pleaded his amendments in vain. Jayakar, the Conference president, rejected them as contrary to the decisions of the Conference in August and incompatible with a national constitution.

The Jinnah–Jayakar debate marked a turning-point in Hindu–Muslim negotiations for an agreed solution to the communal problem. Jinnah's demands embodied the essential principle behind the constitutional strategy that the Muslims had been developing since 1921 in order to secure their position in a free India: autonomous communal provinces within a federal structure in which the Muslims would have weighted representation. Furthermore, the redress of present anomalies, such as the separation of Sind and reforms in the N.W.F.P., should not await the achievement of Indian freedom. Jayakar, backed by the full weight of Hindu orthodoxy, and stiffened by Moonje in particular, was opposed to communal provinces and provincial autonomy as inimical to national unity. The only circumstance in which communal provinces could be conceded was if their divisive influence were counterbalanced by the unifying effect of a strong Indian government at the centre. If progressive concessions were made to the Muslims then nothing would remain of Indian unity by the time that dominionhood was achieved. If, on the other hand, immediate freedom were assured then communal provinces could be conceded safely. Here, in embryo, was the conflict between the bargaining positions that the Muslims and the Hindu communalists were henceforth to assume. The Muslims would make assurance of safeguards the condition of their support for dominionhood, while the Hindus would make dominionhood the condition of their acceptance of Muslim demands. These bargaining positions left little room for communal agreement.

Jinnah departed from the All-Parties Conference a bitter opponent of Jayakar and less hopeful than ever before of achieving a *rapprochement* with the Hindus. He is reported to have said that December 1928 marked 'the parting of the ways' with the Hindus.

Muslim opinion was virtually unanimous in its rejection of the Nehru Report, and even the old Khilafatist leaders turned against the Congress. On 31 December 1928 and 1 January 1929 there gathered at Delhi 'probably the most representative Muslim meeting ever held',[1] the All-Parties Moslem Conference. The Aga Khan presided and the prime movers were Shafi from the Punjab, Ibrahim Rahimtoolah from the Independent Party in the Legislative Assembly, A. H. Ghaznavi from Bengal, and Shafa'at Ahmad Khan from the U.P. Muhammad Ali was prominent in the discussions but Jinnah did not attend. The Conference promulgated a manifesto, in which the following demands were the most important: 'a federal system with complete autonomy and residuary powers vested in the constituent States, the Central Government having control only of such matters of common interest as may be specifically entrusted to it by the Constitution'; separate electorates and weightage on the existing basis, and 'as long as Musalmans are not satisfied that their rights and interests are adequately safeguarded in the constitution, they will in no way consent to the establishment of joint electorates, whether with or without conditions'; the three-quarters safeguard; one third of the centre seats and an 'adequate share ... in all services of the State and on all statutory self-governing bodies'; the concession of provincial status to Sind, the N.W.F.P., and Baluchistan.[2] No constitution would be acceptable unless it conformed to these requirements. Here was a decisive Muslim rejection of the Nehru Report.

In March 1929 Jinnah drafted his famous fourteen points in an effort to bring together the Shafi League, the Khilafatists, the Congress Muslims, and his own followers.[3] The points were less rigid and gave more opportunities for compromise than the Delhi resolutions. In particular, the provision for a federal constitution and provincial autonomy dropped the resolutions' insistence that no matter should be federal unless specifically

---

[1] Paper on 'The Muhammadan Situation', n.d. (probably written by J. Coatman in 1930), Reading Coll. 56 f.
[2] Philips, *Documents*, p. 234.
[3] Ibid., p. 235.

ceded by the constitution. Jinnah's points also allowed separate electorates to be abandoned by 'any community at any time', whereas the resolutions insisted upon the prior satisfaction of the Muslims that their interests were safeguarded in the constitution. In other respects Jinnah's points were essentially the same as the Delhi resolutions. Neither the Congress Muslims, who had endorsed the Nehru Report, nor the Shafi League nor the Khilafatists accepted Jinnah's points. In July the Congress Muslims seceded from the Jinnah League and formed the All-India Nationalist Muslim Party. Jinnah's standing was indeed reduced, and for several years he was to occupy an awkward middle position between the politics of nationalism and the politics of communalism. His lead had been rejected by the Muslims of the majority provinces, by the Muslim Congressmen, and, of course, by Hindu nationalists. He did continue to seek accommodation direct with Gandhi and with the Liberals, but after mid-1929 he could not be said to represent any significant body of Muslim opinion.

The Hinduization of Indian national politics was apparent during the debates of the legislative assembly in March 1929. In previous years when Motilal had reiterated the National Demand for Dominion Status and a Round Table Conference he had been supported by Muslim speakers. In 1929, first a Punjab Muslim, and then one after another of his co-religionists, including Jinnah, repudiated the Nehru Report. Only one Muslim, the Congressman T. A. Sherwani, supported Motilal.

At the end of March the Mahasabha withdrew its acceptance of the narrow concessions that the Nehru Report had allowed the Muslims. As the Muslims had rejected the condition on which communal provinces had been conceded, that is, the simultaneous establishment of a unitary dominion government, the Mahasabha chose to consider its position afresh.

In December 1928 the Congress, meeting at Calcutta, imparted a certain urgency to India's demand for a dominion constitution. The years of frustration that followed the non-co-operation movement had made the younger generation of Congressmen impatient. The older generation was smarting under the Simon Commission insult. At Madras in 1927 the Congress had resolved to seek 'complete independence' from Britain, thereby giving an interpretation to the demand for swaraj from which the absent Gandhi and the more moderate Congressmen dissented. In the Nehru Report the term 'independence' was avoided in favour of 'Dominion Status', much to the irritation of Jawaharlal and the recently formed Independence Youth League. At Calcutta Gandhi emerged from retirement to effect a compromise. The Congress avowed the objective of Dominion Status but demanded its realization within one year. If dominionhood were not conceded by 31 December 1929 then the Congress would resort to civil disobedience in order to secure complete independence.

By 1929 the Indian situation had become explosive. Congress was united on the heads of a constitution that was anathema to Indian Muslims and to the princes. A decade of devolution had, on the one hand, sharpened the conflict between the majority community in British India and the minorities, and, on the other hand, menaced the Indian states. In January 1929, when Motilal invited the princes to join in a bipartite conference with British Indian representatives they were caught between two stools: the paramountcy-claiming democrats of British India and the paramountcy-exercising British Raj.

If Britain intended to bestow responsible government upon a united India, it behoved her to reconsider the method of doing so.

CHAPTER 2

The Promise of Partnership: December 1928—December 1929

> ... I am authorized on behalf of His Majesty's Government to state clearly that in their judgement it is implicit in the declaration of 1917 that the natural issue of India's constitutional progress, as there contemplated, is the attainment of Dominion Status. . . . They will propose to invite representatives of different parties and interests in British India and representatives of the Indian States to meet them ... for the purpose of conference and discussion in regard both to the British–Indian and the all-Indian problems.
>
> LORD IRWIN, 31 October 1929

I. THE ROUND TABLE CONFERENCE INITIATIVE

LORD IRWIN, the Conservative viceroy, was no less culpable than the secretary of state, Lord Birkenhead, for the error of appointing an all-white parliamentary commission to inquire into the Indian constitution. He had reasoned falsely that if one of the major communities collaborated then communal rivalry would lead the other to follow suit. However, he had sufficient insight to realize that the consequences of his miscalculation demanded a drastic reappraisal of the situation.

By summer 1928 Irwin was at once disturbed by the apparent unity of the Hindu nationalist front and aware of certain tensions within it, particularly between the older Liberals and the younger members of the Congress who had been responsible for the 1927 'complete independence' resolution. He wrote to his friend, Geoffrey Dawson, editor of *The Times*, that the Liberals would be happy to detach themselves from the boycotters and that he would be 'glad enough to help them save their face if anything can be done by changes of form that will not affect ... the essential points of substance', that is, the Commission's inquiry.[1] When Sir Chimanlal Setalvad, the Bombay Liberal, suggested 'the lines of a possible agreement with the more reasonable boycotters',[2]

---
[1] Irwin to Dawson, 2 June 1928, Irwin Coll. (hereafter cited as I.C.), 18.
[2] Irwin to Lane Fox, 13 June 1928, I.C. 18.

Irwin recommended them to Birkenhead and requested their consideration by the Cabinet. The suggestion was to elevate the status of the Indian Central and Provincial Committees, which had been appointed from the willing Indian non-official members of the central and provincial legislatures to hear evidence in 'joint conference' with the Commission. Setalvad and Irwin envisaged amending the Royal Warrant appointing the Commission in order that the Commission might extend cooptive membership to the members of the Committees. The Central Committee should also be empowered to present a separate report to the King. Birkenhead, in Irwin's words, thought the plan 'too Bolshie to be considered', and the Conservative Cabinet rejected it unanimously.[1] Sir John Simon, the chairman of the Commission, who was in England at the time, was not consulted but his later comments reveal that he agreed with the Cabinet decision.

By early December 1928 Simon, too, was seriously worried at the low standing in India of the collaborators on the Central Committee. He suggested to Irwin that their position as against the boycotters might be strengthened by announcing that they would in due course go to England to continue their joint deliberations with the Commission. He also suggested clarifying the arrangements for the hearing of Indian views by a Joint Parliamentary Committee, which had always been regarded as the appropriate medium for the eventual consideration of any government proposals that might emanate from the Commission's report. Irwin thought Simon too sanguine of the beneficial effect of making such announcements, and that the report should be completed before the nature of the Joint Committee was indicated.

However, Simon's suggestions, an impending meeting with Simon at Calcutta, and his own mounting concern over the political situation, now led Irwin to give expression to a plan for bridging the gap between the official and the nationalist positions.

The first hint of Irwin's intention to take an initiative that would induce a thaw in the icy implacability of the nationalist opposition appears in a letter that Irwin wrote to Sir Malcolm Hailey, governor of the United Provinces, on 10 December

[1] Irwin to Lane Fox, 26 June, 20 July 1928, I.C. 18.

1928.¹ He enclosed 'a note that I have had revolving in my mind for some time and have eventually reduced to paper'. He thought that he 'might possibly throw a fly over Simon in conversation in Calcutta to see how his mind reacted to the general idea', which would require Simon's support if it were to be adopted.

Irwin's 'Note' represents a historic reappraisal of British constitutional policy in India. It took stock of nationalist politics and discerned 'a clear tendency ... to move towards the left'.² The Nehru Report had called for 'full dominion status', which had 'come to mean something indistinguishable from independence, except for the link with the Crown'. It called for popular control of all subjects, including defence, foreign affairs, and political relations with the states. At the Lucknow All-Parties Conference meeting in September the moderate or Dominion Status speakers seemed 'apologetic' and content to present dominionhood as a 'stepping stone to full independence'. Irwin attributed this 'decided impetus to a more extreme Nationalist policy' only in part to resentment against the Simon Commission. The fundamental causes were the spread of political consciousness, education, and the popular press. He did not expect that the obstacles to constitutional advance—communal tension, the princely states, and the divergence between the aims of provincial and all-India politicians—would stem the drift of the movement against British control. He envisaged the possibility of a general boycott by Hindu politicians of the Simon Commission's report and of any new constitution that was based upon it. The government would then be forced to rely 'more than is wholesome on Moslem support' and to resort to 'stern measures' to crush opposition. Irwin's stock-taking led him to the conclusion: '... we must endeavour so to change the approach to the problem as to give us some hope of getting a substantial portion of Indian political opinion to accept the degree of control that Parliament is likely to deem essential.'

Irwin drew hope from his opinion that in India 'all problems are 90% psychological and 10% rational'. The Nehru Report's demand for full Dominion Status was a worthy reply to taunting remarks that Birkenhead had made about India's reliance on

¹ Irwin to Hailey, 10 December 1928, I.C. 23.
² Note by Irwin, signed and dated December 1928, shown to Simon at Calcutta on 21 December, Simon Commission Coll., Box 34 (hereafter cited as S.C.C.).

British rule, but it did not necessarily reflect what *'might* be accepted, possibly by the majority, or at least by considerable sections, of organized political thought'. If an acceptable approach to the nationalists could be discovered, they might respond by agreeing to 'control in essential subjects'.[1] Irwin appreciated nationalist dissatisfaction with the procedure, which Britain had sketched, for the consideration by a Joint Parliamentary Committee of government proposals based on the Simon report. Assuredly Indian delegates might put their views before the Committee, but they would do so in a 'subordinate capacity'. The Committee's agenda would consist solely of official proposals for reform that Indians would have no part in framing. Irwin proposed a different procedure.

Irwin believed it a serious flaw in the existing scheme of approach that the position of the Indian states was excluded from the purview of the Commission and of the proposed Joint Committee. By the time that the Commission had finished its inquiries, the Butler Committee would have reported. Irwin envisaged that after the government had considered the Simon report, but before it placed proposals before parliament, the prime minister might, in order to secure as much assent as possible from Indian political thought, invite representatives of parliament, British India, and the states to discuss the constitutional problem together. It would be difficult for the nationalists to boycott such a meeting. As 'the discussion would not be restricted to *proposals framed on the Commission's Report*', the 'principal obstacle to the co-operation of those who have hitherto stood aside' would be removed.

Here was the embryo of the scheme for a Round Table Conference. The scheme would not only create a bridge between Britain and the Hindu nationalists but would contribute to unity between Hindu India and Muslim India, and between British India and the states. Irwin expected objections, chiefly on the ground that the proposal involved the depreciation of the value of the Commission's work. The materials before the Conference would be the Simon report, the Butler report, and 'any other

[1] Irwin's comments in his December Note suggest what he made explicit in correspondence early in 1929: that Britain could 'not carry on without introducing an element of responsibility in the Centre' (Irwin to Lane Fox, 14 February 1929, I.C. 23).

documents that either His Majesty's Government, or the Indian representatives, British Indian or States, desired to submit'. Irwin stressed that the procedure must be proposed as 'complementary to and not superseding the work of the Commission'. Still, Irwin recognized his need of Simon's help: 'If Sir John Simon and his colleagues were disposed to agree that on the long view of probable political developments some such scheme promised advantage, and saw fit to recommend something of the kind in their report, the position would be greatly simplified.'

When Irwin showed his Note to Simon at Calcutta on 21 December some comments of Hailey's were appended.[1] Hailey stressed that the status of a conference would have to be advisory rather than authoritative. While the Liberals might attend such a conference, the Swarajists might well continue to hold aloof. It would be essential to sound Indian opinion in order to avoid commitment to a scheme that might prove unacceptable. Further, Hailey regarded the Commission's support as a *sine qua non*. To gain maximum impact the conference should be held prior to the government's formulation of its views on the Simon report, and an announcement to this effect should be based upon a statement by the Commission itself.

The plan took the festivity out of Simon's Christmas. The 'kernel of the proposal', wrote Simon, was that 'the Report of the Commission, ... instead of being treated as the material out of which the British Government ... would frame the new scheme which would be put before the Joint Committee of both Houses, would be set up as a target at which "representatives of Indian political opinion" would be invited to direct their criticism'.[2] Higher authorities would reserve their judgement while the 'whole fire' was concentrated on the Commission. This was tantamount to admitting that the appointment of the Commission had been an 'error' and that the 'boycotters have won'. There was little chance of a sound 'agreed solution' emerging from a conference of Indians and British parliamentary representatives. Indeed, accommodation of the nationalist viewpoint could occur only through a dangerous drift in official policy.

During January 1929 Irwin had two interviews that confirmed his judgement that it was both possible and essential to take an

[1] Hailey's comments attached to Note, 17 December 1928.
[2] Simon's Note, 23 December 1928, marked 'shown to Viceroy', S.C.C.

initiative that would 'detach moderate opinion from the artificial anti-Government unity' that prevailed among 'Hindu politicians'.[1] In a letter to Lord Peel, who had become secretary of state when Birkenhead resigned in October, Irwin expressed the conviction that 'F. E. [Birkenhead] and the Cabinet made a mistake in refusing to permit me to make an attempt to rope in the Liberals last summer'. Interviews with the Swarajist Vithalbhai Patel, president of the Indian Legislative Assembly, and Setalvad now convinced him that a judicious approach might also secure the co-operation of the Congress moderates.

Irwin discussed with Patel the true meaning of the resolution passed by the Congress at Calcutta in December. The resolution threatened that if Dominion Status were not granted by 31 December 1929 a non-co-operation campaign to achieve complete independence would be launched. Patel reported that 'Gandhi had said to him quite categorically that he was in favour of the British connection and that he would not make difficulty about an accommodation of the Dominion Status idea by which Foreign Affairs, Political and possibly Defence should be reserved in some manner to be defined'.[2] Irwin took Patel to favour a declaration of British purpose and a meeting with Gandhi, Motilal Nehru, and Sapru. Reacting stiffly, he confided nothing of the direction of his own thoughts. He could not go behind Simon's back to negotiate with Indian leaders while the Commission was sitting. Further, 'mere assertions of goodwill, even if these were couched in the form of saying that it was the purpose of Great Britain to confer Dominion Status on India as rapidly as this could be done, would have little influence'.

Setalvad had seen Gandhi after visiting Sapru in Allahabad. He told Irwin 'very positively . . . that neither Sapru, nor Motilal, nor Gandhi, expected or wanted full Dominion Status by either the end of this year or next year or probably for many years'.[3] They would accept parliament's retention of control over Foreign Affairs, Political Relations, and Defence. Setalvad contended that what was required was for 'His Majesty's Government [to] make it plain that it was our object to lead India to Dominion Status, and that once this had been said the ways and

---

[1] Irwin to Lord Peel, 17 January 1929, I.C. 5.
[2] Note on conversation with Patel, 11 January 1929, I.C. 5.
[3] Irwin to Peel, 24 January 1929, I.C. 5.

The Promise of Partnership

means of doing so would be less intractable'. Again Irwin put the case against such an announcement, for the Simon Commission might recommend 'going back instead of forward'.

At this stage, Irwin felt that a statement of purpose would be both ineffective and inappropriate. However, he was deeply impressed by the assurances of Patel and Setalvad that for the moderates 'Dominion Status' meant a measure of central responsibility with some portfolios reserved to parliament, 'provided all this could be made to look as if it was consistent with growth towards the ideal'.[1] Here was a possible area of common ground, and an enlightened approach might enable moderate nationalists to save face and agree to explore it with the government. Together with Dawson, who was staying with him for ten days, he set to work on a revise of his December Note, which he now headed 'Memorandum for the Secretary of State for India'.[2] At some stage 'a phrase ... about Dominion Status' appeared in a draft, but, wrote Dawson, 'this we removed'.[3] On 16 February Irwin sent the Memorandum to Simon, with a covering letter.[4]

The Memorandum took account of two of Simon's original objections. First, Irwin admitted that to place the Commission's report before a Round Table Conference, prior to the government's formulation of proposals, amounted to using it as 'a cockshy for everybody to try and knock down'. The Memorandum proposed, therefore, that His Majesty's Government should place its 'provisional conclusions' before the Conference. Secondly, Irwin conceded the danger of seeking an agreed solution at a Conference composed of parliamentary representatives and Indians. For a British delegation of representative parliamentarians the Memorandum substituted 'representatives of His Majesty's Government'.

However, Irwin now swept aside Simon's December doubts about a change of procedure achieving nationalist acceptance of a reasonable solution to the constitutional problem. He claimed to have recently received 'a pretty good indication from almost every political quarter, except that of pure Independence', that

---

[1] Irwin to Lane Fox, 24 January 1929, I.C. 23.
[2] Dated February 1929, S.C.C.
[3] J. E. Wrench, *Geoffrey Dawson and Our Times*, London, 1955, p. 271.
[4] Irwin to Simon, 16 February 1929, S.C.C.

his new proposal would 'have a very good chance of yielding the result we desire'. In the confident February Memorandum he claimed that 'Gandhi, Motilal Nehru, Malaviya, Jayakar, and certainly Liberals and those who follow Jinnah, would be glad to find a way of escape from a position of which they see the dangers'.

A further change in the revise was that Irwin now favoured an early announcement of the plan for a conference. Before the summer dissolution of parliament, the prime minister, after consulting the leaders of the other parties, should announce the plan in answer to an agreed question in the House of Commons. Dawson drafted the prime minister's reply and Irwin incorporated it in the Memorandum. An early announcement would ensure that India was kept out of party politics during the May general election.

Irwin appreciated the importance of Simon endorsing the plan and addressed a strong personal appeal to him. It would be 'a very fine laurel wreath to lay at the feet of the College if you and I together could point the way to a solution of this most baffling problem'. They were both fellows of All Souls.

Simon's reaction is described by a Conservative member of the Statutory Commission, Colonel George Lane Fox, who was married to Irwin's sister: 'Your recent correspondence as to an announcement of a Conference has produced a temporary collapse of Simon, such as I have not seen before. . . . For three days everybody has been asking me whether I knew what was the matter with him, as he was so obviously not himself. . . .'[1] Simon's first response was to dash off a letter to Irwin about the centrifugal effect of an announcement upon the Commission.[2] Unanimity within the Commission would begin to seem less important than agreement between the views of individual members and Indian opinion. Next, he wrote a letter urging Irwin to let the Commission get out of India before any announcement was made.[3] Simon clearly felt that Irwin's readiness to conciliate the opponents of the Commission made the Commission's task more difficult. He thought better of the letter and held it back. Then he wrote a note to himself and sent a

[1] Lane Fox to Irwin, 28 February 1929, I.C. 23.
[2] Simon to Irwin, 22 February 1929, S.C.C.
[3] Simon to Irwin, 25 February 1929, marked 'never sent', S.C.C.

The Promise of Partnership 49

copy to Irwin.¹ This was characteristic of Simon's method, its advantage being that it seemed to give the recipient a window on his innermost thoughts. It was the device of one to whom intimacy of intellectual contact was difficult, a sort of self-defence against imagined charges of a conscious but uncontrollable remoteness.² In fact there remained recesses of reserve behind the confidences implied in Simon's notes.³ The present note showed concern that an early announcement would jeopardize the Commission's work. It would be represented as a victory for the boycotters while the Commission was still deliberating, and they would be strongly placed to sweep the report aside. The only element of concession in Simon's note was that it found 'a great deal that is attractive in Hailey's suggestion that the Report of the Commission should recommend a Conference of some sort', which was very different from an early announcement.

Irwin was 'greatly disappointed'.⁴ He chid Simon gently with trying to elevate the Commissioners to the status of 'law givers' from that of '*rapporteurs*'. Surely the announcement of a conference would help to get the Commission's report considered sensibly rather than opposed unreasonably. However, he assured Simon that he would not send the Memorandum to the secretary of state until they had discussed it together, during the Commission's visit to Delhi towards the end of March. The announcement could be delayed, but certainly not beyond the expiry of the Congress ultimatum in December.

A few days before he proceeded to Delhi, Simon sent on his mature meditations.⁵ He was 'still unconverted, though not I hope, stiff necked or obstinate'. The matter weighed heavily upon him: 'The choice of the right course at this moment may

---

¹ Simon to Irwin, 26 February 1929, and enclosure, S.C.C.
² A further advantage of the note, as opposed to the letter, was that it did not commit the writer as firmly to the opinions that it expressed. For a cautious, indecisive man, as Simon later showed himself to be, there was substantial advantage in being able to dismiss the expression of a view as simply the thoughts of the moment, or the exploration of a hypothesis.
³ What Simon really thought of Irwin's proposals is often suggested by the annotations with which he embellished them. (See, e.g., his copy of the Memorandum.) He suspected Irwin of negotiating with the boycotters and of sabotaging his Commission. (See Simon's memorandum to himself, 23 February 1929, S.C.C.) Irwin sensed this.
⁴ Irwin to Simon, 27 February, 5 March 1929, S.C.C.
⁵ Simon to Irwin, 14 March 1929, and enclosure, S.C.C.

influence the whole future development of the relations of Britain and India and alter the history of the world.' While he repeated that he was 'not . . . at all enthusiastic about the plan', and expected his colleagues to be 'strongly opposed' to it, he felt that if Irwin were determined to go ahead then 'no public purpose would be served' by his refusal to endorse it. '. . . my duty would be, with whatever secret misgivings, to acquiesce', he wrote. Then he added, 'but I could not do this behind the backs of my colleagues. It would be absolutely necessary to get their concurrence.' Simon was anything but simple.

Simon arrived in Delhi on 18 March and made out a convincing case against an early announcement. The Commission might well be split by such a course. Apart from its Liberal chairman, it was composed of two Labour members, Mr. Clement Attlee and Mr. V. Hartshorn, and four Conservatives, Viscount Burnham, Lord Strathcona, Colonel George Lane Fox, and Mr. E. C. G. Cadogan. If, as was likely, it divided along party lines then India would become an issue in British politics. Irwin reverted to Hailey's suggestion that the Commission might propose the conference. Simon 'jumped rather readily at this'.[1] Irwin noted that 'some such plan' would probably be pursued. After further discussions with Simon and his colleagues (except the diehard Lord Burnham, who had become ill and returned to England), it was agreed that Simon should take the initiative. He would write to the prime minister after the Commission had returned home but before it had completed its report. In a summary of the discussions, Irwin noted that Simon's letter on behalf of his Commission would be 'ostensibly for the purpose of satisfying themselves that Government concurred in their giving a sufficiently wide interpretation to their terms of reference to permit them to enter upon a thorough review of the states' problem'.[2] However, the letter would go on to suggest that a tripartite conference should be convened to consider constitutional proposals drafted by the government. The prime minister would send an agreeable reply and indicate that he was supported by the leaders of the other parties.

On 11 April, the day that the Commission left Delhi on its way to England, Irwin related the scheme to Dawson, with the

---

[1] Irwin to Dawson, 20 March 1929, I.C. 18.
[2] Note by Irwin, 4 April 1929, S.C.C.

comment that it gave him 'the substance of what I want'.[1] He regretted that the announcement would not precede the general election, for he had hoped to have the outgoing Tory Cabinet pledged to it. Still, Dawson had told Baldwin of the conference scheme and found him favourable. He cabled in code to Irwin: 'Solon [Baldwin] thoroughly interested, sympathises your ideas, thinks Panourgos [MacDonald] would co-operate but regards consultation Demosthenes [Simon] essential.'[2] Irwin must have felt confident that he and Baldwin could ensure Tory support. The Labour members of the Simon Commission, Attlee and Hartshorn, were sure of Ramsay MacDonald's backing. Finally, Irwin believed that he could 'trust Simon not to let the Liberals bring it into party politics'.[3] His confidence of a common party front was perhaps justified, though Simon had some misgivings about the attitude likely to be taken by the Tories, other than Baldwin.

However, by early April there were already in train events and influences that would so extend the initiative as to strain the common party front until it broke.

II. THE DOMINION STATUS INITIATIVE

On 25 February Irwin received a private letter from Sir Laurie Hammond, the governor of Assam, recounting a conversation with Sir Grimwood Mears, Chief Justice of the High Court at Allahabad.[4] Mears took a 'very gloomy view of the present trend of Indian politics' and was anxious to help find a way out of the impasse. He was on 'very intimate terms not only with Dr. Sapru ... but also with Pandit Motilal and his son, and with Malaviya and Sir Ali Imam'. He offered to 'ascertain their views and the extent to which they are prepared to go in the direction of meeting either Your Excellency or His Majesty's Government'. He was confident that his professional and personal relationship with the Indian leaders was such that 'they would all speak to me without reservation'. Irwin wrote back of the difficulty of meeting Indian leaders until Simon had reported. Mears

[1] Irwin to Dawson, 11 April 1929, I.C. 18.
[2] Dawson to Irwin, 8 April 1929 (t/g), I.C. 18. In a letter of the same date Dawson describes Baldwin as 'extraordinarily receptive' to Irwin's scheme (I.C. 18).
[3] Irwin to Dawson, 11 April 1929, I.C. 18.
[4] Hammond to Irwin, 25 February 1929, and enclosed Mears to Hammond, 25 February, I.C. 23.

expressed willingness to visit Delhi himself, on some pretext, and to tell Sapru that he would be glad to represent Sapru's views, and those of Motilal and Malaviya, to the viceroy. He believed that the Indian leaders might agree to meet the Simon Commission at a Round Table Conference in London, and there put their case for Dominion Status. He explored this possibility during the next month.

Mears had an exploratory discussion with Sapru on 12 March. Sapru promised to arrange a meeting with Motilal, Malaviya, and the Congress Muslim, Ali Imam. He would investigate whether representatives of the Dominion Status group of nationalists would be prepared to go to England 'to discuss formally with a small committee (appointed by the Cabinet) the question whether Dominion Status was not the one method with which alone India would become contented, ... whether conceding the principle of Dominion Status would not be merely carrying out what had already been promised, [and whether] as the result of a favourable discussion it was in principle conceded ... the "group" would be prepared to discuss the details'.[1] Sapru 'felt sure' that 'every representative would ... give way time and time again, if only they could secure the acknowledgement that India's future form of government would proceed along lines of Dominion Status with whatever special conditions and limitations Parliament might think fit to attach'.

A meeting between Sapru, Motilal, Ali Imam, and Mears took place at Sapru's house on 24 March. Mears asked, first, whether they would go to England to urge upon a committee appointed by the Cabinet the desirability of conceding the principle that India was to achieve freedom along the lines of Dominion Status; and secondly, if the principle were conceded, whether they would be prepared to discuss the details. While Sapru and Ali Imam answered the first question in the affirmative, Motilal 'said that Dominion Status must first be conceded as the agreed step, and the "group" should go [to England] merely to discuss details'.[2] All three leaders wished to proceed independently of the Simon Commission and would welcome an opportunity to talk with Irwin.

The meeting established that the primary concern of the

[1] Mears to Irwin, 26 March 1929, I.C. 23.
[2] Ibid.

The Promise of Partnership

moderate nationalists was to obtain an assurance of Britain's ultimate purpose. Their secondary concern was to obtain Dominion Status in a limited form at an early stage. Mears reported:

The Pandit said to me—'Assume Dominion Status to consist of 1, 2, 3, 4, 5, 6, 7, 8, 9, 10 ingredients. If in the discussion the least objection is taken to our having 2, 5 and 7, we shall acquiesce readily. Once we get Dominion Status of any quality—in however limited a degree —we shall be content to prove ourselves responsible and then readily and without argument be given other and wider powers as with the passing of time we prove ourselves capable'.... They believe that there would be an immediate and favourable national response if Dominion Status were put in the foreground. They want a decision on policy—the acknowledged aim being Dominion Status—the details being matters upon which as between India and Great Britain there would be no disagreement and no suspicion of any attempt to drive a hard bargain.

On 31 March Irwin wrote to Mears that he would be prepared to meet Sapru and Motilal if they would request an interview and tell the press that they were doing so.[1] He would agree to put their views to His Majesty's Government, but no meeting between the 'group' and the government would be possible until the Simon report had appeared. He also demanded strict secrecy about the terms under discussion. This overture was peremptorily withdrawn when, the next day, an article headlined 'Viceregal Conversations—A Possible Formula' appeared in the *Pioneer* of Allahabad.[2]

The article claimed to report discussions between Indian leaders and the viceroy; and wrote of an 'attempt to instigate, through the medium of an influential personage, negotiations between the Viceroy and the leader of the Swaraj party in order to see whether it is possible to produce an agreed solution for India's present political problems'. Irwin was said to be seeking the terms on which Indian leaders would co-operate in framing a new constitution. The leaders' reply would be 'based on a demand for the immediate recognition of Dominion Status'. This did not mean handing over all powers to India at once. The time and method of transferring powers were a question of expediency. The substantive question was one of status, which could

[1] Note by viceroy for Mears, 31 March 1929, I.C. 23.
[2] *The Pioneer*, 1 April 1929.

be conceded without altering the existing constitution, except in one respect: the passing through parliament of a single clause Bill recognizing 'India's right to Dominion Status'. The object of Indian leaders was parity with the other dominions, which should be symbolized by changing the name of the India Office to the India Department of the Dominions Office. The 'whole spirit of the Government of India' would be changed by an assurance of status.

Irwin construed the article as inspired by a 'deplorable' disclosure of the group's confidential discussions with Mears.[1] The latter's immediate reaction was to suppose that one of the group was in 'breach of the express agreement that everything said was to be a complete secret between us'.[2] A few days later, after investigating the apparent leak, Mears concluded that the *Pioneer* had merely written up what various of the moderate leaders had said to its editor, F. W. Wilson, from time to time in the past. It was the conclusion of a charitable man of goodwill.

Irwin had not concealed the Mears intervention from Simon. And now Simon suggested an arrangement that commended itself to Motilal. Irwin moved to carry it out. On 1 April he gave Mears a note to discuss with Sapru. It stressed that during his summer visit to England on half-term leave Irwin would certainly not go 'behind back of Commission'. No government would anticipate the Commission's report and no policy statement could precede it. Hence, only through Simon could an immediate contribution to a constitutional solution be made. Irwin pointed out that the Commission had now dispersed but that Sapru might well meet Simon personally and state his views. If Sapru would enter his name in the visitors' book at Viceregal Lodge he would be asked to luncheon to meet Simon secretly. Sapru agreed to sign the book at 10 a.m. on 5 April. Accordingly, he met Irwin and Simon for a long and friendly chat and put the case for an announcement of Britain's purpose.

Between December 1928, when he began planning his Round Table Conference initiative, and the following April, Irwin felt a number of objections to declaring that Britain's objective was Indian dominionhood. These were removed one by one. First, in December, he believed that the nationalists were using the

[1] Note by viceroy for Mears, 1 April 1929, I.C. 23.
[2] Mears to Irwin, 1 April 1929, I.C. 23.

The Promise of Partnership

term 'Dominion Status' to mean independence, except for the link with the Crown. By April it was clear, from his conversations with Patel and Setalvad, from Dawson's account of an interview with Motilal and from Mears's reports, that to the moderates Dominion Status meant a measure of responsibility in the central government but the reservation to British control of certain portfolios. Secondly, in January, Irwin argued that mere professions of aim could be of little help in transforming the political scene. By April it was clear that the moderates regarded a declaration of purpose as a *sine qua non*. Thirdly, he had told Mears that no policy statement could be made until the Commission had reported. The luncheon conversation with Sapru removed this objection.

Though Irwin and Simon both opposed Sapru's case for a declaration, the conversation lingered overnight in Irwin's mind. Next morning, 'inspired by our talk yesterday', he did 'what I had not done lately, . . . looked at the Governor General's Instructions'.[1] There he found: 'IX. For above all things it is Our will and pleasure that the plans laid by Our Parliament for the progressive realization of responsible government in British India as an integral part of Our Empire may come to fruition, to the end that British India may attain its due place among Our Dominions.' This, Irwin wrote to Simon, 'perhaps suggests that the respective positions in which we (jointly) and our third party found ourselves yesterday are not incapable of reconciliation'.

Almost at once Irwin took the first step towards a declaration of purpose. On 29 March Simon had completed the first draft of the letter to the prime minister in which he would suggest that his Commission should extend its inquiry to embrace the princely states, and that a 'triangular' conference be convened to consider proposals tabled by the government.[2] Irwin amended his copy of the draft in several respects and returned it to Simon.[3] The major change was the insertion of the following passage into the sentence in which Simon argued the need for the Commission to consider the position of the states in a new constitution: '. . . if the goal of British India is, as defined in His Majesty's message in 1921, to the Indian Legislatures, the attainment of

---

[1] Irwin to Simon, 6 April 1929, S.C.C.
[2] Simon to P.M., first draft of proposed letter, 29 March 1929, S.C.C.
[3] Irwin's notes attached to preceding.

that political liberty which is enjoyed by the other Dominions of the Crown. . . .' In Irwin's draft of the prime minister's reply, a tacit acknowledgement of this goal would be given. Yet it seems that Irwin was even now not fully convinced of the need for such a statement. After further discussions with Simon he was prepared to see the following 'definitely innocuous wording'[1] substituted for his proposed insertion: '. . . whatever may be the scheme which Parliament will ultimately approve for the future constitution and governance of British India. . . .' Only after he had discussed the letters with Hailey did he give further thought to the inclusion of a passage declaring Britain's purpose.

Hailey returned to India a week after Simon departed. He had been on home leave for three months. He met Irwin on 21 April, on his way back to take up duty. They discussed the plan for the exchange of letters in July and Hailey approved it warmly. An indication that he also mooted important changes is given by Irwin's request to Simon that they discuss the drafts further when Irwin arrived in England in July. As governor of the U.P. Hailey was well placed to interpret the mind of the nationalist leaders of the Allahabad Bar. He was also able to advise Irwin of the importance of the term 'Dominion Status' in the constitutional dialogue between British spokesmen and Indian nationalists.

On 8 February 1924 Hailey had made a declaration that still rankled with the Indians.[2] The occasion was the legislative assembly debate on a resolution by Diwan Bahadur Rangachariar calling for 'full self-governing Dominion Status within the British Empire', to which the Swaraj Party appended an amendment embodying the National Demand (a round table conference with power to devise a new constitution). Reading discussed with Hailey, then Home Member and leader of the House, the course that the government should pursue in the debate. Hailey was free to choose his own words, but on 7 February Reading acquainted the secretary of state that he would point out that the Act of 1919 was 'framed with a view to the progressive realization of responsible government in British India' and that 'the plan under the Act is carefully devised with the object of India's attaining,

---

[1] Simon to P.M., second draft, n.d., with covering note by Irwin marked 'Thursday' [11 April 1929], S.C.C.
[2] *Indian Legislative Assembly Debates*, vol. 4, Pt. I, p. 349.

by successive stages, full responsible self-government'.[1] Hailey stated that the demand for immediate Dominion Status was at odds with the policy of advancing by stages and that the obstacles to Dominion Status were the problems of defence, relations between British India and the states, and the position of the minorities. These problems could mean that India's status would fall short of that of the dominions. Indeed, Hailey pointed out that India had not been promised 'full self-governing Dominion Status' but simply 'responsible government', which did not preclude the retention of certain powers by parliament. Dominion Status might be a step beyond responsible government.

The Nehru Report contested Hailey's distinction by referring (as Irwin himself was to do in April 1929) to the viceroy's Instrument of Instructions. Hailey noted shortly afterwards: '. . . I do not think that at the time I myself attached any great importance to this part of my argument. I was mainly concerned to emphasize the fact that, whatever the Act purported to grant to India in the future, it certainly did not contemplate the grant of Dominion Status in 1929.'[2] Nevertheless, the declaration did, as Irwin came to realize, raise the question whether Britain's purpose was not 'to create a political entity in India that will permanently occupy a subordinate position in an Empire of white nations'.[3]

In April 1929 Irwin referred to his Home Department three questions associated with Dominion Status: '(a) what it would mean in practice as applied to India; (b) how far any undertaking has been given to work up to it; (c) how far Indian opinion has demanded it'.[4] In June the Special Branch of the Home Department reported that 'no explicit undertaking has hitherto been given by Parliament that it has accepted Dominion Status (in the sense in which that status is enjoyed by Canada, Australia and South Africa) as the goal of its policy for India or for British India'. The distinction between responsible government and Dominion Status was that whereas the former term referred to 'the system of government set up in the country', the latter concerned 'the "status" of the country in international

[1] Viceroy to Sec. of S., 7 February 1924, Cabinet Memoranda, 1924, no. 91.
[2] Hailey's memorandum of 27 October 1928, Hailey Coll. 30.
[3] Irwin to Lord Linlithgow, 31 December 1929, I.C. 18.
[4] 'Dominion Status and Responsible Government', 4 June 1929, Government of India Home Dept., Special Branch, Reforms Note 100.

and Inter-Imperial relationships'. In the years after 1917 the Imperial Government had, by giving India representation at international and imperial conferences, consistently accepted Dominion Status as 'the goal of its policy'. Dominion Status and responsible government were 'two possible parallel policies, closely connected with each other, and likely in their consummation to coalesce':

... the difficulty of accepting Dominion Status as the goal for British policy may be little, if at all, greater than the difficulty involved when Responsible Government was adopted as the declared policy of Parliament; and the connection between the two may be found to be so intimate that the final consummation of full Responsible Government may automatically involve the realization of Dominion Status.

However, 'in view of the international status of India, Dominion Status could no longer be a policy applicable to British India alone. If ever the policy comes to maturity, the Dominion will be the Dominion of India and not of British India'. The settlement of the relationship between British India and the states was essential to the achievement of Dominion Status.

While the Special Branch was preparing this advice, Irwin had a long and useful talk with Jinnah that probably reinforced his inclination to act upon it.

Jinnah spoke of an anxiety among nationalist leaders to co-operate with the government and proposed that the Simon report should be discussed at a Round Table Conference. Indians would feel that a conference would give them 'an effective share' in making the constitution and most Congressmen would agree to participate.[1] Irwin reported the interview to Dawson and Simon but stressed that the tripartite nature of the conference was not discussed. Though Irwin made no mention in his letters of any discussion of a policy declaration it is difficult to believe that Jinnah had not pressed him for a declaration of purpose. A letter that Jinnah wrote to Ramsay MacDonald, the Labour prime minister, shortly afterwards shows the importance that he attached to a declaration. He argued that India had 'lost her faith in the word of Great Britain' and that the 'first and foremost' need was to restore it.[2] He stressed that Hailey's 1924 speech

[1] Irwin to Simon, 30 May 1929, S.C.C.
[2] Jinnah to MacDonald, 19 June 1929, cited in M. H. Saiyid, *Muhammad Ali Jinnah: A Political Study*, Lahore, 1962, pp. 201–9.

had seemed to repudiate the goal of Dominion Status: 'I would most earnestly urge upon you at this moment to persuade His Majesty's Government without delay to make a declaration that Great Britain is unequivocally pledged to the policy of granting to India full responsible government with Dominion Status.'

Now fully aware of the views of moderate Hindu and Muslim nationalists, and fully briefed by his constitutional advisers, Irwin met Hailey at Simla a few days before he sailed for England. He also saw Sir Geoffrey de Montmorency, governor of the Punjab. The Simla discussions are not recorded but their content may be deduced from the documents that Irwin laid before MacDonald and the secretary of state, Wedgwood Benn, when he met them in mid-July.

Irwin showed Benn drafts of the proposed exchange of letters. Simon's letter was substantially in the form agreed by Simon and Irwin in April.[1] It made no reference to Dominion Status and included Irwin's 'innocuous wording' of 11 April. However, the prime minister's reply now contained a long passage, written by Hailey, in which Britain's purpose was discussed and avowed explicitly.[2] The key sentence read: 'It is the definite policy of His Majesty's Government that India shall, through the realization of full responsible government, be enabled to obtain in due season recognition as a self-governing Dominion.' Hailey, whose speech of 1924 had caused so much mistrust, was a prime mover in the preparation of the declaration that was now intended to remove suspicion and create goodwill.

III. THE CAMPAIGN TO PREVENT THE DECLARATION

Irwin found MacDonald and Benn receptive to his scheme. Benn was new to Indian affairs, but MacDonald had visited India twice and written two books about Indian politics. A year earlier he had looked forward to the creation of an Indian dominion 'within a period of a few months'.[3] It was now arranged for viceroy and secretary of state to discuss the draft correspondence

[1] Copy headed '3rd draft. Revise incorporating Viceroy's suggestions', 24 June 1929, S.C.C.
[2] Copy headed '4th draft. Given me by Irwin on July 18, 1929', signed 'I. 23.5.29'; with separate interpolation 'A', sent by Irwin to Simon with covering explanation of provenance, 18 July 1929; S.C.C.
[3] Mehrotra, *India and the Commonwealth*, p. 140.

with Simon on 18 July. That was the first occasion on which Simon saw Hailey's extensive interpolation.

Simon circulated to his colleagues a note of the meeting with Irwin and Benn, together with the draft of his letter to the prime minister.[1] The note made much of the argument that the appearance of the Butler Report in March, and the princes' growing awareness of the imminence of constitutional reforms, made necessary, first, the extension of the Commission's inquiry to include relations between the states and British India; and secondly, a procedure through which the states might express their views. Simon emphasized that the proposed tripartite conference would consider not the Commission's report but government proposals based on the report. He also pointed out that before replying to his letter, the prime minister would 'take into consultation the Leaders of the other Parties'. The reply (which was not circulated in draft to the Commission) would be 'the result of an agreement between all parties'. This, Simon noted, 'seems to me important'.

The Commission approved of the draft of Simon's letter on 23 July. Two days later Irwin described the plan to the Cabinet, which accepted that the prime minister's reply should contain a statement that Britain's aim was to help India achieve Dominion Status by stages, and agreed that after the Commission had reported the government should draft proposals for consideration by a tripartite conference.

Simon met Benn again on 26 July and the next day Irwin joined them for further informal discussions on the drafts. The main changes to the drafts at this stage were to shorten and somewhat weaken Hailey's interpolation.[2] The key sentence on Dominion Status became: 'His Majesty's Government regard it as implicit in this [the 1917] statement of policy that India should, through the realization of responsible government, be enabled to obtain in due season the full status of a self-governing Dominion. . . .' Simon joined freely in the redrafting of the declaration. For this reason Irwin and Benn received the impression that he had no objection to the declaration being made, though of course they knew that he was acting in his individual capacity and that the Commission had no official knowledge of

[1] 'Note by Chairman' to Commissioners, 18 July 1929, S.C.C.
[2] P. M. to Simon, 'latest draft to be considered on Saturday 27 July', S.C.C.

the Dominion Status passage. Irwin later recalled a luncheon at which Simon had minimized the difference between responsible government and Dominion Status by likening it to the distinction between a sunflower shoot and the same plant grown to its full height. Simon later claimed that his co-operation was based upon his clear understanding that the making of the declaration depended upon the assents of the Liberal and Tory leaders being first obtained. On 1 August he left London for a holiday and remained away until 17 September. Just as the scheme had become more radical when he had left India so now, when he left London, did it become even more extreme.

The drafts, in the form that they had assumed by 27 July, were telegraphed to the acting governor-general, Lord Goschen, and sent to the prime minister. Irwin was himself quite content with them. He did what he could to 'prepare the ground, directly in one case, and through Reading in the other', for their reception by the leaders of the opposition parties, Baldwin and Lloyd George.[1] This was premature. MacDonald began to doubt whether the plan was sufficiently liberal to transform the Indian scene. His instinct was sound, for when Goschen consulted Hailey, de Montmorency, and Sir James Crerar (the Home Member of the Government of India), advice of the same tenor was proffered. Benn sent to Irwin the following note from MacDonald: 'Prime Minister is willing to sign the letter provided he is advised it will really improve the position. If it does not it will only make matters worse. I gathered from Lord Irwin that it would make a difference. A final draft for me to sign should be prepared provided the Secretary of State still thinks that it will be effective.'[2] Hailey felt that 'neither the proposed Declaration about Dominion Status nor the invitation to the Conference' was sufficiently 'full-hearted'.[3] The former did 'not convey that determination to see the status achieved which might win a good deal of sympathy in India', while the latter did 'not . . . make it clear that the whole range of subjects will be discussed (and not only the position of the Indian States etc.)'. Goschen reported that all three of his counsellors thought that

---

[1] Irwin to Goschen, 6 August 1929, I.C. 28.
[2] MacDonald to Benn, 12 August 1929, enclosed with Benn to Irwin, 14 August 1929, I.C. 28.
[3] Hailey to Irwin, 8 August 1929, I.C. 28.

it should be made clear that the conference would deal 'frankly and fully and without limitation with the entire problem'.¹

On 4 September Benn and Irwin considered MacDonald's doubts about the efficacy of the drafts. Later that day Irwin had conversations with two visitors to London who had, earlier in the year, contributed to the development of the initiative: Setalvad and Mears. Setalvad favoured 'the proposal of a free Conference after the Government had been able to consider Simon's Report, coupled with a declaration that Dominion Status was the goal towards which British policy was directed'.² When Irwin put the point about the 'Government formulating draft proposals' for the conference, Setalvad replied that it would 'spoil the effect of a free Conference' to table 'any formulation that suggested the issues were prejudged'. To do so 'would deprive the action of much of its usefulness'. Both Mears and Setalvad were confident that a liberal initiative would do 'great good'.

After a few days' reflection, Irwin intimated to Benn his view that 'we should stick to the plan already laid down, with, if you so desire, such amendments of the Prime Minister's letter as may be required (a) to make the declaration about Dominion Status more explicit, and (b) to emphasize the freedom of the Conference'.³ He sent a redraft of the prime minister's letter, in which the declaration was more 'full-blooded' and the freedom of the conference made more apparent. Britain's goal became Dominion Status 'as soon as may be', and reference to the government framing proposals for the conference was omitted. While these changes accommodated the wishes of the advisers in India and would assuage MacDonald's doubts, Irwin anticipated that Simon would resist the excision of the provision for the government to formulate proposals: '... on this point I am, as regards him, in a position of some delicacy.' Irwin had only induced Simon 'to go forward with the scheme at all by conceding the point to him' earlier in the year. However, as neither Benn nor MacDonald was similarly committed, Irwin suggested that Benn should argue the case with Simon 'on its present merits ..., reinforced by the sense of the Prime Minister's minute'.

¹ Goschen to Irwin, 14 August 1929, I.C. 28.
² Irwin to Benn, 9 Spetember 1929, I.C. 28.
³ Ibid.

The Promise of Partnership

On 17 September Irwin and Benn discussed the redraft with MacDonald, who was 'strongly of opinion that these were the only lines on which the government could profitably move'.[1] It was agreed to go ahead regardless of Simon's reaction. If Simon or his Commission objected then Simon's letter should be confined to the question of extending the Commission's terms of reference to include relations with the states, leaving the prime minister to make such observations as he chose about a conference. That day Benn telegraphed to Simon in Wales to ask him to see the prime minister.

Simon met MacDonald, Benn, and Irwin on 19 September and the fresh drafts were shown to him. The prime minister explained that in this form the drafts would be referred to the opposition party leaders for their approval. Simon expressed a wish to consult the Commission about the drafts and MacDonald assented. Later in the day MacDonald referred his draft reply formally to Simon. He sent copies of the draft for each of Simon's colleagues, together with a covering note expressing an earnest hope that the Commission would feel able to participate in the correspondence.[2] Simon distributed the drafts at once, together with drafts of his own letter. In a note to his colleagues he explained that the other party leaders were to be consulted and that the government intended to issue the declaration about Dominion Status regardless of any opinions that the Commission might advance.[3] Somewhat later, he circulated copies of a different draft of his letter.[4] This represented the form of letter that Simon believed MacDonald would expect from him if the Commission rejected the proposal for a free conference. It made no mention of a conference at all.

When the Commission met, on 24 September, it was quick to realize its dilemma over the free conference proposal. Previously, it had insisted that if its report were not to be a cockshy, the government must place a formulation before the conference. Now it saw that if it failed to agree to a free conference it would be deprived of the opportunity to propose a conference at all. It could either propose a free conference that might

[1] Benn to Simon, 17 September 1929, S.C.C.
[2] MacDonald to Simon, 19 September 1929, S.C.C.
[3] Simon's Note to Commissioners, 19 September 1929, S.C.C.
[4] S. F. Stewart to Commissioners, 21 September 1929, S.C.C.

attack the Commission's report, and thereby receive some credit for its liberality, or it could adhere to its principles and lose credit for an initiative that the government would then take. Not surprisingly the Commission agreed that Simon's letter should contain no reference to a government formulation. Its decision was eased somewhat by Simon's being able to report that MacDonald had assured him that the government 'would regard the Conference not as an organ for negotiation but as a means of ascertaining views which ought to be heard'.[1]

However, the Commission 'could not agree to any interchange of letters that would evoke [the intended] gloss on the Montagu declaration'.[2] Only the two Labour members of the Commission were prepared to condone the inclusion of the declaration in the prime minister's letter.

Simon's personal position in regard to the declaration is difficult to understand. In July he had not demurred over the Dominion Status passage. In his note to the Commission, dated 19 September, he was non-committal. It is not recorded that he spoke against the declaration when he met the Commission on 24 September. Irwin and Benn had expected him to oppose a free conference but not to object to the declaration. It is true that the declaration had become more 'full-blooded' during his summer absence, but he seems not to have opposed it when it was shown to him on 19 September. Yet six days later he told the Commission that while 'he felt it was not for the Commission to dictate future policy, ... he was disturbed at the prospect of any declaration with regard to Dominion Status being made by the Government while the Commission was sitting'.[3] His argument was that the declaration would be interpreted as a surrender to the boycotters and so prejudice the reception of the Commission's report. He had previously deployed this argument against the scheme for a free conference. It seems not inaccurate to speak of a change in Simon's attitude.

Several factors might explain the change. First, Simon may have begun to feel that he and his Commission were being treated shabbily. The government had effectively outflanked his position on the free conference. Perhaps he felt that he had

[1] Simon's dictated Note of 23 October 1929, S.C.C.
[2] Résumé of Commission's discussion on 24 September 1929, S.C.C.
[3] Continuation of preceding, 25 September 1929.

The Promise of Partnership

been gulled into co-operating with the initiative by the concession of a condition, only to find that concession later withdrawn. Secondly, he was compelled to tread warily among colleagues who included four Tories, one of them a diehard. When all four spoke out against the declaration he had to insist that it be struck out of the correspondence. Thirdly, he may have been influenced by the Liberal Party's elder statesman on Indian affairs, Lord Reading.

Simon's relationship with Reading was close and of long standing. They were of the same party and the same profession. Though their judgement of particular situations might differ they shared a world of values and ideas. They had both worked their way from quite modest backgrounds to the top of two fiercely competitive professions, law and politics. Simon's first taste of office was as solicitor-general from 1910 to 1913, when Reading was attorney-general. At Reading's invitation Simon had visited India during his old chief's viceroyalty. He had taken the chair of the Statutory Commission with Reading's full backing.

It was on 20 September that Reading received from Benn copies of the proposed correspondence.[1] The drafts were in their 'full-blooded' form. In conversation with Benn, Reading made no objection to the free conference but he expressed 'dislike' of the declaration.[2] It is certain that Reading and Simon were in communication on 23 September, the day before the Commission discussed the drafts.[3] Irwin, among others, later supposed that Simon's change of mind about the Dominion Status passage was caused by Reading having 'got at' him.

It is one thing to explain Simon's change of mind but another to explain why he did not make clear to Benn, Irwin, or MacDonald what, on 25 September, he made clear to the Commission: that he was disturbed at the prospect of any declaration being made while the Commission was sitting, even if the Commission were not associated with it. Again, it is surprising that he did not tell them of Burnham's warning, also voiced at the meeting of the Commission on 25 September, that if the government

[1] Copies of drafts in Reading Coll. (hereafter cited as 'R.C.'), 57.
[2] Benn's narrative of events leading up to the publication of letters between Simon and the P.M. and of the viceroy's statement, 4 November 1929, Cabinet Paper in I.C. 5.
[3] Note initialled 'P.S.C.', 23 September 1929, R.C. 57.

made the declaration independently he would feel free to protest in the House of Lords. Simon's failure to make the position of the Commission clear left Irwin and the government with the impression that Simon and his colleagues merely wished to dissociate themselves from the declaration, not that they wished to register a protest against its being made at all.

The truth of the matter is that Simon's own attitude was ambivalent at this stage. Though he had come to dislike the declaration, he had co-operated in drafting it and he did not feel sufficiently strongly to oppose it. He was also inhibited from outright opposition by the fact that MacDonald had undertaken to secure assents from the Tory and Liberal leaders before making any declaration. He knew of Reading's opposition and that Baldwin had been consulted. Baldwin's reply had been received on 21 September. Simon must have assumed that it was favourable to the exchange of the 'full-blooded' drafts. Otherwise there would have been no point in the draft of the prime minister's letter, claiming the assent of the opposition leaders, being discussed by the Commission on 24 September. Of course Simon knew that Lloyd George's assent had not been obtained, but he could well have assumed that the leader of some fifty-odd parliamentarians would not oppose the will of the two great parties.

By 25 September the assumed common party front, and the failure that flowed from it of Simon or the Commission to protest against the declaration, rested, in fact, upon the construction placed upon Baldwin's reaction to the proposed correspondence. On 20 September a secretary from the India Office gave the 'full-blooded' drafts to Baldwin at Bourges. A covering letter of MacDonald's explained that the drafts were to be considered by the Commission on the 24th: 'I am therefore sending these papers to you at the present stage on the supposition that the Commission will, in fact, agree to the course proposed and on the understanding that, should they fail to do so, a new situation would be created which may necessitate other treatment.'[1] In his reply, Baldwin mentioned that Irwin had discussed the scheme with him. However, he was in some difficulty, for he was unable to consult his colleagues. Peel was in the Highlands, Birkenhead and Churchill in America, Austen Chamberlain in

[1] MacDonald to Baldwin, 19 September 1929, cited in Baldwin to Snowden, 28 October 1929, S.C.C.

The Promise of Partnership

the Mediterranean, Amery in Canada, and Hailsham in the Far East. Yet he was prepared to assent to the proposed correspondence, in the terms of MacDonald's letter to him, and to do all that he could to secure his party's unanimous support. He later explained that he 'understood that the proposed declaration had the concurrence of Sir John Simon and had been arranged in consultation with him'.[1] This was not an incorrect understanding of the position as the government knew it at that stage. However, three days later, the position had changed by dint of the Commission's refusal to be associated with the declaration. The 'new situation', to which MacDonald's letter to Baldwin had adverted, now existed; and it did indeed 'necessitate other treatment'. On 25 September the Cabinet considered the situation and agreed upon the treatment. Simon's letter should suggest and MacDonald's reply accept the idea of a free conference. The Dominion Status passage would be deleted from the reply and form the basis of a viceregal statement to be issued by Irwin at the end of October, soon after his return to India.

The government did not consult Baldwin formally about the new situation. On 26 September MacDonald, somewhat carelessly and in the flurry of preparation for his imminent departure for the U.S.A., wrote to Snowden, who was to act as prime minister in his absence, that the declaration had 'already been approved by Baldwin'.[2] He was in breach of his implied agreement with Baldwin. However, as Irwin is known to have shown Baldwin drafts of his declaration, Baldwin certainly knew of the new arrangement. Like Irwin, MacDonald, and Benn, he probably believed that while the Commission did not wish to be involved in the declaration it nevertheless had no objection to the declaration being made independently. Benn later recalled that Simon 'had represented his Commission as taking up an attitude of detachment, but never one of active hostility'.[3]

In truth, Simon forebore from opposing the declaration because he believed it to have Baldwin's support, while Baldwin let the matter drift because he believed that Simon had given his tacit approval.

Before Irwin left England, he made some attempt to forestall opposition to his declaration by explaining his initiative to such

[1] Ibid.   [2] Benn's Narrative.
[3] Benn to Irwin, 14 November 1929, I.C. 5.

old and powerful Tory friends as Lord Winterton and Lord Salisbury. Winterton had twice served as Peel's under-secretary at the India Office and he talked over the declaration with his former chief. He also sent a reasoned note of protest to Irwin, who showed it to Baldwin. Irwin later reminded Baldwin, who had stayed with him in Yorkshire on 29 September, that he had told him 'quite frankly' that some of his lieutenants disliked the declaration.[1] He wrote to Hoare that he had gone over the declaration 'very carefully' with Baldwin and 'warned him in express terms' that Peel, Birkenhead, and other Tories might 'raise a row'.[2] He also acquainted Baldwin of Reading's opposition, and of Lloyd George's hope of attracting Conservative diehards to 'his Imperial flag'.

From late September Reading played a role of growing importance in the declaration drama. At the outset he interpreted the scheme for Lloyd George. It was to him that Benn gave the 'full-blooded' drafts on 20 September, and, later, the redraft of the prime minister's letter with the declaration excised. Reading secured from Benn the assent of Lloyd George to the emasculated draft. He also conveyed to Benn, on 27 September and 1 October, objections that he and his leader felt about the use of the term 'full Dominion Status' in any declaration, either in a letter from the prime minister or a viceregal statement.[3] First, they 'could not see within any measurable distance of time India being put on a footing with the other Dominions, and ... a statement now would become the text of immediate demands for its fulfilment; second, a Commission had been appointed to deal with the matter and it was not a moment, therefore, to anticipate the decisions of the Commission whose work would be rendered valueless and its report discounted in advance'.[4]

Irwin drafted his declaration early in October. The Cabinet approved it on the 7th. The next day he discussed it with Reading and accepted two changes that Reading, supported by Lloyd George, requested. The more significant altered the key sentence, which originally read: 'I am authorized on behalf of His Majesty's Government to state clearly that, in their judgement, it is impli-

---

[1] Irwin to Baldwin, 26 November 1929, I.C. 18.
[2] Irwin to Hoare, 19 November 1929, I.C. 18.
[3] Benn's Narrative; Reading memorandum, 1 October 1929, R.C. 57.
[4] Benn's Narrative.

cit in the Declaration of 1917, that the attainment of Dominion Status must be regarded as the natural issue of India's constitutional progress.' Irwin agreed to substitute for the words following '1917', 'that the natural issue of India's constitutional progress, *as there contemplated*, is the attainment of Dominion Status'.[1] It is clear that Reading really wanted to limit the announcement to a reiteration of the 1917 declaration. He sought 'an explicit statement that the qualifications and conditions applicable to responsible Government in the preamble to the 1919 Act [notably that responsible government was to be achieved by progressive stages and at parliament's discretion] remain unchanged'.[2] If this were not clear, 'misapprehensions' would arise in India and the question of a change of policy would 'assuredly be raised in Parliament'. Irwin's view, Reading realized, was that 'the pronouncement did not involve any change of policy'. But he still urged that the ground be cleared in advance, and thus 'obviate any adverse comment'. Irwin refused to go further in order to meet Reading's wishes. On 9 October, the eve of his sailing for India, he gave Reading a note, which he hoped would convince him that the declaration was necessary and involved no change of policy.

Irwin's note[3] argued that the announcement merely repeated Britain's declared purpose; that it in no way affected the Commission's inquiry, which concerned policy for the fulfilment of that purpose. Irwin isolated for criticism the only possible substantive objection to the announcement: that it avowed a purpose which its opponents wished to disown. That is to say, those who opposed the announcement did so because they viewed Britain's purpose as 'a form of restricted Responsible Government', and not as 'full Responsible Government', or Dominion Status. Irwin could not reconcile their view with his Instrument of Instructions or with Britain's numerous statements about the relationship with India being one of partnership. While he recognized that Dominion Status would 'take a long time' to achieve, he stressed that Britain's task would become even more difficult 'if by refusal, in the face of alleged doubts, to make our

[1] Ibid.
[2] Reading to Irwin, 8 October 1929, I.C. 28.
[3] Irwin's Note [datable to 4 October 1929 from Templewood Coll. 25] on his proposed statement, enclosed with Benn's Narrative.

ultimate purpose plain, we were to afford ground to our enemies to say that we intended India to occupy a permanently subordinate place in an Empire of white nations'. Irwin was clear that the stakes of the declaration game were, for his opponents, India as a dependency of the Empire, and for himself, India as a partner in the Commonwealth.

Irwin had taken up a strong moral position. Strategically, too, he seemed to be on high ground. He was supported by the Labour Government, while he had been appointed by the Tories and now felt sure of the backing of their leader. He also believed that Simon had conceded the merits of his scheme. He did not of course realize that the assents of Simon and Baldwin were contingent each upon the other. Neither did he appreciate that Reading's veiled threats or innuendoes of trouble in Parliament reflected a determination to prevent the making of the declaration.

There is no reason to suppose that Reading was opposed to the achievement of dominionhood in due course. As viceroy he had been ahead of the home government and the provincial governors in following out what he regarded as the logical implications of Montagu's declaration. He had written emphatically of the need to Indianize the civil and military services. He had been prepared to convene a conference in 1922 to discuss further constitutional changes. He had resisted pressures for a harsh policy towards non-co-operation. He had wanted to placate Indian Muslims over the Turkish peace treaty. Despite his unquestioned acumen in the interpretation of legal niceties he had shown no tendency to distinguish the avowed policy of responsible government from Dominion Status. On three occasions, in the context of remarks about the civil services, the army, and his proposed round table conference, he had assumed the object of Britain's policy to be 'Dominion Status' or 'full Dominion Status'. However, on all three matters he was rebuffed by the government in England. His experience must have made him acutely aware of the danger of raising expectations in India without first being certain of full support from home. He had also come to realize that the princes were anxious about the growth of democracy in British India and that they saw the withering of paramountcy as its logical concomitant. The states problem must be solved before Dominion Status could be conferred, yet in 1926 Reading had felt unable to accept any limitation of paramountcy. He became more concerned than ever to insist, as he had always insisted, that the goal could be achieved only, as the preamble to the 1919 Act pointed out, by progressive 'successive stages'. He could clearly expect no good result from a declaration which failed to reiterate the preamble, for its omission would surely suggest to Indians that a change of policy had taken place. Such a declaration would only encourage demands for Dominion Status at once, and thereby provoke a parliamentary reaction.

On 18 October Reading asked Benn to see him within the next few days.[1] They met on the 23rd and Reading urged postponing any declaration until the Commission had reported. He claimed that 'considerable unrest had been created amongst Conservatives by newspaper rumours of some momentous declaration'.[2] Questions were bound to be raised in Parliament. Benn later recalled that from the first Reading had 'frankly warned me of what he intended to do, not only with the Liberal but, so far as he was able, with the Conservative Party'.[3] Conservative observers were, in fact, aware that Reading was engaged in an intrigue with some members of their party, including Birkenhead.

The jurists, Reading and Birkenhead, knew each other well. They had worked in harmony as viceroy and secretary of state, from 1924 to 1926. The third jurist in the story, Simon, aware of mounting Liberal and Tory opposition to the declaration, now began to edge towards outright hostility himself.

Simon and Birkenhead were old friends. They had played rugby together in the Wadham College fifteen. Later, when they both had thriving practices at the Bar they played golf at weekends near Oxford. To some extent Simon lived in the shadow of Birkenhead's brilliance. It was, of course, to Birkenhead that Simon owed his chairmanship of the Statutory Commission. On 21 October Birkenhead made a point of seeing Simon to discover the Commission's attitude to the declaration. He was told plainly that the Commission was opposed to it. This news soon reached Peel.

[1] Reading to Benn, 18 October, 1929, R.C. 57.
[2] Benn's Narrative.
[3] Benn to Irwin, 14 November 1929, I.C. 5.

Wednesday 23 October was the day chosen by Baldwin to disclose Irwin's initiative to the Shadow Cabinet. Sir Samuel Hoare arrived early for the meeting with his colleagues and 'found Willie Peel in a great state about [Irwin's] projected statement'.[1] When the matter came before the meeting there was 'a veritable explosion'. Baldwin, who indicated his 'personal support of the whole plan', found the meeting almost unanimously against him.[2] When asked about the Commission's attitude, he said that he understood Simon 'concurred', whereupon Peel contradicted him. The meeting dispersed with Baldwin resolved to see Benn. Peel had arranged to meet Simon later in the day. Birkenhead intended to write a letter to *The Times*, reproaching the government for short-circuiting the Commission and ignoring the views of the opposition parties.

Also on that Wednesday, later than the meeting but before he saw Peel, Simon dictated a Note of protest against the making of a declaration. He had in fact never been shown the text of Irwin's statement. He took the Note to Benn's office and read it aloud:

> I am becoming more and more uneasy as to the possible reactions to the announcement which Irwin is to make early next month to the effect that the goal of responsible government referred to in the Montagu declaration is indistinguishable from Dominion Status.... I greatly fear that this announcement will bring India within the region of Party controversy.... I hear rumours that important members of the Conservative Party are very strongly opposed to any announcement being made; Reading and Lloyd George also think it unwise and inopportune.[3]

The Note added that the declaration would be taken to embody a new decision, but if the government were challenged in parliament it would be forced to deny this implication. It was to be feared that questions would be asked whether the declaration was made with the Commission's approval. Benn's response disappointed Simon: 'He made no comment.... Obviously he did not wish to discuss it.'

That evening, when Peel came to see him, Simon said that the Commission 'had not been consulted' about the declaration

---

[1] Hoare to Irwin, 28 October 1929, I.C. 18.
[2] Simon's Note of 23 October 1929, S.C.C.
[3] Ibid.

and that they 'did not approve' of it.[1] At this stage, it was the impression of Peel, Birkenhead, Reading, and Lloyd George that Simon was prepared to resign if the declaration were made.

The same night, Birkenhead sent to *The Times* his letter attacking the government for its intended side-stepping of the Commission and the other parties. Dawson, whom Irwin had kept apprised of the facts as he knew them, questioned the justification for the letter and sent it back. Birkenhead claimed to have checked his facts with Simon, Reading, and all of his Shadow Cabinet colleagues save one (presumably Baldwin). He sent the letter to the *Daily Telegraph* at once, and it appeared the following morning (Thursday).

On Thursday Baldwin confronted Benn, who confirmed that Simon and the Commission had declined to be implicated in the declaration and that they had not seen the text of the declaration. He was now in an embarrassing position, and he went away to ruminate. Benn, too, was in difficulties. He had been the junior member of a triumvirate that included the prime minister and the viceroy. Now, with the former in America and the latter in India, with erstwhile sympathizers, Simon and Baldwin, becoming critics, and with a Liberal ex-viceroy and two Tory ex-secretaries of state gathering forces to attack the declaration, he had to decide between inaction and capitulation. He allowed events to run their course and the pressures upon him mounted steadily. The evidence of circumstance suggests that during the weekend Reading and Simon joined forces.

On Sunday 27th Reading dispatched a missive to Benn. He urged that in order to prevent Irwin's statement being misinterpreted it should make 'clear and explicit' that the 'conditions and reservations' of the 1917 declaration and the 1919 Preamble were still in force.[2] Otherwise the declaration should be postponed until the Commission had reported. He emphasized that neither the Liberal nor the Conservative Party would support the declaration and that the Commission had not assented to it.

On Monday Simon placed the draft of a letter to Benn before the Commission and obtained authority to send it. The letter[3]

[1] Simon's Note of 5 November 1929, S.C.C.
[2] Reading to Benn, 27 October 1929, enclosed with Benn's Narrative.
[3] Simon to Benn, 28 October 1929, S.C.C.

registered the Commission's protest against the declaration being made. It referred to press reports which indicated that the declaration would be challenged in parliament. Such an outcome would be 'wholly deplorable' and was 'bound to involve questions to the Government as to whether the Commission has been consulted on the subject'. The letter reminded Benn that the Commission had 'not been consulted upon, or made aware of, the terms of the proposed announcement', and affirmed that 'the assent of all parties in Parliament' had not been obtained.

The timing and content of the Reading and Simon letters were clearly similar. When Simon put his draft to the Commission he reported that 'Lord Reading and the Conservative leaders were extremely anxious'.[1] Burnham said that he would resign if a new policy were declared. Cadogan reported that 'the Conservatives hoped that Lord Reading had saved the situation'. Reading had done his work well. The declaration hung in the balance.

The contretemps at the Shadow Cabinet on Wednesday 23rd and his discussion with Benn the next day convinced Baldwin of the need for firm action. He soon decided to call his Indian experts together and concert a policy. Meanwhile, on the Friday, three experts, Birkenhead, Peel, and Winterton, met independently for luncheon at the Carlton. They were intimately critical of Baldwin's rash conditional assent to such a revolutionary declaration. When, at the weekend, Baldwin discussed the situation with the ex-secretaries of state and Lord Salisbury they were all of one mind. They removed any gloss that Benn might have placed upon Simon's attitude and left Baldwin in no doubt that Simon and his Commission were hostile to the declaration. It was agreed that the declaration must be stopped. Baldwin was forced to write to Snowden what Benn described accurately as an 'ultimatum'.[2]

Baldwin based his indictment on the opposition to the declaration of a Commission that contained members of each of the parties and that had been appointed with the agreement of each of them. The procedure of appointing a Commission had been laid down in the 1919 Act:

[1] Notes on Commission's meeting, 28 October 1929, S.C.C.
[2] Benn to Irwin, 14 November 1929, I.C. 5.

The Promise of Partnership

The Statutory Commission is therefore not like other Commissions, the creation of a Government of the day acting *proprio motu*, but the fulfilment of a provision definitely made by Parliament for the careful review after a lapse of years of the results obtained and an unprejudiced report on the lessons and conclusions to be drawn from them. As a result of the procedure so carefully thought out and so definitely laid down in the Government of India Act, India has remained... outside the field of party controversy....[1]

The declaration, whatever its merits, 'would amount to a sudden reversal by executive action of the considered decision of Parliament'. To anticipate the Commission's report would 'impair the authority of the Commission, would defeat the intention of Parliament... and most gravely compromise its liberty of action when the question comes before it'.

Baldwin claimed, with justice, that his earlier assent was based upon the assumption that the declaration had Simon's concurrence. Now he learned that Simon, like others who had been intimately concerned with the government of India in recent years, viewed the consequences of the declaration 'with grave anxiety'. This put 'the matter in an entirely new light': 'I was prepared to run a considerable personal risk as long as I believed that the Government, this Commission and the Viceroy, were in agreement. I never applied my mind or indeed was given the opportunity of doing so to the contingency that the Chairman of the Commission vigorously dissented from the proposals put before me.' Baldwin now demanded the postponement of the declaration until the prime minister was back in England. (He had sailed from Canada on the 25th.)

Snowden showed the letter to Benn at 11.30 p.m. on Monday 28th. Benn could hardly challenge Baldwin's account of his conditional assent. Snowden could recognize that MacDonald himself had proceeded on the assumption of Baldwin's assent and overlooked the condition. Nevertheless, there was serious likelihood of a parliamentary crisis and Snowden, as acting prime minister, was responsible for the fate of the government. There and then an urgent private telegram was composed, and dispatched to Irwin at 3 a.m. It told of Baldwin's letter and requested the postponement of the declaration from the coming Thursday until the following Sunday or Monday. It stressed that

[1] Baldwin to Snowden, 28 October 1929, S.C.C.

the Cabinet had not receded but that Snowden was prepared to wait until MacDonald returned. Benn added his personal view: 'This opposition is the outcome of Reading's campaign assisted by Birkenhead and others. Simon as you know originally assented to declaration. . . . If you will refuse to budge I will support you absolutely and we can succeed. I do not believe there is any real danger in the House of Commons.'[1] Considering the weight of his adversaries, Benn deserves some praise for stubborn courage, though he was clearly shaken by Baldwin's epistle.

When Simon came to see him at noon on the Tuesday, to discuss the date for the release of the exchange of letters, Benn 'appeared to be in a great state of excitement': 'I was unable to understand a good deal of what he was saying, for his language was vague and rhetorical to a degree; but at last I gathered that he wished to get my comments on a passage in some letter which Baldwin had sent to the Government.'[2] Simon inferred that a telegram had been sent to Irwin, postponing the declaration. Benn was apparently distressed by Baldwin's resentment that he had been misled into assuming Simon's assent to the declaration. Not without reason, Benn was honestly in doubt about the real attitude of Simon and the Commission towards the declaration. He asked Simon whether the Commission objected to being associated with the statement or to the government making it independently. Simon had probably never brought the issue to so clear a definition in his own mind, for now he refused to give an answer until he had consulted the Commission. He left Benn in high dudgeon, for Benn refused to show him the document that had given rise to the interrogation: 'He appeared to be most anxious to dismiss my request for the letter, and asked me, in reference to this part of his conversation, to "wash it out".'

There now occurred 'two amazing coincidences'. As Simon left the India Office, at about 2.30, he 'happened by pure chance to cross Baldwin and Davidson striding down Whitehall to the House'.[3] He stopped Baldwin to inquire about the letter. Baldwin at once pulled a copy of it from his pocket and offered it to him. Simon refused to look at it until he had obtained Benn's

[1] Sec. of S. to viceroy, 29 October 1929 (t/g), enclosed with Benn's Narrative.
[2] Simon's Note of 5 November 1929, S.C.C.
[3] Ibid.

The Promise of Partnership

permission, turned, and went back to the India Office. Benn told him that he would consult Snowden. Simon then went off to the House, where, 'again by pure chance', he met Snowden. The latter assented to his seeing the letter and he at once went off to Baldwin to accept his offer and to take a copy of the letter.

Later that afternoon Simon told the Commission of the telegram that had been sent and asked his colleagues to define their attitude towards the declaration. He said that 'he thought that the attitude of the Commission had all along been not to protest against any statement being made, but to say that it strongly objected to being involved in any statement, and that the Government must make such a statement on its own responsibility'.[1] He was authorized to report this summary of the Commission's position to the secretary of state.

Next, Simon drafted a note for Snowden.[2] He wrote that in the light of Baldwin's letter 'the true situation becomes clear'. Baldwin's assent had been conditional upon the Commission's assent. As early as 24 September he had told Benn that the Commission would be no party to the declaration, but this fact had never been relayed to Baldwin. Simon had been 'in complete ignorance of this omission': 'We were willing to acquiesce in an interim statement if agreed by all Parties, but did not contemplate the making of a declaration which did not satisfy this condition.' Baldwin and his colleagues must now be told that 'there is no question of the Commission assenting to or agreeing with the contents of this document', which, indeed, neither Simon nor the Commission had ever seen.

That night, at 10.30, Simon took his note to Snowden's room at the House of Commons. He found Snowden and Benn together and he read his note to them. A second purpose of the visit was to demand a time gap between the release of his exchange of letters with MacDonald and the publication of the declaration. Earlier in the day Benn had insisted that the documents should appear simultaneously, despite Simon's objection that such a course would encourage the supposition that the Commission complied with the contents of the declaration. Benn's object was, of course, to make it clear in India that the statement of purpose and the adoption of the conference procedure were integral parts

[1] Notes of Commission meeting, 29 October 1929, afternoon, S.C.C.
[2] 'Note for Mr. Snowden', 29 October 1929, S.C.C.

of a peace offer. The timing of the press releases was a second bone of contention between Benn and Simon. Benn, MacDonald, and the Cabinet had decided upon the need for simultaneous publication, but Simon had understood from MacDonald that it was agreed there should be a time lapse. In Snowden's room an altercation developed over the matter, Simon arguing vigorously for his point, and Benn claiming that all the arrangements had been made and that it was too late to change them. Simon was in a position of strength, for he had not yet handed over a signed copy of his letter to the prime minister. Snowden recognized the point and agreed that the letters should appear in the English newspapers on the day preceding the publication of the viceroy's statement.[1]

Simon's attitude to Benn was now one of mistrust spiced with bitterness. To a letter that he dashed off early on Wednesday morning, ostensibly to thank Snowden for his 'considerate treatment', he added:

> I consider that the Commission has been very badly used.... It seems to me outrageous that we should have dissociated ourselves from any declaration five weeks ago ... and yet that the impression should have been maintained that we were cognisant of and approved whatever this precious document may contain. I'll wager that some of Benn's Cabinet colleagues imagine at this moment that I have been consulted and approve.[2]

He was determined that Baldwin should be left in no doubt of the true position.

At 10 o'clock that morning Simon was on Baldwin's doorstep in Upper Brook Street. He read aloud the note that he had read to Snowden and Benn twelve hours earlier, and then put the following questions to Baldwin:

1. Did the Government ever inform you that the Commission would not agree to the draft reply of the Prime Minister in one respect, and objected to being responsible for any interim explanation of the Montagu declaration?
2. Were you ever made to understand that the proposed declaration

---

[1] Simon to Benn, 28 October 1929; Notes on Commission meetings of 29 October, morning, and 30 October; Stopford to Simon, 29 October 1929; Simon's Note of 5 November 1929; all S.C.C. And: Benn's Narrative; Benn to Irwin, 14 November 1929, I.C. 5.

[2] Simon to Snowden, 30 October 1929, S.C.C.

was being settled without the co-operation of the Commission, and that neither I nor any member of the Commission was aware of or had been consulted about its terms?[1]

Baldwin answered 'No' to both questions.

At 10.30 Simon reported his meetings with Snowden and Baldwin to the Commission. He sought authority to write to Snowden that 'the position was altered by the failure of the other Parties to agree to the proposed statement', and that the best course now was to delay the statement until the government could consult the leaders of the other parties, with a view to avoiding disagreement in parliament and 'disaster in India'.[2] Questioned by Hartshorn on the reason for writing to Snowden, Simon answered 'that the Cabinet must know of the situation, and that he was not sure that Mr. Benn would tell them'. He averred that he would not proceed with the exchange of letters unless the Labour Cabinet knew that Benn had never told Baldwin of the Commission's attitude towards the declaration. The Commission authorized Simon to write to Snowden, telling of his interview with Baldwin, stressing the Commission's dissent from any declaration that was not agreed by all parties, and proposing the postponement of the declaration pending a meeting of party leaders. At noon the letter was handed to the prime minister's private secretary at Downing Street and delivered to Snowden in the Cabinet room.

The letter failed to influence the Cabinet, chiefly because of the firm line that Irwin had taken in his reply to Benn's telegram. Irwin had already prepared the princes and the leading nationalists for the declaration. Their response had been enthusiastic and gave reason to hope that the statement would transform the political scene in India. To delay now would revive mistrust and could be 'disastrous'.[3] Responding to his plea, the Cabinet authorized Irwin to proceed as planned.

Baldwin was very upset indeed when Snowden showed him the exchange of telegrams. On Wednesday 30th, the day of the Cabinet's decision, he wrote to Snowden in strong terms about the inadequacies of Benn's telegram to Irwin. Irwin was not there told that Baldwin's September assent had been given on

[1] Simon's Note of 30 October 1929, S.C.C.
[2] Notes on Commission meeting, 30 October 1929, S.C.C.
[3] Viceroy to Sec. of S., 29 October 1929 (t/g), enclosed with Benn's Narrative.

the express assumption of the Commission's concurrence in the declaration. He was not told that Baldwin and his colleagues, on discovering that Simon and the Commission resented the making of a declaration, refused unanimously to be parties to it. Nor was he told that Reading and the Liberals had adopted the same attitude. Finally, he was not told that Simon had informed the government that the Commission regarded the declaration as 'gravely subversive' of its authority. In consequence of these omissions, Irwin had given his reply 'in ignorance of facts which it was essential that he should know'.[1] Baldwin concluded: 'I must press most earnestly upon you, even at the eleventh hour, the grave responsibility which the Government will assume if they authorize a statement which in our deliberate judgement may render impossible that co-operation between all parties upon which the whole future of India may be found to depend.' The government was immovable, and, in spite of a personal cable that he received from Baldwin that night, so was Irwin.

The exchange of letters occurred at 8.30 p.m. on 30 October and appeared in the British press next morning. Irwin's statement was released at 6 p.m. on 31 October and appeared in the following morning's newspapers. In India, the statement was gazetted on 31 October and appeared, together with the exchange of letters, in the newspapers the next day. The attempt to stop the declaration had failed.

IV. THE DEBATES OVER DOMINIONHOOD

The campaign to prevent the announcement had brought together a formidable combination of forces against the government. Among the Liberals it included Lloyd George and Reading and, at the end, Simon. Among the Conservatives it comprised Birkenhead and Peel, then the Shadow Cabinet, and, at last, Baldwin. From the Thursday night on which the statement was released until a full week later the government's fate hung in the balance. That night Lloyd George put down a private notice question for the following morning in the Commons. On the Friday night Reading put down notice of a question in the Lords.

More than the government's fate hung in the balance. On Thursday the *Daily Mail* launched a savage attack on Baldwin's leadership of his party. Under the headline 'MR BALDWIN'S

[1] Baldwin to Snowden, 30 October 1929, enclosed with Benn's Narrative.

CROWNING BLUNDER' it charged him with committing his party to the declaration without consulting his colleagues. He had joined with the Socialists to imperil the empire by promising 'full Home Rule' to the 'natives', the 'countless races', of India. When his colleagues found him out they were 'aghast'. The 'rank and file' were 'furious', and he had been coerced into retracting his 'pledges'. The 'most acute political crisis for many years' had arisen and the party leadership was 'in urgent question'. Very soon the Rothermere press was joined by the Beaverbrook newspapers in an anti-Baldwin, save the Empire, campaign. The *Daily Mail* story was variously attributed to Birkenhead and Lloyd George. Lane Fox wrote: 'There seems general belief that L.G. gave to the *Daily Mail* the story of S.B.'s betrayal of his party, especially as he has since denied giving it.'[1] J. C. C. Davidson, Baldwin's *fidus Achates* and the Conservative Party Organizer at the 1929 elections, named Birkenhead as the source and noted suspicions that he had been in 'collusion with the "Goat".'[2] Suspicions were strengthened by the simultaneous publication of the *Mail*'s story in the Liberal provincial newspapers.

Conservative feeling against Baldwin had been developing since the Labour victory at the 1929 elections. In July, Birkenhead and Worthington-Evans had joined with Lord Melchett to form an Empire Economic Union with the object of developing empire free trade. Melchett was chairman of Imperial Chemical Industries. He was related to Reading by marriage. Reading was president of I.C.I and Birkenhead a director. During a visit to the U.S.A. in August Melchett had said that 'the next Government will be Conservative, but I do not think that Mr. Baldwin will be the next Prime Minister'.[3] He expected the next prime minister to be a protectionist. Melchett's initiative ran parallel with the launching by the press lords, Beaverbrook and Rothermere, of an empire free-trade campaign. All believed that Britain should set up tariffs against non-empire goods and that the countries of the empire should lower tariffs in favour of British imports. The day before Baldwin's stormy Shadow Cabinet (23 October) a large group of business leaders met to consider a

[1] Lane Fox to Irwin, 13 November 1929, I.C. 18.
[2] J. C. Davidson to Irwin, 9 November 1929, I.C. 18. The 'Goat' = Lloyd George.
[3] Quoted in J. K. Middlemas and A. J. L. Barnes, *Baldwin, A Biography*, London, 1969, p. 550.

manifesto of Melchett's on empire economic policy. A couple of days later Beaverbrook published his own manifesto on this question and Neville Chamberlain was aware that he was trying to oust Baldwin. By early November there were, therefore, converging campaigns against Baldwin, the one centred on empire free trade, the other on the Indian question.

Baldwinite Tories had no doubt that there was an intrigue afoot to exploit the Indian situation: to overthrow the government by a combination of Liberals and dissident Tories; to displace Baldwin; and to set up a coalition under Lloyd George along the lines of his 1919–22 government. Davidson confided to Irwin on 9 November:

> About three weeks ago those who regard Stanley as an ineffective, supine Leader, and whose sympathies are clearly Coalition in character, decided to use the Indian situation to get rid of him once and for all, and the opportunity was so favourable that there can be no doubt that they believed they would be successful, aided by the *Daily Express*, *Daily Mail* and Lloyd George.[1]

Dawson wrote as early as 31 October:

> F. E. has taken an active hand in the game, which I suspect being at bottom a relic of the old Coalition intrigue. It must have been a tempting thought that a firm stand for the Empire might get rid of the Government and Baldwin simultaneously.[2]

When Baldwin visited Dawson at home on 2 November they talked about the crisis for two hours. Baldwin was 'rather worried about it all and by the intrigue behind it'.[3] Next day Dawson wrote to Irwin:

> There is no doubt at all that the combination of which I warned you—Lloyd George, Reading, Rothermere, Beaverbrook and Birkenhead, aided and abetted I greatly fear by Simon, and supported by a certain number of stupid Conservatives, some of them told that Labour is selling the Empire and some corrupted by the Goat—has succeeded in producing an almighty row.[4]

Hoare, Winterton, Lytton, and Goschen (then visiting England) wrote in similar terms of the alignment of forces against the

---

[1] Davidson to Irwin, 9 November 1929, I.C. 18.
[2] Dawson to Irwin, 31 October 1929, I.C. 18.
[3] Wrench, *Dawson*, p. 278.
[4] Dawson to Irwin, 3 November 1929, I.C. 18.

government and Baldwin. It was generally thought that Lloyd George was making the most of an opportunity to fell the sapling Labour Government and the sturdy old Tory oak with one blow. Rothermere and Beaverbrook were said to fear a Snowden budget and, with Birkenhead, Austen Chamberlain, Churchill, and Worthington-Evans, to favour a Lloyd George coalition.

When Lloyd George put down his motion Baldwin, as well as the government, was faced with a fight. In an opening skirmish Baldwin prevented Lloyd George from putting down a motion of censure. He had a delicate operation to perform in parliament: to remove the *Daily Mail* smear, rescue his leadership, and restore unity in his party; yet uphold the authority of Irwin (his own appointment), and defend the high principle behind the declaration, which he accepted with sincerity. At this stage, he was more of an ally than an opponent of the government.

The events of 31 October caused Simon similarly to reappraise his position in relation to the anti-government alliance. He could hardly hope to hold his Commission together if a parliamentary dispute along party lines developed. He wrote to an intermediary of the need to impress upon Baldwin the importance of diminishing the debate: 'The all-important thing now is to restore the unity of the Home Front, get everyone to stand by the Commission and await its Report, and to support Irwin's effort.'[1]

Upon the outcome of the debates in parliament depended the Labour Government, Baldwin's leadership, the Simon Commission, and, of course, the success of Irwin's initiative. All hung together.

Lloyd George's question was:

To ask the Secretary of State for India whether the Statutory Commission on Indian Government was consulted with reference to the passage in the important statement made by the Viceroy yesterday, which relates to the constitutional status of India in the Empire; if so, whether the Commission concurred, and whether that passage is intended to indicate any change, either in substance or in point of time, in the policy announced by previous Governments.[2]

When Simon received the notice on the evening of the 31st he at once wrote to Benn to offer his help. Benn's reply to Lloyd

[1] Simon to 'Bobby', 2 November 1929, S.C.C. Simon asked his intermediary to approach Baldwin through Davidson.
[2] *Commons' Debates*, 1 November 1929.

George would 'probably decide whether [the] Commission remains intact and in being'.[1] They met at 10.30 that night for a 'not very fruitful' discussion. Next morning, Simon wrote to Benn to suggest that the answers to the first two parts of Lloyd George's question were 'No' and 'Does not arise'.[2] He believed, however, that a simple 'No' would *provoke* supplementaries', and proposed a form of words 'to soothe feelings which are ready to burst'. Benn should say that it was 'due to the Statutory Commission' that he should 'make it perfectly clear that they were not consulted'. If Benn accepted this proposal, Simon would at once 'tell Lloyd George that I personally gravely deprecate supplementaries'. Simon's stand warrants emphasis for there was some contemporary tittle-tattle about 'Lloyd George's little dinners with Simon in a private room at Claridge's'.[3] Goschen wrote to Irwin of Simon having 'brought some sticks' to feed Lloyd George's fire.[4] He also helped to damp it down.

Benn welcomed Simon's form of words and read it later that morning in answer to the first two parts of the question. His answer to the third part amounted to a rearrangement of the Irwin declaration. A supplementary on the attitude of the leaders of the other parties gave Baldwin the opportunity to rise and affirm the falsity of every fact, expressed or implied, in the *Daily Mail*'s attack upon him. He promised a full personal statement, and a debate was put down for Thursday 7 November.

Reading's motion showed that he was not to be put off by Benn's answer, or by Simon's deprecation of further questions. Simon regarded Reading's intervention over the declaration as sincere and dignified throughout: '[He] . . . held unyieldingly by his view that there was ambiguity in the phraseology employed about Dominion Status, and that this would lead to more harm than good.'[5] Similarly, Goschen described him as 'entirely honest and straightforward', and Davidson as 'frightened, quite genuinely, of the effect [of the declaration] on Indian opinion'.[6] Dawson wrote less charitably that he 'always has cold feet, is a

[1] Simon to Benn, 31 October 1929, S.C.C.
[2] Simon to Benn, 1 November 1929, S.C.C.
[3] Dawson to Irwin, 9 November 1929, I.C. 18.
[4] Goschen to Irwin, 14 November 1929, I.C. 18.
[5] Simon to Irwin, 14 November 1929, S.C.C.
[6] Goschen to Irwin, 20 November 1929; Davidson to Irwin, 9 November 1929; I.C. 18.

The Promise of Partnership 85

natural intriguer, and is perhaps slightly jealous'.[1] Certainly, Reading had stirred up the crisis and now kept it on the boil with his question. He demanded to know, first, why the declaration had been made without consulting the Commission and in advance of its report; second, whether the conditions and provisions of the 1917 and 1919 statements remained in force; third, whether the declaration represented a change in the object of policy or in the time for achieving that object. The question was put down for Tuesday, 5 November: Guy Fawkes Day!

In a long speech, Reading attacked the government's 'extraordinary course', told of his efforts to prevent it, and expressed anxiety about the construction that Indians would place upon the announcement.[2] They would see it as the harbinger of a major change of policy, and that would prejudice the work of the Commission. Benn described the speech privately as 'a terrific rhodomontade in such a grandiose form as to obscure entirely the minute point he was labouring'.[3]

Reading's questions were answered in dismal fashion by the aged Lord Parmoor. He said, in essence, that no change of policy or timing was involved in the declaration, nor could the provisions of the 1919 Act be altered except by statute. He read haltingly from a text that Benn had prepared for him, stopping now and then to interpolate an observation of his own. He sometimes seemed to lose his place, confused his dates and referred throughout to 'Her Majesty's Government' and 'Lord MacDonald'. Benn, whose twenty-five years in parliament had made him the sharpest of sharp-shooters in the Commons, was a witty penman of the Lords' debates. He wrote of Parmoor's 'watery excursus': 'He reminded me of non-Conformist pastors whom I have often heard in chapels reading the Scriptures and breaking off into personal exegesis which I always thought added little to the force of Holy Writ.'[4] Parmoor's inadequacies seemed to enrage Birkenhead, who was next to speak. The night before, Simon had sent his private secretary to Birkenhead in order to correct some serious misrepresentations of the Commission's initial attitude to the declaration, which Birkenhead had put

[1] Dawson to Irwin, 3 November 1929, I.C. 18.
[2] *Lords' Debates*, 5 November 1929.
[3] Benn to Irwin, 14 November 1929, I.C. 5.
[4] Ibid.

forward in the *Daily Telegraph*.[1] Though the secretary had pleaded that the debates must 'improve the situation', Birkenhead's speech was calculated to make it worse. Birkenhead committed a cruel and bullying assault upon Parmoor. Benn called it 'a first-rate old Bailey address'.[2] But Parmoor was no 'accused' and the jury of their Lordships were embarrassed. They were also shocked by the irresponsibility of his remarks about India and by his offensive tone towards Irwin. The term 'appeasement' had not then the associations that it acquired later, but Birkenhead pronounced it with a sneer as he attacked the declaration as a submission to threats of civil disobedience. 'The way to discharge our fiduciary obligations in India is never to yield to threats', he roared, 'never, never!' His speech overshadowed those of the peers who followed him, Crewe, Peel, and Salisbury. It alienated many of his party. Burnham stayed silent, partly because Simon had enlisted the King's support to dissuade him from taking any action that might break up the Commission, but partly because Tory friends exerted pressure upon him. Lord Passfield, for the government, reiterated Parmoor's assurances to Reading, who, to the relief of the House, accepted them and closed the debate.

The Commons' debate was tense.[3] Baldwin told of the conditional and personal nature of his September assent, of the government's failure to consult him subsequently, and of the action that he had taken during the last week of October. He gave measured praise to the viceroy's character and ability but was critical of the government's course after it had failed to secure the support of the Commission. He then questioned Benn on the policy implications of the declaration, which were of real concern to many in his party. The refutation of the *Daily Mail*'s charges was complete and the speech as a whole was impressive, but Baldwin was heard in virtual silence from the Conservative benches. Lloyd George followed him with, by contrast, a full-scale attack upon the government. His every sentence was punctuated with 'Hear, Hears' from Churchill and Worthington-Evans. The speech is better remembered for a brilliant interruption of Benn's,

[1] Stopford's Note of 4 November 1929, S.C.C. See *Daily Telegraph*, 2 November 1929.
[2] Benn to Irwin, 14 November 1929.
[3] *Commons' Debates*, 7 November 1929.

intended to puncture the speaker rather than punctuate his
address. Lloyd George was warming to a florid indictment of
the government's departure from agreed all-party policy and
alluded derisively to Benn as a 'pocket-sized edition of Moses'
who had smashed the tablets of the Covenant and replaced them
with new ones of his own. Benn, a follower of George's until
1927, produced as an immediate riposte an allusion to George's
collection and personal administration of a political 'fighting
fund' believed to exceed a million pounds: 'But I never worshipped the Golden Calf.' The House roared with laughter for
several minutes.

Benn's own speech disappointed some friends and angered
many opponents. Davidson thought it a 'lamentable parliamentary performance', Hoare, 'unworthy of a great occasion'.[1]
Benn did graciously confirm Baldwin's personal statement in a
reference that Winterton called 'one of the most generous things
I have ever heard'.[2] However, although he was pressed very
hard, he refused to give a clear answer to the all-important
question of whether the declaration represented a change of
policy. It was a fighting speech and gave Birkenhead and Lloyd
George as good as they had given. But it was a party speech and
it exacerbated feelings in the House. Simon, who was to speak
next, felt that Benn had made more difficult his own task of
restoring harmony. He later wrote complainingly to Reading:
'... "Getting rid of the Birkenhead tone" [Benn's phrase] was
all very well, but that was no reason for degrading an Indian
debate by smart repartees on Lloyd George and party jeers at
the expense of the party he had deserted.'[3]

Simon spoke for the Commission as a whole. His colleagues
had seen and endorsed the text of his speech. He later recalled
that his aim was 'to reduce the temperature and enable my
colleagues and myself to finish our work'.[4] He spoke of the Commission as representative of all the parties, as an instrument of
parliament with a duty to parliament. He asked that it be left in
peace to complete the difficult task entrusted to it. As he spoke,
he felt 'both a surge of sympathy towards the Commission in its

[1] Davidson to Irwin, 9 November 1929; Hoare to Irwin, 13 November 1929;
I.C. 18.
[2] Winterton to Irwin, 11 November 1929, I.C. 18.
[3] Simon to Reading, 12 November 1929, S.C.C.
[4] Viscount Simon, *Retrospect*, London, 1952, p. 153.

interrupted task and an acceptance of the view that further controversy about the Government's intervention could do nothing but harm'.[1] Benn wrote satirically: 'He chid those who wished to drag the Commission in, and the curtain fell on a beautiful light shed through a stained glass window in which Simon, the principal figure, was a man of unflinching courage and steady purpose.'[2] Benn owed much to Simon's intervention. He knew it, and he did acknowledge the debt directly and charmingly to Simon. Yet the satire showed that the sense of obligation to one whom he mistrusted rankled with him.

Simon's speech was acclaimed as 'a perfect parliamentary performance'.[3] Simon expected bouquets and valued the following from Reading: 'You made a great speech and set an example of dignity and regard for the public interest which had the immediate effect of bringing the debate to an end. You restored the Commission to its high place and, I have no doubt, settled any doubts in the minds of individual Members.'[4] The speech enabled MacDonald to move for the closure of the debate. The Speaker accepted the motion quickly, to the relief of some Tories that it was not pressed to a division. Davidson feared that some Conservatives would fall into 'the trap' which it was 'obvious that that arch-tactician, the "Goat", was setting'.[5] Lytton believed that had the House divided then a half of the Conservatives would have trooped into the lobby behind Lloyd George, the remainder behind Baldwin and the government. With the Tories split, Baldwin would have been forced to resign.

In the event, Baldwin, the Simon Commission, and the government were all saved. But what of Irwin's declaration?

On 11 November, under pressure from his colleagues, Baldwin wrote to MacDonald of Benn's failure to answer the question 'whether this statement implies any change in the policy hitherto declared or in the time when this status may be obtained'. Benn drafted Macdonald's reply: 'The answer to both parts of the question . . . is "No". The policy, as you will remember, is set out in the Preamble of the Government of India Act, 1919, and it

[1] Ibid., p. 154.
[2] Benn to Irwin, 14 November 1929.
[3] Davidson to Irwin, 9 November 1929, I.C. 18. The newspapers were uniformly enthusiastic.
[4] Reading to Simon, 12 November 1929, S.C.C.
[5] Davidson to Irwin, 9 November 1929, I.C. 18.

stands unchanged unless and until Parliament decides to amend that Act.'[1] Churchill regarded the letter as 'rather a snub' to Irwin.[2] Benn noted that 'it was something of a puzzle and a disappointment' for the Labour Party.[3] Certainly, linking the Dominion Status declaration to the 1919 Preamble was to reaffirm that Britain's purpose was only to be achieved by stages and at parliament's discretion. Assuredly, Hailey's 1924 distinction between 'responsible government' and Dominion Status remained in force. However, the declaration of Britain's ultimate purpose as the latter, and not the former, remained intact.

The controversy over Irwin's declaration was, in fact, the great debate over the demission of power to the non-white nations of the British empire. The avowal of Dominion Status as the purpose of the Raj represented the decision that the Empire was to become a Commonwealth of equals. Irwin had the insight, the imagination, the sensitiveness, and the statesmanship to realize that there could be no other lasting basis for the relationship between the metropolitan power and her erstwhile dependencies. What the Durham Report did for the white dominions in 1839 the Irwin declaration did for the non-white ninety years later.

In retrospect it seems remarkable that the decision should have been taken so early. The rare conjunction of a Tory viceroy, with a finely tuned intuition, and a Labour government was required. As Simon had realized in March 1929, even a Round Table Conference would be anathema to the Tory Cabinet. The previous summer such a Cabinet dismissed unanimously Irwin's proposed 'window-dressing' to upgrade the Indian Central Committee, Simon's Indian collaborators. Further, the making of the declaration required an extraordinary juxtaposition of events, individuals, and relationships.

Irwin's cordial relationship with Baldwin and the latter's somewhat casual treatment of the draft letters in September were responsible for a crucial conditional assent. If Baldwin had been consulted in London, with his colleagues around him, he must surely have sounded them. As it was, he remained overconfident of his ability to handle them until it was too late for them to stop the declaration.

[1] *Daily Telegraph*, 12 November 1929.
[2] Lytton to Irwin, 20 November 1929, I.C. 18.
[3] Benn to Irwin, 21 November 1929, I.C. 5.

Simon's tacit acceptance of the declaration until the last week in October was grounded on ambivalence. In July he had helped Irwin and Benn with the drafting of a Dominion Status paragraph for the prime minister's letter. In September he required the deletion of the paragraph but took a detached stand in relation to the issue of a separate declaration. A more straightforward person would surely have conveyed his objections to Irwin and Benn. But, as Irwin had written in March, Simon was 'a very strange man, wholly lacking in the simpler human qualities'.[1]

When he was touring India, Simon everywhere gave an impression of oddness. Irwin wrote to several correspondents in India and England of his two extreme forms of behaviour, 'either the rather cynical manner that suggests he is wise and everyone else a fool, or the other of excess of somewhat unctuous politeness'.[2] (Irwin preferred the former because it gave 'more opportunities for self-defence'.) Simon had 'given an impression ... of keeping all his own personality within locked doors while inviting other people to disclose theirs'.[3] H. A. L. Fisher wrote back of 'something lacking in him, a central coldness perhaps', and confided that he had 'never yet succeeded in feeling quite comfortable in his company'.[4] Neville Chamberlain and Irwin agreed that 'one never seems quite to get to the point with him of complete understanding'.[5] The comments of the Earl of Crawford and Balcarres were even more damning: '... everything this brilliant man does seems shifty, or even worse; he has a lamentable reputation as a twister. . . .'[6] Benn cast a satiric shaft of nicety when he once wrote of Simon's 'agony of punctilio'.[7] Baldwin found amusement in Simon's pique at not being shown formally an advance copy of Irwin's statement, yet steadfastly refusing offers from all and sundry to view it informally.

It is all too easy to do Simon an injustice. Irwin could never understand his apparent change from indifference to hostility over the declaration, and like many others, including Benn, he was prepared to attribute it to Reading's influence. In fact, they

[1] Irwin to Goschen, 25 March 1929, I.C. 23.   [2] Ibid.
[3] Irwin to Archbishop of Canterbury, 15 April 1929, I.C. 18.
[4] Fisher to Irwin, 9 May 1929, I.C. 18.
[5] Irwin to Chamberlain, 15 April 1929, I.C. 18.
[6] Crawford and Balcarres to Irwin, 13 May 1929, I.C. 18.
[7] Benn to Irwin, 14 November 1929.

failed to appreciate the delicacy of his position. His uneasiness arose from concern at the possibility of parliamentary opposition, and his final hostility sprang from the rupture in the all-party front and the realization that Baldwin's attitude was not what he had been left to assume. It was surely natural for the head of an all-party Commission to become alarmed at a break in the all-party front in parliament.

The long neutrality of the Tory leader and the chairman of the Commission rested on a misunderstanding. Both Baldwin and Simon were partly responsible for the misunderstanding. Baldwin ought to have asked why the declaration was removed from the prime minister's letter. Simon ought to have made quite explicit the condition of his own neutrality. However, the primary responsibility for the misunderstanding lay with the government. MacDonald was at fault for not acquainting Baldwin of the Commission's refusal to be associated with the declaration. Benn ought to have put the busy prime minister right.

At the end of October it was Benn's stonewalling, in the face of attacks from Reading, Simon, and Baldwin, that saved the declaration from mutilation. If the incumbent of the India Office had been easily daunted by criticism, or perhaps even a more experienced minister, or a wiser politician, then the declaration might have been stopped. The declaration owed much to Benn's belief in Irwin's policy and to his carelessness of the consequences in following it through. Benn was reckless rather than cunning, though he was suspected of cheap trickery in misrepresenting to Baldwin and Simon the attitude of each to the other.

The Irwin declaration was lucky to be born on 31 October 1929 and lucky to survive during the following week. If its birth owed much to the interplay of personalities, its survival in parliament is attributable to the skill and practical wisdom of Baldwin and Simon. However, what is most remarkable is the great victory of principle. Had the principle of multi-racialism been fully and freely discussed in advance by elder statesmen and constitutional lawyers, the declaration would surely have been aborted. The great British authorities on India would have seen to that. Reading, Birkenhead, Peel, Simon, Winterton, Austen Chamberlain, and Crewe would have overborne Irwin and Benn in any ordinary combat.

The empire's eminent jurists were under no illusion that a fundamental change in the Indian constitution was embodied in the term 'Dominion Status'. As Reading said in the Lords, in 1929 the term conjured up a position in advance of responsible government. It meant the full status of the existing Dominions, which had never been promised previously.

Birkenhead asked incredulously whether Britain could really imagine that the viceroy of India should ever decline to the level of the governor-general of Canada or Australia. His own prejudices were clear. He had viewed the Montagu–Chelmsford constitution as a profound error. In 1924 he told Reading that it was 'frankly inconceivable that India will ever be fit for Dominion self-government'.[1] Those who used the term 'Dominion Status' in relation to India did not know what they were doing:

> Here is this word loosely and ignorantly employed, employed as I believe for the first time, employed with a certain significance, and I am persuaded, in the hope that, in order to deal with a disloyal campaign and with seditious threats, men would be persuaded they would receive that which ... they never can receive. ... Here with crude ignorance you have flung into the disputations of India an indication never made before. ...[2]

Similarly, Crewe opposed the use of the term, and Peel spoke of a 'new phrase' of 'indefinite meaning' being employed. Hoare reported that 'scarcely anyone' in the Conservative Party liked the declaration.[3] Salisbury wrote that 'the assurance as to Dominion Status came as a shock'.[4]

The recoil from the application of the term 'Dominion Status' to India in 1929 seems strangely inconsistent with the frequent use of the term 'Dominion' in relation to India during the preceding decade. The idea of dominionhood would appear to be implied in the Montagu declaration and the 1919 Preamble, while partnership with the other Dominions was referred to in the viceroy's Instructions and in the King's message to the Indian Legislature in 1921.[5] The paradox was explained during the

---

[1] Birkenhead to Reading, 4 December 1924, in F. W. E. Smith (Lord Birkenhead), *Frederick Edwin, Earl of Birkenhead: The Last Phase*, London, 1935, p. 245.
[2] *Lords' Debates*, 5 November 1929.
[3] Hoare to Irwin, 13 November 1929, I.C. 18.
[4] Salisbury to Irwin, 14 November 1929, I.C. 18.
[5] See Mehrotra, op. cit., pp. 228–9, and *The Times*, 5 November 1929, for

parliamentary debates. Birkenhead asked rhetorically: 'Does Dominion Status at this moment mean the same thing that it meant a month before the last Imperial Conference? Most plainly not.' Peel noted the change of meaning since 1926. Winterton, who had discussed with the two ex-secretaries of state the implications of Irwin's declaration, had made a note after their luncheon on 25 October: 'Now "Dominion Status" has a very special meaning (especially since the Imperial Conference of 1926), and use of the term would be in advance of any definitions hitherto attempted, such as "self-government within the Empire", because of that meaning. . . .'[1] Before 1926 'Dominion Status' had still implied a measure of subordination to the British parliament, by such means as the Colonial Laws Validity Act and the governor-general's powers to reserve Dominion legislation. In 1926 Balfour defined the Dominions as 'autonomous communities within the British Empire, equal in status, in no way subordinate one to another in any aspect of their domestic or external affairs, though united by a common allegiance to the Crown, and freely associated as members of the British Commonwealth of Nations'.[2] When, somewhat belatedly in February 1930, Simon realized that the Irwin declaration committed Britain to applying to India any definition of Dominion Status that the white Dominions might obtain at the forthcoming Imperial Conference, he was alarmed. He would dodge the issue by 'not saying anything about this sort of subject in our Report'.[3]

Irwin, as his papers reveal, accepted the change with realism and imagination. He recalled his attitude succinctly in the course of criticizing his adversaries: '. . . whatever might be the exact definition of Dominion Status worked out by ingenious disciples of the law, it in no way touched my conviction that you could not, without losing India from the Commonwealth, hold out a future for her less honourable than that to which constitutional development had brought Canada or Australia.'[4] Baldwin

illustrations of the widespread use of the term 'Dominion Status' in relation to India.

[1] Earl of Winterton, Diary of 25 October 1929, in *Orders of the Day*, London, 1953, p. 158.
[2] D. L. Keir, *The Constitutional History of Modern Britain, 1485–1937*, London, 1948 ed., p. 543.
[3] Simon to Irwin, 20 February 1930, S.C.C.
[4] Earl of Halifax, *Fulness of Days*, London, 1957, p. 122.

backed him admirably on this cardinal principle: '... can there be any doubt whatever ... that the position of an India, with full, responsible Government in the Empire, when attained, ... must be one of equality with the other States in the Empire? ... surely no one dreams of a self-governing India with an inferior status.'¹ Benn, pressed hard to say whether the declaration involved a change of policy, sidestepped the question in its legalistic form and spoke of 'a new spirit' in policy: 'There has been an effort made to make the Indian people realize the position which they occupy in the British Commonwealth, to give them an assurance of equality.'²

Birkenhead was prepared to make an ultimate appeal to a racial distinction: 'We are not dealing with the case of a daughter nation of our own creed and of our own blood.'³ Benn was proud to have 'got rid of the Birkenhead tone',⁴ which Irwin regarded as a standing offence to the people of India. It is significant, however, that the racial test could not, in 1929, be swept contemptuously aside. Baldwin could not ignore it, and his Commons speech contained a long passage on the common Aryan background of Indians and Europeans.

Still, the 1929 declaration does mark the tangible beginning of the multi-racial Commonwealth.

V. THE INDIAN RESPONSE

Irwin's immediate aim in defining Britain's purpose was to transform the Indian political scene. Throughout October Irwin's initiative seemed likely to win Indian Liberal and moderate Congress support for a Round Table Conference. Early in the month, Hailey wrote: 'It is clear that many of the older men in the Congress itself as well as the Liberals would not be unwilling to find a temporary landing-place in which they could rest awhile, and avoid being swept out into the stream of "Independence" and "Young India" politics.'⁵ Goschen mentioned that

¹ *Commons' Debates*, 7 November 1929.
² Ibid.
³ *Lords' Debates*, 5 November 1929. Lord Crewe's speech showed that he had not advanced from his 1912 position. Then, as secretary of state in Asquith's Liberal government, he had opposed conferring 'real self-government ... upon a race which is not our own race' (*Lords' Debates*, 24 January 1912).
⁴ *Commons' Debates*, 7 November 1929.
⁵ Hailey to Irwin, 7 October 1929, I.C. 23.

Motilal as well as Jinnah and Jayakar were anxious to counteract the 'Youth Movement'. Motilal had told him that 'a Round Table Conference ... would help him considerably'.[1] The omens remained favourable after the Congress leaders had received advance notice of the contents of the declaration. On 25 October Mears reported that Sapru's attitude was 'most encouraging' and that of Motilal, whom he had visited, 'quite encouraging enough'.[2] Further: 'Your Excellency may take it as a *matter of certainty* that Mr. *Gandhi* (if health permits), Motilal and Sapru will most readily go to London.' As regards Gandhi, Mears's authority was Sapru, who was 'quite sure about it'. There was good reason for the confidence to which Irwin gave expression in his cable entreating the Cabinet not to delay the declaration: '... I have now little doubt that the Congress ... will be disposed to accept it, and I see a real possibility of the thing coming off as well as the Cabinet have always hoped.'[3]

On 31 October the declaration was welcomed at Bombay by a group of leaders that included Setalvad, Jayakar, Jinnah, Mrs. Sarojini Naidu, and the business magnate, Sir Purshotamdas Thakurdas. Motilal called a meeting for 1 and 2 November at Patel's house in Delhi. Some thirty leaders attended, among them Gandhi, Motilal and Jawaharlal, Malaviya, Moonje, Mrs. Besant, Subhas Chandra Bose, Muhammad Ali, Ansari, Sapru, and Sastri. The moderates were warm in their reception of the declaration, and the manifesto that was issued was generally regarded as a victory for them. All except Bose, the young Independence League leader, signed the Delhi Manifesto on 2 November. It offered co-operation with Britain in the framing of a new constitution. The offer was not conditional but was accompanied by the expectation that political prisoners should be released and that the Congress should send the majority of the Indian delegates to the conference. The Manifesto also interpreted Irwin's declaration to mean that the conference was 'to meet not to discuss when Dominion Status was to be established, but to frame a scheme of Dominion constitution for India'.[4] Irwin felt that these elements of the Manifesto were included

[1] Goschen to Irwin, 8 October 1929, I.C. 23.
[2] Mears to Irwin, 25 October 1929, I.C. 23.
[3] Viceroy to Sec. of S., 29 October 1929, I.C. 5.
[4] *Sunday Times* and *Observer*, 3 November 1929.

in order to help the extremists to save face, and he regarded the Liberals' signatures as an assurance that they would not be pressed as conditions of co-operation. It was, of course, impossible for Irwin to accept the Manifesto's interpretation of the purpose of the Conference. That would certainly have involved the supersession of the Simon Commission, and Simon had accepted the plan for a free conference on the assurance of MacDonald that it was to be 'a means of ascertaining views', not an 'organ for negotiating'.

The Manifesto masked for a brief moment the divisions within the nationalist ranks over the declaration. Some Liberals were critical of their representatives signing it. Sivaswamy Aiyer and Setalvad took Sapru to task for accepting the Congress demand for a majority at a Round Table Conference, and the former objected to the 'condition' claiming Dominion Status at once. When Sapru explained that he viewed the 'conditions' as recommendations Sivaswamy replied that Gandhi could plausibly present them as conditions and attack Sapru for inconsistency if he rejected them.[1] Sastri emphasized that the term 'conditions' was purposely avoided at the Liberals' request and argued that the Liberals would be foolish to break with the Congress over the Manifesto.[2] At the other end of the political spectrum, Jawaharlal bitterly regretted adding his signature. He had done so only under extreme pressure from Gandhi, who insisted that as a member of the Congress Working Committee and president elect he could not override the will of his colleagues.[3] On 4 November Jawaharlal wrote to Gandhi that his signature was inconsistent with his position as president of the Indian Trade Union Congress and secretary of the Independence for India League. He favoured resigning his offices of secretary and president elect of the Congress. He was soothed by Gandhi's reassurance of the correctness of his actions.[4] Motilal stressed that as the conditions would not be accepted Jawaharlal need not feel bound to the Congress right wingers and the Liberals. The parliamentary debates would produce a rejection of the Mani-

[1] Aiyer to Sapru, 6 November 1929, and Sapru to Aiyer, 12 November 1929, Sapru Coll., Ser. 1, A. 138, A. 157.
[2] Sastri to Vaman Rao, 7 November 1929, Sastri Coll. No. 525.
[3] B. S. Moonje's Diary, 2 November 1929; Mears to Benn, 1 December 1929, India Office, L/PO/14.
[4] In J. Nehru (ed.), *A Bunch of Old Letters*, London, 1960 ed., pp. 76-8.

festo and the C.W.C. would have to advocate 'a campaign of civil disobedience with complete independence as the goal'.[1] On 7 November, when news of the Lords' debate reached India, Motilal wrote to Jawaharlal that the Delhi statement must now be consigned to the dustbin: 'The matter for immediate consideration is the mobilization of our forces.'

In view of the parliamentary debates and the exchange of letters between Baldwin and MacDonald, Gandhi was inclined to mistrust Britain's sincerity of purpose. Even at the time of the Manifesto he was not enthusiastic for a Round Table Conference. When Sastri warned him that steep conditions would break the Conference scheme, Gandhi replied that 'he did not mind it a bit'.[2] He looked forward to an early victory in any event and felt that the way of ultimata and direct action was more likely to be fruitful than the Conference. Nor did Gandhi much care for the constitutional niceties of Dominion Status. He wrote in *Young India* on 14 November:

> I can wait for the dominion status constitution, if I can get the real dominion status in action, if today, there is a real change of heart, a real desire on the part of the British people to see India a free and self-respecting nation and on the part of the officials in India a true spirit of service. This means substitution of the steel bayonet by that of the goodwill of the people. Are Englishmen and Englishwomen prepared to rely for the safety of their lives and property upon the goodwill of the people rather than upon their gun-mounted forts? If they are not yet ready, there is no dominion status that would satisfy me. My conception of dominion status implies present ability to sever the British connection if I wish to. Therefore, there can be no such thing as compulsion in the regulation of relations between Britain and India. If I choose to remain in the empire, it is to make the partnership a power for promoting peace and goodwill in the world, never to promote exploitation or what is known as Britain's imperialistic greed.

The same day he wrote to a friend in England that above all he needed evidence of British good faith if he were to commend the Conference to the Congress:

> ... you will be patient with me if I do not take things quite on trust.

---

[1] Motilal to Jawaharlal, 7 November 1929 (2 letters), Jawaharlal–Motilal Correspondence, Nehru Coll.

[2] Cited in Sastri to Vaman Rao, 7 November 1929, loc. cit.

I want some absolute guarantee that things are not what they seem. The two Parliamentary debates contain nothing, not even in Benn's speech, that would give me assurance that I may approach the Conference with confidence and safety. I would far rather wait and watch and pray than run into what may after all be a dangerous trap, [though it] may be quite unintended. The Montagu reforms have proved illusory.... The price that was paid for the reforms was altogether too heavy. I want to pay no price for Dominion Status or whatever name the reality is called by. Why should a creditor have to pay anything for the repayment of debts due to him? I will follow the methods that I have adopted throughout life, and as for instance in South Africa. Immediately I found that Smuts meant well I capitulated but I did so after having taken a written assurance from him. How the events will shape themselves in the next few days I do not know.[1]

British statesmen scratched their heads in wonder at what Gandhi meant by Dominion Status. Irwin felt that he meant a certain right to achieve freedom from British control, rather than the achievement itself. Hailey wrote that Gandhi thought of Dominion Status as 'a frame of mind, which asserts itself in amnesties, suppression of police activity, and a general kind of political kiss-in-the-ring'.[2]

On 18 November, when the Delhi signatories met again at the Nehrus' house in Allahabad, Sapru noted that the moderates' task had been made difficult by the parliamentary debates and the Baldwin–MacDonald exchange of letters. Jawaharlal cited extracts from the debates to illustrate Britain's hypocrisy. Gandhi sympathized with the young Congressmen's mistrust of Britain and looked for some further evidence of a 'change of heart': a release of prisoners or a more liberal spirit in provincial administration. However, the cry of the signatories who favoured attending the Conference was, according to Mears: 'Are you going to wreck everything for this young man?'[3] Gandhi supported the Manifesto and it was reaffirmed.

By the beginning of December, Vithalbhai Patel, who with his brother Vallabhbhai was anxious to accept the Conference offer, appealed to Irwin to see Gandhi before the Congress met

[1] Gandhi to Fenner Brockway, 14 November 1929, Gandhi Coll. No. 15731.
[2] Irwin to Lord Lytton, 24 December 1929, I.C. 18.
[3] Mears to Benn, 1 December 1929, loc. cit.; Sapru to Irwin, 25 November 1929, S.C.C.

in annual session at Lahore. He stressed the immense difficulties of Gandhi and his co-workers and that if they insisted upon conditions they did so 'not in a spirit of bargaining but with a view to enable them to take the Congress with them'.[1] In the middle of December Jawaharlal, as president of the All-India Federation of Trade Unions, declared his opposition to settling the constitutional issue by negotiation. Vithalbhai observed that he was backed by 'all the younger and more radical elements in the country [and] that a split was inevitable in the Congress ranks'.[2]

By 23 December, when Gandhi, Motilal, Patel, Jinnah, and Sapru met Irwin at his magnificent new residence, Viceroy's House, New Delhi, Gandhi and Motilal had decided to attend a Round Table Conference only if Irwin assured them that the British Cabinet would support their demand for immediate Dominion Status, both at the Conference and in parliament. Gandhi put their demand bluntly at the beginning of the meeting and observed that 'unless agreement was reached on this point he felt it fruitless to proceed to any other question'.[3] Irwin indicated that it was impossible for the government to support a demand for immediate Dominion Status or to define the Conference's task as drafting a Dominion constitution. He stressed the freedom of the Conference to propose Dominion Status and to discuss the obstacles to achieving it. He challenged Gandhi to say whether he believed in the sincerity of Britain's declared purpose. When Gandhi said that he doubted Britain's sincerity but not Irwin's, Irwin observed that there was 'obviously no common ground between himself and Mr. Gandhi'. Irwin regarded the Congress mistrust of Britain's goodwill as directly attributable to the British reaction to his declaration. Long afterwards he continued to lament a missed opportunity and to hold his British opponents of November 1929 responsible for it. In 1953 he noted that Congress rejection of his initiative 'was the direct consequence of the clatter created in England by my Declaration, which ... did so much to undermine the confidence of Indian leaders in our purpose, or at least in our capacity to

[1] Vithalbhai to Irwin, 2 December 1929, in G. I. Patel, *Vithalbhai Patel: Life and Times*, 2 vols., Bombay, 1951, II. 1067.
[2] Ibid. II. 1080.
[3] Minutes of meeting at Viceroy's House on 23 December 1929, India Office, L/PO/14; and Motilal to Gandhi, 18 February 1930, Motilal Corr., Nehru Coll.

give our purpose effective shape'.[1] Indians felt that 'however nice the Viceroy might be a very influential chunk of the Conservative Party was against them'.[2] In his memoirs, Irwin deplored the 'missing of this opportunity, if such it was, to bring into closer harmony the political thought of the two countries', for which 'a large part of the blame must rest upon British shoulders'.[3] Such an interpretation of Gandhi's behaviour has the attraction of finding consistency in Gandhi's choice of the occasions for his great campaigns. As in 1920, when Gandhi turned to non-co-operation largely because of British public and parliamentary responses to the Amritsar wrong and the Hunter Report, so now in 1929 did he move towards civil disobedience because of the reactions to the Irwin declaration.

However, there were deeper currents in the troubled waters of Indian politics. As the Viceroy's House meeting wore on Jinnah and Sapru reasoned with Gandhi and Nehru, urging them to realize that the avowal of Dominion Status and the offer of a Conference were tangible advances in British policy. Gandhi then said that

> he did not want his people to go to the Conference in their weakness. While India was disunited as she was at present, and while there were these vast differences of opinion among his friends, there was no use in going to London. . . . For this lack of unity he blamed British rule and said that he had learned the lesson of divide and rule from the British. . . . Could the Round Table Conference bring about unity in England? . . . The only difficulty he saw was the lack of unity. If there were complete unity, His Majesty's Government could not refuse to admit the grant of Dominion Status.

It is quite clear that Gandhi was not referring to the left and right wings of the Congress but to the Hindu–Muslim conflict. When Motilal wrote to Gandhi in complaint against the viceroy's secretary's transcript of the discussion, he was explicit about the thrust of Gandhi's remarks: that 'owing to [the] weakness in [the] communal position the British Cabinet's assurance of support was necessary'. There was 'no use going to London while communal differences persisted', unless the Indian leaders knew that the viceroy and the Cabinet would support their claims. To

---
[1] Halifax to Hoare, 1 September 1953, Templewood Coll. 24.
[2] Halifax to Hoare, 13 July 1953, ibid.
[3] *Fulness of Days*, p. 123.

The Promise of Partnership

go to a Conference divided and without assured British backing for Dominion Status would be to invite Britain to play off the communities against each other and to deny constitutional advance in view of their disunity.

To appreciate Gandhi's preoccupation with unity it is necessary only to recall the communal impasse that had been reached in the aftermath of the Nehru Report. Coatman wrote of a hardening of communal lines from that time:

> From 1928 onwards there is quite definitely a new model of Hindu–Moslem antagonism which shows itself in organized political action for political ends. It is something deeper, more enduring, more embracing in its objectives than the old traditional, semi-instinctive antagonism which vented itself in street fights, and stone-throwing, and quarter-staff play on days of religious ceremonies or festivals. The Moslems are manoeuvring for position in readiness for the coming of responsible self-government....[1]

In mid-1929, when Mrs. Sarojini Naidu, the poetess, an ardent follower of Gandhi, arranged a meeting between Gandhi and Jinnah, the Hindu Mahasabha at once brought pressure to bear upon Gandhi. The Mahasabha had not wavered after its rejection of Jinnah's demands in December 1928. It remained 'uncompromisingly opposed' to separate electorates and insistent upon 'unconditional joint electorates'.[2] Provinces must not be reorganized to produce statutory communal majorities and residuary powers must lie with the central government. Moonje advised Jayakar that if Gandhi yielded to the Muslims he would forfeit Hindu support and he urged Malaviya not to negotiate with Jinnah.[3] He was deeply suspicious of the Congress Muslim leaders, Dr. Ansari and Abul Kalam Azad.[4] Moonje wrote direct to Gandhi to urge him not to agree to any modification of the Nehru Report in order to placate the Muslims, and a group of Bombay Hindus proffered similar advice.[5] Jayakar counselled him that no concession could possibly be made except at the stage when a Dominion consitution was being framed.[6] Earlier

---

[1] J. Coatman, *Years of Destiny: India, 1926–32*, London, 1932, p. 215–16.
[2] Moonje to Raja Narendra Nath, 25 June 1929, Jayakar Coll. 437.
[3] Moonje to Jayakar, 31 July 1929, ibid.
[4] Moonje to Malaviya, 31 July 1929, ibid.
[5] Moonje to Gandhi, 5 August 1929, and Jayakar to Moonje, 21 August 1929, ibid.
[6] Jayakar to Gandhi, 23 August 1929, Jayakar Coll. 407.

concessions would be plucked from their context and become the basis for further demands. Clearly, Gandhi could foresee that he would have no room for manoeuvre on the communal question unless the government were prepared to back his demand for Dominion Status.

It is scarcely surprising that Gandhi refused to attend a Conference in London without being assured of either Indian unity or government support for Indian freedom.

On 31 December 1929 at Lahore the Congress, under Gandhi's guidance, rejected the Round Table Conference initiative and resolved to resort to civil disobedience for the achievement of complete independence. Gandhi preserved the substantial unity of the Congress by bowing to the younger Nehru, though older Congressmen—moderates, Muslims, Hindu communalists, and industrialists—regarded the resolution as a mistake, and the Responsive Co-operators did not accept it at once.[1] Gandhi was now to launch his own experiment in national solidarity and swaraj.

[1] B. Shiva Rao to Sapru, 9 January 1930, Sapru Coll., Ser. 2, R. 129.

CHAPTER 3

The Formula for All-India Federation: January 1930—January 1931

His Majesty's Government has taken note of the fact that the deliberations of the Conference have proceeded on the basis, accepted by all parties, that the Central Government should be a Federation of all-India, embracing both the Indian States and British India in a bi-cameral legislature.... With a Legislature constituted on a federal basis, His Majesty's Government will be prepared to recognise the principle of the responsibility of the Executive to the Legislature.

RAMSAY MACDONALD, 19 January 1931

I. OVERTURES TO THE CONFERENCE

IN the sharply divided world of Indian politics the price of conciliatoriness was often isolation. Jinnah, the 'ambassador of Indian unity', had split the Muslim League in an attempt to reach a communal accommodation with the Congress. He had become mistrusted by the Muslim leaders of the Muslim-majority provinces and the Congress Muslims had deserted him. Sapru had endured criticism from Liberal colleagues for his efforts to accommodate the Congress point of view in the Delhi Manifesto. He had felt in November 1929 that 'if there is no room for me in the Congress there is also very little for me in the Liberal Party'.[1] He was 'dejected and disgusted' by what he regarded as the betrayal by Gandhi and Motilal on 23 December.[2] Irwin himself had suffered ignominy in his own party only to be rebuffed by Gandhi. The Congress rejection of the Round Table Conference offer left all three with the problem of finding sufficient support to make effective the policy in which they had collaborated.

Both Sapru and Jinnah believed that Indians must as a first priority solve the communal problem. If India could not achieve

[1] Sapru to Srinivasa Sastri, 10 November 1929, Sapru Coll. (hereafter referred to as S.C.), Ser. 2, S. 101.
[2] Sapru to Nawab Sir Muhammad Ahmad Said Khan, 6 January 1930, S.C. 2, K. 55.

her own unity then she could scarcely expect to achieve dominionhood. In December 1929, when Sapru urged Jinnah to take an initiative towards a communal settlement, Jinnah replied that there was 'no fundamental difference' between their views and suggested that Sapru 'fearlessly criticize' any of the fourteen points that seemed 'unreasonable'.[1] The ensuing correspondence revealed some sharp differences but also sincere determination to find means of accommodating them.

Sapru challenged several of the fourteen points and doubted whether Jinnah would 'find many people outside the Muslim League who could agree to them'.[2] In particular, Sapru held 'very strong views as to residuary powers'. While Jinnah and the League saw the devolution of residuary powers upon the provinces as a check on a central Hindu raj enforcing its will on Muslim-majority provinces, Sapru regarded it as subversive of national strength. A united nation required a strong central government: 'On this point I feel so very strongly that I cannot agree to any compromise.'[3]

Sapru also attacked other points that seemed inimical to territorial patriotism and protective of social institutions based on religion. To give religious groups a veto on social legislation would paralyse society. To provide separate avenues for entry into public life, either by separate electorates or the statutory reservation of posts in the public services or seats in cabinets, would retard the emergence of a common nationhood.

However, Sapru was not insensitive to Muslim anxieties. He accepted the inviolability of the Muslim majorities in the Punjab and Bengal, and was responsive to the case for giving full provincial status to the North-West Frontier Province, Sind, and Baluchistan.

Indeed, for the sake of a communal settlement Sapru was prepared for any concession or compromise (including separate electorates) that did not positively prevent the creation of a strong central government. Constitutional anomalies and religious prejudices should be tolerated for the sake of reassuring the minorities.

At the end of December 1929, the annual meeting of the National Liberal Federation endorsed a proposal of Sapru's that

[1] Jinnah to Sapru, 14 December 1929, S.C. 2, J. 41.
[2] Sapru to Jinnah, 19 December 1929, S.C. 2, J. 42.   [3] Ibid.

he should work for a loose organization of all parties that espoused the goal of Dominion Status but repudiated Jawaharlal's objective of an independent, socialist India. During the early months of 1930 he wrote hundreds of letters, to leaders of the Muslim parties, the Hindu Mahasabha, and the Justice Party, to Responsivists, Liberals, Anglo-Indians, and Indian Christians, to merchants, landlords, and princes, in order to convene a meeting or 'federation' of parties that would frame a united demand. He wanted, in particular, a communal agreement.

Sapru encountered most difficulty with the Hindu communalists. Suspicion of the Liberals led Malaviya and Kelkar to lay plans of their own for an all-party convention, making endorsement of the Delhi Manifesto a condition of attendance. Moonje was morbidly apprehensive of any move that might conciliate the Muslims. On 26 January he noted in his diary:

This is a time of great crisis for the Hindu community; there is a conspiracy between the bureaucracy, the Anglo-Indians and the Muslims to put down the Hindus forever; because it is the Hindus who are creating all these political struggles. Still the Hindus are disunited, indifferent and bent upon purchasing peace and amity with the Muslims by granting their demands, which are intended to lay an axe on our project of welding India into one nation.[1]

Moonje regarded the Liberals as 'a backboneless people' aspiring to national leadership.[2] Malaviya was 'a hopeless man in the matter of leadership' and 'may also be afraid of the Muslim dagger'. Moonje complained to Jayakar that 'none of these fellows, say Sir Tej Bahadur Sapru, Pandit Malaviyaji and others have the gut in them to oppose Mr. Jinnah'.[3] Jayakar insisted to Sapru that the Liberals must declare themselves on the communal question, stating the limits beyond which they would not go in negotiating with the Muslims. He saw little point in dealing with Jinnah, who was not representative of Muslim opinion. Furthermore, he was averse to negotiating with Muslims unless Britain guaranteed to give self-government to India according to a scheme of India's own devising. Otherwise there was no inducement for Hindus to make concessions.[4]

[1] B. S. Moonje's Diary, 26 January 1930.
[2] Moonje to Jayakar, 8 January 1930, Jayakar Coll. (hereafter referred to as J.C.), 452.   [3] Moonje to Jayakar, 13 January 1930, ibid.
[4] Jayakar to Sapru, 27 January 1930, ibid.

Sapru relied on Colonel Kailas Narain Haksar, a friend and relative by marriage, secretary of the Special Organization of the predominantly Hindu Chamber of Princes, and a Kashmiri Brahman who had been in the service of the old Maratha Confederacy state of Gwalior since 1903, as an intermediary between the Liberals and the Mahasabhites. Haksar succeeded in persuading Malaviya to attend a preliminary conference in Delhi late in February, when the Chamber of Princes would be in session and would provide moral support. However, consistently with the Mahasabha's policy since 1928, Moonje, Kelkar, and Jayakar favoured postponing any meeting until the Round Table Conference, when Simon would have reported and the question could be discussed in 'an atmosphere of finality'.[1] Similar views were held by the Liberal editor of the Allahabad *Leader*, C. Y. Chintamani.

The preliminary meeting achieved merely an airing of views and an agreement to meet again to seek some definite understanding before the Conference delegates proceeded to London. The Liberals and the Muslims held to this agreement but the Mahasabhites retreated from it. The mass support for Gandhi's famous salt march weakened their attachment to the Round Table Conference procedure. Early in May some of the Responsivists, including Malaviya, decided to join the civil disobedience movement by boycotting British goods. Malaviya and Moonje indicated to Sapru that the Mahasabha would not be represented at the all-parties meeting that was soon to be held. The May meeting achieved nothing.

During March Sapru was unable to do any useful work. As his mother lay dying, personal sorrow darkened his view of the political scene. He became alarmed by the development of civil disobedience into 'a mass movement with the deliberate object of defying the law. . . . The very framework of society is being attacked.'[2] He was depressed that the youth of the country spoke of preferring 'chaos for twenty-five years' to the constructive policy of the Round Table Conference.[3] He felt isolated from the main stream of Indian thought. Mears wrote of the change wrought by private grief and public disorder: 'His nerve, I am

---

[1] Sapru to H. N. Kunzru, 23 January 1930, S.C. 2, K. 203.
[2] Sapru to Irwin, 20 April 1930, I.C. 24.
[3] Mears to Irwin, 23 April 1930, I.C. 24.

afraid, is giving out and he told me . . . that he was thinking of leaving India for good and all. He says that the treatment which he receives from people who come to his house is making his life a misery, that he is regarded and spoken of as a traitor. . . .'[1] Sapru appealed to Irwin to rally the 'stable elements of the community' to the support of the Conference policy: princes, taluqdars, zamindars, businessmen, retired officials, former ministers, prominent Hindus, Muslims, Sikhs, and Parsis, Anglo-Indians, and the Depressed Classes.[2] He was desperate to find some counterpoise to the growing influence of the Congress.

Sir Pheroze Sethna, the president of the National Liberal Federation, Setalvad, and Jinnah were similarly worried by the drift of Indian opinion from the Round Table scheme. By the first week of May, when Irwin decided that Gandhi must be arrested, he was being pressed hard to complement his vigorous repression of civil disobedience with a fresh statement about the constructive purpose of the Round Table Conference.

From the time of the Lahore Congress, Irwin was keenly aware of the steady alienation of Indian opinion from his constructive policy. His task of rallying support was often made more difficult by comment in England. In January, Lord Russell, the under-secretary of state for India, was reported as saying in a speech at Cambridge that Dominion Status would not be possible in India for 'a long time'.[3] Russell denied the accuracy of the report but its circulation in India left an impression that even the Labour Government was insincere. A Rothermere press campaign against Irwin added further weight to the Congress argument that British opinion was unreconciled to viceregal plans for dominionhood. Irwin struggled to keep his constructive policy in the foreground. In May he announced that the Conference would be held on or around 20 October. He also urged Simon to include in his report a definition of Dominion Status and a consideration of the steps towards its realization. In an interview with Sapru he intimated that he favoured establishing conventions whereby the governor-general would choose some of his ministers from the elected members of the central assembly and accept their advice on purely Indian questions. However,

[1] Mears to Irwin, 2 May 1930, I.C. 24.
[2] Sapru to Irwin, 20 April 1930, I.C. 24.
[3] *Daily Telegraph*, 9 January 1930.

he insisted that the governor-general must retain power to discharge parliament's responsibility for such great questions as defence, foreign policy, law and order, and the protection of the minorities. Sapru described 'that sort of thing' as 'Dominion Status with safeguards'.[1] Irwin advised Benn that the influence of such men as Sapru could be re-established only by their being able to say that they had obtained 'Dominion Status with safeguards' at the Round Table Conference.

Towards the end of May Irwin cabled to Benn a concise explanation of the drift of Indians into the Congress camp:

... while crowd follows the band great bulk of intelligent opinion associated with it is influenced by genuine nationalist desire to secure political advance. Their faith in policy announced last autumn was badly shaken by contemptuous tone of some speeches in Parliamentary debates at that time and by Rothermere's ill-judged campaign following. This did untold harm. Result is that though many largely disapprove of Gandhi's methods, they sympathise with the broad purpose of getting India free of British control of which he has made himself the expression. This general feeling readily reinforced as it can be at any time by racial consciousness is responsible for present situation.[2]

In June, when Irwin saw an advance copy of the Simon Report, he bitterly regretted the 'very grave lack of imagination' betrayed by its total silence on Dominion Status.[3] Nor did the Report propose any advance towards responsibility in the central government. Irwin recommended that the secretary of state should reaffirm government policy in parliament immediately after the publication of the Report.

The draft statement that he cabled to Benn on 13 June contained five paragraphs.[4] The first was a simple expression of thanks to Simon and his colleagues. The second explained that the next stage was the Round Table Conference to bring Indian opinion freely to bear upon 'British Indian and All-Indian problems'. The third repeated Irwin's declaration that in the government's judgement 'the natural issue of India's constitutional progress, as contemplated in the Declaration of 1917,

---

[1] Irwin to Benn, 8 May. 1930, I.C. 6.
[2] Irwin to Benn, 24 May 1930, I.C. 11.
[3] Irwin to Benn, 19 June 1930, I.C. 6.
[4] Irwin to Benn, 13 June 1930, I.C. 11.

was the attainment of Dominion Status', and stressed the government's desire 'to lend every assistance in their power to India in such development'. The object of the Conference was 'to secure the greatest agreement for proposals consistent with this purpose', and, 'in particular, to explore means of making the most appropriate provision under the new Constitution for such vital matters as foreign policy, defence, internal security and the future position of minorities'. The fourth paragraph refused to anticipate the result of the Conference but appealed to the non-co-operators to attend. The final paragraph stated the government's intention 'that any... agreement at which the Conference is able to arrive will form the basis of proposals which His Majesty's Government will later submit to Parliament'.

Irwin was in fact going quite some way towards meeting Gandhi's conditions of 23 December 1929: that the government should support India's demand for Dominion Status at a Round Table Conference and in parliament. He was proposing an affirmation of the freedom of the Conference, an indication that its function was to consider India's development in relation to the goal of dominionhood and an intimation that its results would be embodied in draft legislation. Though the statement avoided an explicit avowal that the object of the Conference was to frame the heads of a constitution embodying 'Dominion Status with safeguards' it hinted at some advance in the central government, accompanied by special provisions for the continuing responsibility of parliament for certain major matters.

Recalling the parliamentary crisis of November, MacDonald resolved to consult the opposition leaders about the draft statement. To emphasize the government's support for Irwin's proposal he secured its endorsement by the Cabinet on 25 June. The next day, he and Benn met Lloyd George, Reading, Baldwin, and Austen Chamberlain at the House of Commons to consider the statement, which it was proposed to issue simultaneously in parliament and at Delhi by 7 July. It was at once apparent that Irwin and the Labour Government would again be confronted by the united opposition of the Conservative and Liberal parties.

The reactions of the opposition leaders at the 26 June meeting were probably spontaneous expressions of individual opinions. Chamberlain, the chief Tory spokesman, claimed that he had not consulted his colleagues. Reading and Lloyd George had discussed the draft statement with Herbert Samuel and Crewe only at luncheon that day. Nevertheless, though the emphasis of their comments varied the opposition spokesmen were unanimously critical of Irwin's draft. Chamberlain regarded the first paragraph as insufficiently laudatory of the Simon Report and objected to the third paragraph, which 'would lead Indians to believe that the Round Table Conference would have as its main work the framing of a Dominion Status constitution'.[1] Baldwin agreed that the third paragraph was 'a grave error' and would 'inevitably lead to trouble'.[2] Lloyd George similarly opposed the reiteration of the Dominion Status objective, particularly in a context where it 'tended to induce the belief in Indians that the principal subject for discussion at the Conference would be the framing of a Dominion Status Constitution'.[3] Reading pressed for the omission of the paragraph. MacDonald argued the delicacy of the situation in India but agreed to convey the criticisms to Irwin.

Irwin consulted his executive and cabled an appreciation of the seriousness of the situation.[4] The repressive measures introduced to combat civil disobedience had alienated a great deal of non-Congress Hindu sympathy from the government and even sterner measures were almost certain to be required. It was essential to show that 'repression is not the sole policy of the Government'. The limitations of the Simon Report, and in particular its silence over Britain's ultimate purpose, had cast 'very grave doubt on British intentions'. It would be preferable to issue no statement rather than one that suppressed all reference to Dominion Status. On the other hand, grave damage would be caused by an opposition attack in parliament.

Benn circulated copies of the telegram to the opposition leaders and arranged to meet them on 1 July in the prime minister's room at the House of Commons. On the preceding evening Reading consulted Simon about the telegram at ICI House and later at Reading's house in Curzon Street. Simon persuaded Reading that it was unnecessary to suppress the whole

[1] Reading's memorandum on meeting of party leaders, 26 June 1930, R.C. 57.
[2] Ibid.
[3] Ibid.
[4] Irwin to Benn, 28 June 1930, R.C. 57.

of Irwin's third paragraph. The goal of Dominion Status had been avowed in November and its reiteration now need suggest no change of policy. The error lay not in reaffirming the *ultimate* goal but in hinting at its possible realization at the Conference. Simon proposed omitting only the passage that enumerated the subjects requiring special treatment. If the reference to the particular were suppressed then the general purpose of the Conference remained open. Simon was more worried about the undertaking in Irwin's fifth paragraph, to the effect that the government would prepare legislation on the basis of an agreement achieved by the Conference. He feared the government delegation to the Conference reaching an agreement with Indian delegates of the government's choosing, and the presentation of the *fait accompli* to parliament.

Reading's discussions with Simon nourished a suspicion that Irwin and the Labour Government might, as in the previous October, be hatching a scheme in concert with the nationalist leaders. Before the meeting of 1 July Reading discussed the situation with Lloyd George, Samuel, Crewe, and Chamberlain.

In the prime minister's room Reading sympathized with Irwin's difficulties and offered to accept a reaffirmation of the Dominion Status objective, provided that the offensive section of the third paragraph was suppressed, and given an assurance that the government did not regard the statement as a change of policy. Even then he would accept no responsibility for the statement, though he would deprecate a parliamentary debate upon it. He also appealed to MacDonald for reassurance that the government did not contemplate going beyond the Simon Report with regard to the central government.

Chamberlain and Baldwin could not go so far. A reiteration of the Dominion Status objective would produce a Conservative challenge in parliament. Chamberlain supported Reading's appeal for a government undertaking on the future of the central government.

Reading and the Tories failed to extract assurances from MacDonald and they were left with 'distinct uneasiness and even apprehension as to the future policy of the Viceroy and His Majesty's Government'.[1] Reading noted: 'That there is something happening beyond what was disclosed to us is quite

[1] Reading's memorandum on meeting of 1 July 1930, R.C. 57.

clear to me.'¹ He was now less sure that he would deprecate a debate on an amended version of the viceroy's draft.

Irwin relieved Reading of the need to decide the point. The certainty of the Conservatives challenging the statement induced him to drop the plan for its delivery in parliament. In consideration of his so doing he hoped that the opposition parties would agree to his making a speech in which he would emphasize, first, that the 1929 declaration remained official policy; second, that the Conference would not be fettered in any way by the recommendations of the Simon Commission; and third, that if an agreement were reached at the Conference it would be embodied in a bill to be laid before parliament.²

On 4 July copies of Irwin's proposed speech were sent to the opposition leaders. They found much in it to dislike. Pressed by Chamberlain, Baldwin at once cabled to Irwin the unanimous objection of the Tory leaders to the term 'Dominion Status'.³ The preservation of the *status quo* in the central executive was fundamental to the Simon Report and 'essential to the continuation of all-Party agreement on Indian policy'. Chamberlain drafted a Commons motion thanking the Simon Commission and recording a 'sense of the high authority and intrinsic value' of its Report.⁴

Passages in Irwin's proposed speech deepened the suspicions of Reading and Simon that there was a plot in the making. Irwin had stressed that his government must make its own appraisal of the Simon Report and that non-official Indian opinion must be consulted. He had described the Conference as no 'mere meeting for discussion' but a 'Joint Assembly of representatives of both countries, on whose agreement the precise proposals to Parliament should be founded'. On 6 and 7 July Reading discussed such points with Simon, Chamberlain, and Lloyd George. He drafted a memorandum on the implications for future procedure of Irwin's speech, and he gave a copy of it to Chamberlain.⁵

---

¹ Ibid. ² Irwin to Benn, 2 and 3 July 1930, I.C. 11.
³ Baldwin to Irwin, 4 July 1930, enclosed with Benn to Irwin, 4 July 1930, I.C. 11.
⁴ Copy of Chamberlain's draft motion received by Reading on 7 July 1930, R.C. 57.
⁵ Reading's memorandum of [?] 7 July 1930, marked 'copy to A. Chamberlain', R.C. 57.

The Formula for All-India Federation

Reading observed that Irwin's speech revealed that 'Indian leaders are being encouraged to ask for more and to complain that the Report does not propose to establish Dominion Status'. If, in the terms of the November declaration, the Conference delegates were to be members of the Labour Government and Indians selected by the viceroy, it seemed probable that the Conference would 'agree in rejecting the Report and proposing, however vague, something they will call "Dominion Status" '. There seemed therefore to be 'a great deal of significance to be attached to the assurance . . . that whatever agreement is reached at the Round Table Conference thus constituted will be inserted in the Bill which the Government will introduce'. Reading concluded that there was a strong case for extending the all-party approach of the Statutory Commission by providing for all-party representation at the Conference.

At 9.30 p.m. on 7 July the leaders of the three parties met again. Baldwin and Chamberlain agreed that Irwin's proposed speech was 'much less objectionable' than the original draft statement, but they still regarded a parliamentary debate upon it as unavoidable.[1] Chamberlain suggested that mischief might be prevented if MacDonald would propose the motion thanking the Simon Commission that he had himself drafted. He, Baldwin, and Lloyd George agreed that the motion could be followed by a 'not unfriendly' debate on the composition of the Conference, at which, they urged, all three British parties should be represented. MacDonald made no promises but he did say that he would do his best to prevent party conflict over India. He removed some of Reading's fears by denying explicitly that Irwin would negotiate the cessation of civil disobedience by offering Dominion Status with safeguards to the Congress.

Irwin made his speech on 9 July. At once Chamberlain sought MacDonald's agreement to another confabulation.

At a meeting on 10 July MacDonald reported that the Cabinet had agreed to his proposing a motion of thanks to the Simon Commission, though he would stress that its Report was not definitive. The question of party representation at the Conference was again aired, and it became apparent that Reading and Chamberlain would be predisposed to uphold the Simon Report at the Conference.

[1] Reading memo. on meeting of leaders, 7 July 1930, R.C. 57.

Benn consulted Irwin about party representation. Earlier in the year Irwin had been quite prepared to accept it but now he believed that co-operative Indians would regard it as a 'breach of faith'.[1] It was bound to be construed as a device to consolidate British opinion against Indian and so prejudge the outcome of the Conference. Correspondents such as Hoare, Lane Fox, and Dawson assured Irwin that the opposition demand was irresistible. Failure to accept it would precipitate a parliamentary motion to secure a definite endorsement of Simon's recommendations. Certainly the opposition leaders were unmoved by Irwin's protests. Indeed, they added the further demand that Simon should attend the Conference in an independent capacity.

The question was settled at the end of July when MacDonald announced that each of the opposition parties would be invited to send separate delegations to the Conference but that the government would retain its freedom of executive action at and after the Conference. There would be not one all-party delegation but three individual delegations, the Tories and the Liberals each having four members while the government would be represented by six to eight members of the Cabinet. Pressure for the representation of the Simon Commission was resisted effectively in both houses of parliament, partly because it was known that Baldwin would not support the demand.

After three years the Indian problem was now freed from the iron grip of the Simon Commission. The Conference would be untrammelled by Simon's presence. Irwin was free to draft his own proposals on constitutional reform. However, the meetings of June and July had shown that the opposition representatives would go to the Conference disposed to resist an advance in the central executive.

The dispute over Irwin's mid-year proposals for a policy declaration indicated a new and significant divergence between Conservative and Liberal attitudes. Reading and Simon were prepared to give their tacit assent to a parliamentary avowal of the Dominion Status objective whereas the Conservatives, on the whole, were not. Here was a shift in the Liberal position. Of course Simon had originally been receptive to the idea of the November declaration, but then Burnham's opposition to the declaration had shown that the issue might split the Commission.

[1] Irwin to Benn, 17 July 1930, I.C. 11.

The Formula for All-India Federation

Reading had expected that Indians would use the declaration to secure the conferment of Dominion Status at once and saw insuperable difficulties in advancing otherwise than by stages. Burnham's continued hostility was a good tactical reason for Simon's avoidance of the question in his Report, though he defended the omission in terms of the obscurity of 'Dominion Status' as an expression and the contradiction inherent in the phrase 'Dominion Status with safeguards'. Once the Commission had reported neither Reading nor Simon objected to the avowal of Dominion Status as the *ultimate* goal, provided that the government was prepared to retain a 'strong' central executive to control its achievement by stages.

However, the opposition parties were still in accord over immediate policy. Both thought that the Simon proposals afforded the necessary strength in the central executive. When, during July, they began to suspect Irwin and the government of antipathy towards the Simon centre they entertained a common fear of a 'sell out' on Dominion Status.

Here they did Irwin an injustice. He was not contemplating central responsibility or even central dyarchy. His hostility to Simon's centre sprang from a conviction that Simon misunderstood the prerequisites of strong government and that the strength in his scheme was illusory. As at the time of the 1929 declaration so now with the appearance of the Report, Irwin identified Simon's shortcomings in terms of integrity, candour, and intellectual rigour. Harold Laski, watching developments from the sidelines, agreed. He thought it 'queer how all Simon's defects come out in the document—it is brilliantly written, clear, logical, concise, but lacking in generosity, cold, even, in places, callous, and wanting in that power to make the reader feel he *ought* to go along with the writer'.[1]

Irwin believed that Simon's 'strong centre' was 'quite unworkable', a 'conjuring trick', the 'biggest fraud that has ever been attempted'.[2]

Simon had earlier confessed to Irwin that he felt 'very great difficulty indeed about the Central Government'.[3] For the pro-

[1] Laski to Mr. Justice Holmes, 28 June 1930, in M. de Wolfe Howe (ed.), *Holmes–Laski Letters*, 2 vols., London, 1953, II. 1264.

[2] Irwin to Dawson, 22 July and 9 September 1930, I.C. 19; Irwin to Benn, 19 September 1930, I.C. 6.

[3] Simon to Irwin, 27 March 1930, I.C. 19.

vinces he confidently proposed the abolition of dyarchy and the introduction of full responsible government, subject to the governors' retention of certain reserve powers. While this 'experiment' was in operation a strong central government seemed essential. The Montagu–Chelmsford reforms had set up a central assembly of 145 members, of whom 26 were nominated officials, 14 nominated non-officials, and 105 elected through a system of territorial (including communal) constituencies. Though the viceroy's executive of seven members contained three Indians they were not drawn from the legislature or responsible to it. Nevertheless, the moral influence of the popular legislature was large, and if a state of friction between the two arms of government was to be avoided it behoved the viceroy to harmonize executive action with opinion in the legislature. Throughout the twenties relations between the central executive and the legislature had been strained. The same was generally true, *a fortiori*, in the provinces, where the experience of dyarchy suggested that departure from the unitary principle in the executive enhanced tension between the two arms of government. Simon's recommendations sought refuge in leaving the executive intact while reconstructing the legislature. In place of the central assembly, returned by direct election through territorial constituencies, they proposed a federal assembly, composed of members elected indirectly by the provincial legislatures.

Irwin recognized the advantage of an indirectly elected legislature, but he thought it a quite inadequate answer to the question of the development of the central government. It was a 'profound delusion' to imagine that a 'tame' legislature could be obtained through a process of indirect election: 'How does [Simon] suppose that any Executive Government labelled *strong* will in fact get its business through an elected Assembly of 280 with something like 15 or 17 official votes only?'[1] Irwin had experienced great difficulty in getting legislation through an assembly with a far higher proportion of official to elected members. Irwin assumed that if Simon had thought the problem through he must have envisaged the viceroy's appointment of popular Indians to his executive. Only the representation of popular opinion in the executive could ensure a harmonious re-

[1] Irwin to Benn, 19 September 1930, I.C. 6; Irwin to W.G.A. Ormsby-Gore, 18 July 1930, I.C. 19.

lationship with an elected legislature. Irwin suspected that Simon realized this implication of his scheme and that he suppressed it because political opinion in Britain would regard it with hostility.

Irwin's misgivings were shared by a conference of provincial governors that Irwin called in July. It agreed upon the need 'either to go back or forward' from the Simon scheme.[1] Some governors favoured advance, others the *status quo*.

Irwin thought it 'illogical' to proceed to a full transfer of power in the provinces and yet withhold all power at the centre.[2] In September he and his councillors embodied in a Dispatch a proposal to make the executive 'responsive' to a central legislature.[3] The main departure of the Dispatch from the Report lay in its attempt at a precise formulation of 'Parliamentary purposes' over which Britain must retain control, and in its readiness to entrust all other matters to popular Indians appointed to the viceroy's executive. Except for such matters as 'defence, foreign relations, internal security, financial obligations, financial stability, protection of minorities and of the rights of services recruited by the Secretary of State, and prevention of unfair discrimination',[4] the Government of India should rule in accordance with the desires of the Indian legislature. Irwin believed that such an arrangement would advance India from a position of 'subordination' to one of 'partnership'.[5]

It could be argued that the Dispatch did little more than spell out the implications of the Simon Report. When, eventually, Reading learnt of its contents he regarded them with remarkable equanimity. However, during August, September, and October, while Irwin's intentions remained unknown, he was possessed by fears of radical concessions being made in the central government. As the Liberal and Conservative delegations made their preparations for the Conference they continued to look for security in standing firmly behind the Simon centre.

II. THE CONFERENCE DELEGATIONS

The government delegation to the first Round Table Conference was eight strong and included the prime minister, the

[1] Irwin to Dawson, 22 July 1930, I.C. 19.
[2] Irwin to Linlithgow, 4 August 1930, I.C. 19.
[3] *Govt. of India Despatch on Proposals for Constitutional Reforms, 20 September 1930*, Cd. 3700, 1930. [4] Para. 116.
[5] Irwin to Viscount Cecil of Chelwood, 1 October 1930, I.C. 19.

lord chancellor (Lord Sankey), and Benn. The Conservative delegation was younger and less diehard than Irwin or the Labour Government could have dared to hope. Baldwin declined to lead it himself, partly to reserve his energies to defend his own shaky leadership, partly because he reasoned, correctly, that if he stood aside Lloyd George would do so too. Baldwin had lethargically allowed Chamberlain to mould the Shadow Cabinet's Indian policy during the July discussions with the other parties, and he now invited him to lead the Tory team at the Conference. Chamberlain hesitated, partly because Baldwin had not supported his claim to have Simon appointed to membership of the Conference, but more particularly because he sensed that Lord Salisbury and the diehards had never fully trusted his judgement since his negotiation of the Irish treaty of settlement in 1921. When Baldwin sounded Salisbury and learnt that he felt no confidence in Chamberlain, the latter declined to lead the Tory delegation. As Baldwin observed to Irwin, Salisbury blundered in thinking that Chamberlain would 'give everything away. . . . Austen's rigidity would have been the danger.'[1] Peel was given the leadership of the delegation. He was joined by the Marquess of Zetland, a former governor of Bengal with a sincere interest in India. At the behest of Sir Samuel Hoare, who saw India as a means of advancing his own political career, Irwin had already urged Baldwin to appoint some younger Tories to the delegation. Hoare himself was empanelled, together with Oliver Stanley, who admitted to knowing 'nothing about India except that it is very big and rather black'.[2] Irwin was 'delighted' with the team.[3]

Hoare soon became the most active member of the Conservative delegation. Peel was content to leave much of the work to him. Hoare swiftly obtained as the delegation's secretary R. J. Stopford, Simon's personal assistant throughout the Commission's inquiries. He arranged for the delegation to keep in close touch with the India Committee of the Conservative Party, of which Winterton now became chairman in place of Chamberlain, and which was open to all Conservative parliamentarians. He also arranged for the delegation to meet members of the

[1] Baldwin to Irwin, 16 October 1930, I.C. 19.
[2] Stanley to Hoare, n.d., Templewood Coll. 29.
[3] Irwin to Benn, 3 October 1930, I.C. 6.

diehard Indian Empire Society and the conservative committee of ex-governors of Indian provinces. Hoare was somewhat less liberally inclined than he presented himself to Irwin as being. Observers of the Conference were to note that he was apt to think less in terms of the best policy for India than of what would be acceptable to the Party.

The Liberal delegation was inevitably led by Reading. He had determined to give his full attention to the Indian question and he was to become the dominant opposition delegate. He was joined by Lord Lothian, the former Philip Kerr and one of Milner's kindergarten, ex-editor of the *Round Table*, and secretary to Lloyd George during his premiership. He had a profound belief in the Commonwealth ideal and had long been interested in Indian reform. The other Liberal delegates were Sir Robert Hamilton and Isaac Foot, neither of whom was steeped in the Indian question. The delegation's secretary was John Coatman, who knew India well from fifteen years in the Indian Police Service (1911–26) and five years as Director of Public Information and nominated member of the legislative assembly (1926–30). Reading's colleagues and Coatman were less impressed than their leader with the adequacy of the Simon Report, and they were more disposed to evaluate the Indian situation from the standpoint of liberal political theory. They were perhaps closer to the view of the Liberal Party worker in the constituency, or to the Liberal press, from which Reading's eminence naturally placed him at some distance.

During the second half of October, as the Indian delegates were arriving in London, Reading began to press Benn for an undertaking that the British delegations would work as a single parliamentary team. However, Benn had taken to heart Irwin's entreaties that the Indian delegates must be given no reason to suspect that the British parties were concerting a common policy in advance of the Conference. He also resented what he took to be Reading's wish to run the Conference, and determined that procedure must be decided by the members themselves. He remained aloof from the opposition delegates and refused to be drawn into any statement of government policy. Reading found it intolerable to contemplate the possibility that the opposition delegates would be left to fight the claims of the Indians to Dominion Status, while the government stood 'aloft in the position of a judge, remote from the strife in the arena.... After which they would come down from the Olympian heights and deliver judgement.'[1]

Towards the end of October some of the officials whom Irwin had sent home as advisers to the British delegations had interviews with Reading. Sir George Schuster (Finance Member of the Government of India) and Mr. H. G. Haig (Secretary of the Home Department) explained the policy of the Dispatch on reforms. They found Reading to be remarkably flexible. Coatman, too, reported his saying: 'I will go as far as I possibly can to support Lord Irwin.'[2] On 10 November Reading told a joint meeting of opposition delegates that he 'did not by any means rule out the Government of India's proposals'.[3] His fear now was that the Labour Government would feel a need to go further than the Conservative viceroy.

Reading was concerned above all else to avoid the government delivering judgement in favour of Dominion Status with temporary safeguards. On 10 November, with Peel's support, he issued an ultimatum to Benn:

Our view was that a demand would be made from the Indian side to know if we were prepared to agree to Dominion Status with certain reservations. We Liberals took the view that we and the Conservatives should not be put in the position of fighting this demand, with the Government doing nothing.... I said that if the Government was in favour of Dominion Status for India with temporary reservations, as far as I was concerned there was no good going on with the Conference. We said that presumably the Government would not want to go further than the Government of India's Despatch, but this we have not yet been able to learn from the Government. I said that we must have an answer before [the opening of the Conference on] 17 November.[4]

A crisis seemed to be in the making. It failed to develop because of the convergence of two sets of events. First, the British Indian delegates failed to achieve the communal settlement that was the precondition of a united demand for Dominion Status.

[1] Minutes of Liberal delegation meeting, 5 November 1930, R.C. 56 f.
[2] Coatman to Irwin, 31 October 1930, I.C. 19.
[3] Minutes of Liberal and Conservative delegations meeting, 10 November 1930, R.C. 56 g.
[4] Ibid.

The Formula for All-India Federation

Secondly, the Indian constitutional problem was transformed by the intervention of the Indian states' delegation.

Compared with the British delegations' total strength of sixteen members, British India sent some fifty-eight delegates.

A strong sixteen-member Muslim delegation was led by the Aga Khan. From the Punjab came the verteran politican Sir Muhammad Shafi and the brilliant young Chaudhuri Zafrullah Khan; from the U.P. the aged Khilafatist Muhammad Ali, the Nawab of Chittari, and the educationalist and professor of history at Allahabad University, Dr. Shafa'at Ahmad Khan; from Bengal there were Fazlul Huq and A. H. Ghaznavi; and from Bombay, of course, Jinnah. However, the greatest Muslim influence on the Conference, Mian Fazl-i-Husain, remained in India. Fazl-i-Husain had developed a strong political base as leader of the Unionist Party in the Punjab. He later extended his influence to all India through the Muslim Conference and by his membership of the viceroy's executive (1929–35). In the latter capacity he was well placed to learn the mind of the bureaucracy on communal and constitutional questions and to influence the membership of the Muslim delegation. He was hostile to Jinnah's conciliatoriness and relied upon his own favoured appointees, Zafrullah and Shafa'at, and of course the Aga Khan, to keep him in check. As the dominant politician in the Punjab, Fazl-i-Husain could act as arbiter of the conditions for a communal settlement. Coatman described him as the *eminence grise* behind the delegation, 'a man of inflexible will and immutable purpose, with a mind like a diamond which can cut its way through anything'.[1] De Montmorency made the following appraisal of him when he recommended his appointment to the viceroy's council.

He is extremely able and long-sighted and has a great power to grasp the essential principles of a difficult case. He is an excellent debater. He is excellent also at dealing with non-official members of a Legislature, keeping together a party in support of Government and warding off prejudice and opposition by private discussion. His faults are a sometimes too ardent communalism and sometimes a degree of cleverness in negotiation which higher standards than his own do not pass as within the legitimate sphere of action by a Government Member.[2]

---

[1] *Years of Destiny*, p. 107.
[2] De Montmorency to Irwin, 24 February 1929, I.C. 23.

The Liberals were powerfully represented by a delegation with a strong element of lawyer politicians whose exercise of high office had made them elder statesmen. The major figure, indeed, the dominant British Indian at the Conference, was Sir Tej Bahadur Sapru, a Kashmiri Brahman leader of the Allahabad Bar and former member of the viceroy's executive, who was steeped in constitutional law. It is possible, wrote Coatman ironically, 'that he does not, in his innermost heart, believe that the voice of the people is the voice of God'.[1] Srinivasa Sastri, the eminent imperial envoy, and Sir C. P. Ramaswami Aiyer (soon to be Law Member of the Government of India) came from Madras, Chintamani from the U.P., and Sir Cowasji Jehangir, Setalvad, and Sethna from Bombay.

The Hindu Responsivists and the Mahasabha were represented by the Poona eye surgeon, Dr. Balkrishna Shivaram Moonje, working president of the Mahasabha (1927–35), M. R. Jayakar and S. B. Tambe. 'Sturdy, stocky, ... [and with a] vivacious yet determined face and square, iron-grey beard',[2] Moonje combined the Maratha Brahman's conception of Hindu nationhood with a disregard for personal popularity. No conciliator, he was at the opposite communal pole from Fazl-i-Husain. He exerted great influence at the Round Table Conference simply by saying 'No' and by pressing Jayakar and, later, Gandhi to do the same. Even Jayakar, who was perhaps closer to his political outlook than any other delegate, wrote of him as 'a tactless and unpopular man whom nearly everybody dislikes'.[3] Raja Narendra Nath, the Hindu leader from the Punjab, also represented the Hindu communal point of view at the Conference.

The 'minor minorities' had delegations at the Conference: the Sikhs from the Punjab, Ujjal Singh and Sampuran Singh; the Depressed Classes, led by Dr. B. R. Ambedkar; the Justice Party, represented by Sir A. P. Patro and Ramaswami Mudaliyar; the Anglo-Indians or Eurasians (Lieutenant-Colonel H. A. J. Gidney); the Indian Christians (K. T. Paul) and the European resident non-official community (Sir Hubert Carr). In addition, there were representatives of Indian women (Begum Shah

---

[1] *Years of Destiny*, p. 101.
[2] Ibid., p. 98.
[3] Jayakar's Diary, 25 September 1931, J.C.

Nawaz), of the trade unions (N. M. Joshi), industry (H. P. Mody), and the landholders.

Though the delegates were mere nominees of the viceroy and as such held no mandate from the groups they claimed to represent, they were so eminent that any agreements that they endorsed would carry great weight in India.

The Simon recommendations, which reopened the question of representation by abolishing the blocs of official members in the provincial councils, predisposed the Muslim delegates to come to terms with the Hindus and present joint claims to the government. The Muslims wanted separate electorates to continue, with weightage on the existing basis in the Hindu-majority provinces, but on a population basis in the Punjab and Bengal. The Simon Report conceded the continuation of separate electorates everywhere and with the existing weightage in the Hindu-majority provinces. But it denied Muslims the enlargement of their share of seats in the Punjab and Bengal on a population basis, for that would give them unalterable statutory majorities. The Muslims must earn their majorities by capturing some seats in the general constituencies. In effect, the Commission offered Muslims either separate electorates on a population basis everywhere (which meant majorities in the Punjab and Bengal but loss of weightage in the Hindu-majority provinces), or general electorates in the Punjab and Bengal, and separate electorates with weightage in the Hindu-majority provinces.

In August, Fazl-i-Husain explained to Irwin that the Report undercut the 'fairly satisfactory' existing position of the Muslims.[1] In the Muslim-majority provinces of the Punjab and Bengal, where their majority position had been secured by the official blocs, Simon's recommendations would leave them with a minority of the seats. In the other, Hindu-majority, provinces the abolition of the official blocs would also undermine their position. In the Simon federal legislature they would be worse off than in the existing central assembly. Fazl-i-Husain outlined the conditions of Muslim co-operation with constitutional reform: the concession of a majority of the seats in the Punjab and Bengal; the separation of Sind from Bombay; and the elevation of the North-West Frontier Province to the status of a governor's province. He took separate electorates so much for granted, as

[1] Fazl-i-Husain to Irwin, 18 August 1930, I.C. 6.

a victory long since won, that he did not even mention them in this context. Muhammad Ali made clear his demands in his letter accepting the viceroy's invitation to the Conference. Separate electorates and weightage in the Hindu-majority provinces were

> not sufficient safeguards . . . under a so-called democratic and nationalist constitution. What we need is the strengthening of our position in the Provinces in which we constitute a majority such as the reformed Frontier, in the separated Sindh, the 56% Punjab and the 55% Bengal. The strengthening of our position there would protect the Muslim minorities in other Provinces far more effectively than mere weightage or even separate electorates.[1]

The Government of India's Reforms Dispatch of 20 September, to which of course Fazl-i-Husain was party, treated the Muslims more favourably than had the Simon Report. It agreed to the preservation of separate electorates and weightage in the Hindu-majority provinces, but felt that it would be unfair on that account to deny the Muslims their Bengal and Punjab majorities. It was disinclined to allow an outright statutory majority through separate electorates. However, it favoured some scheme by which the Muslims received separate electorates that would ensure them predominance commensurate with their numbers, but not a majority of seats. To secure majorities they would need to win some of the special seats to be allotted to the interests of labour, landholding, etc.

The contents of the Dispatch were not officially known to delegates until 13 November, a day after the ceremonial opening of the Conference. In consequence, during the voyage to London and for some time after their arrival, Muslim delegates were more inclined towards negotiation over separate electorates than they were likely to be after the tenor of the Dispatch leaked through to them.

Serious negotiations began on the communal issue aboard the *Viceroy of India*, which sailed from Bombay on 4 October and arrived in England a fortnight later. Its passengers included Sapru, Jayakar, Moonje, Patro, Ambedkar, Jinnah, and Shafa'at Ahmad. Moonje put the orthodox Mahasabha view that 'we

---

[1] Muhammad Ali to G. Cunningham (Irwin's private sec.), n.d. [August 1930], Md. Ali Coll.

must first pin down the British Government and then it won't take us 24 hours to settle terms between us'.¹ The Hindu communalists would make no concessions unless the Muslims backed a demand for Dominion Status. On the other hand, the Muslims would not agree to support a demand for Dominion Status without a prior agreement on the communal question. Moonje noted that the Non-Brahman and Untouchable representatives were apprehensive of the Brahmans and inclined to yield to the Muslims. In the early days after their arrival in London the Liberal, Muslim, and Mahasabha delegates met at the Savoy Hotel but failed to make any significant progress.

Soon after the Muslim delegates began to arrive in London, Sir Michael O'Dwyer renewed some old acquaintanceships. He reported to Reading the fears of some of them that 'if they ... go back to India with nothing in advance of the Simon proposals, they won't be able to face their own people'.² The delegation was divided but some Muslims were clearly predisposed to come to terms with the Hindus.

On 22 October, at his first interview with Benn, Sapru was encouraged to reach an agreement with the Muslims:

I told Wedgwood Benn that while I admired Lord Irwin I was not prepared to support him in all his recommendations and that I wanted nothing short of responsibility at the Centre.... [Benn said that] if we could come to a mutual understanding among ourselves we should win all along the line, and even though Labour might come out of office, the Government that succeeded it would not and could not go behind that agreement.³

Benn warned Sapru against Reading but said that Lothian and Hoare were 'good friends'. The Indian Liberals, as Sapru explained to a correspondent, had every inducement to settle the communal question: 'If we can present a united front it is the opinion of some of my most intimate friends, and I share that opinion, that we have more than got a chance of achieving Dominion Status with certain temporary safeguards.'⁴ It would seem that Reading had good reason for suspecting Benn of being

---

[1] Moonje's Diary, 7 October 1930.
[2] O'Dwyer to Reading, 4 November 1930, R.C. 56 j.
[3] Sapru letter of 23 October 1930, S.C. 1, Misc. 15.
[4] Sapru to Iswar Saran, 12 November 1930, S.C. 1, S. 18.

prepared to concede Dominion Status with temporary safeguards to a united Indian delegation.

At the beginning of November Sapru, Sastri, and Setalvad initiated talks with the Aga Khan, Jinnah, and Shafi at the Nawab of Bhopal's house, 25 Upper Brook Street. The group met almost nightly until the Conference opened on 17 November, with Jayakar and Moonje, Ambedkar, Ujjal Singh, and others often joining them. The Liberals offered to concede the Muslim claims for majorities in the Punjab and Bengal, the reforms in the N.W.F.P., the separation of Sind, weightage in Hindu-majority provinces, one third of the seats in a federal legislature, and a share in the executive government and administration in the various provinces. Instead of separate electorates the Liberals offered the reservation of seats. According to O'Dwyer, the attitude of some Muslims to these overtures was *timeo Danaos et dona ferentes*.[1] However, it seems clear that the main Muslim spokesmen, the Aga Khan, Jinnah, and Shafi, were prepared to join the Liberals to demand Dominion Status with temporary reservations if these concessions were agreed.

During the second week of November the obstacle to agreement came not from the Muslims but from Moonje and Jayakar. Moonje felt that he and Jayakar were being isolated by the Liberals' capitulations. On 14 November he noted that Sapru, Sastri, and their ilk were 'theorists, philosophers, metaphysicists [*sic*] and moralists. They are not fit for executive duties and have no executive mentality.'[2] He and Jayakar quibbled over the separation of Sind and refused to allow a Muslim majority in the Punjab or weightage in the provincial legislatures. They frustrated the achievement of a quick settlement. On 16 November, the eve of the Conference, a compromise was reached at Bhopal's house between the Aga Khan, Shafi, Jinnah, Sapru, Setalvad, Jayakar, and Moonje. The Muslims agreed to joint electorates in the provinces and at the centre, with reservation of seats for provincial minorities on a population basis; except that Bengal and the Punjab were to negotiate their own communal arrangements. Sind and the N.W.F.P. would become full provinces. There would be no social legislation inimical to the interests of a community. The Muslims would have

[1] O'Dwyer to Reading, loc. cit.
[2] Moonje's Diary, 14 November 1930.

The Formula for All-India Federation

30 per cent of the seats at the centre. However, not surprisingly, when the deal was put to the Muslim delegation they rejected it, thereby preventing the presentation of a united demand, supported by a Hindu–Muslim agreement, at the opening of the Conference.

The Indian States delegation was sixteen strong. It included representatives of the great south Indian states, Sir Akbar Hydari for Hyderabad and Sir Mirza Ismail for Mysore, Travancore, Cochin, and Pudakottai, the rulers of Rewa and Sangli, representing respectively the conservative and the smaller states, and twelve delegates for the generality of states, eight of them nominated by the Standing Committee of the Chamber of Princes. The leading Chamber members were the Chancellor, the Maharaja of Patiala, and the ex-Chancellor, the Maharaja of Bikaner. Colonel Haksar acted as secretary-general to the delegation and, with a team of some half dozen advisers, including K. M. Panikkai and Rushbrook Williams, he was poised to exert a substantial influence upon the Conference. Similarly, Hydari, representing the largest state, and having a team of four advisers and close relations with Mysore, Travancore, and Cochin, was well placed to influence proceedings. There existed, in fact, the lines of a broad cleavage between the central, northern, and western states of middling size, with full membership of the Chamber, and the large south Indian states, which did not frequent the Chamber.

The states, like the Muslims, set off for the Conference predisposed by recent events to seek a redefinition of their constitutional rights. In March 1929 the Indian States (Butler) Committee had reported upon the relationship between the Paramount power and the states, and upon the financial and economic relationships between British India and the states. To the chagrin of the princes the Committee rejected their submission that the Crown's paramountcy rested upon treaty relationships between sovereign states. Paramountcy, it declared, was no 'contractual relationship' capable of judicial definition but 'a living, growing relationship shaped by circumstances and policy'.[1] 'Paramountcy must remain paramount',[2] and it would continue to be exercised at the Crown's discretion, on the advice

---
[1] *Report of the Indian States Committee 1928–29*, Cd. 3302, 1929, para. 39.
[2] Para. 57.

of the Political Department of the Government of India. However, the Committee commended the appointment of advisory tribunals or commissions of inquiry into disputes over justiciable issues between states or a state and the government. Some consolation for autocratic rulers apprehensive of the growth of democracy in British India was provided by the Committee's assurance that paramountcy was not transferable from the Crown to a self-governing Indian dominion. Consistently with this reasoning, the Committee proposed that the princes' relations should be with the viceroy, as the agent of the Crown, and not with the governor-general-in-council.

In its consideration of the machinery governing the economic and financial relations of the states with British India the Committee gave emphasis to the separateness of 'the two Indias'. No 'constructive proposal' for combining the two Indias had been put to the Committee and any scheme of a 'federal character' seemed 'wholly premature'.[1] Thus 'for the present it is a practical necessity to recognize the existence of two Indias.... There is need for great caution in dealing with any question of federation at the present time, so passionately are the Princes as a whole attached to the maintenance in its entirety and unimpaired of their individual sovereignty within their states.'[2]

The Chamber of Princes met at Bombay in June 1929 under Bikaner's chairmanship and agreed to place its views on the Butler Report before the viceroy. It deplored the doctrine of unlimited paramountcy and proposed the creation of a tribunal to hear disputes over its exercise. The Chamber also stated its willingness 'to open avenues of negotiation with a view to the closer association of the two Indias in the future'.[3]

In February 1930 Patiala welcomed the Irwin Round Table Conference initiative. The next month Irwin, concerned that the princes might convert the Conference discussions into an opportunity for attacking paramountcy, suggested a 'friendly talk' with the leading princes at Simla.[4] A meeting was arranged for 14 July. Prior to the meeting, the Standing Committee, the Hyderabad External Relations Committee, and representatives of Mysore and Baroda would assemble for informal deliberations.

[1] Para. 66. [2] Paras. 67, 78. [3] *The Times*, 26 June 1929.
[4] Viceroy to Sec. of S., 14 March 1930, Foreign and Political Dept., Special, 1930, No. 22.

The Formula for All-India Federation   129

In the interval between the appearance of the Butler Report and the Simla meeting the princes showed no serious inclination to gather together for discussions with British Indian politicians. In January 1929 the All-Parties Convention had resolved to invite the princes to participate in discussions on the future constitution of India, and in August Motilal invited the Chamber to appoint representatives for this purpose. After consulting the Political Department, Patiala declined the invitation. In March 1930 there was an inconclusive meeting at Delhi between some twenty-five or thirty British Indian leaders (who were present at Sapru's preliminary gathering of parties) and some princes. Sir Manubhai Mehta and Haksar were deputed by the Chamber to discuss with British Indian representatives—Ramaswami Aiyer, H. S. Gour, Shafi, and Muhammad Ali—ways of reaching an agreement. However, no meeting occurred.

On the British side there was some speculation about the princes' likely attitudes to closer constitutional relations with British India. The secretary of state believed that the princes might well assume that paragraph 58 of the Butler Report, adverting to an eventual federation, foreshadowed likely developments, and that they would 'bargain for restriction of right of intervention of paramount power in return for co-operation in any scheme of Federation'.[1] Sir Charles Watson, the Political Secretary of the Government in India, thought the secretary of state

> wrong in thinking that the Princes will require to be tempted to co-operate in any scheme of Federation. I doubt if any, with the exception possibly of Mysore and Travancore, will agree to any Federation which involves the grant of constitutional government to the States' subjects; and without such a grant true Federation Scheme with British India seems impracticable. On the other hand any Federation with British India which would leave the internal administration of the States unchanged and intact would be welcome to the Princes and they will undoubtedly press for it. For example, they will demand a voice, if only in consultation, in All-India matters and in international affairs.[2]

The opinion is important for its scepticism towards the notion of a federation in which the princes could retain their internal

[1] Sec. of S. to viceroy, 26 March 1930, ibid.
[2] Watson's memo. of 28 March 1930, ibid.

autocracy. It is exceptional in believing that the princes might be ready to embrace federation.

The Simon Commission accepted the Butler doctrine of the two Indias. Though 'the essential unity of Greater India will one day be expressed in some form of federal association . . . the evolution will be slow and cannot be rashly pressed'. The Commission contented itself with proposing a small beginning towards ultimate federation by creating a Council of Greater India, containing representatives of the states and of British India, to have 'consultative and deliberative functions in regard to a scheduled list of "matters of common concern" '.[1]

The Simla meetings in July 1930 were attended by the Standing Committee princes, Bikaner, Patiala, Kashmir, Bhopal, Dholpur, Rewa, Alwar, and Sangli, the ministers of the first four of them and of Baroda, together with Haksar, Mirza Ismail, Hydari, and three other Hyderabad delegates. On 11 July the delegates submitted a memorandum for the viceroy's consideration. It proposed that the Round Table Conference discussions should be limited to the future relations between the government of British India and the states and the method of closer co-operation between British India and the states. On the former question the princes sought to safeguard treaty rights by the creation of a federal court with power to declare legislative or executive encroachments *ultra vires*. Issues might be vetted by a standing committee of provincial and states' representatives before being referred to the court. On the latter question the princes sought an adequate voice in matters of common concern and to this end favoured a 'union Council' representing the states and the provinces.

After discussions among themselves the states' delegates passed a number of resolutions, the chief of which was:

> . . . the Princes are in cordial agreement with the suggestion that they should co-operate with British India in matters of common concern. They realize that an All-India Federation may possibly prove the most satisfactory solution of India's problem. The Princes further realize that offer of the Council of Greater India should be accepted without hesitation subject to safeguards . . . dealing with matters of common concern. . . .[2]

[1] *Report of Indian Statutory Commission*, Cd. 3569, 1930, II, paras 228, 368.
[2] Summary of Princes' suggestions, 13 July 1930, For. and Pol. Dept., Spl. 1930, 22.

The Formula for All-India Federation

The princes welcomed the Butler Committee's recommendation that in future their relations should be with the viceroy and not the governor-general-in-council. They also advocated the immediate creation of a supreme court to settle 'justiciable issues' as a prerequisite of a federal constitution.

These matters were discussed with the viceroy on 14 and 15 July. The viceroy argued for *ad hoc* courts instead of a federal court to consider justiciable disputes. He claimed absolute discretion to decide which issues were justiciable and opposed automatic reference to any body. Haksar contended for setting up an impartial tribunal to determine whether a case was justiciable, and for a federal court to decide such cases. Bikaner pressed for the states having a 'really effective voice on the proposed Council of Greater India'.[1]

It is clear that at this stage the princes' main concerns were, first, the removal of justiciable issues from the absolute discretion of the viceroy (resting on the doctrine of paramountcy) to the purview of suitable tribunals; and secondly, the creation of a council of greater India for the consideration of matters of common concern to the states and the provinces. The Hyderabad delegation reported on the question of federation: 'So far as we have been able to ascertain all States including Mysore are at present opposed to any commitment for entering immediately into federation.'[2] Panikkar later recalled that while he himself spoke in favour of federation at the Simla meetings, the princes and their ministers were unanimously against it.[3]

The Government of India's Reforms Dispatch of September endorsed the Simon Commission's 'distant ideal' of an all-India federation but recognized 'that the time has not yet come when the general body of Indian States would be prepared to take a step so far-reaching in its character as to enter into any formal federal relations with British India'.[4] On 1 October Irwin wrote to H. A. L. Fisher of the princes: 'Whatever lip-service [they] may pay to the federal idea, they will, when it comes to the point, want it to begin through some consultative machinery at the outset before they burn any boats.'[5] The process of

[1] Discussions at Viceregal Lodge, Simla, 14–15 July 1930, ibid.
[2] Hyderabad delegation to Nizam, 11 July 1930 (t/g), ibid.
[3] K. M. Panikkar, *Autobiography*, 2 vols., Trichur [1953 and 1964], 1967 ed., in Malayalam, I. 184.
[4] Para. 16.   [5] I.C. 19.

developing any 'organic' relationship with British India must be 'very gradual'. In November, he recalled that 'during all the talks that I have had with [the princes] they have never left me in any doubt that they would be quite unprepared to adopt a policy of immediate entry into an organic federation'.[1]

The declarations of the Chamber and the inquiries of Simon, Butler, and the Government of India gave no reason to expect that the states' delegation to the Conference would emerge as the champions of the early creation of an all-India federation. Yet on 14 November, Sapru, in the midst of vain attempts to unite Muslims and Hindus on a common platform, observed: 'The only organized party here is that of the Princes and they are taking very progressive lines. They are ready to join the All-Indian federation which will give us Dominion Status with safeguards at once.'[2] The princes' intervention rendered obsolete the one-sided concentration of Simon and Irwin on the British Indian problem. As Reading observed on 19 November: 'If the Simon Commission and the Government of India had known what we now know they'd have written very different reports.'[3] No longer were the Simon Report and the Dispatch the foci of attention. The Conference delegates were busily engaged in appraising the new situation.

III. SCHEMES FOR FEDERATION

The move towards an immediate all-India federation began in the largest of the states, in the dominions of His Exalted Highness, Our Faithful Ally, the Nizam of Hyderabad. It was the consequence of a change of policy induced by the persuasiveness of the British Resident, Lieutenant-Colonel Terence H. Keyes, who took up duty in February 1930.

During the twenties Hyderabad had been the leading exponent of the argument that paramountcy was limited by treaties. It was the Nizam's insistence upon the appointment of a judicial commission to settle his claim for the restoration of the ceded territories of Berar that provoked Reading to affirm the universality of the Crown's paramountcy, and to declare that the doctrine of *res judicata* applied to the Berar case. The argument

[1] Irwin to Sir W. Lawrence, 17 November 1930, I.C. 19.
[2] Sapru to his son, Ranjit, 14 November 1930, S.C. 1, R. 66.
[3] Minutes of Liberal delegation meeting, 19 November 1930, R.C. 56 g.

The Formula for All-India Federation

for the contractual nature of paramountcy was put before the Butler Committee by Sir Leslie Scott on behalf of the Chamber of Princes. The Nizam had remained aloof from the Chamber but he did help to finance its activities. In February 1930 he agreed to award the Chamber a lakh of rupees towards the costs of representation at the Conference, and half a lakh per annum for the following six years. Soon afterwards the Special Organization of the Chamber sent emissaries south to induce the Nizam to raise the Berar question again in London and to claim freedom from intervention in Hyderabad's internal affairs. Keyes wrote to his predecessor, Sir William Barton, that he was able to persuade the Nizam to repulse the emissaries and to accept that he owed his sovereignty to Britain. He explained the change to Sir Denys Bray, Foreign Secretary to the Government of India:

The Nizam, as you know, made, when claiming the rendition of the Berars, more excessive claims than any other Chief to independence. I have now got him to acknowledge that his sovereignty grew up with that of the [East India] Company and only reached its present stage when we freed him from paying chauth to the Peshwas and assumed responsibility for all his external relations. He has put it in writing that the British Government is the successor of the Moghal Emperors; and he and his ancestors always recognised the suzerainty of the Moghals till the very end.[1]

Proof of the Nizam's change of policy is contained in a telegram that he sent to his delegation at the Simla conference of princes on 9 July 1930: 'H.E.H. considers that [the] present is not suitable time for raking up old grievances and for endeavouring to define future relations of States with Crown Agents. Latter can be more suitably done in London after Round Table Conference.'[2] Keyes interpreted the telegram for Irwin as 'meant to be a public recantation of his previous attitude'.[3] The greatest prince had gone beyond the others in admitting the paramountcy of the British Crown.

The Nizam's recognition of the Crown's paramountcy was one major aspect of his new readiness to pursue a policy quite independently of the dominant group of central and western

[1] Letter of 21 July 1930, Keyes Coll. (hereafter referred to as K.C.), 28.
[2] K.C. 28.
[3] Keyes to Irwin, 6 September 1930, K.C. 28.

Indian rulers in the Chamber. He was also prepared to adopt an independent stand on constitutional development.

On 14 June Keyes reported to Watson that the Nizam was willing to declare that Hyderabad aimed at 'coming into a federation on an equality with the Provinces'.[1] Keyes supported an early federation enthusiastically as the best means of securing Hyderabad against the regional movements in Maharashtra, Andhra, and Berar. He sent on a draft agenda (in which federation appeared prominently) for the viceroy's July meetings with the princes, and asked whether the viceroy wished the south Indian states to declare for federation on that occasion. The Political Department telegrammed a polite snub: Keyes was thanked for his 'interesting observations', but 'further action in the direction suggested by you is hardly practicable'.[2] The latter remark echoes Watson's March observation that prior to the introduction of constitutional government in the states federation 'seems impracticable'. Undeterred, Keyes wrote again to Watson to offer his services at the Simla meetings. Kenneth Fitze of the Foreign Department sneered: 'Colonel Keyes's missionary zeal appears to be unabated by our telegram.'[3] Irwin's instruction was kinder: 'Political Secretary will no doubt couch the reply in terms as sympathetic as possible to Keyes's general desire to help.'[4] When Keyes wrote to Watson yet again to point out the need for the states to enter a federation at once in order to influence its form from the start, Watson noted sourly: 'If these are Colonel Keyes's ideas I think it as well he did not come to Simla!'[5]

Keyes was very much responsible for the development of Hyderabad's policy towards federation. On 2 July he summarized the advice he had given to the Nizam, at the latter's request, in a letter to the viceroy's private secretary, Sir George Cunningham:

The advice I gave to His Exalted Highness was:
To declare his desire to enter into an all-India federation under certain safeguards from the other units in the Act of Federation and from

---

[1] Keyes to Watson, 14 June 1930, F. and P. D. Spl., 1930, 22.
[2] Political Dept. to Keyes, 20 June 1930 (t/g), ibid.
[3] Fitze's note of 28 June 1930, ibid.
[4] Irwin's note of 28 June 1930, ibid.
[5] Watson's note of 10 July 1930, ibid.

H.M.G. by Act of Parliament. To define those safeguards in consultation with other States of a like frame of mind. To endeavour to have the conditions of federation laid down by the Simon Commision so altered as to make the Federation attractive to the States and Provinces alike.[1]

On 9 July, after a private talk, the Nizam asked Keyes to send the following telegram to his delegation to the meeting of princes at Simla.

I. H.E.H. is prepared to enter into all-India Federation under due safeguards with provision for contracting out should Federation adopt course contrary to interests of Greater India.

IV. If Viceroy approves delegation may make open declaration re I; but should in any case make this the basis of negotiation with other States.[2]

The telegram arrived too late to influence proceedings at Simla. The Hyderabad delegation had already supported the Chamber policy, and they advised the Nizam that to declare his position at that stage would be 'calamitous'.[3]

However, the Nizam regarded his telegram as embodying a departure of 'historic value',[4] and it was not to be reversed by the princes' Simla resolutions. In September, when the Hyderabad delegation left for the Round Table Conference, Keyes wrote: 'I hope that they will pull their weight in London, and manage to modify the vicious attitude of the Chamber of Princes Organization, which is entirely in the hands of that charlatan Haksar. Their instructions to them to do so are very clear.'[5] The Nizam had briefed Hydari as follows:

Towards an All-India Federation the attitude of my Delegation should be one of sympathy but also of wise caution. While, on the one hand, it must be careful not to give its support to any scheme that may threaten the continuance of my relations with the British Crown or the interests of the Empire and my State, it will, on the other, if the deliberations of the Round Table Conference should show that the welfare

---

[1] Keyes to Cunningham, 2 July 1930, K.C. 28.
[2] Nizam to Hyderabad delegation, 9 July 1930, K.C. 28.
[3] Hyderabad delegation to Nizam, 11 July 1930, K.C. 28.
[4] Nizam to Keyes, 9 July 1930, K.C. 28. 'In memory' of the occasion he presented Keyes with a silver pencil.
[5] Keyes to Barton, [?] September 1930, K.C. 28.

of the States, as well as of British India, lies in that direction, use its influence towards securing from British India a Constitution that will facilitate an All-India Federation when the moment for it is ripe.[1]

Keyes had put a powerful case to the Nizam for his adoption of a new and independent policy. The Simon scheme for the separate political development of the British provinces and the states meant that autonomous provinces, and, later, a powerful British Indian federation, would arise to threaten the very existence of the southern states. Hyderabad, Mysore, and the Madras states lay in the midst of British Indian provinces: 'They are isolated and surrounded; their economic life is bound up with that of their neighbours.'[2] They would be at the mercy of British India. Of course they had treaty rights, but who could feel confident that Britain would be able to maintain them against the claims of a democratic Indian dominion? Simon's British Indian federation would grow in strength until it could overwhelm the southern landlocked states: 'I see no future for India but a series of economic quarrels and eventually civil wars if the country is split in two.'[3] The fate of 'that great mass of states' which included Baroda, Gwalior, and the Rajput and Central and Western Indian States was not so gloomy, for their geographical position and access to the sea would enable them to resist the incursions of the British Indian provinces. Neither would they appear as anomalous as the Nizam's autocratic Muhammadan dynasty, set in a Hindu-majority state and surrounded by democratic Hindu provinces. The Nizam's only salvation lay in his *immediate* negotiation of favourable terms of entry to an organic all-India federation. If a British India federation were once set up on democratic lines then the states could never hope to accede to it on favourable terms.

Once Keyes had convinced the Nizam of his case he began campaigning against the Simon scheme in every quarter available to him. Early in July he wrote to Cunningham: 'The alternative to an all-India Federation is not a British India and an Indian India with a Council of Greater India and the Viceroy holding the balance, but a Swaraj India and a Rajahs' India

[1] Quoted by Hydari before Joint Committee on Indian Constitutional Reform, 25 May 1933.
[2] Keyes to Nizam, 30 June 1930, K.C. 28.
[3] Ibid.

The Formula for All-India Federation

with friction at every point of contact, and the Viceroy's authority continually strained to the breaking point.'[1]

Later in July, Keyes wrote at very great length to Bray, whom Sapru was to regard as Benn's 'right-hand man' at the Conference. He derided Haksar as 'a very ordinary intelligence', a 'most bitter Brahman' who was out for a revival of Maratha Brahman dominance in Central India and the Deccan, based on the unity of the Bombay states, the Marathi-speaking parts of Berar and the Central Provinces, and Baroda, Indore, and possibly Gwalior.[2] He criticized the Political Department for succumbing to the influence of Haksar's Special Organization of the Chamber in the appointment of the princes' delegates to the Conference. The states would be represented by a 'solid phalanx of Rolls Royce rajahs' who had opted for the Simon 'escape from Federation', the Council of Greater India. The Standing Committee of the Chamber stood for all that was worst in autocracy: 'corruption, tyranny and the wildest extravagance'.[3] Both the Political Department and the Chamber accepted the fatuous doctrine of the two Indias: 'To me this is the madness of the gods sent before destruction. . . . What Butler calls British India is just that part of India that is trying to repudiate all that is British. . . . What he calls Indian India is the part that wants to retain its British connection.' Between 'swaraj India' and 'maharajas' India' there were hundreds of causes of potential friction, economic, racial, and religious, and the Crown would never be able to settle them. If Britain were not to destroy 150 years of nation building she must create a central authority to bind the northern Muhammadan areas to the central and southern Hindu areas. In this process of unification Hyderabad, as a southern state and the largest Muhammadan state, had a unique role to play. Keyes concluded: 'I am a fanatic of the creed that unity can only come by federation, and that federation must come through the States.'

Early in October, Keyes appealed to an old friend in England, F. S. Oliver, to place notes of his views on all-India federation

[1] Keyes to Cunningham, 5 July 1930, K.C. 28.
[2] Keyes to Bray, 21 July 1930, K.C. 28.
[3] In 1930 the Chancellor, the Maharaja of Patiala, was deeply in debt and hoped, in vain, that the Nizam would make him a loan of Rs. 1.8 lakhs. The indiscretions of the Pro-Chancellor, the Maharaja of Kashmir, as 'Mr. A.' are sufficiently known.

before two public men of Oliver's acquaintance—Dawson and Lothian. The notes expressed regret that the predominance of the Chamber group in the states' delegation might prevent the Conference from taking as its 'first issue' the question of 'unitary or federal government'.[1] Dawson and Lothian duly received the notes. Lothian found them 'extraordinarily interesting'.[2]

Keyes's success was not limited to Hyderabad. In June Mirza Ismail readily agreed with Keyes upon the need for the southern states to enter an all-India federation, and Cochin and Travancore followed suit. All-India federation was, in fact, no new passion for Mysore. The state suffered disabilities under the conditions imposed by Britain when she restored it to the raja in 1881, and it had long recognized the possibility of enhancing its freedom through negotiated entry into a federation. At a conference of south Indian states at Bangalore in August 1930, Ismail anticipated a more rapid accession of the states to a federation than was contemplated in Simon's vision of 'the misty twilight of a distant future'.[3] He was prepared for the immediate entry of the states into a federal senate, while British India achieved responsibility in a British Indian central government.

At the end of September, on the voyage to England, Hydari explained the Hyderabad position to Schuster. On the basis of the Nizam's instructions, Hydari had developed a rough plan for a small 'aristocratic' federal assembly, to contain some thirty-six provincial representatives, twenty-four states' representatives, and twelve Crown nominees. Schuster reported to Irwin:

> This is in fact *the* feature of the scheme, the idea being that, if the Federal Legislature is constituted on these lines, eliminating the popular demagogues from British India and giving the States and the Crown due weight, the Indian States would come in *at once*; but, if a Central Legislature for British India is allowed to develop on democratic lines, and to make itself the dominating political influence in India and the main stage for political manoeuvre and publicity, then the States will never come in, for no basis of partnership with such a body could be found which did not mean the overwhelming [of] the states.[4]

[1] Keyes to Oliver, 9 October 1930 and enclosures; Oliver to Keyes, 30 October 1930; K.C. 28.
[2] Lothian to Oliver, 3 November 1930, K.C. 28.
[3] Ismail's speech, 19 August 1930, in R.C. 56 e.
[4] Schuster to Irwin, 9 October 1930, I.C. 19.

At Schuster's behest Hydari committed his scheme to paper on 2 October. It defined the federation's jurisdiction as 'matters of common concern' made over by the states and the provinces. Hydari provided for powers to be distributed among the states and provinces, the federation, and the Crown. The provinces would, like the states, enjoy full autonomy except in matters handed over to the federation and those reserved to the Crown (notably foreign affairs, political relations, defence, finance, and ultimate responsibility for law and order). Disputes over the exercise of powers would be referred to a federal court.[1]

Under Hydari's original scheme there was to be no central authority for British India alone, for that could overwhelm the princes. Schuster pointed out the difficulty of abolishing the British Indian centre. It performed functions, for example in relation to finance and law, that could prove inconvenient to distribute to the provinces or to a federal body dealing with all-Indian matters. Further, the politicians of British India seemed unlikely to accept the elimination of their central stage. Such arguments persuaded Hydari to append to his scheme a provision for a central authority for British India.[2] However, he rigidly segregated the activities of the all-India federation and the British Indian centre, from fear of the latter dominating the former. The British Indian representatives in the federal body would be returned by the provinces directly and severally, not by their spokesmen acting in concert in the British Indian forum.

Hydari counted on the support of Ismail, and thereby of Mysore, Travancore, Cochin, and Pudakottai. Several observers did in fact view the south Indian states as a united team. In that the southern states were completely sincere in their vigorous advocacy of an immediate all-India federation they were at one. However, tension developed between Hydari and Ismail when the latter continued to talk somewhat loosely, as he had in August, of the princes joining the British Indian central authority to create a federation. Ismail exacerbated the tension by expounding a scheme of his own that contemplated an organic relationship between a federal senate or upper house, dealing with all-Indian affairs, and a central assembly or lower house dealing with British Indian affairs. All matters of common

[1] Dated 2 October 1930, R.C. 56 e.
[2] Hydari's 'later supplement', ibid.

concern, except defence and external affairs, were to be transferred from the Crown to a federal executive responsible to the federal senate. Hydari was apprehensive of the avenue for pressure and influence that would be afforded by the upper–lower house relationship between the federal and British Indian bodies. The federal authority must 'not have anything to do with' the British Indian authority. He was also uneasy about the extreme transfer of power that Ismail contemplated.[1]

It seems likely that Ismail was influenced by the arguments that Haksar elaborated after his arrival in London. As his relationship with Sapru in February suggested, Haksar's political interest extended beyond the states. Coatman described him as a 'Swarajist'.[2] Haksar's attitude to federation is set out in *Federal India* (London, 1930), which he and Panikkar completed jointly on 18 August 1930. Panikkar tells the story of the book's composition in his autobiography.[3] He claims to have been an advocate of all-India federation since his student days. Certainly, in 1919 he published an article on 'The Native States and Indian Nationalism', in which he argued for the mediatization of the small states and for guaranteeing the sovereignty of the larger states in order to get their support for swaraj.[4] He was disappointed when the princes and the diwans opposed federation at the Simla meetings in July 1930, and he decided to write a book to explain the advantages of federation. He completed a draft in mid-August and submitted it to Haksar, who praised it as 'very good and very timely'. Haksar proposed joint publication, made some corrections to the manuscript, and added an introduction. The book appeared on the opening day of the Conference.

Federal India contemplated the extension of complete responsible government to a British Indian centre, except for the transfer to a federal authority of matters concerning both the states and British India. A federal council would contain some 100 British Indian representatives elected by the British Indian central

[1] Ismail's Bangalore speech of 20 August 1930, R.C. 56 e; Sir Charles Todhunter (secretary to the Maharaja of Mysore) to Keyes, 13 November 1930, K.C. 28.
[2] Coatman's appreciation of 'The Position with Regard to Federation', n.d. [? November 1930], R.C. 56 e.
[3] *Autobiography*, I. 184–7
[4] *Modern Review*, xxv (1919), 37–44.

assembly, and some fifty princely nominees. The grand theme of the book was, however, the devolution upon the states of complete internal autonomy, safeguarded by a supreme court. The terms of the scheme implied a deal between the princes and the British Indian politicians: full responsible government for British India underwritten by the princes in return for full internal autonomy for the princes underwritten by British India.

Federal India defined a desirable goal towards which progress might be made at the Round Table Conference. It foreshadowed a substantial change from the Chamber's Conference policy as it had been defined at Simla in July: acceptance of Simon's goal but no immediate commitment to federation. However, it seems to have made converts rapidly. On 9 and 25 September Sastri reported that Bikaner was 'hopeful he can bring all his Order to agree to some federal scheme *immediately*', and that he had one 'up his sleeve'.[1] It is likely that when Bikaner and Haksar learnt that Hydari had a scheme for instant federation they turned to *Federal India* as a manual of immediate political application. In London Haksar and his cohorts began to push their ideas before the princes, the British press, and British Indian politicians.

Haksar's argument to the Chamber princes was quite different from Keyes's case for federation. The latter stressed the need for immediate federation to secure a conservative centre, with continuing Crown influence, that would enforce Hyderabad's right to protection against aggression and secure her economic interests. Haksar emphasized that by joining forces with the British Indian politicians on the common platform of Dominion Status for an all-India federation, the princes would win British Indian support for freedom from the operation of paramountcy. As their territorial integrity and economic interests seemed less exposed than Hyderabad's to menace from British India, so were the states of Rajputana and Western and Central India less worried by the prospect of responsible government in British India, and by the forging of an organic link between a British Indian central and an all-Indian federal authority. Doubtless Ismail was attracted by Haksar's arguments and Haksar by Ismail's alternative to Hydari's scheme.

By the beginning of November Haksar's ideas had spread

[1] Sastri to T. R. V. Sastri, 9 September, and to D. V. Gundappa, 25 September 1930, in *Sastri's Letters*, pp. 195–7.

among the Chamber princes, while the schemes of Hydari and Ismail were becoming well known. On Sunday 2 November the states' delegation appointed a committee to consider the attitude that it should adopt towards all-India federation. Hydari was elected to the chair and Ismail, Haksar, Manubhai Mehta (Bikaner), V. T. Krishnamachari (Baroda), Sir P. Pattani (Bhavnagar), and K. C. Neogy (Orissa States) were appointed members. States' delegates and advisers were consulted and a report was produced on 6 November.[1] It recommended that the states should agree to join a federal structure for joint control with British India over matters of common concern; provided that the states were admitted to the federation at its inception, were given their due share in its deliberations, and were assured of their internal autonomy. Each state should be free to accede or abstain from the federation. A federal court should be set up to settle disputes over the legislative authority of the federation and the states, and between the individual states and British India. The report thus embodies the essential aspect of the Hydari scheme (accession by the states at the outset) and the Chamber group's scheme to circumvent paramountcy.

The idea of an all-India federation was discussed vaguely by British officials and delegates from about the first week in October, when Hydari and Schuster arrived. A month later it had found some favour among the British Indian Hindus, with Bikaner 'playing hard as an ally of the Hindu politicians'[2] and Sapru showing an interest. On 10 November Benn called together an Agenda Committee, representative of all delegations, and including, for the states, Hydari, Ismail, Haksar, Bikaner, and Alwar. Reading suggested and Sapru agreed that the first discussions of the Conference should concentrate upon the question of an Indian federation. On 12 November, after the formal ceremony to open the Conference, it was decided that the first three days, commencing on the 17th, should be devoted to federation. Reading had found deliverance from the menace of a united British Indian demand for Dominion Status at the opening of the Conference; and Sapru from the danger of an open rupture between the British Indian communities.

[1] Report of committee appointed by informal conference of the Indian states' delegation on 2 November 1930, R.C. 56 e.
[2] Schuster to Irwin, 7 November 1930, I.C. 19.

The Formula for All-India Federation 143

All-India federation was the dominant principle throughout the nine weeks of the Round Table Conference. All of the major delegations subscribed to it. By the end of the Conference the abolition of the British Indian centre had been negotiated, and it had been agreed that a bicameral federal legislature, with the princes and the provinces represented in both houses, should be established. The government had declared its intention to transfer the reserved subjects in the provinces and to confer responsible government, with safeguards and reserves, upon the federal authority. This new direction of constitutional development owed much to Hydari's initiative. The agreed arrangements did, however, differ in detail from Hydari's original scheme, and Keyes and Hydari were to address themselves to the resultant problems in 1931.

The transformation of the political scene was aided by the intervention of the Chamber princes. Ismail had intended to declare for federation at the first plenary session of the Conference. That would have occasioned no surprise. However, he deferred to the Chamber group's wish that one of its senior members should be the first to proclaim the princes' new policy. Experienced officials and statesmen were amazed at the princes expressing, one after another, their willingness to join a federation. Irwin rubbed his eyes in disbelief and exchanged doubts with Hailey and Sir Walter Lawrence over whether they realized what they were doing. For federation implied the administration of matters of common concern by a federal body and the presence of federal agents in the states. Sacrifice of sovereignty was bound to be involved. Haksar, noted Coatman, was more far-sighted than the princes and realized that federation would take them further than they wished to go.

However, their Highnesses were careful to make their conditions clear. Bikaner made the first pledge of support for an all-India federation. On the evening before his speech he conferred with Patiala and other princes, together with Sir Leslie Scott, in his room at the Carlton Hotel. It was agreed that he should make acceptance of federation conditional upon the recognition of the states' treaty rights. Patiala made his acceptance dependent upon the establishment of a federal court to interpret the treaties. The limitation of paramountcy, implying an enlargement of the princes' sovereignty, was regarded by all of the major princes as a prerequisite to accession to a federation. Irwin anticipated their strategy, even though they had a gentlemen's agreement with him not to raise the paramountcy question at the Conference: 'I am not sure... that they may not have some idea in their minds of using federation to get rid of the exercise of paramountcy.'[1] Hailey, who was in London as a constitutional adviser to the Conference, observed the princes' reluctance to surrender any of their own sovereignty to the federation. 'Most of them seem prepared to surrender only the powers they claim but have not got.'[2] Again: 'They seem to be out for the extinction of the Political Department, rather than the creation of a federal constitution.'[3] The apparent opportunism of some of the Chamber princes, including Patiala and Alwar, repelled a sincere federationist like Ismail. Coatman found him to be 'very angry with the Northern Princes' and saying quite openly that they 'do not want to do real business'.[4]

An all-India federation had obvious attractions to Indian Muslims. On the journey to England Hydari told Schuster that he counted on 'the backing of the Mussalman representatives from British India', and he explicitly claimed Jinnah's interest.[5] The extinction of the unitary central government of British India and the distribution of powers between a conservative federal authority and autonomous provinces were features of the scheme bound to appeal to Muslims. The Nizam and the Muslims of northern India shared an aversion to Hindu raj. Nevertheless, an all-India federation was not in itself sufficient safeguard against Hindu raj. In November the progressive Muslim delegates, Jinnah, the Aga Khan, and Shafi, impressed by the Hindu Liberals' sincere concern to effect a communal agreement, welcomed the federal idea with enthusiasm and left the question of safeguards for later determination. This was a temporary and short-lived departure from the established Muslim policy of making support for any constitutional development contingent upon the prior satisfaction of the demand for specific safeguards. The Muslim delegates were soon bombarded with telegrams insisting that they adhere to that policy.

[1] Irwin to Lawrence, 17 November 1930, I.C. 19.
[2] Hailey to Miss S. Charnaud (Reading's secretary, later his wife), 11 November 1930, R.C. 56 g.   [3] Hailey to Irwin, 20 November 1930, I.C. 19.
[4] 'The Position with Regard to Federation', R.C. 56 e.
[5] Schuster to Irwin, 9 October 1930, I.C. 19.

The Formula for All-India Federation

At first British observers were doubtful of the Hydari scheme attracting any Hindu nationalist support. Even late in October Haig believed that neither it nor any of the variant schemes of federation was 'likely to find much response among the British Indian Delegates'.[1] The association of the princes with the determination of all-Indian policies was at odds with nationalist demands for a democratic constitution. To Sastri and Chintamani it seemed a dangerous departure from the ideal of a British Indian executive responsible to a British Indian legislature. It exposed British India to the whim of the princes and seemed a betrayal of the states' peoples.

It was Sapru who took up the federal idea with resolution and swept most British Indian delegates along with him. Hailey reported that at first he had shown some 'resentment' towards it.[2] Like the other Liberals Sapru had staked his political career on the Conference. Vilified by the Congress as a collaborator he was determined not to accept a constitutional settlement that would lend substance to the accusation. His opening strategy in London was to achieve a communal agreement and present a united Hindu–Muslim demand for Dominion Status with safeguards, backed, Hailey reported, by the threat of a walk out. It is likely that his preoccupation with this strategy, and a certain scepticism towards the princes' initiative, explains any early coolness in his attitude towards all-India federation. However, he soon warmed to the idea. By 23 October he had joined with Haksar, Panikkar, and Manubhai Mehta in an attempt to enlist Sastri's support for federation.[3] As the prospect of a quick communal settlement receded, and once the princes' committee had defined the states' delegation's attitude towards federation, he became seized of the need for a change of strategy. On 14 November Hailey noted that Sapru was 'trying hard to get [Haksar's scheme] into a form in which it can actually be put forward by the British Indian delegation itself and adopted by the Princes'.[4] Some southern nationalists were speaking sourly of his being 'in the pay of the Northern Princes'.[5]

[1] Haig to Irwin, 31 October 1930, I.C. 19.
[2] Hailey to Irwin, 14 November 1930, I.C. 19.
[3] K. M. Panikkar, quoted in T. N. Jagadisan, *V. S. Srinivasa Sastri*, New Delhi, 1969, p. 120.
[4] Hailey to Irwin, 14 November 1930, I.C. 19.
[5] Coatman, 'The Position with Regard to Federation'.

Sapru knew that with Haksar's help he could form an alliance with the princes on the policy of Dominion Status with safeguards for an all-India federation. He could also count on Muslim approval of the principle. The acceptance by Britain of the demand would give the moderates a fresh lease of life in Indian politics, for it could be presented as the achievement in principle of 'equality with other Dominions'.[1] However, Sapru's bid for an alliance with the princes was no mere expediency. The 'tyrannical' methods of the Congress during the civil disobedience movement led him to observe that 'along with patriotism there are equally other strong incentives at work—prestige, bravado, love of power'.[2] The intolerance of the Hindu communalists caused him to doubt the existence of true nationalism in India. He had seen the social order under attack and he had looked for the organization of notables to protect it. His acceptance now of a strong autocratic element in the government of an Indian dominion was but a short step. His Liberal colleagues had 'despised [the princes] as autocratic', but now he saw them as 'statesmanlike, progressive, and patriotic'. Sapru, indeed, favoured the abolition of the existing central legislature. He accepted that India, though ready to govern itself in most matters, was yet unready for the rule of numbers. He was, in Sastri's words, 'all for giving whether to Princes or Moslems',[3] and he accepted the need for Britain's retention of safeguards over several departments of state.

Sapru could not have won the Hindu Liberals' support for an all-India federation by appeals to such a political philosophy. Indeed, Chintamani fought him tooth and nail over the dereliction of democratic principle and repeatedly demanded that the Conference discuss the question of central responsibility in British India. He remained a true representative of the philosophical liberalism of that eminent constitutionalist, Sivaswamy Aiyer, who had been appalled when Simon seemed to postpone the achievement of Dominion Status until after the emergence of Greater India. More typical than either Sapru or Chintamani in his attitude to federation was Sastri. Hostile in principle and uneasy about its practical implications, by 23 October Sastri

[1] Innes to Irwin, 19 November 1930, I.C. 19.
[2] Sapru to Iswar Saran, 12 November 1930, S.C. 1, S. 18.
[3] Sastri to D. V. Gundappa, 15 December 1930, in *Sastri's Letters*, p. 203.

was nevertheless prepared to follow Sapru in accepting the federal idea. For here seemed to be the only means of prising responsible government out of the British parliament.

Sapru prided himself on his knowledge of the British official mind. After talks with representatives of the party delegations and their advisers he concluded that 'if we leave the States out, we shall get nothing, and certainly responsibility at the Centre, with a Unitary form of Government, is not going to come to us'.[1] This was an accurate appraisal of the Liberal and Conservative position, and, in the absence of a united British Indian demand, of the position that Labour would have to assume. He reasoned that, on the other hand, Britain might well respond to an appeal for Dominion Status with safeguards within an all-India federation. His commitment to such a policy was a desperate but courageous gamble. He declared himself unequivocally at the opening session of the Conference, on 17 November, before either his own party or the British parties had determined their policies. He might have been repudiated by his own party and have failed to win British support. He was, indeed, frequently attacked by Hindu Liberals and at the end of November he felt compelled to resign from the party:

> It has been suggested time without number, by several of the members both at the meetings and outside that by accepting the Federal basis of the Constitution we are weakening the case for Dominion Status. That is a view which I cannot accept, on the contrary we have satisfactorily achieved the idea of responsibility at the Centre and made it a real live issue.... My critics might have given me some credit for Political judgement and experience and some knowledge of the official mind....[2]

He was indeed right about the British official mind.

As soon as Schuster learnt of the Hydari scheme he realized that it could create a 'new situation' at the Conference.[3] Haig and Hailey were also quick to see its implications as an alternative to the two Indias approach. The key official, the adviser most in demand among the British delegates, was Hailey, who welcomed the princes' initiative.

[1] Sapru to P. N. Sapru, 19 November 1930, S.C. 1, S. 17.
[2] Sapru to Setalvad, 29 November 1930, S.C. 1, S. 131.
[3] Schuster to Irwin, 9 October 1930, I.C. 19.

Hailey found in neither the Simon Report nor the Reforms Dispatch a convincing solution to the problem of the central government. He shared Irwin's view that Simon had failed to harmonize the central executive with the legislature, but he argued that the Dispatch suffered from the same weakness. It failed to give the governor-general, the agent of parliament, a legislative authority that would, without his recourse to his extraordinary power of certification, enable him to discharge his responsibilities. Under either the Simon or the Irwin schemes the legislature would seek to invade fields of administration reserved to the executive as the responsibilities of parliament. Simon's weak executive would be overwhelmed by the legislature; Irwin's was 'divided in itself'.[1] Hailey was convinced, too, that a democratic legislature would be unable to find experienced ministers for the major departments of state. In the absence of a convincing solution to the problem of development he favoured the *status quo*, in spite of its disadvantages. The princes' initiative now offered an escape from the agonizing dilemma of either sitting pat and provoking nationalist hostility or making a change that would place more weapons in the nationalists' hands. All-India federation gave 'hope of creating a legislature which could with confidence be given charge over the executive', for the states contained princes and ministers of long experience in practical administration.[2] An all-India federation would also solve the 'constitutional puzzle' of how to give Dominion Status to British India without giving it to the 'inter-set territories' of the states.

An appreciation similar to Hailey's was made independently by J. T. Gwynn, the Indian correspondent in London of the leading Liberal newspaper, the *Manchester Guardian*. Gwynn had been at a loss to discern a safe point of advance in the central government that would stop short of Dominion Status. Yet the viceroy adjudged advance to be necessary. On 26 October he was disposed to 'back anything like a reasonable scheme commanding weighty support at the Conference'.[3] Four days later he had 'fallen to Colonel Haksar', whose scheme showed 'how a strong Indian central government might be formed—

[1] Hailey's memo. of 18 November 1930, R.C. 56 g.
[2] Ibid.
[3] Gwynn to Charnaud, 26 October 1930, R.C. 56 j.

a native government to which it would be possible to make a genuine transfer of responsibility'.[1] If the British Indian delegation shunned it because of their 'pedantic ideas about democracy' they deserved to remain under British rule for ever. The *Guardian* backed the Haksar scheme on 5 November.[2] A week later Hailey traced the start of a strong federation movement to 'a kind of pact between Haksar and the *Manchester Guardian*'.[3]

Both Hailey and Gwynn were in touch with Reading. Gwynn fed him with information and gave him prior notice that the *Guardian* would support all-India federation. As the movement gathered strength, Reading too welcomed it as the solution to his difficulties. Since summer his abiding fear had been that the government would succumb to the Indian Liberal pressure for Dominion Status with temporary safeguards. He found it impossible to reconcile an advance towards central responsibility in British India with safeguards that could be anything but temporary. He had always disliked declarations of the Dominion Status objective because he could see no means of advancing by stages. Any concession strengthened the pressure and the case for further concessions.

Hoare and Zetland also welcomed the federal movement as providing an alternative constitutional road to that of parliamentary democracy.

During the second week of November, when it was agreed to open the Conference with a discussion of the federal question, the strength of the movement was still uncertain. At that stage British officials and opposition delegates saw the main attraction of the movement as a tactical one: it would enable the Conference to get down to business without Britain having first to respond to a demand for Dominion Status. The way was opened for an initial discussion that would not expose a fundamental split between the government and opposition delegations, as a discussion on status would have done.

On the eve of the Conference the opposition delegations met the government and pressed for a clarification of its attitude on all-India federation. Hailey had advised Hoare to seek 'an undertaking that there will be no dyarchy at the Centre except

[1] Gwynn to Charnaud, 30 October 1930, R.C. 56j.
[2] See also Haksar's letter in the *Manchester Guardian*, 10 November 1930.
[3] Hailey to Irwin, 14 November 1930, I.C. 19.

on the basis of a federal central assembly'.¹ Reading was also disposed to seek such an assurance. True to its intention to avoid masterminding the Conference the government disclosed little. MacDonald was infuriatingly evasive. He would say only that he accepted the need for some reserved subjects and that 'he would state the facts sometime during the debate in such a way as to make federation appear to be the most favourable line of advance'.²

In fact the Labour mind was following much the same line of thought as the minds of the officials and the opposition delegations. Before the Conference opened Benn wrote a long memorandum which suggests that all-India federation appealed strongly to the government.³ He proposed a major devolution of power upon a federal centre and recognized that the states' accession would provide a stable element to allay opposition apprehensions of central responsibility. An all-India federation could provide a 'safe' legislature, containing experienced statesmen and not 'lawyer demagogues' dependent upon direct election. It might also have an executive not dependent upon day-to-day manoeuvre in the legislature. Both of these ideas were 'worth exploring, for there is a very large body of thinkers in India and England who in their secret hearts feel that "responsible" government based on Parliamentary democracy is not a suitable system for India'.

On 17 November, when the various Indians declared for all-India federation, the British delegates agreed that the matter should be pursued by a committee. Thereafter the real work of the Conference was done by the Federal Structure Committee, expertly chaired by Sankey. Its membership included Mr. H. B. Lees Smith (for the government), Reading and Lothian, Hoare and Peel; Bikaner, Bhopal, Hydari, Ismail, and Haksar; Sapru, Sastri, C. P. R. Aiyer, Jayakar, Jinnah, Shafi, Sir Sayed Sultan Ahmed, Mudaliyar, Ujjal Singh, and T. F. Gavin Jones. It produced an interim report on 16 December and a second report on 15 January. It favoured a bicameral federal legislature with British Indian and states' representatives in both houses. The

[1] Hoare's note of Hailey's advice, 13 November 1930, Templewood Coll. (hereafter referred to as T.C.), 1.
[2] Hoare's note of meeting with the government, 16 November 1930, T.C. 19.
[3] Memorandum circulated upon the P.M.'s instructions, 19 November 1930, India Office, L/PO/269.

federal legislature would replace the existing central legislature. To that extent the Committee's (or Sankey) scheme resembled the original Hydari plan as against that of Haksar and Panikkar. However, the administrative unity of British India was to be maintained intact, and the federal authority was, in course of time, to assume the powers that the Government of India then exercised. That is to say, Britain was to devolve British Indian powers upon a federal authority rather than upon the provinces. This ran counter to the Hydari scheme for the federal authority to exercise authority only in matters of common concern, and to Muslim plans for avoiding a concentration of powers in a Hindu-dominated central authority. In short, the Federal Structure Committee reports envisaged a strong federal government rather than a weak one. This was largely because of Sapru's effective committee work. The proposed structure reflected Hindu nationalist aspirations rather than Muslim or princely preferences.

As the Federal Structure Committee advanced with its consideration of the organization and powers of a federal authority, Reading warmed to the attractions of all-India federation. His attitude was of crucial importance. Reading was the respected spokesman of the party that held the balance of power between the government and the Conservative Party. He could defeat or uphold the principle upon which the Indian delegations were agreed and to which the government was prepared to accede. On Monday, 5 January 1931, before the Federal Structure Committee, he responded to an overture of Sapru's by giving his verdict in favour of central responsibility, with safeguards, within an all-India federation. His reserved subjects included defence, the army, foreign affairs, and relations with the states, while there were to be safeguards for finance, the services, the minorities, and law and order. The speech was seen at once as marking the turning-point of the Conference. It enabled MacDonald to close the Conference on 19 January with a pledge of central responsibility with safeguards. It enabled Sapru and the Liberals to go home with the claim that they had extracted a promise of Dominion Status with safeguards. It left Irwin and Benn to reflect that a year of civil disobedience might have been avoided if only Reading had been so liberal in 1929.

Benn and Irwin had difficulty in following the development

of Reading's thought. On 30 December Benn accounted for his advance in terms of the influence of the other Liberal Party delegates (Benn's own former colleagues): 'Reading has been pushed along by his colleagues, who gleefully point privately to this fact.'[1] Certainly, Lothian, Foot, and Hamilton were quick to respond to the idea of federation. At the beginning of November Lothian found Keyes's notes 'extraordinarily interesting' and soon afterwards Haig and Schuster reported that while he was against transferring responsibility to a British Indian democracy he was not opposed to devolving powers upon a stable federal authority.[2] On 18 November he wrote at length to appeal to Reading to respond to the Indian nationalists' demand by expressing 'in unmistakable terms the idealism of Fox, Gladstone, Campbell-Bannerman and the Parliament of 1906'.[3] In the first place, he argued that the Indian Liberals must be supported if Britain were not to be 'left to confront a strengthened Congress'. Secondly, he felt that the mass of British Liberal voters and readers of the *Manchester Guardian* would 'certainly respond whole-heartedly' to such speeches as those of Sapru, Jayakar, and Shafi. It was essential 'to sound the traditional note of Liberal sympathy with national self-government'. Thirdly, if the Liberal Party failed to sound the note the government would assuredly do so. At meetings of the Liberal delegation during November and December, Lothian, Hamilton, and Foot continued to talk of the Indian nationalist demand being 'the legitimate child of English liberalism'.[4] On 21 November Coatman noted that Reading's three colleagues wanted to go as far as possible to meet Indian opinion.[5]

However, it seems most unlikely that Reading needed to be pushed along by his colleagues, though he must have been reassured by their views. He had quickly seized the princes' federal initiative as effecting a dramatic change in the terms of the Conference, a possible solution to a constitutional problem that he had long tried to solve. His denials of the Dominion Status objective had been essentially strategic, and he responded

[1] Benn to Irwin, 30 December 1930, I.C. 6.
[2] Haig to Irwin, 7 November 1930; Schuster to Irwin, 13 November 1930; I.C. 19.
[3] Lothian to Reading, 18 November 1930, R.C. 56 j.
[4] Minutes of Liberal delegation meeting, 19 November 1930, R.C. 56 g.
[5] Coatman to Irwin, 21 November 1930, I.C. 19.

The Formula for All-India Federation

at once to his colleagues' appeals to the Liberal tradition: 'English Liberals were the lawful inheritors of the democratic tradition and must certainly act up to their character as such.'[1] He saw the need to strengthen the Liberals' position in India. On 19 November he told his delegation that Britain must 'at all costs avoid a state of things in which the soldiers would have to be called out in India'. He was also politician enough to see the advantage to the Liberal party in taking the credit for putting all-India on the road to dominionhood. In Benn's words, he made himself the 'hero of the Conference and creamed the milk the Prime Minister was due to deliver'.[2] Lloyd George waxed euphoric over his triumph:

> Circumstances combined to make the Liberal Party to a very large extent the arbiters of the fate of the Conference. . . . On the one hand any hasty or insufficiently considered acceptance of Indian claims for extensive and fundamental changes . . . must inevitably have provoked a dangerous, indeed, a fatal reaction, in this country. On the other hand, a stiff and unyielding opposition to the demand . . . for an appreciable measure of responsibility at the centre, must have produced equally calamitous results in India. It is the great merit of the Liberal delegates that . . . when the Conference had reached a critical moment at which its success or failure hung in the balance, they, through their leader, made it known that they and their party accepted the principle of a responsible Federal Government for all India, accompanied by certain safeguards designed primarily in the interests of India herself. In taking this step the Liberal delegates correctly interpreted both the necessities of the situation and the will of responsible leaders of most sections of opinion, in this country and also in India. This result was achieved by Liberals working assiduously in the light of historic Liberal doctrine, guided throughout by your great knowledge of Indian affairs, by your statesmanship, and by your great personal influence and prestige. . . . [It] will always be reckoned one of British Liberalism's foremost achievements in the realm of constructive statesmanship.[3]

Reading joined the line of those whose commitment to all-India federation established it as the constitutional formula that was to tantalize British and Indian politicians for a decade:

[1] Minutes of Liberal delegation meeting, 19 November 1930, R.C. 56 g.
[2] Benn's enclosure to his letter to Irwin, 15 January 1931, I.C. 6.
[3] Lloyd George to Reading, 4 February 1931, R.C. 56 g.

Keyes, Hydari, Panikkar, Haksar, Bikaner, Sapru, Benn, Reading. But even before the first Round Table Conference ended there were signs that the definition of the terms of the formula might prove an enigma within a riddle.

IV. FEDERATION: CONSENSUS OR CHAMELEON?

Though the Tory delegation acquiesced in the scrutiny by the Conference of the all-India federation principle, it approached the question of responsibility with circumspection. Tension developed between Zetland, who was not unfavourable to devolving responsibility upon a stable centre, and Peel. Both Peel and Hoare believed that the Party would accuse its delegation of having 'given way' if it declared itself 'favourable to responsibility in the Central Government'.[1]

Hoare saw difficulty in shaking the Party's attachment to Simon's irresponsible 'strong centre' while the democratic experiment was on trial in the provinces. But he also saw that the Party's position might become untenable if the other parties moved with the tide of Indian opinion. It might then be better to accept a change at the centre while limiting it to the minimum and presenting it to the Party as broadly consistent with Simon's admired strategy. Lane Fox knew of his thoughts immediately after the Conference opened:

> He hopes to avoid the question of a Central Assembly, with its Dominion Status application, for British India, by securing a Federal body representing the two bodies of Princes on the one hand and Provinces on the other, and that they [Indian nationalists] will all be so pleased with this that they will be content for it to have little real power, so long as it exists, leaving the Provinces and States respectively autonomous in domestic matters.[2]

Hoare, Peel, and Stanley thought a good model for Indian federation would leave residuary powers with the provinces. They wrestled with harmonizing the Simon scheme with immediate federation. On 26 November Hoare consulted Simon and received the following policy recommendation: 'Try to get out of the Conference general resolutions in favour of federation of

[1] Minutes of Liberal and Conservative delegations meeting, 21 November 1930, R.C. 56 g; Coatman to Irwin, 21 November 1930, I.C. 19.
[2] Lane Fox to Irwin, 19 November 1930, I.C. 19.

The Formula for All-India Federation

all-India, and provided that all-India is federated, then a cautious acceptance of Government corresponding to responsible Government.'[1]

On 12 December Hoare submitted a memorandum[2] for the consideration of the Conservative delegation and of the Conservative Party Business Committee, which at that stage comprised Baldwin, Neville Chamberlain, Churchill, Lord Hailsham Stanley, Peel, and Hoare himself. It presented all-India federation as the fulfilment of Simon's scheme and as an opportunity of avoiding democracy in the central government. There was no difference between the Simon vision and the Conference model of federation 'except that the unexpected support of the Princes has brought federation from the distant horizon on to the immediate foreground'. The Conference was taking the 'very remarkable step' of eliminating the British Indian centre and thus extricating 'British India from the morass into which the doctrinaire liberalism of Montagu had plunged it'. The question now was whether 'the picture is so much changed as to justify us giving responsibility of any kind to an Indian executive'. All-India federation would provide a stable centre while the provincial experiment was being tried and Conservatives could insist that central responsibility must be 'entirely dependent upon an effective federation being in actual existence'. Indeed, as a federation would take years to create, the *status quo* would continue at the centre for a considerable time. This interpretation of federation contrasted strongly with Sapru's expectation that central responsibility would be real at the outset and complete within a few years.

Hoare explained that Britain could yield 'a semblance of responsible government and yet retain in our hands the realities and verities of British control'. The viceroy should have large overriding powers. The army would be reserved to British control. Finance could be 'tied up' through a statutory currency board, a reserve bank, and special provisions to make service salaries and pensions, the army, and the interest on loans prior charges on the revenues. Some 80 per cent of the Indian revenues could be kept out of the hands of an Indian finance minister. A commercial agreement could be attached to the constitution

---
[1] Hoare's note of Simon's advice, 26 November 1930, T.C. 19.
[2] Memo in T.C. 1.

and there could be a statutory railway commission. Furthermore, the federal executive would not be responsible or removable in the British sense, for it would depend partly on the princes' nominations as well as on British Indian elections. Hoare also commended central 'responsibility' as expedient. The concession would create goodwill in India and its endorsement by the Conservatives would avert their becoming isolated politically.

Hoare's advice to support central responsibility given certain conditions was accepted by the Party's Business Committee, with only Churchill dissenting. However, from a large Party meeting in December Hoare could obtain agreement only that the delegation should not oppose responsibility in principle. The Party would not commit itself in general terms to responsibility in an all-India federation, and it reserved judgement until the government produced a detailed proposal. Hoare was not the man to press the Party against what he sensed to be its general will. Coatman, reporting the Party's decision, noted that 'his eyes [were] more on the Conservative Party outside than on the Conference'.[1] Hailey observed a strong disinclination in the Party at large to concede central responsibility.[2] By the beginning of 1931 Dawson could see that Hoare had become rigidly noncommittal.[3] Even after Reading's speech of 5 January the Tories remained immovable. Haig wrote of them just before the end of the Conference: 'They stand now isolated in the Conference —the only element which has not committed itself to the principle of responsibility at the Centre.... They stand immobile in the middle of a flood, seeing their foothold gradually being washed away.'[4]

On 26 January Hoare did state in parliament that while his Party did not wish to block the federal solution it must insist on certain safeguards being real. He had cleared his speech with Baldwin in advance, so that after Churchill had leapt to the attack, Baldwin, determined that the Indian problem should never assume the character of the Irish question, responded with a pledge to back the federal solution developed by the Conference. The speech was reassuring to an extent. However,

[1] Coatman to Irwin, 19 December 1930, I.C. 19.
[2] Hailey to Irwin, 24 and 30 December 1930, I.C. 19.
[3] Dawson to Irwin, 2 January 1930, I.C. 19.
[4] Haig to Irwin, 9 January 1930, I.C. 19.

Churchill now resigned from the Shadow Cabinet, the diehards' resentment was strong, and the new Tory expert on India had hardly emerged from the Conference a staunch advocate of the federal solution. His memorandum of December, like his caution throughout the Conference and his concern for Party opinion, suggested that he was as likely to retard as to advance the creation of a federation. In February he delivered the ominous claim: 'During ten weeks of almost incessant discussion, basing ourselves on the Simon Report, we steadily maintained our position.'[1] As he accepted the princes' initiative as justifying an acceleration of the Simon timetable for federation, so might he be expected to backpedal if the princes' attitudes changed.

By the close of the Conference there were signs that the northern princes' initial enthusiasm for federation was evaporating. Divisions were appearing in their ranks as it became clear that different federal solutions were contemplated by different sections of princes. Benn observed at least three schools of thought on the question of princely representation in the federal legislature and executive: the southern states wanted separate representation; Bikaner wanted representation to be arranged by the Chamber of Princes; the small states wanted a special scheme of their own.[2] Indeed, some princes were already talking of the need for a federation of states as a prerequisite to an all-India federation. As for the great southern states, the Federal Structure Committee's scheme for 'central' British Indian powers to be retained by a federal government, rather than provincialized, was contrary to the Hydari scheme. The F.S.C scheme contemplated a close relationship between the central British Indian and federal authorities, the very thing that Hydari had wanted to avoid. Again, the financial implications of federation were different in the case of each state, and a general settlement would clearly be difficult to achieve. Finally, the princes had pressed the prime minister on the question of paramountcy and it was agreed that Irwin should take it up with them. Irwin had the wit to see that if the princes were satisfied on the question of paramountcy then the basis of much of the federal movement would vanish. Yet some of them would make satisfaction on

---

[1] Hoare's pamphlet, 'India, an Official Statement of Conservative Policy', reprinted from *Morning Post* of 5 February 1931.
[2] Benn to Irwin, 15 January 1931, I.C. 6.

paramountcy a condition of their accession. Clearly, opportunities would not be wanting for dissident Tories seeking to deconvert princes from their recent attachment to a federal solution.

There would also be opportunities to play discontented Muslims off against the friends of all-India federation. The failure to solve the communal problem was the most disappointing and portentous feature of the first Round Table Conference. The agreement of the leading Muslim delegates to support the federal solution momentarily papered over the communal cracks in the nationalist front. However, his experience of the Hindu–Muslim negotiations at the Conference led the sober Sapru to observe that the language of national unity was a transparently thin veil drawn across the harsh realities of communal division.[1]

After the meeting at Bhopal's house that extended into the early hours of the first morning of the Conference, it was clear that the initial informal round of negotiations had broken down. Despite the Liberals' entreaties, Moonje and Jayakar had refused to accede Muslim weightage in the Muslim minority provinces, or a statutory majority of Muslims in the Punjab legislature. On the latter point they were supported by the Hindu Punjabi delegate, Narendra Nath, and the Sikh, Ujjal Singh. The Liberals blamed the Mahasabhites and the Sikhs for the breakdown and felt that the Aga Khan, Jinnah, and Shafi were seeking an agreement. However, it is likely that the Muslim negotiators would have found their agreement to abolish separate electorates repudiated by their co-religionists. British observers noted that Jinnah was widely mistrusted by his own people, that the Aga Khan failed to give a strong lead, and that Shafi's ultimate willingness to make a concession of substance was doubtful. O'Dwyer perceived suspicions among conservative Muslim delegates.[2] On 19 November, Ismail Khan, the president of the All-India Moslem Conference, which Fazl-i-Husain had revived, cabled to Reading: 'All-India Moslem Conference in session at Lucknow unanimously reaffirms its Delhi resolution of 1 January 1929 and hopes Moslem delegates nominated by Viceroy for Round Table Conference would abide by it. Further

[1] Sapru to Edward Thompson, 29 December 1930, S.C. 1, T. 19; Hailey to Irwin, 15 December 1930, I.C. 19.
[2] O'Dwyer to Reading, 4 November 1930, R.C. 56 j.

The Formula for All-India Federation

declares clearly that no constitution modifying it agreed by Moslem delegates will be acceptable to Moslems.'[1] For the time being there was, as the Aga Khan told Benn, 'nothing doing' on the question of communal settlement.[2] Hailey noted wrily: 'Not all the beef and ham pies of our London lunches seem able to bring the two communities closer together.'[3]

By late November the two chief peacemakers, Sapru and Jinnah, were spurned by many of their respective co-religionists. The Muhammadan extremists were 'not prepared to follow the coaxings of Jinnah, and the Hindu Mahasabha are equally distrustful of Sapru'.[4] Jinnah was called 'a little liar' by a Muslim delegate.[5] He was to stay on after the Conference, living in Hampstead and practising at the Privy Council bar until 1934. Sapru resigned from the Liberal Party, partly because many of its members suspected him of having become pro-Muslim.

During the second week of December, Sapru took a fresh initiative. Its basis was joint electorates but the concession of the other Muslim demands for the provinces, which, except for the majority in the Punjab, the Mahasabhites now seemed ready to approve. The prime minister himself undertook to chair discussions. The *Daily Telegraph* attacked the government for pressing the Muslims to accept joint electorates. This charge, though denied by Benn, was widely believed by delegates for the Indian minorities and it was publicized in India. O'Dwyer noted 'much anxiety among [the minorities] and some resentment over the persistent efforts of the Government to abandon the right of separate electorates'.[6] None the less, when the Muslim delegates met on 9 December to consider the fresh Hindu offer they agreed to surrender separate electorates if seats were reserved to the Muslims on a population basis in Bengal and the Punjab and on a weightage basis in other provinces. On Saturday 13 December the Hindu and Muslim delegates went down to Chequers by bus. Hailey noted his prognosis: the Muslims would give up separate electorates if they got bare majorities in Bengal and the Punjab and weightage elsewhere; the Hindus would

[1] Telegram, R.C. 56 j.
[2] Benn to Irwin, 5 December 1930, I.C. 6.
[3] Hailey to Irwin, 28 November 1930, I.C. 19.
[4] Haig to Irwin, 27 November 1930, I.C. 19.
[5] Hailey to Irwin, 28 November 1930, I.C. 19.
[6] O'Dwyer to Reading, 11 December 1930, R.C. 56 j.

accept these conditions if a satisfactory position were achieved in the central government.[1]

Hailey was wrong. The results of the Chequers meeting were 'staggering'.[2] The Muslims refused to give up separate electorates and sat pat on all of Jinnah's fourteen points. The Hindu Mahasabhites retracted their concessions. There was a 'complete deadlock'. Sapru 'broke into a fierce attack on Moonje, saying that ... there was in India no spirit of nationalism and to talk of it was a farce', and that 'there was no foundation on which a British Government could grant responsibility in India'. The breakdown, wrote Haig during the following week, was 'loosening the whole fabric of the Conference' and 'little trace' of Indian unity remained.[3] Bhopal spoke of 'confirmed pessimism, almost despair', over the communal situation.[4]

What had happened was that on 10 and 11 December over a hundred cables, protesting against yielding separate electorates, poured in upon the Muslim delegates. Opinion in India was now firmly against concessions. Reading received a strong plea from Waris Ameer Ali;[5] Irwin complaints from Fazl-i-Husain about official pressure being exerted on Muslim delegates, together with a request to acquaint Benn of Indian Muslim opinion.[6] Irwin cabled that the Muslims were 'greatly disturbed at the least suggestion of the abandonment of communal electorates' and that the possibility of negotiating a settlement that would not be repudiated in India was 'very faint'.[7] Coatman noticed the effects of Indian pressures upon Shafi. At the beginning of December he was urging Muslims to give up separate electorates, by Christmas he was an extreme communalist.[8]

During the week before Christmas the Aga Khan and other Muslims were responding to pressure by seeking reassurance from the opposition delegations. The Muslim delegates were no longer able to talk of giving up separate electorates. Within the delegation the reactionaries, Shafa'at Ahmad Khan and Ghaz-

[1] Hailey to Irwin, 13 December 1930, I.C. 19.
[2] Hailey to Irwin, 15 December 1930, I.C. 19.
[3] Haig to Irwin, 18 December 1930, I.C. 19.
[4] Bhopal to Irwin, 19 December 1930, I.C. 19.
[5] Ameer Ali to Reading, 11 December 1930, R.C. 56 j.
[6] Irwin to Benn, 15 and 26 December 1930, I.C. 11.
[7] Irwin to Hailey, 22 December 1930, I.C. 19.
[8] Coatman to Irwin, 19 December 1930, I.C. 19. For Fazl-i-Husain's excoriation of conciliatory Muslims see A. Husain, *Fazl-i-Husain*, pp. 252-7.

navi, had emerged as the dominant influence. They were seen as the true spokesmen of Muslim feeling in India. The Muslims now made much of their community's loyalty to Britain and intimated that if Britain failed to support them then they would have to reappraise their attitude towards civil disobedience. On 19 December the Aga Khan met Peel, Stanley, Foot, and Reading at the latter's house. Peel promised to defend the Muslims' electoral claims but Reading was evasive.

On 19 December, too, several Hindu Liberals met and decided to send a letter to the Aga Khan and Jinnah, reaffirming the Bhopal house terms and offering the Muslims 51 per cent majorities in Bengal and the Punjab. The Sikhs spurned the proposals. Narendra Nath, though not hostile in private, was not prepared to stand out publicly for such a settlement in the Punjab. Moonje declined to join in the initiative. Jayakar at first agreed to the proposals but soon retracted, probably after discussing them with Moonje. At this stage, cables from Hindu Sabhas were raining down upon the viceroy and Hindu delegates, objecting to any agreement that might give statutory majorities to the Muslims in Bengal and the Punjab.[1]

On 21 December Sastri, Setalvad, and Sapru met the Aga Khan, Jinnah, and Shafi. Further Hindu–Muslim talks followed. By the end of the year Sapru had accepted that 'the whole Conference will now proceed ... on the basis of Separate Electorates'.[2] They would certainly place Hindus at a disadvantage and they were indefensible 'on strictly logical grounds and from a purely nationalistic point of view'. However:

I cannot get over the feeling that in the present circumstances of India we cannot be always logical and no compromise has any chance of success in India unless it satisfies the minorities that they have a distinct place of honourable equality in the future Constitution. . . . As far as I can foresee it almost seems to be certain that Separate Electorates must hold the field. I shall regret these results, but I shall not stand in the way of a settlement even on the basis of Separate Electorates, which I very much hate.[3]

The prime minister, advised by Hailey and other officials,

[1] In Government of India Reforms Branch, 1931, 15; P.M. to Jayakar, 12 January 1931, J.C. 455.
[2] Sapru to Raina, 22 December 1930, S.C. 1, R. 17.
[3] Sapru to Thompson, 29 December 1930, S.C. 1, T. 19.

spent the last weekend of the year at Chequers preparing the statement with which he would close the Conference. He would promise provincial responsibility, and central responsibility with safeguards provided an all-India federation was established. Sapru was delighted that such a promise would be made in spite of the communal deadlock. However, on New Year's Eve, MacDonald's private secretary alerted him to Muslim feelings of alarm: 'It appears that [Jinnah and Shafi] are very much afraid that the Government may give a large amount of responsibility at the Centre while at the same time doing nothing to safeguard the Mohammadans beyond using a few general phrases such as that "the interests of the Minorities must be protected". This they fear will leave them at the mercy of a Hindu Government at the Centre.'[1] The Muslims wanted a communal settlement to accompany the prime minister's statement. At an all-night meeting with the prime minister on 1 January the Hindu Liberals expressed their readiness to yield to the Muslims, but Moonje and Narendra Nath remained obstinate.

On 12 January the prime minister obtained Cabinet approval for the virtual retention of the *status quo* on communal representation. He reasoned that to issue an award at that stage would increase friction between Britain and India. It seemed better to leave the question open to further negotiation between the Indian parties.[2]

The next day Jinnah and Shafi announced that they did not want a declaration on central responsibility unless it was accompanied by adequate assurances as to safeguards. If the Hindus obtained the promise that they sought then they would no longer have any motive for accommodating the Muslims. Fazlul Huq from Bengal joined in this chorus. Irwin cabled to Benn of the 'hardening of Muslim opinion in India' and of anxiety over the Government's policy.[3]

On 14 January Shafi presented the final Muslim offer: separate electorates, a 50:50 position in the Punjab, and a near approach to a majority position in Bengal. It was debated for

[1] Brown's note to P.M., 31 December 1930, Brown Coll.
[2] Cabinet Paper by P.M. on Hindu–Muslim representation, 12 January 1931, T.C. 14.
[3] Irwin to Benn, 15 January 1931, I.C. 11.

four hours and the point of difference between the communities was narrowed to 1 or 2 per cent of the seats in the Punjab. In the end Ujjal Singh, pressed hard by the Sikhs in India, and Narendra Nath refused to accept the Muslim demand. Hailey believed that the Sikhs were being used by the Mahasabhites to prevent a settlement that they themselves wished not to seem to frustrate.

At the end of that week the Aga Khan delivered a 'bombshell' to the prime minister and cabled in urgent tones to Irwin. The Muslim delegation was alarmed as to the likely contents of the prime minister's statement. The Aga Khan now made 'the whole future work of the Conference and the examination of the constitutional question strictly contingent upon a settlement of the Mohammadan difficulties'. If the Muslims were not satisfied with the prime minister's assurances they would 'dissociate' themselves from the Conference and its proceedings.[1] Here was the return to a position very like that which the Moslem Conference had assumed in January 1929: Muslims would not accept any constitution that did not embody the safeguards that they demanded. Hailey and Benn spent an anxious weekend drafting passages on the communal question for inclusion in the prime minister's speech. To their relief, though MacDonald departed from the text, and seemed lost in a sea of light during the Movietone filming of the closing session, he did allude to the need for adequate safeguards. He also undertook to deliver an award if the communities themselves failed to agree.

The Conference ended with a clear realization that the Muslims could wreck the putative federation if their demands were not met. Even with conciliatory delegates and a fund of goodwill the communal problem had not been solved. Furthermore, the question of residuary powers had yet to be tackled, and on that matter the division of opinion, even between Sapru and Jinnah, was sharp. The retention within the Sankey scheme of the 'central' powers associated with British India was not calculated to appeal to the Muslims.

It would clearly be a matter of great difficulty to devise a federal constitution that satisfied the conflicting demands and expectations of Sapru and the Hindu Liberals, the British Conservative Party, the various groups of princes, and the Muslims

[1] Benn to Irwin, 17 January 1931, I.C. 6.

of British India. And, of course, the Indian National Congress, which had still to be consulted, was likely to expect the formula to yield freedom within a more unitary structure than was envisaged by the Conference devotees of federation. There was good reason for scepticism about the consensual character of the federal formula that the Conference espoused. Like the chameleon, the formula acquired colour according to the background against which it was set.

CHAPTER 4

The Way of Satyagraha: January 1930—August 1931

... for the sake of liberty people have fought, people have lost their lives, people have killed and have sought death at the hands of those whom they have sought to oust. The Congress then comes upon the scene and devises a new method not known to history, namely, that of civil disobedience, and the Congress has been following that method up.

M. K. GANDHI, 30 November 1931

I. 'SWARAJ' AND SOLIDARITY

GANDHI left the Lahore Congress perturbed at the dangerous divisions within the nationalist movement. While the Congress remained united many of its leaders and supporters, including the Patel brothers, Mrs. Naidu, and Rangaswami Iyengar, the Hindu communalists, Malaviya and Kelkar, the nationalist Muslims, Dr. Ansari and A. K. Azad, and commercial magnates such as G. D. Birla, were disappointed with the rejection of Irwin's initiative and regarded the wilderness of civil disobedience with undisguised apprehension. Early in January 1930 Gandhi was disposed to leave the Congress to Jawaharlal and to undertake an experiment in civil disobedience that would be strictly limited in scope. He wrote to Jawaharlal:

Ever since we have separated at Lahore, I have been evolving schemes of civil disobedience. I have not seen my way clear as yet. But I have come so far that in the present state of the Congress no civil disobedience can be or should be offered in its name, and that it should be offered by me alone or jointly with a few companions.... I want to do nothing that would cross your purpose or thwart your plans.... I cannot conceive a more favourable opportunity for me for making my experiment than when you are the helmsman of the Congress.[1]

However, Jawaharlal hastened to associate both himself and the Congress with the civil disobedience experiment. The 26th

[1] Gandhi to Jawaharlal, 10 January 1930, All-India Congress Committee (hereafter A.I.C.C.), G. 26, 1930.

of January was proclaimed Independence Day and a pledge was taken: 'We will . . . prepare ourselves, by withdrawing, so far as we can, all voluntary association from the British Government, and will prepare for civil disobedience, including non-payment of taxes. . . . We . . . hereby solemnly resolve to carry out Congress instructions issued from time to time for the purpose of establishing Purna Swaraj.'[1] The pledge affirmed 'the inalienable right of the Indian people . . . to have freedom and to enjoy the fruits of their toil and have the necessities of life'. It indicted British rule, which denied freedom and based itself on the exploitation of the masses and the ruination of India economically, politically, culturally, and spiritually. Gandhi welcomed the taking of the pledge throughout the cities and villages of India as evidence of the masses' 'unity in their starvation' and of their hope for 'the glow of freedom'.[2]

Early in 1930 Gandhi's problem was to define the ends and the means of civil disobedience in terms attractive to the disparate elements of Indian society. To nationalist Liberals and others who appreciated the value of ordered progress under the *pax Britannica*, Gandhi's objectives and techniques smacked of anarchy. Sastri described him as a 'philosophical anarch': 'If you say to him: "What you are doing is bad for all Government", he says, "That is exactly what I desire". If you say, "It will lead to chaos", he says, "Only by chaos perhaps can we get back to natural society."'[3] Sapru was alarmed at the implications of civil disobedience for the structure of Indian society and feared a headlong plunge into violence. Gandhi had tried to forestall such criticism by arguing that British rule itself rested on the subtle and sinister manipulation of violence. By assailing authority by non-violent non-co-operation he would draw out the violence that underlay the Raj. He explained his outlook to Liberal friends:

We must cease to dread violence, if we will have the country to be free. Can we not see that we are tightly pressed in the coil of violence? The peace we seem to prize is a mere makeshift, and it is bought with the blood of the starving millions. If critics could only realize the torture of their slow and lingering death brought about by forced

[1] In D. G. Tendulkar, *Mahatma*, 8 vols., Bombay, 1951–4, III. 10–12.
[2] Quoted ibid. III. 12.
[3] Irwin to Lord Halifax, 31 March 1930, I.C. 27.

starvation, they would risk anarchy and worse in order to end that agony. The agony will not end till the existing rule of spoliation has ended. It is a sin, with that knowledge, to sit supine, and for fear of imaginary anarchy or worse, to stop action that may prevent anarchy....[1]

The message was simple. Britain ruled India by force for her own selfish ends. If Indians refused to co-operate with the Raj, British interests would at once be affected and naked violence would appear to enforce obedience. This philosophy did not appeal to the Liberals, but Gandhi's clever formulation of India's interests did win the support of many elements in society that had much to lose from the disorder inseparable from civil disobedience. Gandhi was able to secure the backing of India's mercantile community for an experiment in anarchy.

At the end of January Gandhi formulated eleven demands which, he insisted, epitomized independence. If they were met then the government would hear no more of civil disobedience. Remarkably, the eleven points made no reference to constitutional issues. They summed up the essence of Britain's economic exploitation of India and the violent methods by which she enforced it. They concerned the liquor trade (which was degrading as well as extortionately taxed), the exchange rate, the land revenue, the salt tax, customs duties, coastal shipping, military expenditure, civil service salaries, political prisoners, the Criminal Investigation Department, and the embargo on armaments. To the Nehrus, the points read 'more like a surrender than anything else'.[2] After the grand Lahore independence resolution and the pledge, Gandhi seemed to have 'gone back to the Delhi Manifesto only in greater detail, with perhaps the addition of one or two fresh items'. Gandhi chid Jawaharlal: 'I never thought you would miss the importance of the 11 points.'[3] As he claimed, the points strengthened the nationalist case. Their predictable rejection by the viceroy enabled him to taunt Britain with her refusal to yield her 'ill-gotten gains' or to modify a regime which, in order to extract enormous riches, had organized violence 'on a scale unknown before, and manipulated in

[1] In *Mahatma*, III. 8.
[2] Motilal to Jawaharlal, 4 February 1930, in Jawaharlal-Motilal Corr., Nehru Coll.
[3] Gandhi to Jawaharlal, 6 February 1930, in Jawaharlal Corr., Nehru Coll.

so insidious a manner as not to be easily seen or felt'.[1] By his eleven points Gandhi elevated his case to a higher moral plane and sharpened Indians' awareness of the conflict between their own material interests and those of Britain.

The strategic effectiveness of Gandhi's formulation is evidenced by a letter of the great Bombay entrepreneur, Lalji Naranji:

Gandhiji's 11 points or demands are more of economic nature than of mere political nature. It is therefore that commercial community have put more explicit faith in Gandhiji or his organizations.... I can give you a number of instances where we see Government lives only for the vested interests of Great Britain, firstly by keeping India as their market for their manufactured goods, 2ndly by milking India dry through their (a) banking policy which preserves banking and exchange etc. for their Banks, (b) shipping of even their coastal traffic for Inchcape interests, (c) insurance policy through their bankers, (d) transport on railway under their management, (e) currency, exchange and fiscal policy in such a way that India is not only robbed by Great Britain but by Italy, Japan etc.... We capitalists to work with Socialistic organizations like Congress clearly shows that Government indifference to us has driven us into their camp.[2]

For the capitalist as for the peasant Gandhi's programme now comprehended the economic interests of India as against those of Britain.

Gandhi's next move was to identify a symbol of imperial exploitation to which all Indians could respond. He found it in the salt laws, by which Britain imposed an excise of some $3\frac{1}{2}$ annas ($4d.$) per head per annum upon a necessary of life. As the salt excise yielded only some Rs. 70,000,000, or about 4 per cent of the Indian revenues, its non-payment could not cause major embarrassment to the Raj. Still, the identification of the tax as a target established the moral basis of Gandhi's campaign. All Indians paid the salt tax. All could easily participate in defiance of the law by making their own salt. Gandhi planned to inaugurate civil disobedience by making salt at Dandi on the sea, after marching there from his ashram at Sabarmati, near Ahmedabad, with a band of his followers. The scheme was brilliantly conceived. The 241-mile march would become an

[1] *Young India*, quoted in *Mahatma*, III. 14.
[2] Naranji to Jayakar, 27 January 1932, J.C. 456.

The Way of Satyagraha 169

epic, with the eyes of the world riveted upon its progress. When Gandhi picked up salt from the shore civil disobedience might begin everywhere. At first the salt laws alone would be violated; but soon liquor and foreign cloth shops would be picketed, British imports would be boycotted, and land taxes would be withheld.

While the programme went far towards establishing a sense of common interest against Britain, Muslim leaders felt that it ignored the need for communal unity. In January, such old non-co-operators as the Ali brothers entreated Muslims to abjure civil disobedience. In February, even the nationalist Muslims were out of sympathy with the movement. It seemed that Gandhi had shelved the communal issue. The Congress Muslims, Dr. M. A. Ansari, C. Khaliquzzaman, T. A. Sherwani, R. A. Kidwai, and Dr. Syed Mahmud had all welcomed the Irwin declaration as a 'God-send' and were aggrieved by the Lahore resolution.[1] On 13 February Ansari, as the Nationalist Muslim spokesman, wrote to Gandhi that although he would not leave the Congress he must insist that the quest for Hindu–Muslim unity be given top priority in its programme. In reply, Gandhi explained his new approach to the communal question:

I agree that the Hindu–Muslim problem is the problem of problems. But I feel it has to be approached in a different manner from the one we have hitherto adopted—not at present by adjustment of the political power but by one or the other acting on the square under all circumstances. Give and take is possible only when there is some trust between the respective communities and their representatives. If Congress can command such trust the matter can proceed further, not before. The Congress can do so only by becoming fearless and strictly just. But meanwhile the third party—the evil British power—has got to be sterilized. There will be no charter of independence before the Hindus and the Muslims have met but there can be virtual independence before the charter is received. Hence must civil disobedience be forced from day to day. . . .

Again:

You can not achieve unity through any Conference. But we can through fighting for common causes. . . . I want you to realize the new orientation I have given to the struggle. I seek independence through a redress of the age-long grievances which touch the masses

[1] Ansari to Gandhi, 13 February 1930, Ansari Coll.

more than us. I want you to throw yourself heart and soul into this battle.[1]

Motilal, too, stressed the futility of negotiations for Hindu–Muslim unity: 'This can only be done on an economic basis and in the course of the fight for freedom from the usurper. . . . The master mind has amidst much ridicule and misrepresentation discovered one such economic basis in the breaking of the salt laws.'[2]

The 1930 satyagraha was to be not merely the way to achieve Indian freedom but also the means of creating national unity, of bridging the gaps that separated disparate interests and communities.

The Government of India's response was to avoid, as far as possible, taking any step that would enhance Gandhi's popularity. The great salt march, which began on 12 March, ended on 5 April. Next day, Gandhi inaugurated mass civil disobedience by ceremonially breaking the salt law. The Government of India adopted a policy of studied forbearance towards the march. It decided that if the march were peaceful then it could not be prohibited. To arrest non-violent demonstrators would be to play into their hands. H. G. Haig, the Home Department Secretary, wrote to the provincial governments that 'every effort should be made to avoid being drawn into struggles of this kind'.[3] If non-violent crowds became troublesome the *minimum* of force should be used. When the district magistrate at Borsad arrested Vallabhbhai Patel early in March for inciting villagers to make salt, he was rapped over the knuckles.

The government's treatment of the salt satyagraha was guided by purely tactical considerations: 'to neutralize in such ways as may be found most convenient the practical effects of a breach of the law and prosecute such leaders as it may suit Government to deal with'.[4] The government recognized that the purpose of the campaign was to educate Indians in civil disobedience, and that Gandhi planned to use his arrest for breaking the salt laws as the signal for a mass response on a wide range of issues. They unobligingly determined not to arrest him so long as he seemed

[1] Gandhi to Ansari, 16 February and 3 March 1930, Ansari Coll.
[2] Motilal to Ansari, 17 February 1930, Ansari Coll.
[3] Haig to local governments, 26 March 1930, Home Pol. 213/30.
[4] Govt. of India to Govt. of Bombay, 5 April 1930, Home Pol. 247/II/30.

The Way of Satyagraha

likely to provoke less excitement by being free than he would by being arrested. They would deny him the mass sympathy that his arrest would arouse. However, they would not ignore the transgression of the salt laws by any other leader if a clear case could be proved against him. From the official viewpoint Gandhi's choice of the salt tax as the first object of civil disobedience had the advantage of exposing the satyagrahis to *penal* action. The government could pick off the leaders at will. It hoped that the agitation would soon be defeated by such tactics.

Towards the end of 'National Week', the first week of civil disobedience (6–13 April), the viceroy's council was satisfied that 'no modification of policy was required and that unless he forced our hands by some quite new development we should continue to avoid the arrest of Gandhi'.[1] Illicit salt was being seized and Congress leaders arrested (notably, Jawaharlal on 14 April) without any apparent growth of revulsion towards the government. However, from about the third week in April Gandhi's breaches of the salt laws in the Surat district of Gujarat, Bombay province, were causing acute embarrassment to the local authorities. Rioting occurred in one city after another. More alarmingly, on 18 April the police armouries at Chittagong were raided. On 21 April the viceroy's council decided to sound the provincial authorities about the desirability of arresting Gandhi. On 22 April a telegram to all local governments explained that the policy of treating Gandhi differently from other salt satyagrahis had created in Gujarat a situation in which 'the authority of Government is perhaps becoming increasingly difficult to maintain'.[2] Furthermore, the campaign had now been extended beyond salt to include picketing of liquor and foreign cloth and the persuasion of Indian officials to resign their appointments. The local governments were asked whether the movement was more likely to subside if Gandhi were left free or if he were apprehended. Was government forbearance unsettling its loyal supporters and weakening its authority; or would Gandhi's arrest attract to the movement groups that had not hitherto been involved, for example, the Muslims?

Most local governments despaired of improvement unless

---

[1] Home Member to P.S.V., 11 April 1930, ibid.
[2] Govt of India to local govts., 22 April 1930 (t/g), Home Pol. 257/VIII/30.

Gandhi were apprehended. They expected his arrest to encourage rather than alienate loyalists. The decisive opinion came from Bombay, the most disturbed province:

The hope that was entertained in many quarters that the movement will be discredited must be abandoned. On the contrary, day by day individuals and bodies of men hitherto regarded as sane and reasonable are joining the movement, not because any definite results from anti-salt laws campaign are expected by them, but because among the educated Hindus, Gujaratis mostly but others also, the belief that the British connection is morally indefensible and economically intolerable is gaining strength. Movement has therefore developed beyond point at which even the arrest of Gandhi will break it down unless very early steps are taken to afford a rallying point for moderate and minority opinion and to maintain Government's prestige and restore public confidence.[1]

While this opinion was being prepared a massive demonstration was held at Peshawar against the arrest of Abdul Ghaffar Khan, 'the Frontier Gandhi', leader of the Khudai Khidmatgars (Servants of God) or 'Red Shirts', a Muslim organization in the N.W.F.P. that supported the Congress. From 25 April until 4 May the N.W.F.P. government lost control of its leading city. The case for Gandhi's arrest gained strength rapidly. To official embarrassment in Gujarat and apprehension over events at Chittagong and Peshawar were added fears of disaffection in the army and a threat from Gandhi to raid the salt works at Dharsana. By the end of April Irwin had reached the broad conclusion that 'unless Government is to abdicate in favour of Gandhi and Congress by admitting to ourselves and the public our inability to arrest him at all we must be prepared to make plain without further delay our intention to continue governing'.[2] With Benn's consent plans were laid to arrest Gandhi. On 5 May he was interned under a Bombay regulation.

Gandhi had won far more support than almost anyone had anticipated. His disappointment was that the Muslims played a relatively insignificant part in civil disobedience, except in the N.W.F.P. The All-Parties Moslem Conference dissociated itself from the movement. His great successes were to win over the right-wing Hindu nationalists and, even more important, the

---

[1] Govt. of Bombay to Govt. of India, 26 April 1930, ibid.
[2] Irwin to Benn, 29 April 1930, I.C. 11.

commercial classes, especially in Bombay. In April the government lost the co-operation of Vithalbhai Patel, the president of the legislative assembly, and the Responsive Co-operation Party, led by Malaviya and Moonje. Patel and Malaviya resigned their assembly seats in protest against the government's cotton duties bill, which made imperial preference a condition of protection for Indian-manufactured piecegoods. The bill also provoked G. D. Birla, the industrialist and merchant, to resign. His fellow magnate, Sir Purshotamdas Thakurdas, reacted against the government when, on 27 April, it introduced an ordinance to reimpose the Press Act (1910). Though Thakurdas disapproved of the Lahore resolution and the salt satyagraha he felt sure that repression would exacerbate civil disobedience. He reported to Irwin that the committee of the Indian Merchants' Chamber was being pressed to identify itself with Gandhi's campaign. It was impossible to hold a public meeting in Bombay 'to point out the dangers of this movement'.[1] In May, Thakurdas wrote to Sir Joseph Bhore, an Indian member of the viceroy's executive, that the views of his electorate, 'the vast Indian commercial community', had forced him to the decision that he must resign from the assembly.[2]

The disposition of the commercial collaborators with the Raj was of major importance. Thakurdas represented it faithfully. Though never a creature of political party, he occupied a strategic position as an intermediary between the Congress and the government. Originally a Bombay cotton trader, he had, by the 1920s, become a director of over fifty companies engaged in industry, commerce, and finance. He had been a nominated member of the Bombay legislative council, a representative of the Bombay cotton trade in the Bombay legislative assembly, a nominated member of the Indian council of state, and a representative of commerce in the Indian legislative assembly. He was knighted in 1923. He sat on the Retrenchment Committee in 1922 and the Royal Commission on Indian Finance and Currency in 1925–6. He was a leading member of the Indian Merchants' Chamber, and in 1927 he joined with Birla and others to form the Federation of Indian Chambers of Commerce

[1] Thakurdas to Irwin, 28 April 1930, Purshotamdas Thakurdas Coll. (hereafter P.T.C.), 99.
[2] Thakurdas to Bhore, 14 May 1930, P.T.C. 99.

and Industry. In 1930 the former body boycotted the government's cotton tariff legislation and the latter resolved, on 16 May, to non-co-operate with the Round Table Conference unless Gandhi agreed to attend it.

The mercantile community wanted the government to declare that under the reformed constitution 'the economic exploitation of India' would be terminated by the transfer of full control over finance, currency, fiscal policy, and the railways to popular ministers responsible to the central legislature. A week after Gandhi's arrest Thakurdas called upon Irwin to declare that Indians would become masters in their own house, except over military, foreign, and political (states') matters. The commercial community's support for Gandhi owed much to the exiguous economic conditions of 1930. The depressed prices of agricultural produce on the world markets had caused a sharp decline in the demand for imported and manufactured articles. Indian financial leaders had long pressed for the devaluation of the rupee against sterling, which would enhance the rupee earnings of exporters and consequently stimulate home demand. For India's business classes Gandhi's campaign promised financial autonomy and all its attendant benefits.

For Gandhi, mercantile support was a double-edged sword. Civil disobedience was bad for business. Indian merchants were often involved with British manufacturers, as importers, processors, and distributors. The boycott movement was marvellously effective, and as time passed its effects upon Indian merchants became serious. Valuable working capital was committed to unsaleable stock. Hartals had caused commercial dislocation on a large scale. In early June Thakurdas evinced signs of uneasiness. The affairs of the commercial classes were becoming 'more and more entangled.... I am getting more nervous about a crop of insolvencies and consequent disaster.'[1] With the steady escalation of the conflict between Congress and the government commercial men and moderate politicians began seeking an opening for the restoration of peace. When, on 30 May, the government introduced ordinances against intimidation and unlawful instigation, respectable middle-class nationalist sympathizers became increasingly disturbed at their complicity in such illegal activities as picketing.

[1] Thakurdas to Rangaswami Iyengar, 4 June 1930, P.T.C. 91.

The Way of Satyagraha

II. THE NEGOTIATION OF A TRUCE

The disparateness of Gandhi's following was an impressive demonstration of national unity. However, when the time came for Gandhi to articulate the conditions of peace the varied objectives of his supporters and sympathizers were bound to create difficulties. At Lahore the declared aim was complete independence; at the end of January 1930 it was the eleven points; for the merchants it was financial autonomy; for the more moderate Hindus it was Dominion Status with safeguards. After the first flush of success Gandhi's problem became to secure in peace the unity achieved in conflict. That meant deciding how much freedom to demand.

On 20 May a *Daily Herald* journalist, George Slocombe, obtained an interview with Gandhi, who intimated that Congress would attend a Round Table Conference that was authorized to frame a constitution embodying the 'substance of independence'. His prior conditions were the release of political prisoners, the repeal of the salt tax, and the prohibition of liquor and foreign cloth. Gandhi's idiosyncratic usage of such terms as 'independence' made his meaning difficult to follow, though he seems to have been concerned to secure evidence of India's equality of status with Britain. Gandhi was ready to negotiate on terms of equality, though he stressed that he would do nothing without the agreement of Motilal, the acting president of the Congress, who was still at liberty. In the third week of June Jayakar, Sethna, Setalvad, Jinnah, Lalji Naranji, Bikaner, and Sir Prabhashankar Pattani (diwan of Bhavnagar) met to formulate constitutional terms that Gandhi and the government might accept. They pressed for a declaration that the Round Table Conference would frame 'a scheme of full responsible Government subject to transitory safeguards' for the army, foreign and political relations, and the interests of the minorities.[1] At this stage Motilal and Thakurdas met in Bombay and the former confided the belief that the satyagraha movement would not last longer than three months all told. This suggested a return to peace by early July.

On 25 June, after meeting Jayakar and Slocombe at Bombay, Motilal agreed to the terms on which Congress would participate

[1] P. Sethna to Sapru, 18 June 1930, Sethna Coll.

in a Round Table Conference. The governments of India and Britain must offer a private assurance that they would support the demand for 'full responsible government for India, subject to such mutual adjustments and terms of transfer as are required by the special needs and conditions of India and by her long association with Great Britain, and as may be decided by the Round Table Conference'.[1] Motilal would convey the assurance to Gandhi and Jawaharlal and if it were accepted civil disobedience would be called off, the government's repressive measures would be repealed, and political prisoners would be pardoned. This formulation was indeed close to the proposed parliamentary declaration that Irwin had cabled home on 13 June: 'The object of the Conference... will... be to secure the greatest agreement for proposals consistent with the purpose' of India's attaining Dominion Status; the Conference would be free to examine any Indian proposals for 'the realization of His Majesty's Government's declared policy and in particular to explore' provisions for foreign policy, defence, internal security, and the minorities.[2] Regrettably, the opposition parties demurred at Irwin's proposal. They allowed only that the viceroy should himself say, on 9 July, that he wished to see India enjoying 'as large a degree of management of her own affairs as ... [is] compatible with the necessity to make provision for those matters in regard to which India is not yet ready to assume full responsibility'.[3] Unfortunately, too, on the day that Motilal agreed to Slocombe's formulation, the Congress Working Committee confirmed a resolution of 7 June calling upon police and troops to disobey orders. The government's response was to do now, on 30 June, what it had refrained from doing during three months of civil disobedience: declare the C.W.C. an unlawful institution. Motilal was arrested at once.

In spite of the guarded verbiage of Irwin's 9 July declaration, Jayakar and Sapru still hoped for a *rapprochement* between the Congress and the Raj. Though Irwin disclaimed the possibility of further concessions to Congress, he allowed the two intermediaries to meet Gandhi in gaol on 23 and 24 July. The result was not discouraging. Gandhi gave Sapru and Jayakar a note

[1] J. Nehru, *Autobiography*, London, 1936, p. 227 n. 1.
[2] See above, pp. 108–9.
[3] Irwin's speech in Imperial Legislative Assembly, 9 July 1930.

The Way of Satyagraha 177

for the Nehrus. It suggested that 'the Conference be restricted to a discussion of the safeguards that may be necessary in connection with the self-government during the period of transition'.[1] Civil disobedience would be called off simultaneously with the release of prisoners. Property confiscated for non-payment of the land tax should be restored, fines refunded, officials who had withdrawn their labour reinstated, and ordinances repealed. Salt manufacture and peaceful picketing should continue. However, the note specified that 'Jawaharlal's must be the final voice' and that Gandhi would support 'any stronger position up to the letter of the Lahore resolution'.[2] Here was a readiness to attend a Conference concerned not with Dominion Status but with 'safeguards'!

It is remarkable that Gandhi was prepared to subordinate his judgement to that of Jawaharlal as president of the Congress. So too was Motilal. In Jawaharlal's presence Motilal's conciliatoriness, so conspicuous during his June talks with Slocombe and Thakurdas, disappeared. Doubtless he had been angered by the outlawing of the C.W.C. and by being arrested. Possibly, the government's evident reluctance to take such action had made him over-confident of their early willingness to accept Congress on its own terms. Jayakar recorded that Motilal was now 'very bitter, perhaps because he had been clapped in gaol just at the time when he evinced a desire to become reasonable. He said that the *status quo ante* had been altered, and he had, in consequence, altered his views also.'[3] Jawaharlal, recalling the visit of Sapru and Jayakar to him and his father at Naini prison on 27 July, later wrote that Motilal regretted his statement to Slocombe and that there was now 'not the faintest chance of any peace between Congress and the Government'.[4] The Nehrus gave the emissaries a letter for Gandhi that rejected his suggested Conference about 'safeguards'. They reasserted the Lahore demand for complete independence. However, they expressed a wish to consult Gandhi and the C.W.C. before they issued a final statement.

The July *pourparlers* reveal a clear distinction between the inclinations of Gandhi and those of Jawaharlal. Even the Home

[1] *Mahatma*, III. 57. [2] Ibid.
[3] Jayakar's account of the peace negotiations, 2 October 1930, R.C. 56 g.
[4] Nehru, *Autobiography*, p. 228.

Department accepted that Gandhi's suggestion of a Conference about safeguards was not unreasonable, whereas Jawaharlal's response was 'bellicose' in its insistence upon independence.[1] Jayakar gave Sapru an account of a meeting with Gandhi on 31 July:

> I asked him what his view was about continuing the present agitation for another period of six months on the ground that the proper time for a settlement had not arrived. He said that he did not agree with that view. He was not fighting, he said, for the sake of a victory, but desired to create an intensity of feeling as a demonstration and thought that he had done so sufficiently long.[2]

On the other hand, Jawaharlal had gloried in the 'epic greatness' that 'the new India' had achieved through civil disobedience and believed that the pressure must be maintained until the government made an 'appreciable advance'.[3] His attitude affected Gandhi, who now indicated that he would press for a constitution that enabled India to secede from the empire and for control over the subjects involved in the eleven points. Yet he still shrank from defining these terms as conditions precedent to attending a Conference. He merely wanted the viceroy to be 'aware of my views in order that, when I press them at the Round Table Conference, it might not be said that I was springing new points and taking the Government by surprise'.[4]

Gandhi's overriding concern remained Indian unity rather than any external constitutional embodiment of freedom. On 23–4 July he had stressed that he could not guarantee to attend a Conference on safeguards unless, upon his release from prison, he became sure that the Indian delegates were in 'agreement as to the minimum by which they should stand under all circumstances'.[5] On 31 July he pressed Jayakar to clarify his own intentions and those of Sapru in the event of the government failing to offer a satisfactory advance. Given a consensus among Indians Gandhi was prepared to go to a Conference without prior assurances from Britain. Since Jawaharlal's response, as Congress

---

[1] Note by M. G. Hallett on July–August negotiations, Home Pol. 31/97/32 Secret.
[2] Jayakar to Sapru, 4 August 1930, J.C. 15.
[3] Jawaharlal to Gandhi, 28 July 1930, Jayakar's account, loc. cit.
[4] Quoted in Jayakar to Sapru, 4 August 1930, J.C. 15.
[5] Jayakar's account, loc. cit.

president, made a consensus impossible, Gandhi allowed himself to be associated with the framing of extreme constitutional conditions of co-operation.

From 13 to 15 August a meeting between Gandhi, the Nehrus, Vallabhbhai Patel, Mrs. Naidu, Jayakar, and Sapru occurred at Yervada gaol. The Congress leaders put forth the impossibly high demand that no settlement was acceptable that did not provide for: India's right to secede from the empire; an Indian national government responsible to the people for all matters, including defence, finance, and the subjects contained in the eleven points; India's right to refer to an independent tribunal such British claims (e.g. the public debt) as the national government considered unjust or contrary to India's interests. The Congress leaders rejoiced in the 'marvellous mass awakening' aroused by civil disobedience and regretted that the 'great sufferings' had been insufficient to convert Britain to the acceptance of Indian freedom. The Congress demand was weighed down by references to 'past wrongs', 'ruin', 'exploitation', and the 'dwarfing process' of British domination. It also insisted upon the right to make salt and to peaceful picketing of liquor and foreign cloth.[1]

Such terms may have been necessary in order to satisfy the young left wing of the Congress after their early triumph. But they alienated the Liberals and some Hindu moderates and placed the mercantile community in alarming financial straits. Jayakar adjudged Congress intransigence 'a great mistake'. A sympathetic viceroy, who had given 'as good terms as it was possible for him to do', had been treated 'in a scurvy manner'.[2] Sethna wrote of 'a great chance missed by the Congress'.[3] Moonje broke with the Congress boycott and attended the Conference. Birla counselled Thakurdas that it was 'the general opinion of the [Bengal] mercantile community . . . that it would not be a bad idea if you accepted the [Conference] invitation'.[4] Thakurdas declined, out of deference to the wishes of the Federation of Indian Chambers of Commerce and Industry, and from a conviction that he would be running a fool's errand unless the

[1] Congress leaders to Sapru and Jayakar, 15 August 1930, in Nehru, *Autobiography*, pp. 603–5.
[2] Jayakar to B. Das, 13 September 1930, J.C. 453.
[3] Sethna to Sapru, 11 September 1930, Sethna Coll.
[4] Birla to Thakurdas, 6 September 1930, P.T.C. 104.

government were 'prepared to concede complete self-government to us in all domestic matters, barring the usual, military, political, etc. for which consideration will have to be given at the Conference'.[1]

Thakurdas personified the dilemma of the commercial community. When Jayakar visited Gandhi at Yervada the community showered upon him expressions of concern at the economic depression and of hope for an honourable peace. In his July conversations with the Nehrus Jayakar stressed that though the Bombay merchants were still prepared to support Congress they were at the end of their tether financially. He bore tidings of the evaporation of credit and financial confidence, of the slump in raw material prices, of closures of the share market, and of cotton mills. Britain was certainly losing exports but the impact was affecting Indian shippers, bankers, and traders. Still, the commercial community wanted a substantial not a shadowy compromise with Britain. It meant financial autonomy.

In August, leading merchants and industrialists began to divide over the need for a truce in order for business to recover. Sir H. P. Mody urged the Millowners' Association of Bombay, of which he was chairman from 1927 to 1935, to review its political policy in the light of economic conditions. Trade and industry were at a standstill, credit was largely destroyed, and unemployment was widespread. In Bombay there was 'a paralysis of the economic structure'.[2] Continued civil disobedience would spell 'economic disaster'. On 11 August F. E. Dinshaw, of the Parsi merchant family, put much the same case to Jayakar:

> The view I beg to urge is that Bombay has come to the end of her resources, and if the fight continues, her trade will be entirely gone, her people will be starving, and she will cease to be the powerful supporter she has been of the National cause.... These are not mere words, and I am prepared to put before you the opinions of all important firms which are interested in trade and industry in Bombay. ... Tradespeople have no resources, have no business and have no credit.... Our troubles have been exaggerated by the foreign piecegoods situation. Some crores of capital invested in this business is for the time being as good as lost.... As to cotton mills, it is certain that by the end of this month about 25 mills will completely shut down....[3]

[1] Thakurdas to Birla, 16 September 1930, P.T.C. 104.
[2] H. P. Mody draft, n.d. [? August 1930], P.T.C. 100.
[3] Dinshaw to Jayakar, 11 August 1930, J.C. 17.

After the failure of the Sapru–Jayakar intervention Thakurdas wrote to ask Motilal's advice upon ways of extracting internal autonomy from Britain: 'Our anxiety is to ensure the Congress the success that its activities have earned, and prevent the country an economic shock which may weaken the popular enthusiasm.'[1] But for the moment there was no way of delivering the business community from its agony. While in London the Conference assembled, with H. P. Mody attending, in India Thakurdas continued to lament the evidences of depression yet insist upon domestic self-government as the irreducible demand. Nobody wanted to deal in jute, wheat, and cotton at the depressed prices prevailing. The purchasing power of the masses was 'completely shattered'.[2] Devaluation of the rupee was essential. Yet if Congress remained intransigent it would certainly lose support. At Delhi, Cawnpore, and Amritsar piecegoods importers and dealers were 'getting tired of picketing'.[3] Congress would 'certainly have a severe set back'.

On the eve of the Conference the Government of India was confident that civil disobedience would 'on the whole die out before long'.[4] For the moment, Gandhi had lost the opportunity to cash in the success of his experiment with freedom and unity.

MacDonald's declaration at the close of the Conference—that Britain would devolve responsible government upon an all-India federation subject to safeguards for defence, external relations, the states, the minorities, the services, and finance—came close to satisfying the commercial community's demands. The British Indian delegates, especially Sapru and Jayakar, believed that in view of the achievements of the Conference an amnesty for political prisoners would now suffice to induce the Congress to reappraise its policy. They pressed His Majesty's Government for a display of clemency. Benn urged Irwin to consider 'whether any action could be taken directly or indirectly to persuade authoritative Congress leaders to make some statement which would justify an amnesty'.[5] On 22 January Irwin replied that he had withdrawn the notification declaring the C.W.C. illegal and released unconditionally the members and ex-members of

[1] Thakurdas to Motilal, 22 September 1930, P.T.C. 104.
[2] Thakurdas to E. J. Bunbury, 3 October 1930, P.T.C. 104.
[3] Thakurdas to D. P. Khaitan, 8 October 1930, P.T.C. 99.
[4] Ibid.
[5] Benn to Irwin, 19 January 1931, I.C. 11.

the Committee so that they might discuss the prime minister's statement.

At the end of January the Home Department sounded local governments on their attitudes towards a general release of the 25,000-odd civil disobedience prisoners, given, first, an assurance from Congress that civil disobedience would be abandoned, and secondly, evidence that Congress would pursue constitutional methods and co-operate in the task of constitutional reform. The local governments' replies revealed serious apprehension about the intentions of the governments at Whitehall and New Delhi, and grave misgivings for the future. Concern was expressed at the effects of any general release and at the dangers that lay ahead. Summarizing the replies, H. W. Emerson, secretary of the Home Department, generalized: 'In short, doubts are current regarding the will and the capacity of Government to protect their friends and servants.'[1] The Muslims, who had stood aloof from civil disobedience, had not been reassured by the prime minister's generalities about safeguards for the minorities and were in a depressed mood. If the government gave reason for apprehension that Congress was the power of the future then the Muslims might well shift camps, while the services and the police would become demoralized. The government must assess courses of action by reference to their probable effects upon friends and supporters: 'The issue is in the balance as to whether we shall within a few months, or even within a few weeks, be able to command support.' There was a strong conviction that government had conquered civil disobedience. If Congress were now sufficiently chastened to co-operate, well and good; but there must be no government retreat. In short, Congress should be given the opportunity to join the constitutional discussions; but if they did not do so whole-heartedly, accepting the prime minister's declared objectives, then 'it is essential that government should show unmistakably that they are able and willing to govern'.

After his release Gandhi was subject to conflicting pressures. Jawaharlal's remained the voice of revolution, whereas the Hindu moderates and Liberals, Jayakar, Sapru, and Sastri, and the commercial community counselled conciliation. On 7 February the governor of Bombay advised Irwin of 'clear indications

[1] H. W. Emerson's minute of 12 February 1931, Home Pol. 5/45/31 and K.W.

that a number of Gandhi's followers, particularly among the mercantile community, are contemplating a breach with him, unless he adopts a reasonable attitude'.[1] Thakurdas told Irwin that the men of commerce would 'put all the pressure on him that they could', for 'they now definitely want to find ways of peace'.[2] He also pointed out the significance of the recent death of Motilal, who had thrown a 'cloak of moderation' over Jawaharlal's 'extremer programme'. The younger Nehru would probably be less influential in the future.

On 7 February Sapru arrived home at Allahabad. During the next few days he met Gandhi and other Congress leaders to acquaint them of the inwardness of the developments at the Conference. He found Malaviya and Ansari 'obviously very anxious that a settlement should take place and they approved in substance the scheme outlined at the Round Table Conference'.[3] Jawaharlal was, however, 'very hostile'. He objected to the scheme's failure to place the army and civil service salaries in Indian hands, the transfer of power to reactionary princes and landlords, and the probability that financial safeguards would leave little scope for improving the lot of the masses. Sapru found Gandhi's own preliminary conditions such that he could support: release of political prisoners and withdrawal of the repressive ordinances. He sympathized, too, with Gandhi's concern for peaceful picketing of liquor and foreign cloth to continue. He found that Gandhi also wanted to ensure the right of the poor to make salt.

At Gandhi's behest Sapru summoned Jayakar and Sastri to discussions with the C.W.C. He kept Irwin *au fait* with proceedings. On 14 February, following a decision of the C.W.C., Gandhi wrote to Irwin to request a 'heart to heart talk'.[4] 'Friends' who had attended the Conference read into its proceedings 'a meaning and a hope I would like to share'. Gandhi's resultant parleys with Irwin began at Viceroy's House on 17 February and continued, by fits and starts, until terms of peace, the so-called 'Delhi Pact', were agreed on 5 March. Sapru and Jayakar acted throughout to smooth over rough patches in the dialogue. Jayakar served as a channel of communication between anxious Bombay merchants and the Mahatma. Sapru felt that Gandhi's

[1] I.C. 11.   [2] Irwin to Benn, 9 February 1931, I.C. 6.
[3] Sapru to Bikaner, 11 February 1931, S.C. 2, S. 174.   [4] I.C. 6.

attitude 'left no room for doubt that he was anxious for peace', as were 'the vast majority of Congressmen' who had assembled at Delhi.[1]

It was significant of the eagerness of Gandhi and the C.W.C. for peace that during the Gandhi–Irwin talks little difficulty was experienced with the constitutional issue. Gandhi agreed that Congress should co-operate in 'considering further the scheme for the constitutional Government of India discussed at the Round Table Conference', of which federation was 'an essential part', as were 'Indian responsibility, and reservation or safeguards in the interests of India, for such matters, as for instance, defence; external affairs; the position of minorities; the financial credit of India, and the discharge of obligations'.[2] It was understood in conversation, however, that at the Conference Gandhi should be free to raise the question of secession from the empire, and that the specific reserves and safeguards agreed at the first Conference session were provisional rather than definitive. Gandhi also established that the agreement did not preclude his raising the question of the Indian states' peoples' rights and their representation at the Conference. He knew that Jawaharlal felt deeply about these points, and he wanted to be able to assure him that the agreement to explore the federation with safeguards scheme did not prevent Congress from pursuing the implications of its demand for independence. However, he could have been in no doubt that the government regarded the freedom to raise such points as of no practical effect, for the Conference had laid bare the limits to which the British were prepared to go.

The Gandhi–Irwin talks became contentious over the conditions of peace and the treatment of the eleven points. Ultimately, Gandhi agreed to 'discontinue' civil disobedience, including the organized defiance of the law, the non-payment of land taxes and rents, attempts to incite civil and military servants and officials against authority, and the dissemination of civil disobedience propaganda. The government agreed to withdraw repressive ordinances and release civil disobedience prisoners. Most difficulty occurred over picketing, salt making, the resto-

[1] Sapru to Bikaner, 10 March 1931, and MacDonald, 14 March 1932, S.C. 1, S. 175, and M. 10.
[2] Text of settlement published on 5 March 1931, in *India in 1930–31*, Calcutta, 1932, pp. 655–9.

ration of lands forfeited for non-payment of tax and rent (especially in Gujarat, where the non-payment campaign had been most effective), the reinstatement of officials who had non-co-operated, and Gandhi's demand for an inquiry into alleged police excesses. Irwin allowed peaceful picketing as an economic measure to stimulate Indian industry, but not as a political weapon, and conceded the right to make salt in certain areas. Negotiations almost foundered over the question of an inquiry into police excesses. Here Irwin dared not yield for fear of the effect upon police morale, despite the urgings of Sapru and Jayakar. Gandhi settled eventually for having it noted that he had represented the need for an inquiry but had refrained from demanding one. Finally, Irwin agreed to the restoration of forfeited lands, provided that they were still in official possession, and the liberal reinstatement of officials by local governments. Here was the weakest element in the settlement. In the main area of confiscation, Bardoli taluq in Gandhi's Gujarat homeland, Vallabhbhai Patel had promised peasants that when peace was secured they would recover their holdings. The promise was scarcely redeemable where the lands had already been alienated to third parties. Patel, the Congress president in 1931, made the difficulty clear, but Gandhi could obtain from Irwin only a note to the Bombay government requesting the consideration of confiscation and reinstatement.

The settlement was a truce rather than a peace, the suspension rather than the abandonment of civil disobedience. Gandhi had yielded to pressures from the Hindu moderates and Liberals to examine the federal formula and from the commercial community for a respite. Yet he had not surrendered his freedom of manoeuvre. On 6 March he made clear that the pact was 'most decidedly consistent' with the Lahore resolution and that there was 'nothing to prevent' the Congress at its coming annual session at Karachi, or at the Conference, from reasserting the demand for complete independence.[1] His problem was to achieve a consensus among Indians upon a national demand to be put before the Conference. He had now to encash the success of his civil disobedience experiment in national unity, and convert it into a measure of freedom acceptable to India and extractable from Britain.

[1] Report of press conference, *Mahatma*, III. 75.

186   *The Way of Satyagraha*

In a reflective letter of 25 March, Sir Frederick Sykes, who as governor of Bombay had suffered the brunt of civil disobedience, wrote of the impossibility of the democratically committed Congress reaching agreement with minority communities or autocratic princes or British Conservatives. The elements of the situation portended a constitutional deadlock:

... we now stand on a razor's edge. On the one side there is the danger of reactionaries at Home, or Muhammadans and minorities in India, overdoing the question of safeguards; and, on the other, we have the extremists, such as Jawaharlal, prepared to wreck everything and welcome the resulting chaos. Already all the parties, Congress, Muhammadans and others are sticking their toes in, and it is unlikely that any of them will budge from the position they are taking up. Even if someone is clever enough to bridge thinly over the gulf between the Muhammadans and the Hindus in order to serve present purposes, we can only expect a much worse breach when the real strain comes.... We must therefore anticipate a deadlock sooner or later, either with the Congress, or with the Muhammadans, or with the States or in Parliament. The Congress will then once more stand forth as the champions of Indian independence, and it will be left to us to go ahead with a scheme on the lines already approved by the Round Table Conference with the help of the more moderate elements.[1]

III. THE PURSUIT OF UNITY AND PARITY

In March 1931 Gandhi strove to reconcile the Lahore resolution with the formula for central responsibility given federation and safeguards. This was necessary if he was to placate the young left yet pursue constitutional negotiations. He explained the nub of his own demand to Irwin, who wrote on 10 March:

I saw him a couple of days ago and told him that, if he went on talking about complete independence, although I knew what he meant, he would greatly puzzle and upset British opinion, which would naturally jump to the conclusion that his goal was the break-up of the Empire. This he explained to me was not so. What he really desired was that India and Great Britain should be absolutely equal partners in the Empire, and he was prepared to admit plenty of safeguards or adjustments once this equality was secured, and provided that the safeguards were honestly designed in the interests of India and that India must accept them of her own free-will without being

[1] Sykes to Irwin, 25 March 1931, I.C. 26.

The Way of Satyagraha

coerced thereto by Great Britain. If we could get to this kind of relationship, he would say he had got independence, but it would be independence with partnership. And this he thought a higher conception than independence in isolation.[1]

Recognition of India's equality and a relationship based on partnership: here was the core of Gandhi's demand. With it went an insistence upon the freedom of Congress to question all or any of the proposed safeguards.

When the Congress assembled at Karachi in the last week of March, the young left made no secret of their antipathy for the constitutional terms of the settlement. Their strength was enhanced by the wave of anti-government feeling that followed the execution on 23 March of Bhagat Singh. A leader of a Punjabi youth movement, Singh had been sentenced for the murder of a Lahore police officer in December 1928. In April 1929 he had thrown a bomb in the legislative assembly.

Gandhi managed to secure the approval of the pact and his own appointment as a Round Table Conference delegate, together with such others as the C.W.C. might nominate to serve under his leadership. However, the goal of complete independence was reaffirmed. At any Round Table Conference the Congress would pursue 'this object, and in particular, so as to give the nation control over the army, external affairs, finance and fiscal and economic policy ... and the right ... to end the partnership at will, provided, however, that the Congress delegation will be free to accept such adjustments as may be demonstrably necessary in the interest of India'.[2]

Gandhi paid something of a price for the left's approval of his policy. This was Nehru's resolution on Fundamental Rights and Economic Policy, by which Congress declared that any constitution accepted on its behalf should enable 'the swaraj government' to provide for certain rights and reforms.[3] The rights included freedom of association and combination, of speech and the press, of conscience and religion; the right of the minorities to protection; the right to bear arms, etc. The reforms included adult suffrage and free primary education. Industrial workers would be paid a living wage and be given

[1] Irwin to Halifax, I.C. 27.
[2] *Mahatma*, III. 103.
[3] Ibid., III. 111–12.

certain amenities; peasants' rents would be reduced; there would be a progressive tax on agricultural incomes and a graduated inheritance tax. Military expenditure would be halved and civil service salaries reduced to a maximum of Rs. 500 per month. Indigenous cloth would be protected, liquor would be prohibited, and salt might be manufactured freely. India would control the exchange and currency policies and the state would control key industries.

Nehru's resolution identified a large number of targets for a Congress-dominated government to attack. The princes, already under Congress pressure to allow their subjects to elect representatives to the Round Table Conference, were alarmed at the list of civil and political liberties. The services were appalled at the proposed salary levels. The zamindars were antagonized by the suggested agricultural tax, and the Muslim élites by the notion of an inheritance tax. Industrialists were scarcely likely to take comfort from the socialist elements in the programme. A less fortunate resolution for a body seeking national solidarity can hardly be imagined. Passed at Gandhi's moment of triumph, the resolution indicates the formidable difficulties of his achieving national unity. Yet he was firm about the need for unity prior to negotiation in London. He would go to England 'when unity is attained'; and 'his conception of unity is ... that all differences should be adjusted in India; in England there should be no [?division], at any rate amongst any section of the British Indian delegates'.[1]

The deepest British Indian division continued to be that between Hindus and Muslims. During the civil disobedience movement the Nationalist Muslims and those in the N.W.F.P. rallied to the Congress standard, but otherwise the communal accord of the 1920–22 non-co-operation campaign was not repeated. Indeed civil disturbances often brought communal rioting. As the delegates gathered at Karachi the communal animosity that characterized the first quarter of 1931 reached a climax at Cawnpore. On 25 March Muslim shopkeepers in the city refused to observe a hartal in memory of Bhagat Singh. Fighting broke out and for two days Cawnpore was beyond control.

By the end of the first Round Table Conference the Muslim

[1] Haksar to Sapru, 19 May 1931, S.C. 1, H. 30.

The Way of Satyagraha

delegates had resolved not to co-operate with an advance towards central responsibility until their required safeguards were assured. Early in February, de Montmorency told Irwin of Muslim fears that the prime minister's declaration meant nothing but danger for them. His Majesty's Government seemed to have been preoccupied with gratifying the Hindus and to have shown a callous disregard for the Muslims, who were 'undoubtedly sore'. They had a 'rod in pickle' for Shafi, who had been too ready to surrender their position.[1] On the eve of the Delhi Pact Fazl-i-Husain told Irwin that the Muslims would probably non-co-operate with the development of central responsibility until the communal question was settled. Of course, Irwin's negotiating with Gandhi as an equal fanned Muslim resentments.

Gandhi applied himself to the Hindu–Muslim problem the moment that the Pact was announced. On 7 March he addressed a mass meeting at Delhi:

The settlement that has just been arrived at will fail of effect without a real heart unity between Hindus and Musalmans. Without that unity our going to the conference will be of no avail.[2]

Gandhi claimed that to settle the problem he would be prepared to concede whatever the Muslims demanded. The rub was that the Muslims themselves were never in agreement. The Nationalists had accepted the Nehru Report, and in particular joint electorates and a unitary polity, whereas the preponderance of non-Congress Muslims insisted upon separate electorates and strong provincial governments within a weak federation. On the eve of the Karachi Congress, discussions at Dr. Ansari's house in Delhi showed clearly that these positions were still held tenaciously. After the Congress, when Gandhi asked Shaukat Ali, the president of the All-Parties Moslem Conference, for a statement of the Muslims' demands he was presented with Jinnah's fourteen points. On 5 April non-Congress Muslims met in conference at Delhi and reaffirmed their adherence to the All-Parties Moslem Conference resolutions of January 1929. Two days later Gandhi stated his personal readiness for a 'full surrender to any unanimously expressed wish of the Musalmans

[1] De Montmorency to Irwin, 6 February 1931, I.C. 6.
[2] *Mahatma*, III. 76.

and Sikhs'.[1] But he denied that the resolutions represented a unanimous demand. A communalist settlement of the constitutional problem could be accepted only if it represented the views of almost the entire community.

Towards the end of April Gandhi saw Bhopal at the latter's request. He gave him *carte blanche* to call in Shaukat Ali and 'his other friends and then summon me to Bhopal if he thought that there were anything to be done'.[2] At Mrs. Naidu's instance he also saw Shaukat Ali again. At the beginning of May Shaukat, Shafi, Dr. Iqbal, the renowned poet, and Shafi Daudi of Bengal, as representatives of the Moslem Conference, and Ansari, Sherwani, and Khaliquzzaman, as representatives of the Nationalists, met at Bhopal. The negotiations produced two alternative compromises to settle the electorate problem. The one provided for separate electorates to be replaced by joint electorates with adult suffrage at the end of ten years, or at such earlier stage as the Muslims in any legislature might agree; the other provided for the first elections under the new constitution to be on the basis of separate electorates, and for a referendum on the question after four years. Fazl-i-Husain was aghast at this readiness to accept a time limit for the assurance of separate electorates. In view of his opposition the negotiations failed. Sapru observed truly that there was no possibility of a communal settlement without the conversion of Fazl-i-Husain.

There was a general tendency for Congressmen to misunderstand the position that non-Congress Muslims had assumed. They were inclined to view electoral arrangements as the major plank in the Muslim platform, whereas by early 1931 the Muslims were preoccupied with the distribution of executive authority. The Muslims were out to safeguard themselves in a polity that embodied MacDonald's promised central responsibility. On 14 April Nehru betrayed his failure to grasp the point when he commented that the All-Parties Moslem Conference 'passed most vile resolutions which have nothing to do with communal demands but which go to show that these friends are working in the interests of a third party'.[3] The rationale of the Conference's reiteration of the January 1929 resolutions was explained

---
[1] Statement by Gandhi on 6 April 1931, in A.I.C.C., G. 85, 1931.
[2] Gandhi to Jawaharlal, 8 May 1931, J. Nehru Corr., Nehru Coll.
[3] Jawaharlal to Mustafa Ali, 14 April 1931, A.I.C.C., G. 40, 1931.

to Irwin by the Punjabi, Feroz Khan Noon, with whose help Fazl-i-Husain 'stagemanaged' the Conference.[1] Feroz told of the Muslim insistence upon the establishment of Sind and N.W.F.P. as separate constitutional entities and of Bengal and Punjab as Muslim-majority units: 'He pressed that the delegation of powers from Parliament should be to Provinces in the first instance and that Provinces should then, on the analogy of Indian States, decide what subjects should be made Federal.'[2] Only thus could India's Muslims secure themselves against a Hindu raj in a self-governing India. This position was implicit in the January 1929 resolutions. It had been spelled out by Muhammad Ali and refined by Fazl-i-Husain. Separate electorates were important to Muslims in Hindu-majority provinces, but they were vital as the means of securing majorities in the Muslim provinces.

The April 1931 All-Parties Moslem Conference underlined 'the demand for autonomy of the constituent units and for complete residuary powers to be vested in them'. There was to be no difference between the powers of the federal units, whether states or provinces. 'It was urged that all transfer of power should be made from Parliament to the Provinces, and that no subject should be made Federal without the previous mutual consent of the autonomous units of the Federation.'[3] Sind and the N.W.F.P. must be full and separate provinces and the Muslims must enjoy majorities in Bengal and the Punjab. In June a *Manchester Guardian* correspondent summarized astutely the drift of Muslim opinion:

The Moslems see that the new Federal Government, if and when it comes into existence, will have a large Hindu majority. The entrance of the States has increased the majority, for the States are chiefly Hindu. There is a strong tendency to counteract this permanent majority by trying to form a large northern block of provinces which will be Moslem, and in which the Hindus will be, as it were, hostages for the good behaviour of their co-religionists in the centre and south. The writer found this 'hostage' theory to be very widely held. Many Moslems do not believe in the permanence of a Federal India, and they foresee a Moslem state in the North stretching from Karachi to Northern Bengal....[4]

[1] Jayakar to Sapru, 11 April 1931, J.C. 454.
[2] Irwin to Benn, 2 April 1931, I.C. 6.
[3] *The Times*, 14 April 1931.
[4] *Manchester Guardian*, 19 June 1931.

The first Round Table Conference and Gandhi's successes forced the Muslims to crystallize their views on Muslim India. Their demand in relation to Hindu India was not unlike that of Gandhi in relation to Britain. They wanted partnership not subordination. Their strategy was first to destroy the unitary Raj and consolidate their strength in some of the fragments; then to enter into a voluntary partnership with the Hindu fragments, always retaining the right of secession.

By the end of May there seemed little likelihood of Gandhi achieving agreement with the Muslims. He had long felt that there was 'no going to London without Hindu–Muslim unity'.[1] He now asked Ansari rhetorically: 'What can I ask and what strength can I put forth in the national demand if we are a house divided against itself?'[2]

If Congress again refused to attend the Round Table Conference then Britain must go forward to concert reforms with the other parties. Some officials had disapproved of Irwin's play for Congress support and his apparent recognition of Gandhi as a plenipotentiary. There were also some who did not share his aversion to the Muslim scheme for the provincialization of the Raj. For example, Sir James Crerar, the Home Member of his council, believed that 'the prudent, sound and logical course to take' was to begin the process of reform by establishing autonomous provinces, leaving federation for a later stage.[3] In the first months of Lord Willingdon's viceroyalty (18 April 1931 —18 April 1936) there were rumours of 'the Fazl-i-Husain–Crerar group capturing the Viceroy' to the exclusion of the Sapru–Jayakar influence.[4]

It was extreme to speak of an alliance between the Muslims and the bureaucrats against central responsibility. The main evidence for the claim was the selection of additional delegates for the Round Table Conference. Fazl-i-Husain was suspected of blackmailing the viceroy by threatening a boycott unless additional Muslims of his persuasion were appointed as Conference delegates or members of the Federal Structure Committee. Hindu Liberals feared the Committee being stacked with

[1] Gandhi to Nehru, 8 May 1931, J. Nehru Corr., Nehru Coll.
[2] Gandhi to Ansari, 26 May 1931, Gandhi Coll., vol. 47.
[3] Crerar's minute of 13 May 1931, Reforms 11/31.
[4] Jayakar to Sapru, 8 May 1931, J.C. 455.

Muslim anti-federationists. Certainly, some of Fazl-i-Husain's recommendations secured appointment to the Conference (Shafi Daudi and Dr. Iqbal) and the F.S.C. (Shafa'at and Zafrullah). However, the C.W.C. had itself placed the government in difficulty when on 2 April it nominated Gandhi as its sole delegate. The government could scarcely appoint Congress Muslim delegates. Under pressure, however, it did finally nominate Sir Saiyid Ali Imam as a Nationalist Muslim to replace the Raja of Mahmudabad, who had not taken up his invitation to the first Conference session.

In June the C.W.C. overrode Gandhi's reluctance to attend the Conference without a mandate from both communities. Its preponderance of right wingers, many of whom had discountenanced the Lahore resolution, were determined to have the Congress case represented. In July it framed its own 'compromise between the demands of undiluted nationalism and undiluted communalism'.[1] It rejected separate electorates but favoured manhood suffrage and the reservation of seats on a population basis for minorities comprising less than one quarter of the people in any province. It accepted, too, the separation of Sind, the full provincial status of N.W.F.P. and Baluchistan, and, with some reservations, the bestowal of residuary powers upon provinces within a federal constitution. As the compromise failed to provide the essential security of Muslim majorities based upon separate electorates in Bengal and the Punjab, Shaukat and the Moslem Conference rejected it out of hand. So too did the Mahasabha and the Punjabi Hindus, who resented the Gandhian and Congress anxiety to appease the Muslims. If Gandhi were to go to London it would be encumbered not only with hostile Muslim and Hindu communalists but also with a Congress compromise that both communities abhorred. His room for manoeuvre would indeed be limited.

Even after the C.W.C. overruled his unwillingness to attend the Conference without a national mandate, Gandhi's departure remained doubtful. A further prerequisite of his participation in the London negotiations was the effective operation of the Delhi pact, which was not achieved to his satisfaction until the conclusion of a 'second settlement' on 27 August. From March

[1] Congress Scheme for a communal settlement, in *R.T.C. Progs.*, 2nd Session, pp. 64–5.

Gandhi sought an interpretation of the pact that was acceptable both to the governing authorities and to his own lieutenants. The interpretative problems were most acute in the rural areas of Gujarat and the U.P. that were affected by the Patel and Nehru campaigns against the payment of taxes and rents.

Of all forms of civil disobedience the non-payment of taxes and rents alarmed the administration most. It menaced social as well as financial stability. The land tax was the third-largest source of British Indian revenues, accounting for some 15 per cent of the total receipts as against customs' 22 per cent and railways' 17 per cent. More important, it was the lynchpin of provincial finance, while the land settlement arrangements with the landholders provided the cornerstone of the British administration throughout rural India. Gandhi held the no-land-tax weapon in reserve as the final sanction during the 1920–2 satyagraha. His threatened resort to it in Bardoli taluq in February 1922 never eventuated. In 1928 Vallabhbhai Patel at once established his status as an all-India figure and revealed the potency of the weapon when he organized a non-payment campaign to secure a resettlement of the revenue arrangements for Bardoli. The governor of Bombay, Sir Leslie Wilson, drew sobering lessons from his experience of the Bardoli affair. There was 'no easier way in which [Congress] can embarrass Government than by organizing this passive civil disobedience of non-payment of taxes'.[1] He impressed upon Irwin 'the difficulty . . . of dealing with an organized campaign for the non-payment of taxes', and the need to act with vigour and speed:

> It seems to me imperative that the organizers should themselves be dealt with with great promptitude . . . [by issuing] a proclamation under the Criminal Law Amendment Act declaring the organization an unlawful association. I would strongly urge that, before any such movement had had time to grow it should be possible for any Provincial Government to make it definitely illegal for anyone to organize a campaign advocating non-payment of taxes due to Government. . . .

At Irwin's instance the Home Department prepared a draft on policy, which agreed on the need to deal with such a movement 'at the very beginning; if it is allowed to develop it soon becomes formidable'.[2]

---

[1] Wilson to Irwin, 16 August 1928, Home Pol. 197/28.
[2] Draft prepared in Home Dept. for dispatch to local govts. but not sent, 197/28.

In 1930 Surat district, especially the Bardoli and Borsad taluqs, was the area most seriously affected by the anti-land-tax movement. The Bombay authorities replied by summarily confiscating the lands of defaulting peasants and dismissing local officials who incited the offenders. The pact did not commit the government to restoration and reinstatement but liberality was expected. Difficult cases arose at once and disputes occurred between local officials and Congress workers, especially when third parties (either purchasers of forfeited lands or newly appointed officials) had acquired rights. A further problem was the payment of arrears of rent, for which ryots were legally liable.

In October–November 1930, during a brief spell of liberty, Nehru had launched a no-rent campaign in five districts of the U.P. Because the land tax was payable by the zamindars and taluqdars the withholding of rents had explosive implications for landlord–tenant (*kisan*) relations. Nehru was at once rearrested and the campaign was less serious than in Gujarat. However, the U.P. Congress acquired a certain standing as the kisan's champion against the landlord and the government. As in Gujarat, the Congress workers were loth to forfeit their influence and abandon the peasant to the operation of the law.

The collapse of agricultural prices in 1930–1 compounded the difficulty of collecting arrears of rent and tax. The Government of India had been alive to the dangerous conjunction of civil disobedience and depression. In January 1931 the Home Department called upon local governments for details of their measures to relieve agricultural distress and it kept the situation under review subsequently. On 19 January the U.P. government reported that most statutory, non-occupancy tenants and sub-tenants would be unable to pay their rents in full, for rents were based upon the high agricultural prices of recent years. The government was unwilling to prescribe a general reduction but was making a district-by-district review of hard cases. By March it was observing a policy of leniency towards collection. District officers had been advised not to enforce coercive process where 75 per cent of the rent had been paid. A go-slow had been introduced on proceedings for non-payment of arrears and relief was to be granted where genuine need was established.

In the aftermath of the pact Jawaharlal adjudged the relief

procedure in the U.P. to be inadequate. Though the pact required the suspension of the no-rent movement, he at once set about organizing a campaign for economic relief, backed by the threat of non-payment. In the U.P. and Gujarat the pact was represented to the peasants as a mere 'truce' or temporary suspension of hostilities, during which Congress, the 'victors' of the civil disobedience movement, would present the peasants' demands to the government for redress. For example, in a message of 8 March to the people of Rae Baraeli, Sitla Sahai, a Congress worker, claimed that the Delhi settlement was a Congress victory, a truce to facilitate talks about 'complete swaraj' and 'the troubles of the tenants': 'If the Government agrees to our terms it will be a very good thing, but if we do not get a satisfactory answer, the struggle will begin again.' Congress had agreed to suspend non-payment of taxes but as rents could not be paid fully in the prevailing economic circumstances, 'the tenants should submit their applications in the Congress office, and the Congress workers will see the zamindars, taluqdars and Deputy Commissioner and try to get the rent suspended, remitted or reduced'.[1] The letter was prefaced by the following message from Jawaharlal: 'Our peace is still far away. The more our strength increases the sooner we will have real peace and this is only possible when we obtain complete Swaraj.... We cannot take rest yet. We will take rest only when the troubles of the tenants are over.'

The government regarded such Congress activities as a flagrant breach of the settlement. The Deputy Commissioner of Rae Baraeli saw little likelihood of the Allahabad Congress leaders trying to control their rank and file 'as this [campaign] is the sole bond of their union with the kisans, and I doubt if they would miss the present favourable opportunity for pushing their advantage when their ignorant followers in the rural areas are flushed with what they consider to be a great achievement'.[2] The Commissioner of Lucknow supported his subordinate and sent his views on to the chief secretary of the U.P. government with the comment: 'By calling upon the tenants to submit

---

[1] Sitla Sahai's message to the people of Rae Baraeli, with preface by J. Nehru, 8 March 1931, in Home Pol. 33/11/31.
[2] Deputy Commissioner of Rae Baraeli to Chief Commissioner of Lucknow, 12 March 1931, ibid.

applications for remissions of rent they are encouraging them in ... non-payment of rent.'[1] The U.P. secretariat regarded the Congress activities as the no-rent campaign in another guise. Reporting them to the Government of India, it added a note that the U.P. Provincial Congress Committee had resolved in favour of a 50 to 60 per cent remission of rents. Towards the end of March the secretariat sent to the Indian Home Department a copy of an intercepted letter from the U.P.P.C.C. to the District Congress Committee, Fatehpur: if zamindars and taluqdars would accept 50 to 60 per cent remissions then the kisans should pay their rent; otherwise 'you can tell the kisans to withhold the rent till some settlement is made'.[2]

Emerson minuted that Jawaharlal's message to the people of Rae Baraeli was 'a travesty of the terms of the settlement' and 'directly calculated to keep the agitation alive'.[3] When he took the matter up with Gandhi, the latter defended Jawaharlal: '... all will be well if the local authorities do not repel the advances made by Congress Committees and do not look upon their activities with suspicion.'[4] Emerson was appalled. The object of the U.P. agitation was clearly to enable Congress to 'establish its position in rural areas' so that it might 'come as an intermediary between Government and the landlord or the landlord and the tenant'.[5] This implied a claim to status that the government had never recognized. The appropriate action would be to declare the offending Congress committees unlawful under the Criminal Law Amendment Act (1908) and to revive the Unlawful Instigation Ordinance (May 1930). However, that would certainly destroy the settlement. The only alternative was to rely upon the ordinary law against non-payment (i.e. coercive process) and insist that the settlement required the Congress to refrain from 'any agitation in rural areas regarding the payment of land revenue or rent'.[6] Further to an order-in-council of 6 April, Emerson told Gandhi that he must restrain his followers in U.P. and also in Gujarat, where non-payment

[1] Chief Commissioner of Lucknow to Chief Sec. of U.P., 13 March 1931, ibid.
[2] Sec. of U.P.P.C.C. to District C. C. Fatehpur, 22 March 1931, ibid.
[3] Emerson to Home Member and viceroy, 16 March 1931, ibid.
[4] Gandhi to Emerson, 23 March 1931, A.I.C.C., Misc. 2, 1931.
[5] Emerson's note after interview with governor of U.P. (Sir George Lambert), 3 April 1931, Home Pol. 33/11/31.
[6] Ibid.

was being employed to secure the restoration of lands and the reinstatement of officials.

After meeting Emerson, Gandhi made explicit his claim for the status of Congress as an intermediary:

> I never could surrender the primary function of the Congress, viz., to speak for and represent the peasantry. The Congress... is primarily a peasant and workers' organization. The Congress could not possibly implement the terms of the settlement if local authorities refuse to recognise and treat with sympathy the advances of the Congress when speaking for the peasantry. The difficulties you mentioned about U.P. I am convinced could all have been solved if the local authorities had sent for the Congress officials in their respective districts. Many of the Congress officials are well-known to them. I suggest that any other attitude would be contrary to the spirit of the Settlement and must defeat the very purpose we both have in view. It would be wrong to accuse the Congress of breach of the Settlement if the local authorities by ignoring local Congressmen render it impossible for them to implement it. After all the terms have to be carried out through the people and the Congressmen must fail if they could not interpret the people's wishes and woes to the authorities.[1]

Gandhi pressed the same claim to status in his correspondence with the government of Bombay when he protested against the issue of notices in Borsad for the payment of arrears under threat of coercive process. The notices ignored Congress as 'the intermediary between the Government and the people', and if they were evidence of 'the position to be finally taken up by the Government it will in my opinion be a distinct breach of the settlement'.[2] When the government of Bombay denied the intermediary status of the Congress and affirmed its right to exercise discretion upon the use of coercive process, Gandhi replied:

> If you agree that the settlement is between the Congress and the Government, and if it is the Congress that has to implement its terms so far as they are applicable to the people, it follows that the Congress must be recognised as the intermediary between the Government and the people whom the Congress represents. If such was not the case, I suppose that I should have no right to see you or to correspond with you or to receive your replies in the several matters arising out of the settlement.[3]

[1] Gandhi to Emerson, 9 April 1931, A.I.C.C., Misc. 2, 1931.
[2] Gandhi to J. H. Garrett, 20 April 1931, A.I.C.C., Misc. 3, 1931.
[3] Gandhi to J. H. Garrett, 21 April 1931, ibid.

The Way of Satyagraha

Neither the U.P. nor the Bombay government was prepared to accept such reasoning.

Hailey (now back as governor of U.P.) met Gandhi at Naini Tal late in May. He had already arranged revenue remissions to the tune of Rs. 7,000,000, which involved remitting over Rs. 20,000,000 of the rents payable to the zamindars and taluqdars. Gandhi contended that the rents were still beyond the peasants' means and he sought a summary inquiry. Hailey argued the delays involved in an inquiry. He insisted upon immediate payment, for otherwise some rents would be lost for ever, much to the detriment of the revenues and of landlord–tenant relations. Eventually Gandhi agreed to advise the kisans to pay a certain minimum sum, which had the disadvantage that the minimum would immediately be regarded as the maximum. As Hailey noted, Gandhi was not prepared for Congress to 'retire from its position of championship of tenants and small landowners'.[1] Hailey succeeded only in obtaining Gandhi's assurance that he would discountenance a no-rent campaign, and that he would refrain from setting up Congress tribunals on individual rent cases. The U.P. government continued to collect rents and to evict tenants who withheld payment contumaciously. When Nehru protested to Gandhi that evictions were being pursued ruthlessly he found Gandhi determined to uphold the settlement. If repression occurred Nehru must request an interview with the governor and present details of the offence. Gandhi stressed that 'we must not be in any shape or form, directly or indirectly, party to the breach [of the settlement]. . . . Government and the Congress are supposed to be co-operating with each other.'[2]

In Gujarat Gandhi tried hard to secure the payment of land revenue and the restoration of forfeited lands. Despite official rejection of the doctrine of intermediacy, Gandhi and Patel assumed that if they canvassed payment energetically the government would forbear from coercive process. They were consequently enraged when, after they had persuaded reluctant ryots to pay up, the government deemed the payments inadequate and proceeded to attach property. The dispute came to involve the prestige of Congress and local officials. If the latter accepted

[1] Hailey's note on discussions with Gandhi, 20 May 1931, Home Pol. 33/11/31.
[2] Gandhi to Nehru, 20 June 1931, A.I.C.C., G. 40, K.W. iii, 1931.

the adequacy of payments made under Congress duress then the *de facto* mediation of the Congress seemed in danger of being established. If they rejected Congress-determined payments as inadequate then they undermined Congress and reasserted their own position. Congress assurances to protect the peasants would lose credence. In July, matters approached a climax and Gandhi protested to the Collector of Surat about coerced payments: 'The payments made under these circumstances I regard as payments made under duress and forced in violation of the implied understanding that no processes would be issued except in cases where the Congress workers had no influence and where the people had not taken part in the civil disobedience campaign.'[1] The threat to the Gandhi–Irwin pact seemed so serious that the Home Department asked Bombay to 'give quiet hint to Collector to go slow at present, especially in the use of police'.[2] Emerson wrote: '... we apprehend that a position may easily develop in which the Collector of Surat, in order to maintain his prestige, will feel disposed to carry on coercive processes on a considerable scale and in some cases with the aid of the police, while Congress, and especially Vallabhbhai, will feel compelled to offer open opposition.'[3] It was unwise to allow a break in the settlement to occur unless responsibility could be demonstrably laid on the Congress.

In the U.P. and Gujarat Gandhi skilfully prevented his lieutenants from precipitating a confrontation with the authorities. He himself continued to act out the role of an intermediary. However, Jawaharlal and Vallabhbhai felt their relationships with the peasants to be compromised by the official levels of rents demanded, by breaches of the pact as they construed it, and by the resort to coercive processes. In July, after talking with Jawaharlal, Emerson observed that Congress would find difficulty in suspending its U.P. rent agitation while Gandhi went to London: 'Congress, having gone so far, cannot contract their activities to any considerable extent without suffering a loss of prestige, which it will be very hard for them to tolerate.'[4] Gandhi's proposed solution to the impasse was the appointment

[1] Gandhi to T. T. Kothawala, 25 July 1931, J.C. 474.
[2] Home Dept. (Simla) to Bombay Special, 21 July 1931, Home Pol. 33/19/31.
[3] Emerson to R. S. Bell (Chief Sec. Bombay), [? 23] July 1931, ibid.
[4] Emerson's note on talks with J. Nehru, 19–20 July 1931, Home Pol. 33/23/31.

of a tribunal to arbitrate on alleged breaches of the settlement. Gandhi was rebuffed on several occasions when he advanced the proposal, for its implications were anathema to government. The appointment of a tribunal would be tantamount to recognizing the parity of Congress with the government in administrative matters. It implied the acceptance of the Congress claim to a status coequal with that of government, and that the pact had removed certain subjects from the operation of the ordinary law. Towards the end of July, after conversations with Gandhi at Simla about the problem, Willingdon wrote to Jayakar: 'It is true that my negotiations with Mr. Gandhi failed, and for the reason that he conducted them with me as if he were the head of a parallel administration, which naturally I can't admit!, and brought up proposals which after the most careful consideration with all my colleagues I felt bound to refuse. . . .'[1]

Hailey's government devised a means of easing the situation in the U.P. In July it proposed a provisional scheme of rent and revenue adjustments to meet the economic situation. A committee of the U.P. Legislative Council was set up and a Congressman was invited to join it. The invitation brought out the contrast between the attitudes of Gandhi, who favoured acceptance, and Nehru, who did not.

Hailey's astute initiative limited Gandhi's difficulties to Gujarat. Here Gandhi demanded the cessation of coercion, the refund of monies extracted by coercion, and the withdrawal of notices of attachment; or, as an alternative, the appointment of an impartial tribunal. On 10 August the Bombay government denied breaching the settlement and that the Collector of Surat had committed any breach of faith. Thereupon Gandhi wrote to Willingdon that in view of the dogmatic assertion that government must be the final judge, he found it impossible to go to London. However, he stressed that he did not regard the settlement as terminated. He was receiving complaints about its implementation and sought an official statement about the relief of abuses.

Gandhi's inquiry elicited a ruling that put an end to the pretensions that the pact had nourished, but without terminating the pact itself. On 19 August the Government of India replied that it would continue to observe the settlement, which, however,

[1] Willingdon to Jayakar, 2 August 1931, J.C. 455.

'involved no suspension or abrogation of the ordinary law and left complete discretion to the Government of India and local governments to take what measures might be necessary to deal with particular situations'.[1] Government would continue to avoid 'special measures' as far as possible and action would continue to be restricted to the needs of particular situations. 'But so far as this action may relate to the activities of the Congress its nature and extent must depend primarily on the nature of those activities, and the Government of India are unable to fetter their discretion or that of local Governments in this respect.' Willingdon explained to Benn that the statement of policy was 'in accordance with [the] realities of [the] case. It allows settlement to be merged into ordinary administration. At same time it gives assurance against action in excess of clear requirements while preserving essential discretion of Government.'[2] The government neither denounced the settlement nor allowed the Congress claim to a favoured position. Willingdon emphasized that the statement effectively brought to an end the Congress's parity of status, which the pact had implied. On 28 August Willingdon wrote privately to the new secretary of state, Sir Samuel Hoare (26 August 1931—7 June 1935), that the Delhi pact 'certainly has established a position in the minds of the people of the country that Gandhi had acted as a plenipotentiary in negotiating terms of peace with the Viceroy himself, and that therefore there seemed to be two Kings of Brentford in India. My job has been to reassert the authority of the administration.'[3]

Once made, the policy statement became definitive. When, on 20 August, Gandhi published in *Young India* a charge sheet of alleged official breaches of the pact, the government took it as an ultimatum. No concession could now be made without its being generally construed as a climb-down. The government's response was to publish a full refutation of the charges. Now Gandhi gave further evidence of his anxiety to cling to the shreds of his plenipotentiary status by cabling his willingness to discuss matters at Simla. Though he still held the right of impartial arbitration to be implied in the pact, he would waive it if 'reasonable satisfaction is given to Congress' by some informal

---

[1] Willingdon to Gandhi, 19 August 1931, Gandhi Coll. 17525.
[2] Viceroy to Sec. of S., 22 August 1931, Home Pol. 33/23/31.
[3] Willingdon to Hoare, 28 August 1931, T.C. letter book.

The Way of Satyagraha

means.[1] Willingdon held that Gandhi's gesture 'removed the difficulty which we felt to be insuperable, of making any approach ourselves' so long as the demand was for arbitration.[2] He would make no surrender to Gandhi that set aside the government's responsibilities, even to get him to the Round Table Conference, for the effects would be to encourage him to raise his price, to anger the Muslims, and to disgust officials.

Gandhi went to Simla accompanied by Nehru, Patel, Abdul Ghaffar Khan, and Ansari. After a meeting with Willingdon and Emerson on 25 August and conversations with his lieutenants, Gandhi entered into a 'second settlement' on 27 August. The agreement provided for Gandhi to represent Congress at the Conference; for the continuance of the Delhi pact; for an inquiry by a Collector into Congress complaints about collections in Bardoli; for there to be no inquiry into any other Congress complaint; and for future complaints to be handled through the normal processes of administration. At the suggestion of his colleagues, Gandhi had pressed for the following addition to the last provision: 'Mr. Gandhi, while stating that the Congress was desirous that nothing should be done to the prejudice of peaceful conditions, wished to make it clear that this did not imply any undertaking *restricting the future action of the Congress in the matter of continuing grievances or in respect of unforeseen developments.*'[3] Emerson communicated the government's refusal to accept the amendment, which was 'wholly inconsistent with the essential condition' that, except for the Bardoli inquiry, Congress would not pursue any outstanding matter that was 'not clearly covered by the specific provisions of the settlement'.[4] Gandhi replied that he was seeking recognition of the freedom of Congress to obtain some method of relief, if inquiry into a sorely felt grievance were denied, 'in the shape of defensive direct action... notwithstanding suspension of civil disobedience'.[5] Congress was asserting that defensive direct action should not be held to violate the Delhi pact. The government merely noted Gandhi's view and reiterated its policy statement of 19 August: Congress

---

[1] Gandhi to Willingdon, 21 August 1931, Gandhi Coll. 17550.
[2] Viceroy to Sec. of S., 22 August 1931, Home Pol. 33/23/31.
[3] Gandhi to Emerson, 26 August 1931, Gandhi Coll. 17601.
[4] Emerson to Gandhi, 27 August 1931, ibid.
[5] Gandhi to Emerson, 27 August 1931, ibid.

activities would be evaluated by the appropriate governing authorities and dealt with at their discretion, either by the ordinary law or, if necessary, by special measures.

IV. GANDHI'S DILEMMA

The second settlement served to patch up the Delhi pact to an extent that facilitated Gandhi's departure for London to participate in the second Round Table Conference. He was accompanied by Mrs. Naidu, Malaviya, and the mercantile leaders, Birla and Jamal Muhammad. However, he left India without having established the national unity that he had hoped would flow from the civil disobedience experiment. He had failed to achieve a communal agreement. He was encumbered with the C.W.C.'s unsatisfactory compromise of July, while his dealings with the Muslims had antagonized the Mahasabha. He had substantially united the mercantile classes behind the Congress banner, but the socialist programme of the Karachi Congress had alarmed some of their number. He went fettered by the Congress brief that he must work for complete independence, though he himself was prepared to accept an idiosyncratic definition of complete independence to which it would be difficult to attach his young lieutenants. He left behind in the U.P. a situation made potentially explosive by dint of Nehru's disapproval of revenue arrangements that he had seen fit to accept. And difficulties could arise from the Congress assertion of a general right of defensive direct action, for the government had reserved its discretion to have recourse to the ordinary law or to special measures.

Nor had Gandhi's civil disobedience experiment secured the substance of freedom. During the months following Irwin's departure Willingdon had denied to Gandhi the equality of status and plenipotentiary standing that negotiations with the viceroy and the Delhi pact had seemed to confer.

With the cards so heavily stacked against him, still Gandhi chose to attend the Conference, and to do so without a supporting Congress team commensurate in size with the other delegations. In view of the divisions within the Congress it is not surprising that he should have chosen to go almost alone. One voice was more likely than several to speak consistently. Yet surely Gandhi must have realized that his voice was unlikely to prevail. His readiness to attend the Conference can be explained only if the nature of his dilemma is appreciated.

In India Gandhi would certainly have laboured under difficulties no less formidable than those that lay ahead in Britain. During the months preceding his departure he often believed that British officialdom was out to crush the Congress. Even when he felt unable to attend the Conference unless he could speak for a united India, he offered to go to London to put a case before the Cabinet. A visit to London would enable him to appeal beyond the officials of the Raj to British statesmen and the British public. It was disenchantment with Britain at large that had precipitated his 1920 and 1929 decisions to launch satyagraha. He now hoped for a hearing before a court of appeal above the Raj.

Gandhi's decision to go to London was tactically sound. In March 1931 he had called off civil disobedience when the experiment had achieved the maximum success possible. The pact enabled him to enhance his stature while retaining the allegiance of his followers. The period of the truce diminished rather than supplemented national unity and his own status. The second settlement was a minor recovery, again maximizing the yield from his activities. It headed off an early confrontation between Congress and government, but Gandhi must have anticipated that Congress would face increasingly hard times. He realized that he would find Nehru difficult to control,[1] and that official responses would be firm, if not harsh. The wisdom of his conciliatoriness in August 1931 is revealed clearly by the evidence of the Government of India's preparations to inaugurate a draconian era.

The January 1931 correspondence between the central and local governments had suggested the line of policy that was generally favoured if the Congress did not enter into constitutional discussions. The government should 'show unmistakably that it was able and willing to govern'. When, in the immediate

[1] 'It appears that Gandhi expressed his views to [Lady Willingdon] . . . that his left wing may give him more trouble in the future. . . . He particularly requested Lady Willingdon to invite Jawaharlal when he returns from Ceylon and to speak to him as "a Mother". Gandhi told her that she by her winning ways may influence Jawaharlal far better than others.' (P. Sethna to J. S. Wardlaw Milne, 25 May 1931, Sethna Coll.). The source of this extraordinary story was Lady Willingdon herself. Either Gandhi or Lady Willingdon was naïvely humourless on this occasion.

aftermath of the settlement, it became clear that in several provinces local Congress workers regarded the pact as a mere truce, of which, in de Montmorency's words, 'advantage should be taken to reorganize forces for a further struggle', the Government of India laid down rules for the guidance of local governments.[1] Action by Congress contrary to the ordinary law should be punished according to that law. Local governments and district magistrates should enjoy freedom of action to maintain order, but the Criminal Law Amendment Act (1908) should not be invoked without the consent of the Government of India. As disputes increased, the Government of India set about sounding local governments on the special measures that they would require to deal firmly with a revival of civil disobedience consequent upon the breakdown of the settlement. By June the local governments had agreed upon 'the vital necessity of a hard and immediate blow' if civil disobedience were revived.[2] On 12 August the Home Department circularized them about the detailed course of action to be taken. Several ordinances would be proclaimed, including a new and comprehensive Emergency Powers Ordinance, which had been prepared in autumn 1930 but held back.

The logic of a repressive policy was explained to Benn in a telegram of 4 August:

If a direct challenge is given to Government, an effective reply should be given at the first possible moment. Otherwise our officers and friends will be disheartened and a large number of persons who would otherwise not join the movement will be encouraged to do so. In particular, we simply cannot afford to allow the movement to gain force in rural areas by waiting to watch results. If, for instance, it obtained a hold in the U.P. or the N.W.F.P. the consequences might be extremely serious.[3]

Europeans and Muslims would interpret delay as 'weakness and incapacity'. The government recognized that strong measures could affect the Round Table Conference adversely, but argued that the safety of the state must be the first consideration. It sought authority for the specific measures to be adopted imme-

---

[1] De Montmorency's speech of 25 April 1931, quoted in Government of India, *The Civil Disobedience Movement, 1930-34*, New Delhi, 1936, pp. 10-11.
[2] Govt. of India to Sec. of S., 4 August 1931 (t/g), Home Pol. 14/12/31.
[3] Ibid.

diately civil disobedience was revived: the declaration of the C.W.C. as unlawful and powers for the local governments to declare local Congress organizations unlawful; the arrest of Gandhi within ten days unless he dissociated himself from the movement; the promulgation of the Emergency Powers Ordinance and its extension to appropriate provinces; the promulgation of a Press Ordinance as soon as a press campaign for civil disobedience began; the promulgation of an Unlawful Association Ordinance and its extension at least to Bombay in order to deal with Gujarat; the promulgation of an Unlawful Instigation Ordinance and its extension to provinces threatened by the no-rent movement; and the use of the Emergency Powers Ordinance to arrest and restrain provincial leaders.

In response to a request from Benn for a further appreciation of the dangers of civil disobedience a draft telegram was prepared in the third week of August. It warned of the danger of civil disobedience inflaming communalism and even of 'conflicts approximating to civil war'.[1] A protracted struggle with Congress could not be contemplated. A heavy blow was essential to encourage police and officials. The consolidation of Congress authority in the villages, which had been 'the deliberate policy of Congress since Delhi Settlement', would undermine the administration. The draft was held over when the second settlement was arranged.

The preparation of such heavy artillery from fear of the organized might of the Congress was in itself recognition of the success of Gandhi's experiment. Gandhi did well to turn from confrontation with the monolith of British officialdom in August 1931. However, he was to find no less implacable an adversary in the imperial political and financial establishment in London.

---

[1] Viceroy to Sec. of S., n.d. (draft prepared in reply to Sec. of S. to Viceroy, 14 August 1931), not sent. Home Pol. 14/12/31.

CHAPTER 5

The Failure of Consultation: January—December 1931

It is somewhat likely . . . that so far as I am concerned we have come to the parting of the ways. . . .

M. K. GANDHI, 1 December 1931

I. THE ASCENDANCY OF IMPERIALISM

STANLEY BALDWIN ranked the Indian problem in the same order of importance as the American crisis from the mid-eighteenth century and the Irish question from the late nineteenth. He was determined that at a crucial moment in imperial history Britain should not again rebuff a legitimate demand for liberty, and that India should be kept out of party politics. For his assurance of 26 January 1931 that as head of a Conservative government he would observe the tenor of Labour policy he was regarded 'rather coldly by his back benchers'.[1] The ranks of the latter were stiffened by Winston Churchill, who resigned from the shadow cabinet. A 'considerable proportion' of Conservatives preferred Churchill's antipathy towards central responsibility, even given an all-India federation and safeguards, to Baldwin's acquiescence.

On 5 February 1931 Hoare contributed an article to the *Morning Post* that told Conservatives what they wanted to believe: their delegation to the Round Table Conference had not committed them to anything beyond an elaboration, in terms suitable to the circumstances, of the Simon programme. Irwin was contemptuous of Hoare: 'precise, prudent, logical, without a redeeming streak of warmth of sympathy and imagination'.[2] The *Morning Post* article was 'singularly ill-timed' and led Irwin to complain to Benn: 'I really don't begin to know how anyone in his position can think that the Party interest of the Conservative Party is a more important issue than really trying to get a

[1] H. S. L. Polak to Sapru, 12 February 1931, S.C. 1, P. 80.
[2] Irwin to Benn, 16 February 1931, I.C. 6.

The Failure of Consultation

settlement of what is surely the biggest problem in the world of our or adjacent generations.'[1]

It is a reflection of the decline of the empire that at this stage it was served by such 'experts' as Simon and Hoare, trimmers of outstanding intellect who placed personal or party considerations above principle.

After having demanded a place at the Round Table Conference the Tory delegation now sought to dissociate itself from its future proceedings. When the first conference ended the location of the next session was left undecided. The British Indian delegates favoured a resumption in India. At the beginning of March Hoare and Peel told Benn that their delegation would not participate in deliberations in India. Fearing criticism from the party, they wished to hold themselves free to oppose the plan for central responsibility with safeguards when it emerged in detailed form. On 10 March the Conservative Party's India Committee (which was open to all members of the parliamentary party) published a resolution to withdraw from the next stage of proceedings. The statement left obscure the degree of dissociation and seemed to jeopardize the all-party approach to the Indian problem: '... the Conservative Party cannot be represented at any further Round Table Conference to be held in India as now foreshadowed by the Government.'[2] It was necessary for Baldwin to explain in parliament on 12 March that the resolution signified only the party's unwillingness to participate in a conference in India, where, no doubt, the pressure for advance would seem stronger. The Conservative delegation had taken its decision before the announcement of the Gandhi–Irwin pact, but there is no doubt that the decision was partly the result of Churchill's vituperation against the viceroy's negotiating on terms of equality with the 'seditious fakir'. The Conservative opposition, together with the ill health of Lord Sankey, made the resumption of the Conference in India impossible. In consequence, little progress was made between January, when the first session ended, and September, when the main sub-committees resumed work in London. However, there were Conservative attempts to limit the liberality of the central

---
[1] Irwin to Benn, 23 February 1931, I.C. 16.
[2] Quoted in J. K. Middlemas and A. J. L. Barnes, *Baldwin*, London, 1969, p. 592.

responsibility with safeguards formula. In March questions about the financial safeguards were put to Benn in the Commons and Sankey in the Lords. The result was the government's assurance of its intention to provide for the governor-general to enjoy the large powers to safeguard defence, external relations, finance, commercial discrimination, etc., that were recommended in the second report of the Federal Structure Committee.

Between the first and the second conferences Tory attitudes towards Indian freedom hardened, partly because of the tenor of Indian political activity. The persistence of picketing of British goods after the conclusion of the settlement offended the Lancashire interest. Sympathy for Bhagat Singh and for the murderer of an English officer's wife, to which de Montmorency alluded feelingly in the course of a trenchant speech, provoked hostility. The atrocities of the Cawnpore riots, and the temper of communal feeling generally, gave rise to revulsion. The continued agrarian agitation in the U.P. and Gujarat created mistrust of Congress goodwill. Lothian, a staunch supporter of central responsibility with safeguards, wrote in perturbation that extremism, lawlessness, and communalism were 'driving Government nearer to the necessity of firm measures in order to prevent the structure of order and government, without which the development of democratic self-government itself is impossible, from being undermined before the new constitution can come into effect'.[1] In June, Sastri, C. F. Andrews, and H. S. Polak sent a cable to Gandhi from London to reassure him that Irwin was now steadying the Conservatives, whose view of the Indian situation was coloured by 'Lancashire pressure owing [to] immense unparalleled local distress'.[2] But this was a distortion. Feeling ran deeper than the friends of freedom imagined. Toryism, like officialdom in India, was beginning to demand strong government.

On the eve of the reassembling of the Federal Structure Committee in September, Hoare observed in the party a 'general feeling that defeatism has corroded the machine of government'. Britain was thought to be shuffling out of her imperial responsibilities and liquidating a bankrupt state.[3] Right-wing opinion

[1] Lothian to Sapru, 4 May 1931, S.C. 1, L. 42.
[2] In Sapru to Bikaner, 2 June 1931, S.C. 1, S. 178.
[3] Hoare to Willingdon, 2 September 1931, T.C. letter books (hereafter L.B.).

The Failure of Consultation

favoured the vigorous reassertion of authority if civil disobedience revived. It was 'dead against anything in the nature of a surrender on the lines of the Irish Treaty'. In July, when Sankey had called together the British members of the F.S.C. to discuss the best means of conducting the committee's business, Hoare had insisted that the Round Table Conference was no constituent body and that there must be no question of its making a constitution for India or seeking to agree a bill for the future government of India.

Certainly, the slump was a further reason for the hardening of Conservative feeling against Indian freedom, for its effect was to polarize the economic interests of Britain and India. The slump made plausible the accusation of exploitation that Congress workers carried to the villages. They could point to high rent and revenue charges at a time when incomes were slashed by sharply falling world prices for agricultural produce. The Government of India could remain unconvinced that the illustration proved the Congress case yet respond sympathetically to demands for reasonable remissions. However, in the realm of budgetary and monetary policy, the government accepted the main plank in the nationalist platform. The viceroy's executive advocated, to the point of threatening to lay down their offices, Indian budgetary and monetary policies as against the imperialist alternatives favoured by the British Cabinet.

Since the 1860s duties on India's imports of British cotton piecegoods had been a bone of contention between Lancashire and the Government of India. In the late nineteenth century duties had risen and fallen according to the revenue requirements of the Government and the Lancashire pressures upon susceptible British Cabinets. In the nineties, when the need for revenue tariffs was undeniable, Lancashire had secured favourable treatment by the imposition of countervailing excise duties upon Indian manufactures. In the early years of the twentieth century the export of cotton piecegoods to India was a major British interest. In 1913 cotton manufactures accounted for 21 per cent of all British exports (£110m. out of £525m.). India bought £35m. worth of the cotton exports (3,000m. yds. out of the total of 7,076m. yds.). The Indian cotton market accounted for some 7 per cent of all British exports! Britain supplied 54 per cent of India's consumption of cotton piecegoods and all but a small fraction of her imports. The war reduced consumption and post-war conditions favoured the expansion of Indian production. The fiscal autonomy convention was established in principle in 1919, and with the creation of a tariff board in 1924 there was machinery to ensure that the cotton duties were evaluated according to India's interests. In 1925 the countervailing excise duty was abolished. At that stage the import duty on cotton goods was 11 per cent.

In 1928 British cotton goods exports still accounted for 20 per cent of total exports (£145m. out of £723m.), though the volume of cotton goods exports had fallen dramatically since 1913 (from 7,076m. yds. to 3,968m.). India's share of the cotton exports had fallen to £30m. (1,453m. yds.). Britain supplied only 28 per cent of India's consumption, just over one half of her share of the trade fifteen years earlier. India was supplying almost two-thirds of her own requirements, while Japan had made serious inroads upon British dominance. In 1929–30 Japan captured almost 30 per cent of the piecegoods import trade, as against Britain's 65 per cent. In short, in the late twenties the Indian cotton goods market was worth over £100m., of which the British share was about £30m. This still represented some 4·5 per cent of all British exports and about a third of Britain's exports to India.

Early in 1930 the Government of India was faced with a budgetary prospect that demanded an increase in customs duties, the mainstay of the central revenues. The decline in world prices had cut India's earnings from Rs. 3,610,000,000 in 1929–30 to Rs. 2,570,000,000 in 1930–1, which had caused a fall in revenue from the import duties and the land tax. At the same time, Bombay millowners, recovering from a period of industrial unrest, were pressing for protection. As Lancashire was hit hard by the slump and had recently suffered strikes, the home government urged the Government of India to consider the effect that enhanced duties would have upon the cotton goods trade. The Government of India increased the duty on cotton imports from 11 per cent to 15 per cent. At the same time, it provided for a 5 per cent protective tariff in return for a measure of imperial preference: the tariff would apply only to non-British imports. Sir George Schuster, the finance member, justified this departure from the fiscal autonomy convention by appealing to the interests of the Indian consumer as against the producer. In such hard times it was surely wrong to benefit the producer by a tariff that forced up consumer prices. The bill was passed but it precipitated the resignation of V. J. Patel and Malaviya from the legislature.

In 1930 British cotton goods exports to India fell to 728m. yds. The value of the British cotton exports to India fell from £26m. in 1929 to £13·7m. in 1930. By September 1930 the monthly level was only 25 per cent of the 1929 monthly average. In February 1931, when Schuster prepared his budget for 1931–2, he was again faced with the need for additional revenue. He proposed a 5 per cent surcharge on cotton imports. Benn fought the entire Cabinet in his defence of Schuster. The levy was imposed, but not without a vigorous protest from the president of the board of trade, who complained of the catastrophic fall in British exports to India since the 1930 increase of duty. Irwin was intolerant of Britain's unreal hopes for the revival of the cotton trade: '. . . half the present trouble in India today is due to the many years of Lancashire exploitation.'[1] In 1931 Britain's cotton goods exports to India yielded only £5·5m.

Despite a stringent budget in February 1931, which included severe retrenchment of expenditure on the civil and military services, and increased customs and income tax, by mid-year Schuster was anticipating a steep deficit. It was impossible to collect much of the land revenue because of the collapse in commodity prices.

In a memorandum of mid-June Schuster argued that the financial difficulty was aggravated by the exchange ratio of Re. 1:1s. 6d. stg. Confidence in the rupee was being undermined by the budgetary problem, by the widespread belief that the rupee was overvalued, and by the consequent speculation of financiers and merchants. British investors were also loth to hold rupee stock because of the uncertain political outlook. The Government of India was finding difficulty in providing funds to meet India's sterling obligations in London. However, at this stage Schuster was in favour of maintaining the existing exchange rate. He believed that the Indian financiers and merchants wanted devaluation from self-interested motives. Devaluation

[1] Irwin to J. C. C. Davidson, 31 March 1931, I.C. 19.

would mean lower real wages and higher prices for imports. On neither count would the masses benefit. Devaluation would also compound India's problem of meeting her London obligations. At the same time, of course, devaluation would deal Lancashire another blow and depreciate the value of Indian stock held in London. The value of Britain's India trade (c. £80m. p.a.) and investment (£500m.—£1,000m.) would fall, with serious implications for the strength of sterling. There was also the danger of devaluation causing a panic damaging to both British and Indian interests.

By the beginning of September the drain on India's sterling reserves had convinced Schuster of the need for an emergency budget and for firm British support. If Britain did not guarantee the rupee there was urgent danger of a collapse. Alternatively, in view of the universal Indian opposition to the existing ratio the rupee might be given a lower fixed sterling value or allowed to float. Schuster proposed an immediate cut in all service salaries and a further 5 per cent customs surcharge.

Schuster's proposals, which received the full backing of the Government of India, ran counter to the imperial government's purposes. On 28 August Ramsay MacDonald formed his National Government, with a 'doctor's mandate' to deal with the British economic crisis. Its 'sole purpose', according to Hoare (now secretary of state), was the defence of sterling and the maintenance of British credit.[1] Parliament would meet on 8 September to approve economies agreed by the three-party Cabinet and then dissolve. Hoare emphasized that neither of Schuster's alternative currency proposals was acceptable. The guarantee of a large sterling credit to India or the devaluation of the rupee would smash sterling—and indeed, the government. Furthermore, Schuster's budgetary proposals were anathema. To cut all salaries would mean overriding the statutory contract that guaranteed the conditions of the I.C.S. An act of parliament would be necessary and the Tories would oppose it as tantamount to breach of contract. If parliament could change statutory terms of service then no confidence could be felt in the safeguards subject to which it was proposed to transfer, say, financial responsibility to a federal executive at New Delhi. The Cabinet opposed the salary cut unanimously. They also resisted

[1] Ordinary telegram, 28 August 1931, T.C.

the proposed increase in the cotton duties: 'They feel that it will knock the final nail into the Lancashire coffin, will have the worst possible political reaction here, and will result in pouring more money into the pockets of Congress and Bombay millowners.'[1] The Cabinet suggested that the increase should be accompanied by an excise of equal extent on Indian cottons.

In the second half of September secret cypher cables shuttled between Whitehall and New Delhi. The Government of India and the Cabinet collided. Willingdon and his six colleagues felt unable to remain in office unless they were free to pursue the budgetary policies that they believed to be necessary. When Willingdon demurred over reinstating the cotton excise Hoare had 'enormous difficulty' in talking the Cabinet around.[2] The Conservatives were loth to risk losing Lancashire seats at the imminent general election. The Cabinet advanced the alternative of enhancing the preference that had been accorded British piecegoods in 1930; the effect would be that non-British imports should pay 60 per cent more duty than British.

The budget dispute was pushed into the background by the events of the week following Friday 18 September. That Friday and Saturday the bourses of the world panicked. The conversion of sterling into gold was so massive that the Cabinet decided to relieve the Bank of England of the obligation to sell gold for sterling at the agreed ratio as from the Monday morning. Britain was off the gold standard. Without reference to the Government of India the Cabinet decided that the rupee should leave gold simultaneously but remain tied to sterling at the existing Re. 1:1s. 6d. ratio. The viceroy read of the decision in the press telegrams an hour and a half before he received the news officially.

The Government of India felt injured by the manner in which the decision on the rupee was taken and hostile towards the linkage with sterling. Britain had done nothing to strengthen the rupee or to prepare Indian opinion for its policy. Hoare argued that the decision was concerted by the Cabinet, the India Office, the Treasury, and the Bank of England, that there had been no time to consult the Government of India, and that India's best interests had been served faithfully. To have severed

[1] Hoare to Willingdon, 18 September 1931 (Secret t/g), T.C.
[2] Hoare to Willingdon, 21 September 1931 (Secret t/g), T.C.

the rupee–sterling link would have precipitated panic among holders of rupees and brought chaos to India. The viceroy complained that the pressure on India's sterling reserves was already serious and that like India's gold reserves they would soon be dissipated. Either Britain must guarantee India sterling credits up to £50m. or the rupee must be left to float down to a level at which it could be defended. Cabinet rejected both proposals.

The currency dispute increased the likelihood of the viceroy's council resigning. The members were being required to defend a policy that they considered indefensible economically and politically. They appreciated the practical problems of a floating rupee. Certainly, British holders of rupee stock and savings would lose, while India would find difficulty in meeting her sterling commitments and renewing Treasury Bills that fell due for payment. On the other hand, the rupee would assuredly stabilize at a lower level and Indian exports would be stimulated. As for maintaining the *status quo*, without a sterling guarantee that policy would surely fail. From the strictly economic standpoint, the Government of India criticized imperial policy more for its failure to provide sterling support than for its rejection of devaluation. The case for floating the rupee was primarily political. Here was a chance to harmonize currency policy with Indian opinion. Schuster commented:

England can continue political control in India and retain India as a friendly member of the British Empire provided that she allows her to run her own economic policy. The whole of the Congress movement would have had no force if it had not been for the hostility on economic grounds which brought in all the commercial classes. . . . The worst cause of discord in the last years has been currency policy.[1]

Statesmanship suggested the need to float the rupee.

That the Government of India interpreted Indian opinion on currency policy correctly was soon brought home to Hoare. Gandhi sent on to him cabled protests that he had received from Vallabhbhai, Jamal Muhammad, and the Committee of Bombay Commercial Associations. The Council of Indian Chambers of Commerce in Great Britain protested to Hoare direct against the 'total disregard of the interests of India, her

[1] Schuster to Sir Henry Strakosch, 5 October 1931, T.C. 8.

trade, or even her public finance'.¹ Indian delegates to the Round Table Conference, and in particular Thakurdas and Bikaner, claimed India's right to adjust her currency to the exigencies of her own foreign trade.

On 24 September Hoare sent to Willingdon a secret telegram from the prime minister and Baldwin on behalf of a united Cabinet. It implored him not to resign:

> The political situation with which the Government of India and His Majesty's Government are faced is probably more serious than any that has so far occurred in the relations between India and this country. Anything like resignations upon the scale which you indicate as possible would present the appearance of an open conflict of interest between India on the one hand and Great Britain on the other. In reality this is not so. We and you are solely concerned with the interests of India but unfortunately we take divergent views as to the best means of serving these interests.... We say with great seriousness that any concerted resignations by your colleagues would be comparable to the resignation of a general staff in the face of the enemy.... You have given a lifetime of service to the Empire in many fields and we are sure we can count on you to stand by us now in the greatest Imperial emergency since the war.²

Willingdon and his colleagues agreed to remain and accept the Cabinet's currency policy, though they continued to stress that India's voice must be heard. In the event, the rate of exchange was maintained without a guarantee. With sterling soon selling at 20 to 25 per cent discount on the old gold standard private Indian holders of gold soon began to sell for rupees. Massive exports of privately held gold to Britain helped to restore India's credit and to replenish Britain's gold reserves. The fall in the gold value of the rupee also helped to stimulate India's agricultural exports. Nevertheless, Indian hostility towards British currency policy remained.

The Cabinet capitulated over the civil service cuts, for which an enabling bill was passed by parliament, and the imperial preference on cottons. Willingdon insisted that the provision for imperial preference in April 1930 had cost the government the support of V. J. Patel and Malaviya and exacerbated the boycott

---

¹ Council of Indian Chambers of Commerce in G.B. to Hoare, n.d. [October 1931], P.T.C. 111.

² Sec. of S. to viceroy, 24 September 1931, R.C. 56 i.

movement. The Indian members of the executive felt unable to toe the Cabinet line and Schuster and Sir George Rainy (the Commerce member) could not reconcile discrimination against Japanese imports with the interests of the Indian consumer. In tariff questions India's interests must take precedence. The present members of the Cabinet would, according to Hoare, be disposed to reconsider the fiscal autonomy convention if they were returned to office after the October election. Hoare could placate the Lancashire members of parliament only by arguing that the advantage of the surcharge to Indian manufacturers would be offset by new revenue duties that Schuster had imposed upon imports of machinery and raw cotton.

The budgetary and monetary controversies reveal the Indian government's conviction that the Cabinet was concerned with Britain's interests to the exclusion of India's. Policies devised at New Delhi were consistent with a vision of Indian freedom whereas those developed at Whitehall were inspired by imperial necessities. The Cabinet's outlook did not augur well for Indians who yearned for equality at the conference table and a free partnership with Britain. The economic condition of Britain made the occasion of the second Round Table Conference unpropitious. A long step towards freedom was scarcely to be anticipated in September 1931, as the F.S.C. and the Minorities Committee began to deliberate. However, their proceedings indicate that if evidence of imperial exploitation had a unifying effect upon India, it was insignificant by comparison with the divisive influence of conflicting interests among Indians themselves.

II. THE COMMUNAL IMPASSE

As at the first Round Table Conference so at the second the Hindu nationalists sought to unite Indian opinion before proceeding to discuss the devolution of powers. Gandhi's initial task, if he were to have any chance of extracting swaraj from Britain, was to settle the communal problem. This order also suited the Muslims, who refused to discuss the central government unless their position was secured by safeguards.

At the first formal gathering of the session, the F.S.C. meeting on 14 September, Shafa'at Ahmad made the Muslim delegation's position crystal clear. His statement was explicitly about constitutional structure, but implicit in it was the assumption of electoral arrangements that would secure Muslim majorities in Bengal and the Punjab, and of the full provincial status of Sind and the N.W.F.P. Shafa'at demanded the complete autonomy of the units of the federation. The provinces should have control over law and order. The federal legislature or cabinet should have no right to interfere. Only the governor-general should have such power, and then only in an emergency. The provinces should also enjoy financial autonomy. Here was implied the reduction of the Home Department and the distribution of the Raj's central powers. As for central responsibility: 'Until we know what our position is going to be it would be difficult for us to commit ourselves to any scheme.'[1] In particular the Muslims could not judge any federal proposal until the representation of the predominantly Hindu princely states was known. Such representation should be on a strict population basis.

Shafa'at's statement was revolutionary in its implications. It sought swaraj through the provincialization of the Raj. The Muslims saw therein security against the possibility of large powers falling to a Hindu centre. An India Office departmental note of 25 September commented that the most difficult communal issue was 'whether the Muslim provinces, or the provinces in which the Muslims hope to consolidate their power, should be under any degree of control from a Centre, which will be predominantly Hindu. Their primary object is, no doubt, to establish a "Muslim India".'[2] Shafa'at was giving voice to the conclusion of the orthdodox, led by Fazl-i-Husain: the federation should only exercise such powers as the provinces specifically ceded to it. The conclusion resembled that to which many of the princes were working, and Fazl may well have agreed it with Bhopal and Hydari. Throughout the second conference Fazl remained in close touch with Shafa'at, Zafrullah Khan, and the Aga Khan. The Muslim demands had been clarified and refined. They were most unlikely to be relinquished.

From the outset, the Muslim delegates assumed the need for separate electorates on a population basis in Bengal and the Punjab. Gone now was the willingness that Shafi and Jinnah

[1] *Indian Round Table Conference: Proceedings of Sub-Committees (7 September–1 December 1931)*, H.M.S.O., 1932, p. 4.
[2] India Office Departmental Note regarding the Communal and Minority Problems, 25 September 1931, T.C. 14.

had shown at the first conference to accept joint electorates and the reservation of seats. Gandhi soon realized this in September, during informal discussions with the Muslims. But he would not modify the Congress 'compromise', which conceded separate representation to Muslims only in provinces where they accounted for under 25 per cent of the population, and approached the communal problem in the Punjab through adult suffrage and the separate representation of the Sikhs.

On 28 September, when the Minorities Committee met for the first time, it was agreed to adjourn until 1 October so that informal negotiations might continue. On 1 October a further week's adjournment was proposed by Gandhi and agreed unanimously. From the beginning, Gandhi and Malaviya rejected the principle of special representation for any minority group except the Muslims and the Sikhs, whereas representatives of the minorities, including, most significantly, the Depressed Classes, but also Indian Christians, Anglo-Indians, and Europeans, advanced separate representation as a general principle. Gandhi's objection to extending separate representation to groups other than the Muslims and the Sikhs was the logical corollary of his concern for national unity. Its effect was to offend the 'minor minorities', who now ranged themselves on the Muslim rather than the Congress side. In the words of an observer, they were 'frightened before long by Gandhi's intransigent attitude into active steps to secure their interests'.[1] The bargaining strength of the Muslims was thereby supplemented and Gandhi's difficulties exacerbated.

By about 5 October Gandhi had expressed his willingness to concede separate Muslim electorates, Muslim majorities in Bengal and the Punjab, and weightage in the Muslim-minority provinces. He would also accept that residuary powers should lie with the provinces and that the Muslims should have one third of the seats at the centre. His conditions were that the Muslims should endorse the demand for swaraj and that after the introduction of the new constitution a referendum of Muslim voters should be held on the question of joint electorates. The proposed referendum echoed the Bhopal discussions, and Fazl had briefed his team to oppose it. Moreover, as at the first

[1] G. Laithwaite's summary of communal negotiations, 6 November 1931, T.C. 14.

conference, the Sikhs and the Punjab Hindus refused to contemplate a statutory Muslim majority in their province. Various solutions were suggested, including one from the Sikh delegation that the Punjab should be governed from the centre, and another from Sapru that the Sikhs should concede a Muslim majority provided they obtained substantial weightage. On the evening of 7 October negotiations broke down over the comparatively minor question of whether the Punjab problem should be referred for arbitration to an informal sub-committee of the Minorities Committee (which the Muslims favoured) or to an outside judicial body (which the Hindus and the Sikhs preferred).

On 8 October Gandhi reported the failure of informal negotiations sadly to the Minorities Committee. He proposed that the new constitution should provide for a judicial tribunal to examine communal claims. Though he was opposed to separate representation for the minor minorities, and the untouchables in particular, he would accept the verdict of an arbitral body. The Muslims reiterated their demand that the communal question must be settled prior to the drafting of a new constitution. Together with the Depressed Classes they also opposed reference to arbitration and expressed willingness to accept a government decision. The Depressed Classes had definitely lined up with the Muslims against Gandhi. Like the Sikhs and the Muslims they now insisted upon the protection of their interests as a condition precedent to constitutional advance. The Minorities Committee was adjourned indefinitely.

During the last three weeks of October innumerable informal meetings of the communities' delegates were held. Gandhi worked strenuously to reach agreement with the Muslims and to prevent the separate representation of the minor minorities. On 16 October he met Muslim delegates and offered them three alternatives: first, the package that they had already rejected, including majorities in Bengal and the Punjab, a referendum on joint electorates, weightage in Muslim-minority provinces, one third of the centre seats, and residuary powers with the provinces; secondly, arbitration by a few members of the conference; and thirdly, a Punjab settlement of the type proposed by Sir Geoffrey Corbett, I.C.S. The latter provided for the transfer of Ambala Division to the U.P., which would increase the Muslim percentage of the Punjab population from 55 to 62, thereby assuring the Muslims of a majority under a joint electorate system. Gandhi's conditions were that the Muslims should not support the minor minorities' claims for separate representation and that any agreement must be subject to the approval of the Congress.

On 19 October the Sikh delegates declared that they would not contemplate Corbett's scheme. Their solution to the Punjab problem was to link certain of the Muslim areas to the N.W.F.P., thereby reducing the Muslim population to 43 per cent, increasing the Hindu element to 42 per cent, and leaving the Sikhs holding the balance with 14 per cent. As at the first conference, the Hindu Mahasabha and Sikh position was irreconcilable with that of the Muslims.

Of Gandhi's other alternative offers to the Muslims arbitration was unacceptable and a referendum anathema.

By the end of October it seemed unlikely that the Sikhs and the Mahasabhites could be drawn into any general agreement acceptable to the Muslims and the less communalist Hindus. Much of the controversy now concerned the appropriate body to decide the Punjab question. It was generally believed that any independent arbiter would probably decide in favour of manhood suffrage and against a statutory Muslim majority. In that event Punjab politics would become an open contest, with power being seized by those most successful in mobilizing mass support. The Mahasabhites pressed for arbitration by the League of Nations, a judicial tribunal, or independent Englishmen. Gandhi was prepared to accept arbitration by a non-judicial body of three Englishmen. However, the Muslims would accept only a government decision. On 1 November Gandhi declared that if they would have neither private nor judicial arbitration then time alone could provide a solution. Next day the Sikhs averred that the only hope of solution lay in their eventually reaching a settlement with the Muslims.

At the beginning of November the Muslims, the Depressed Classes, the Indian Christians, the Anglo-Indians, and the Europeans joined forces to demand communal representation through separate electorates and representation in cabinets. The Muslims and the minor minorities were ranged against the Sikhs and the high-caste Hindus. The minorities' pact was presented to a meeting of the Minorities Committee on 13 November.

The Failure of Consultation

The Round Table Conference had declared its failure to solve the communal question. The deadlock was the result of the Muslims having concerted a clear programme in advance and refusing to surrender any part of it. The minorities' pact made their position unassailable. Though Gandhi might have compromised with the Muslims he would do so only if they abandoned the minor minorities. Furthermore, the intransigence of the Sikhs and the Mahasabhites made compromise practically impossible for him.

To Gandhi the communal discussions were agonizing. Not only was India divided between the two great religions. Hinduism was divided into its communalist higher castes on the one side and its Depressed Classes on the other, with the Hindu Liberals and Gandhi himself suspended painfully between them. Before the conference was over he vowed publicly that if necessary he would contest separate untouchable electorates with his life.

The communal impasse affected the status of Indians in constitutional discussions. As an India Office representative wrote to the King's secretary on 2 November, its effect was to deadlock progress on the form and powers of the federal government: 'This deadlock, if it continues, as it probably will, puts an end to the idea of settlement of the general constitutional problem by discussion and agreement which is the essence of round table conference procedure, and His Majesty's Government will have to take the matter into their own hands and announce a policy.'[1] As yet such action was somewhat premature. For a time in November there was an attempt, in which Gandhi participated, to break the deadlock by a fresh approach to the problem of devolution, which meant in effect the concession of the Muslim demand for the provincialization of the Raj. The attempt was encouraged partly by the failure of the princes to enter into constructive discussions at the second conference, which, in its turn, was also partially a consequence of the communal impasse.

III. THE RECOIL OF THE PRINCES

Between the first and the second Round Table Conferences many princes, like the Muslim leaders, defined and hardened

[1] W. D. Croft to Sir Clive Wigram, 2 November 1931, India Office, L/PO/20.

their attitudes towards all-India federation. Objectives and objections that received little emphasis in 1930 were sharpened in 1931. By the end of the second conference it was clear that the princes were deeply divided over such fundamental questions as the powers of the federal authority, the size of the legislature, and the representation of the states. Many were hostile to the form of federation envisaged by the F.S.C. Others would make their accession to a federation contingent upon the satisfaction of demands that were unrelated or peripheral to federation. When the second conference revealed deep communal fissures within British India they were happy to take up the position, akin to that of the Muslims, of making their co-operation dependent upon the acceptance of their terms.

Hyderabad, the prime mover in the federal initiative, continued in 1931 to develop the principles that it had espoused the previous year. Alarmed at the prospect of a strong self-governing British India, it sought safety in the persistence of a strong Crown element capable of discharging Britain's treaty obligations. The federal legislature should be small and businesslike, leaving little scope for demagogues from British India, or for the representation of mere numbers, whether of people or lesser states. Hyderabad was uneasy about the F.S.C. scheme. At the insistence of the Hindu Liberals the Committee had accepted that the federal authority should inherit from the Government of India responsibility for certain central subjects, for example, income tax, civil and criminal law, law and order, etc. Originally Hydari had provided for the complete provincialization of British Indian subjects not reserved to the Crown, and for the cession of matters of common concern to a federal authority by the states and the provinces. When he became aware of the objection to the destruction of the British Indian centre he had proposed a British Indian executive and legislative structure separated rigidly from the federal authority. He was disturbed by the F.S.C. plan for central subjects to be administered by the federal authority. In May 1931 he wrote to Keyes that central subjects were evidence of the Hindus' object to 'preserve under a Federal facade what so far as British India is concerned will be a Unitary Government'.[1] This alarmed the Muslims and was contrary to the interests of the states:

[1] Hydari to Keyes, 11 May 1931, K.C. 28.

I have always understood that Federation postulates a number of Federal units each enjoying an equal degree of sovereignty, however much their forms of administration may differ. The existence of Central Subjects must destroy the symmetry and balance of the Federal Structure, while the creation of a British Indian Centre to deal with them, whether it is merged into the Federal Centre or is set up as a separate authority, cannot fail to import into the Federal domain a British Indian bloc or combination that will prove most embarrassing to the State Federal units.

Hydari suggested reducing central subjects to a minimum and securing 'a co-ordinating authority to deal with them that is rigidly and effectively segregated from the Federal Centre'.

Keyes replied that the success of the federal idea depended upon the states and the Muslims working together for the same five objects: the retention of residuary powers by the federal unit, whether state or province; the strict limitation of federal subjects; the freedom of each state or province to decide its own system of representation in the federation; the creation of a federal court; and the elimination of central subjects from the federal scheme. The only central subjects should be those reserved to the Crown, namely, defence and foreign and political relations. In short, Keyes envisaged the complete provincialization of British India and the retention by states and provinces of all powers not specifically ceded to the federation. He believed that 'the Provinces with a majority of Muhammadans, and the Muhammadans in the other Provinces, ought to join the States openly. . . . Surely the Nawab of Bhopal [now Chancellor of the Chamber of Princes] could stand out as a Chief and a Muhammadan leader to bring this about.'[1] The policies of Hyderabad and Fazl-i-Husain were clearly similar.

During May Hydari and Mirza Ismail reached agreement upon 'five safeguards . . . essential for the Indian States coming into any Federal scheme'.[2] The safeguards were conveyed to Bhopal on 20 May. They provided for the units of the federation to be the states and the provinces; for federal subjects to be limited; for no interference with the units beyond the federal subjects; for the states to select their own federal representatives; and for the Crown to secure the states' treaty rights by retaining

[1] Keyes to Hydari, 26 May 1931, K.C. 28.
[2] Hydari to Keyes, 29 May 1931, K.C. 28.

powers over political relations and defence. The same month Hyderabad put up the money necessary to keep afloat the sinking Bombay newspaper, the *Indian Daily Mail*. Hydari told its managing editor, F. W. Wilson, that the support was dependent upon the paper's espousal of the cause of the states and its friendliness towards the Muslims. The editor wrote to Sapru that Hydari had 'peculiar ideas' about central subjects. He also confided that Bhopal was 'much more of a communalist' than was generally believed.[1]

However, Bhopal, who was virtually Bikaner's nominee Chancellor, pursued a strategy similar to that of Haksar and Bikaner in 1930: to work with the British Indian leaders for central responsibility provided that the internal autonomy of the states was guaranteed. Given freedom from the intrusion of the Political Department and the assurance of a federal court, the leading Chamber princes would co-operate with British India on matters of common concern. The Chamber princes planned to prevent British India from overwhelming them in a federal legislature by securing weighted representation in both houses and seats for all ruling princes who were full members of the Chamber. Though Bhopal was said to be alarmed at Jawaharlal's Fundamental Rights and Economic Policy resolution at the Karachi Congress, he approached Gandhi in April with the hope of arranging a Hindu–Muslim agreement. After all, Congress had passed no resolution on the states. Though its leaders urged the princes to give their subjects representation at the Round Table Conference and to confer fundamental rights upon them, it maintained a policy of non-interference in the administration of the states.

In July Bhopal began to campaign vigorously for British acceptance of a contractual definition of paramountcy such as Sir Leslie Scott had proposed. He presented Willingdon with a note on the subject, contending that paramountcy meant 'practically nothing beyond an obligation on paramount power to protect the States'.[2] He claimed that the note summarized the views of the Standing Committee and the Chamber. Soon afterwards he indicated to Willingdon that the princes would not commit themselves to all-India federation unless the para-

[1] F. W. Wilson to Sapru, 1 June 1931, S.C. 2.
[2] Govt. of India P. and F. Dept. to Sec. of S., 23 July 1931, T.C. 2 A.

mountcy question was settled, even if a federal structure satisfactory to them were evolved. Arguing the urgency of the question, he brought together the implications for the princes of the Butler and the Nehru reports. The former left paramountcy unlimited while the latter demanded its transfer from the Government of India to an Indian commonwealth. While Britain was moving towards redeeming its promise of responsible government for British India it was doing nothing to satisfy the legitimate claims of the princes. Failure to settle the paramountcy issue would 'mean giving an incentive to the future Federal Government of India to make concentrated and most unwelcome onslaughts on the sovereignty and internal independence of the Indian States'.[1] Willingdon urged Bhopal to defer the matter until after the second conference.

In London, Bhopal raised the matter with Hoare. He lodged four main demands. First, the princes' relations with the Raj should be conducted through the viceroy, not the governor-general-in-council; the latter channel had given Indian members of the executive access to files relating to the states. Secondly, the practice of reading the princes' treaties as interrelated should end; this meant that the viceroy's practice in relation to each state should be governed only by that state's treaty. Thirdly, succession should be settled by the dynastic laws of individual states. Finally, all disputes between a state and the viceroy should be settled by arbitration. These claims would indeed abolish the discretionary element in paramountcy. Hoare deferred the whole complex issue for discussion by Willingdon and the princes; but he was left in no doubt that its solution was a major factor in the Chamber's evaluation of federation. It was true, as Willingdon and Indian officials were wont to remark, that as paramountcy was not to be a federal subject it was irrelevant to federation. But the observation ignored the Standing Committee's belief that the princes' future in an Indian commonwealth depended upon Britain guaranteeing their internal sovereignty.

A third strategy, little in evidence at the first Round Table Conference, gained favour among a section of the princes in 1931. This was for the states to form their own federation prior to entering into a constitutional relationship with British India.

[4] Bhopal to Willingdon, 6 August 1931, T.C. 2 A.

Sir Prabhashankar Pattani, the guardian of the ruler of Bhavnagar in Kathiawar, went to the first conference with a scheme for a confederation between British India and a federation of the states. The proposal betrayed an apprehension, shared by Dholpur, Rewa, and Sangli, that the states would be overwhelmed by British India and eventually absorbed into an organic federation. It appealed to the small states. Whereas they could not expect separate representation in an all-India federation they might well hope for representation in a states' federation and, thereby, for a voice in the selection of states' delegates to a confederation with British India.

During 1931 Patiala and his cousin, Dholpur, together with Pattani and the Maharaja of Indore, developed the confederation alternative to the F.S.C. scheme. Patiala's actions were often inspired by a concern for his own *izzat*. At the first conference his policy had been to insist that the precise legal limitation of paramountcy was a necessary precondition of the princes' acceptance of all-India federation. His rivalry with Bikaner for the leadership of the Chamber was so intense that Panikkar suggests that he anticipated strengthening his candidature for the chancellorship by advocating the cause of the small states.

In June 1931 Patiala published a pamphlet, *Federation and the Indian States*. Federation was described as a 'radical innovation' that would destroy the individuality of the states. It was 'at best an empty dream and a delusion pregnant with the greatest dangers to the very existence of the States'. It was 'a revolution as far-reaching as the absorption of the States in British India'.[1] The F.S.C. plan failed to safeguard the interests of the federal units as against a strong federal executive, which would doubtless interfere in non-federal as well as federal subjects. Moreover, as paramountcy lay outside the federal constitution it would continue to be exercised by the Crown. The tract brought together the small states' fear of extinction, the Hyderabadi anxiety over an interfering central executive dominated by British India, and the Chamber group's concern with paramountcy. It proposed expanding the Chamber into a Union of States in order to give the small states individual representation. The enlarged body would elect a standing committee to

[1] Maharaja of Patiala, *Federation and the Indian States*, n.d. [1931], pp. 11–18.

confer with a standing committee of the British Indian legislature on matters of common interest. Here was a return to the 'two Indias' of the Butler and the Simon reports.

In July a meeting of princes at Bombay voted overwhelmingly against Patiala's scheme and avowed their adherence to the F.S.C. plan. Subsequently, Patiala agreed with Dholpur upon a confederationist variation on the federal theme. The Chamber would be expanded into a states' confederation, which would operate as an electoral college for the selection of states' representatives to a bi-cameral all-India federal legislature. The states would have parity of representation with a federation of British India in the upper house and representation on a 40:60 ratio in the lower. There would be an all-India federal executive responsible to the legislature, but its powers would be restricted to specified matters of common interest. British India must have no say in any states' question that was not federal, and the states should have no say in any non-federal question affecting British India.

The Patiala–Dholpur scheme was discussed at an informal conference of princes and ministers from 8 August. It obtained substantial support and at Patiala's request the Government of India agreed to invite Dholpur to join the F.S.C. at the second Round Table Conference. The leading advocates of confederation were Indore, Bhavnagar, Bahawalpur, Panna, Rampur, and Sangli. By the time of the Indian delegates' departure for London almost one hundred states had expressed a predilection for confederation. During the voyage Dholpur and Hydari agreed that the states and British India must have no say in each other's non-federal affairs. Of course, as Hyderabad held aloof from the Chamber it could not accept the selection of the states' federal representatives by a Chamber-based confederation, but Dholpur was willing to allow the reservation of federal seats for nominees of the seven largest states. Yet Hyderabad would certainly have an overriding objection to the scheme: the preservation of the 'two Indias'. As Keyes had argued in 1930, a separate British India must in time secure responsible government and come into conflict with the inter-set territories of Hyderabad.

Confederation was the major development in the constitutional controversy during 1931. It effectively divided the Chamber between the dominant Standing Committee group, led by Bikaner and Bhopal and supported by most of the rulers of the medium-sized states, and the Patiala–Dholpur group, which enjoyed the support of the smaller states' representatives. Confederation alarmed Sapru and the Liberals. They had secured the promise of central responsibility by agreeing to the addition of a conservative states' leaven to a liberal British Indian union. If, in lieu of organic federation, there were to be simply an all-India government with strictly circumscribed jurisdiction, what would become of the British Indian central authority? The diehards would refuse to transfer central subjects to Indian hands. Jayakar saw at once that Patiala was 'playing into the hands of Die-hard politicians'.[1] A confederationist–Tory deal could be imagined: by refusing to join an organic federation the princes would prevent central responsibility in British India, while the British would retain the power to prevent British Indian interference in the states. Confederation might become a cry to rally any interest opposed to Indian constitutional development.

The F.S.C.'s discussions at the second conference were deadlocked by disputes between the advocates of the Sankey scheme on the one hand and the confederationists, as well as the Muslims, on the other. No agreement was possible even on a skeleton structure, let alone on the detailed anatomy: the size of federal houses, the seats available to the states corporately and individually, the vexed issue of central subjects, etc. Furthermore, from a special sub-committee's exploration of the implications of federal finance many states realized that their contributions for the governance of India would be enhanced. For example, they would have to forgo the right to levy inland customs, and help to meet the cost of all-Indian defence. It became apparent, too, that federal officials must obtain a footing in the states, thereby inevitably transgressing their internal sovereignty.

In 1930 several princes had endorsed the federal formula from apprehension of a strong self-governing British India emerging. Such fears were exacerbated by the Gandhi–Irwin pact, and they were the basis of each of the major constitutional strategies that the princes developed during 1931. Hyderabad would eliminate or minimize central subjects, provincialize British India, and maintain the strength of the Crown. Bhopal and Bikaner would secure a ruling on paramountcy that would prevent

[1] Jayakar to Sapru, 17 June 1931, J.C. 454.

The Failure of Consultation

powers of interference from falling to British India. Patiala and Dholpur would consolidate the states as against British India. The second Round Table Conference demonstrated amply that Gandhi did not represent British India as a whole. Princely apprehensions receded before the spectacular communal impasse, and with them princely interest in federal blueprints. The princes now had less reason to seek agreement among themselves, and they were wont to give extra emphasis to the conditions of their co-operation. Hyderabad had already revived the question of Berar, which it wanted to see separated from the C.P. under a federal constitution and governed by the Crown, though subject to the ultimate sovereignty of the Nizam. Mysore began to demand relief from its heavy burden of tribute. Maritime states such as Baroda and Nawanagar pressed claims for port concessions. The principle of the *quid pro quo* was in the ascendant.

A transformation in the princes' attitudes towards federation is illustrated by the expert testimony of Sir Reginald Glancy, a member of the secretary of state's India Council with long experience as a political officer in Hyderabad, Baroda, Jaipur, and Central India. On 1 September 1931 he wrote: 'Too many Princes are now committed to Federation for any general withdrawal to be possible, provided the British Indian Delegates do not insist on terms so onerous as to threaten the very existence of the States.'[1] The 'most powerful motive' for federating was the princes' fear of 'what would happen if a campaign of "satyagraha" were once launched against them'. On 29 October Glancy noted a 'marked change in their attitude':

> Now that the outlook is so gloomy and the chance of agreement between the British Indian parties so remote, the Princes have begun to hope that nothing will become of the Conference, and that they will be able to continue their sheltered existence while Hindus and Muhammadans wage communal war in British India. . . . When the Conference opened the accommodation for the Princes was insufficient: now for the most part their chairs are empty: some have left the country: others will go this week. . . . One is compelled to say there is not one genuine friend of federation left amongst the Princes.[2]

Even Bikaner left the conference in October, though its proceed-

[1] Sir R. I. R. Glancy, memo. on 'Attitude of the Indian States Delegates towards Federation', 1 September 1931, T.C. 2 A.
[2] Glancy's supplementary memo., 29 October 1931, T.C. 2 A.

ings lasted until 1 December. He spoke of federation as 'postponed for five years'.[1] When Willingdon met him at the end of November he 'seemed to have weakened very considerably in his enthusiasm for the Princes entering a Federal scheme'.[2]

Willingdon confided to Hoare his assessment of the prospects of federation: 'My own opinion is . . . that the Princes will decide not to come in at this juncture, that you will then be forced back on to a general advance in British India alone, and that you will have to give the *hookum* [command], both on the Minorities question and in the matter of safeguards.'[3] The collapse of consultation at the second Round Table Conference placed the initiative with the imperial government, and, more particularly, with the Tory secretary of state.

IV. THE RETREAT TOWARDS 'SIMONISM'

It became clear in October that the Indian delegations would not achieve a consensus upon federal structure. The Congress demand for a swaraj constitution seemed unreal in the context of the financial crisis, the communal impasse, and the princes' tergiversation. British policy-makers pondered ways of proceeding.

On 5 October Sankey advocated the division of constitutional reform into two stages. 'A large measure' of provincial autonomy should be promised at once.[4] A sub-committee of the F.S.C. should tackle the outstanding problems of central responsibility and prepare a scheme for the parliamentary draftsman at an early date. Hoare's thought followed similar lines: Indians must be 'more and more forced back upon Provincial Autonomy as the first step to be taken'.[5] However, with the onset of a general election, Indian problems were relegated to the background. The 'doctor's mandate' government could scarcely determine future policy on India.

On 23 October, just before the election, Hoare hazarded a prediction in a letter to Willingdon. The new government would take an interim decision on the communal issue so that provincial autonomy might be introduced immediately. In addition, pre-

[1] Ibid.
[2] Willingdon to Hoare, 30 November 1931, T.C.L.B.   [3] Ibid.
[4] Lord Chancellor's secret memo. on India, 5 October 1931, R.C. 56 i.
[5] Hoare to Willingdon, 2 October 1931, T.C.L.B.

parations for federation would be made by inquiries into outstanding problems and by negotiations with the princes. Britain would undertake to consult the provinces and the states prior to introducing a federal bill, probably by calling Indian assessors before a joint parliamentary committee. In any event, with the close of its second session the old Round Table Conference would perish.

MacDonald re-emerged from the general election of 27 October as a National Premier, now, however, at the head of a predominantly Conservative Cabinet. Sankey and Hoare retained their portfolios. Simon returned to the Cabinet, doubtless delighted to find both of them converted to his old policy of provincial autonomy first. Lothian became Hoare's undersecretary, though he remained a Liberal delegate to the conference. The Labour delegates, Benn and Lees Smith, lost their seats in parliament, which was dominated by 470 Conservative members.

At the beginning of November Hoare sent to MacDonald the procedural recommendations of Sir Geoffrey Corbett. As federation could not be launched during the economic crisis an interval was desirable. Moreover, it was 'obvious that there can be no stable federation without the agreement and support of the unborn self-governing provinces'.[1] Britain's approach should be to intervene in the communal problem and set the provinces free. At a later stage provincial and state representatives should meet the British government to frame a federal constitution. Meanwhile, detailed preparations for federation should be made. This procedure should be sold to the leading Indian delegates, especially Gandhi. While Sapru and the Liberals would oppose it because it recalled Simon's recommendations, Gandhi might be convinced that the resemblance was superficial. He should be persuaded that the phasing of the reforms was intended to expedite federation and that the eventual meeting of representatives would be competent to frame a constitution consistent with Congress demands. The minorities might be expected to accept the procedure.

Hoare took soundings. They suggested that the Muslims and Ambedkar were disposed to advance to provincial autonomy first, provided that the government pledged itself to press on

[1] Sir G. L. Corbett's memo. of 30 October 1931, T.C. 1.

towards federation as quickly as possible. Sapru was implacably opposed to the procedure. Gandhi (who was approached by Sankey) 'was prepared to accept provincial autonomy as a first step, provided it accorded with his conception of provincial autonomy, which in essence involved depriving the Centre of most of its cherished powers, which the Liberals are still willing to invest it with, even when the Federal scheme goes into effect'.[1] Gandhi would not accept an unaltered centre, but he was prepared in effect to consider breaking the deadlock over federal structure by a provincialization of British India. At a meeting at Malaviya's flat Sapru and Sastri took him to task for his unorthodoxy, and subsequently he signed a letter of protest that the moderates sent to the prime minister on Friday 6 November.

Nevertheless, during meetings at Balliol College that weekend he discussed the matter further with Lothian, A. D. Lindsay (Master of Balliol), Malcolm MacDonald (the prime minister's son and under-secretary for the Dominions), Sir Reginald Coupland (Beit Professor of the History of the British Empire), H. S. Polak (of the India Conciliation Group), Corbett, and S. K. Datta (an Indian Christian delegate to the conference). Gandhi and Lothian agreed that the best way to achieve federation was

to free the provinces from the incubus of the present Central Government, realizing of course that this freedom could only be completed when real responsibility was brought about at the Centre. The provinces freed would be in a position with their elected Chambers to take powers from the Central authority more adequately than any scheme at present being considered would permit.[2]

On the Monday Lothian and Malcolm MacDonald returned to London believing that negotiations might begin at once with Gandhi on provincial autonomy of a radical kind, 'the statute to make provision for a national convention elected by the provincial legislatures to implement Federal Constitution'.[3] Here was a possibility of a constructive reopening of the whole constitutional question, in its communal no less than its structural aspect, for the Muslims' main object was autonomous Muslim provinces. In addition, some of the most important states favoured provincialization.

[1] S. K. Datta to J. Nehru, 12 November 1931, A.I.C.C., G. 60, 1931.
[2] Ibid.   [3] Ibid.

The Failure of Consultation

That same Monday Hoare completed a proposal for submission to the Cabinet. Its nub was advance in two stages, first to provincial autonomy without changing the centre, later to federation:

Probably few, if any, of the delegates could be brought to concede in terms—what logic and history assert—that it is premature to consider the plans for an Indian Federation, and still more to attempt to construct it, until those of the units which are to be parties to the pact are in being in the shape of 'autonomous' provinces, with sufficient practical experience of their individual needs and desires as such to be able authoritatively to formulate them and themselves to be parties to the creation, and the endowment with powers, of the Central organism. To concede this position would be to acquiesce in the postponement of the Federal consummation for at least five and more probably for ten years.[1]

The government should, if necessary, issue a communal award to enable a provincial autonomy bill to be introduced in 1932. Hoare envisaged the continuation of separate electorates and a solution to the Punjab and Bengal problems that would give the Muslims effective though not statutory majorities. The N.W.F.P. should become a full province, for that would wean the frontier moderates away from the Congress and make cooperators of them. Sind should be separated provided that its financial viability could be established. In addition, the imperial government should renew its pledge on central responsibility within an all-India federation, given, of course, effective safeguards and reserve powers. As an earnest of its sincerity it should provide for the dispatch to India of expert committees of inquiry into the outstanding problems involved in federation: the franchise, federal finance, and the financial relations with the states. A consultative committee of Indians should then visit London for discussions about federation.

Hoare calculated that his proposal would restore the initiative to the government and attract strong support from all of the minorities. The latter was important: 'there is a grave risk of our having no friends in India at all if we disregard these representatives of the 120 million Indians who have hitherto refused to take part in civil disobedience.' In addition, the Hindus may not unanimously oppose a two-phase approach: 'Mr. Gandhi

[1] Sec. of S.'s memo. of 9 November 1931, T.C. 1.

himself, although he has signed a letter against advance in two stages, has undoubtedly been attracted by it. Moreover, I do not greatly fear Hindu non-co-operation in the provincial autonomy stage. I do not believe that the Hindus can afford to stay out.'[1] Hoare's proposal was much more attractive to British policy-makers than that of Gandhi and Lothian. Tories generally, and the most influential Liberals, Reading and Simon, were opposed to any diminution of the central authority, even through the process of provincialization. It was the outline of the Hoare plan that MacDonald and Sankey placed tactfully before Sapru at dinner on Wednesday, 11 November. Next day a committee of the Cabinet commended the plan to the full Cabinet, which approved it on Friday the 13th. The second session of the Round Table Conference would be concluded with a reaffirmation of the statement with which the prime minister closed the first; but whereas all-India federation would be presented as the ultimate aim, provision would be made for a provincial autonomy bill in summer 1932.

However, on that inauspicious Friday, Sapru, 'very distressed and disappointed', wrote a long letter of protest to MacDonald.[2] Provision for provincial autonomy and federation must be embodied in a single bill. Even if a provincial autonomy bill contained a preamble promising central responsibility at an early date, the overwhelming Tory majority in parliament would prevent Indian aspirations from being satisfied. Furthermore: 'The whole scheme of Federation may be, and probably will be, imperilled if the Provinces are given the right to decide whether they will come into the Federation, or not; or even if they are given a potent voice in the devising of the machinery for the Central Legislature—an idea which seems attractive to Mr. Gandhi, but which does not attract me at all.'[3] The real danger, of course, was that autonomous Muslim and Hindu provinces would be unable to agree upon the form of the central government.

Sapru and the Hindu Liberals marshalled the opposition of Benn, Lees Smith, and the Labour newspaper, the *Daily Herald*,

[1] Ibid.
[2] Sapru to MacDonald and Irwin, 13 November 1931, S.C. 1, M. 12, and S.C. 2, I. 36.
[3] Sapru to MacDonald, 13 November 1931, S.C. 1, M. 12.

to the government's 'policy of back to Simon'. They persuaded Ambedkar and the more liberal Muslims, Jinnah, Shafi, and the Aga Khan, to repudiate publicly the assurances of support that Hoare claimed them to have given him in private. Hoare was bitterly resentful of Sapru and the Labour delegates' intrusion. He charged them with misrepresenting for personal or party purposes a policy that had been endorsed not only by the Tories but also by Sankey, MacDonald, and such experts as Haig and Corbett. MacDonald and Sankey now bent before the opposition of former colleagues and the persuasive Hindu moderates. On 27 November the Cabinet reversed its conclusion of a fortnight earlier. The prime minister's closing statement on 1 December would not propose a two-stage constitutional advance. The government would prepare a single India bill.

The viceroy's response to the deadlock over federal structure was to propose an immediate advance at the British Indian centre. Willingdon could see no reason why the British government should not issue a communal award for the centre as well as for the provinces. As the princes had blocked all-India federation for the moment, they should be set aside while the central government was liberalized. In November, Willingdon felt 'extreme distaste' at having to certify the whole of Schuster's stringent emergency budget because of the legislative assembly's hostility to taxation increases. He criticized the 'unreality' of proceedings in the assembly 'when you have an irresponsible official Executive with an entirely irresponsible unofficial [legislative] majority. The situation really can't go on, and I do trust we shall get forward very quickly to some form of central responsibility.'[1] Here was a statement of the constitutional implications of Willingdon's concern to harmonize budgetary and monetary policy with Indian opinion. New Delhi and Whitehall were now developing divergent constitutional strategies. Willingdon would press ahead with reforms 'to the limits of safety'. At the very least he wanted freedom to select his own executive untrammelled by the existing requirement that three of its six civil members must be Europeans who had spent ten years in the service of the Crown in India.

At the end of November the Government of India protested against the proposed prime ministerial statement. By continuing

[1] Willingdon to Hoare, 22 November 1931, T.C.L.B.

to insist upon all-India federation as a condition of central responsibility the statement precluded advance in British India: 'We think such a declaration unnecessary and dangerous, particularly as it leaves fate of India at the discretion of the States.'[1] Hoare was firm: 'Believe me, the Conservative party will not move in . . . the direction of any responsibility for British India as distinct from an All-India Federation.'[2] Hoare experienced difficulty even in obtaining the party's approval for central responsibility with safeguards within an all-India federation. During a House of Lords debate at the beginning of December Salisbury attacked the policy and would have defeated it if there had been a division. Many peers had taken fright at a recent speech of Willingdon's in which he spoke of becoming a 'constitutional governor' before the end of his term. The party would also be hostile to Willingdon reducing the British official element in his council. Hoare advised him: '. . . it is most essential that we should appear to be taking at the moment no risks with the Central Government. Conservative feeling is very strong on this point, and if it became anxious we should have a complete reversal in the House of Commons . . . of our policy.'[3] England was 'demanding resolute action' in India, and official control at the centre must not be slackened.[4]

On 1 December the prime minister closed the second Round Table Conference with a reiteration of his policy statement of 19 January. He averred that if necessary His Majesty's Government would settle the communal question provisionally. The N.W.F.P. would become a governor's province, as, subject to its financial viability, would Sind. A consultative committee would be set up in India to continue the work of the conference, and expert committees would be sent to India to investigate the major outstanding questions involved in federation: the franchise, federal finance, and the financial arrangements between the states and the federation. Nevertheless, the Hindu delegates left the conference full of misgivings. Moonje made the following assessment:

[1] Viceroy to Sec. of S., 29 November 1931 (t/g), T.C.
[2] Hoare to Willingdon, 17 December 1931, T.C.L.B.
[3] Hoare to Willingdon, 10 December 1931. In fact Churchill had obtained only 43 votes in the House of Commons' division over the government's policy.
[4] Hoare to Willingdon, 17 December 1931, T.C.L.B.

Result of the Conference seems to me to be as follows: Muslims have been placated. N.W.F. Province has been wrested from Mahatma's hands. Muslims of Punjab and Bengal and Muslims generally absolutely weaned away from Mahatmaji by promise of Provincial Autonomy. Civil disobedience movement, if Mahatma were thinking of reviving it, is made terribly more difficult if not impossible. Show of All-India Federation with promise of Central Responsibility with safeguards kept up; as a cloak or as a sweet smelling chloroform under which the whole nation may go to sleep again. As a result the Central Responsibility is indefinitely postponed, because the Princes will be controlled by the Political Department of Government of India to keep at arm's length from Federation. Besides if the Provinces become autonomous, it is nothing more than the scheme of the Simon Commission. While Punjab and Bengal being predominantly Muslim, they may eventually refuse to join the federation; and then the federation may never come into being, and thus there may be no occasion for the Central Responsibility. This is all the result of the original blunder of Sir T. B. Sapru of last year in accepting the idea of the All-India Federation. It was a trap to which he fell an easy victim.[1]

Jayakar wrote to Bikaner in similar vein:

We have averted [difficulties] for the present, but I fear that one of them, viz., the grant of Provincial Autonomy as a first instalment may still raise its head with the help of the Muslims and the officials in India.... Muslims ... will be glad if, instead of Federation, mere Provincial Autonomy is established as the first instalment.[2]

The Hindus sensed that the tide had turned. A Tory-bureaucratic-Muslim alliance was at hand. An era of reaction was opening. Events in India towards the end of 1931 confirmed their suspicions of Britain's determination to break the freedom movement.

V. THE END OF THE TRUCE

Both Gandhi and Willingdon had sought peace as an end in itself, and not merely a cessation of hostilities to permit an experiment in constitution-making. The Raj's overriding concern was law and order, while Gandhi valued 'human contacts

[1] Moonje to Ganpat Rai (secretary of the Hindu Mahasabha), n.d., received by air mail on 16 December 1931, J.C. 356.
[2] Jayakar to Bikaner, 28 December 1931, J.C. 455.

by which one could swear' above 'the securing of a constitution'.[1] During 1931 Gandhi yearned for co-operation with government. He constantly urged his provincial lieutenants to take their grievances to the local authorities, and he stressed that the Delhi pact must be observed whether or not he went to London. Willingdon, for his part, wrote to Jawaharlal and Vallabhbhai at the beginning of September to say that he was 'always accessible' if they were 'in any difficulty'.[2] Nevertheless, no sooner had Gandhi sailed than it became clear that the struggle between officials and Congressmen for power and influence would not abate.

The Gandhi–Willingdon exchange of letters at the end of August had left each side with ready means of ending the truce. Gandhi had reserved the right of resort to defensive satyagraha against specific grievances arising from the Delhi pact. Willingdon had denied that the pact superseded the law of the land and asserted the government's freedom to deal with unlawful activities either by employing normal coercive processes or by assuming special powers.

From early September relations between Congress workers and local officials in the U.P. deteriorated steadily. Congress complained that tenants were being unjustly evicted because of their inability to pay excessive rents at a time of economic distress. It sought a joint investigation with government in order to secure an adequate general remission. The government replied that Congress had rejected an invitation to participate in an official investigation into remissions and that it was now too late to reopen the inquiry. The U.P. Rent and Revenue Committee, which had been established on 10 August, had indeed invited the Congressman, Govind Ballabh Pant, to join it. But by the time that Pant had obtained the U.P.P.C.C.'s consent to his acceptance, the Committee had reported. The government gave immediate effect to the recommendations in August. Rents were reduced by Rs. 41,000,000. In September, even after the onset of the rains, the current season's rents were being collected by forcible processes and attempts were being made to collect arrears. Congress proposed the reduction of current rents by Rs. 100,000,000, the remission of all arrears, and the reinstate-

---

[1] Gandhi to Emerson, 28 August 1931, Gandhi Coll. 17601.
[2] Willingdon to Gandhi, 4 September 1931, Gandhi Coll. 17642.

ment of all tenants evicted for non-pyament. It sought further remissions in the Allahabad district in particular.

From the Provincial Congress office in Allahabad Nehru watched the situation with mounting distaste and impatience. During September and October he and Vallabhbhai, as Congress president, wrote protestingly to the local government, to Emerson, and to Sir Eric Miéville (the viceroy's private secretary). The burden of ultimate responsibility for resort to defensive satyagraha weighed heavily upon Vallabhbhai, who counselled Nehru upon the wisdom of damping down the dispute. On one occasion he urged Nehru 'first [to] see the Viceroy before we do anything', for Willingdon was 'sure to blame us if we ignore his offer of help'.[1] On another, he wrote: 'Keep the door open for a resumption of discussions.'[2] He would avoid placing Congress in the wrong by publishing acrimonious correspondence with the government, and he sought to establish that a U.P. no-rent campaign against official policy would not constitute a breach of the 'second settlement'. Nehru was far less circumspect. He did not shrink from a confrontation that would precipitate total war.

Nehru's letters to Gandhi revealed contempt for the Round Table Conference. On 19 September, after meeting a group of Allahabad kisans who had suffered beatings for non-payment of rent, he wrote:

It is a strange world we live in and daily we add to our experiences. In London city there is peace and harmony—at any rate I suppose so—and the future of India is being discussed and fashioned out. Here, the future seems so distant. The present absorbs our attention. Enough for the day is the evil thereof, and it is a little difficult to feel vastly interested in the constitutional problems that are being discussed at the R.T.C. . . . I wonder when you will come to grips with the real question.[3]

A week later, he wrote:

If I had to listen to my dear friend Mohammed Ali Jinnah talking the most unmitigated nonsense about his 14 points for any length of time, I would have to consider the desirability of retiring to the South

[1] Vallabhbhai to J. Nehru, 19 October 1931, A.I.C.C., G. 60, 1931.
[2] Vallabhbhai to J. Nehru, 1 December 1931, ibid.
[3] J. Nehru to Gandhi, 19 September 1931, J. Nehru Corr.

Sea islands, where there would be some hope of meeting with some people who were intelligent or ignorant enough not to talk of the 14 points.... I marvel at your patience.[1]

By the beginning of October he was expecting the conference to break down any day. On 16 October he cabled about a request from the Allahabad District Congress Committee for permission to advise the kisans to withhold rent. He wrote the same day: 'I do not know how this will affect your work in London. So far as I can see the Round Table Conference is as dead as a doornail and it does not matter much what effect is produced on it.'[2] He warned Miéville that a no-rent movement was possible: '... the question of payment or withholding payment of rent is a vital and urgent one for the tenantry and it cannot afford to be shelved till the conclusion of the London Conference.'[3] Gandhi accepted Jawaharlal's order of priorities: 'You should unhesitatingly take necessary steps meet every situation expect nothing here.'[4]

On 1 November the council of the U.P.P.C.C. considered the Allahabad Committee's request to launch a no-rent satyagraha. Further approaches were then made to the government but they failed to secure relief. On 15 November the provincial committee approved the Allahabad request and Vallabhbhai added his endorsement. On 5 December the U.P.P.C.C. authorized the District Committees of Etawah, Cawnpore, Rae Baraeli, and Unao to advise the non-payment of rent and revenue.

Neither the council of the U.P.P.C.C. nor Nehru himself was concerned to limit the movement to five districts in the U.P. The council's resolutions of 5 December expressed sympathy for the victims of 'repression' in the N.W.F.P. and Bengal.[5] They appealed to people in the U.P. generally 'to hold themselves in readiness for such action [satyagraha] when the call for it may come from the Working Committee of the Congress'. On 7 December Jawaharlal wrote to Vallabhbhai about celebrations to welcome Gandhi home: 'You might call for meetings all over the country to pass an identical resolution conveying our

[1] J. Nehru to Gandhi, 27 September 1931, Gandhi Coll. 17863.
[2] J. Nehru to Gandhi, 16 October 1931, J. Nehru Corr., Nehru Coll.
[3] J. Nehru to Miéville, 16 October 1931, A.I.C.C., G. 7, 1931.
[4] Gandhi to J. Nehru, 17 October 1931, Gandhi Coll. 18223.
[5] Resolution of council of U.P.P.C.C., 5 December 1931, A.I.C.C., P. 21, 1931.

affection and gratitude to Bapu and assurance to stand by him in the struggle for independence and to put up with all the sufferings that the struggle may bring.'[1] Jawaharlal was spoiling for a fight. He would leave Gandhi as little opening as possible to pursue the way of co-operation.

Nehru's activities were not limited to the U.P. In September Patel had asked him to consider the problem of Congress organization in the N.W.F.P. During the civil disobedience movement Abdul Ghaffar Khan's Khudai Khidmatgars had functioned independently of the N.W.F.P.P.C.C. On 9 August 1931 Gandhi had recognized Abdul Ghaffar Khan as a true follower by authorizing him to reorganize the Provincial Congress Committee (the N.W.F.P. Jirga) according to his own discretion. Gandhi admitted to Emerson that he found great difficulty in distinguishing truth from falsehood in his frontier lieutenant's allegations and the official counter-allegations about the implementation of the Delhi pact. However, he represented his disciple's claims that many civil disobedience prisoners were never released and that officials molested Khudai Khidmatgars on the slightest pretext. He had Abdul Ghaffar Khan with him at Simla during the period of the second settlement negotiations, and he impressed upon him the need to talk over his grievances with the viceroy. Willingdon was appalled when Abdul Ghaffar asked his secretary to write to Miéville to arrange a meeting, and dismissed him as 'a gentleman who has wind in the head'.[2] Gandhi wrote from England, asking Willingdon to excuse such rudeness as simply a rustic's ignorance of the proprieties.

Nehru was impressed by a report that Gandhi's son, Devadas, had written on the N.W.F.P. He was prepared to accept its finding that unrest had grown out of harsh repression and that revenue had been extorted by cruelty and torture. He confirmed Abdul Ghaffar as the Congress leader in the province in October, when the old Congress Committee members proved reluctant to vacate their offices. On 16 October (the day that Nehru cabled for Gandhi's sanction of satyagraha in the U.P.) Abdul Ghaffar wrote to Gandhi: 'The Government have started severe repression against the Khudai Khidmatgars. They raid their offices and beat them there. . . . This is how the Government

[1] J. Nehru to Vallabhbhai, 7 December 1931, A.I.C.C., G. 60, 1931.
[2] Willingdon to Gandhi, 4 September 1931, Gandhi Coll. 17642.

are observing the Truce.'[1] The Red Shirt leaders began to withhold land revenue. In some districts orders prohibiting meetings were issued under the Criminal Procedure Code. Abdul Ghaffar defied them and his public speeches became more and more inflammatory. On 1 November he proclaimed that he sought 'to liberate the country from the foreign yoke'.[2] On 23 November Jawaharlal wrote in rousing terms to Dr. Khan Saheb, Abdul Ghaffar's brother:

We are getting involved in a no-tax campaign here owing to the economic distress. It is possible that many of us may be arrested before long. Whether we are arrested or not rest assured that we shall think of our comrades in the Frontier Province frequently, and with the confidence that whenever the time may come they will play a brave and leading part in the struggle for freedom.[3]

On 4 December the Peshawar City Congress Jirga expressed dissatisfaction with the Round Table Conference reforms and declared that 'not a single well-wisher of the soil would ever be content with anything less than complete independence'. It assured the A.I.C.C. that it 'would not lag behind in facing the consequences of a war for freedom'.[4] Next day Nehru wrote to Khan Saheb: '. . . we know that you will face all trials to come without flinching. Very soon we in the U.P. are also going to have a stiff time. All the better.'[5] Solidarity between Congressmen in two troubled provinces had been accomplished.

Nehru also devoted his attention to Bengal, where Congress leaders had long complained of being neglected by the A.I.C.C. Between August and October terrorism broke out and a number of officials were shot. In September Bengali feelings were inflamed by the shooting of two political *détenus* during a disturbance at Hijli. On 29 October the government took special powers by ordinance to arrest suspected terrorists and detain them without trial. In November Nehru toured the province and complained of the use of the ordinance to arrest Congress workers. On 30 November a further ordinance was introduced

---

[1] Abdul Ghaffar Khan to Gandhi, 16 October 1931, Gandhi Coll. 18122.
[2] *India in 1931–32*, Calcutta, 1933, p. 28.
[3] J. Nehru to Dr. Khan Saheb, 23 November 1931, A.I.C.C., P. 17, 1931.
[4] Paper forwarded to Gen. Sec. A.I.C.C., d. 5 December 1931, A.I.C.C., P. 17, 1931.
[5] J. Nehru to Dr. Khan Saheb, 5 December 1931, A.I.C.C., P. 17, 1931.

The Failure of Consultation

to provide for the speedy trial of terrorists and to facilitate combined civil and military operations in Chittagong. The council of the U.P.P.C.C. condemned the ordinance as tantamount to martial law. In December the Bengal P.C.C. set about organizing a boycott of British goods.

As the political situation in the U.P. and the N.W.F.P. and Bengal deteriorated steadily the Government of India prepared for war. On 13 October it sent home the cable that it had drafted in August, seeking the secretary of state's approval for a course of massive retaliation if 'defensive satyagraha' were initiated or if the Frontier Province situation warranted it.[1] The package of repression included several ordinances, notably the comprehensive Emergency Powers Ordinance, and the arrest of Gandhi within ten days of his associating himself with the agitation. On 27 October Hoare signified his agreement to the package in principle but reserved the power to approve the occasion for its introduction. On 7 December the Home Department sent to the local governments drafts of the ordinances concerning Emergency Powers, Unlawful Instigation, Unlawful Association, and the Prevention of Molestation and Boycott. They were to be revealed only to officers who would be responsible for strategies to deal with civil disobedience. The *pièce de résistance* was the Emergency Powers Ordinance, which sanctioned the arrest, detention, and control of suspects, the seizure of buildings and movables, the prohibition of access to places, the control of commodities in general use, of utilities, posts, telegraphs, etc., the search of persons and premises, the introduction of special legal processes, etc. The Government of Bombay expressed the spirit of the policy that was germinating:

In all the suggestions now put forward . . . it has been the assumption of this Government that the policy would be to use every means which past experience could suggest to paralyse the movement at the outset, and it is the firm opinion of the Governor-in-Council that a vigorous and successful offensive during the first few weeks of the movement will do more to limit its intensity and severity than any measures adopted at a later stage.[2]

The conflict between provincial Congress leaders and local

[1] See above, pp. 206–7.
[2] Home Sec. to Govt. of Bombay to Home Sec. to Govt. of India, 12 December 1931, Home Pol. 14/12/31.

governments sharpened in December as the time for Gandhi's return approached. On 14 December the U.P. government took the precaution of introducing an Emergency Powers Ordinance. A week later the U.P.P.C.C. was forbidden to hold its forthcoming conference unless it undertook not to use the occasion to foster the no-rent campaign. The conference was postponed. On 22 December Nehru was instructed to remain in Allahabad. He was arrested four days later on his way to meet Gandhi at Bombay. On 24 December Emergency Powers, Unlawful Instigation, and Unlawful Association Ordinances were promulgated in the N.W.F.P., Abdul Ghaffar Khan was arrested, and Peshawar district was occupied by six mobile columns. The 'Frontier Gandhi' had been prevented from fulfilling his declared intention of meeting the Mahatma at Bombay to discuss the resumption of civil disobedience.

In an order-in-council of 17 December Willingdon drew together the implications of provincial developments for his policy towards Gandhi and the Congress. The document is of such crucial importance to the history of relations between Congress and the Raj as to warrant quotation *in extenso*:

(a) So long as the no-rent campaign is being carried on in the United Provinces, there should be no correspondence with Congress which would suggest even by implication that the Delhi Settlement is in operation.
(b) Government should await the proceedings of the Congress Working Committee to be held on December 29th, before reaching a decision as to whether they should make a formal public announcement to the effect that they regard the Delhi Settlement as no longer operative.
(c) If Mr. Gandhi, as the express or implied representative of Congress, asks for an interview with His Excellency the Viceroy, or a discussion with the Government of India on any matters he should be informed that this is not possible so long as the no-rent campaign is in progress in the U.P.
(d) If the Working Committee pass resolutions
    (1) in favour of revival of civil disobedience either at once or after preparation, or
    (2) in support of U.P. no-rent campaign, or
    (3) in support of boycott of British goods in Bengal or elsewhere,
this should be regarded as a *casus belli* and direct action taken against the Central Congress organization.

The Failure of Consultation

The programme of action would be put into force as necessary. The immediate action required would be as follows:
(1) Mr. Gandhi would be arrested under Regulation if he associates himself with the resolution.
(2) The Working Committee would be declared an unlawful association.
(3) The Emergency Powers Ordinance would be promulgated.
(4) The Prevention of Molestation and Boycott Ordinance would be promulgated if Resolution (3) were passed.
(5) The approval of the Secretary of State be obtained to the above course and local Governments be informed of the Government of India's proposals.

In particular, local Governments be advised in regard to action to be taken, if boycott of British goods is revived.[1]

On 19 December the policy was referred to the secretary of state and obtained his instant approval.

The Government of India had made a decisive change of policy towards Gandhi. In March Irwin had agreed to meet him while civil disobedience was still in operation. In August Willingdon had met him while a no-rent campaign was in progress. Now it was decided that Gandhi must choose between talks with the viceroy and civil disobedience. A major reason for the change was to show the servants and supporters of the Raj who was boss. Willingdon explained the policy to Hoare:

I don't see how I can possibly agree to see him unless he will give me an assurance that he will call off these Congress activities which have been set on foot. If I did agree to see him, it would create a most extraordinarily bad effect among all moderate-minded men and they would say again 'this is the old story—Gandhi coming along to do a deal with the Viceroy'.[2]

The Irwin policy was at an end:

The Delhi Pact at all events is dead and gone, murdered by Jawaharlal Nehru and Abdul Ghaffar. Edward Irwin certainly made a great and gallant effort, but it has proved unsuccessful, and has further proved that, as long as it lasted, it was a great handicap to Government in its administration and an enormous advantage to Congress in promoting their activites.[3]

Hoare agreed that there could be no question of another pact

[1] Order in Council, 17 December 1931, Home Pol. 14/12/31.
[2] Willingdon to Hoare, 20 December 1931, T.C.L.B.
[3] Willingdon to Hoare, 26 December 1931, T.C.L.B.

with Gandhi. The administrative action of the government to deal with terrorism and lawlessness could not be bargained away.

When Gandhi landed at Bombay on 28 December he was ignorant of the new policy. He was disposed to co-operate and unready for a renewal of civil disobedience. He hoped to meet Willingdon and to protest against the 'emasculation'[1] of Bengal and the harsh ordinances in the U.P. and the N.W.F.P. On 29 December he cabled to Willingdon, asking whether the ordinances and the detention of 'valued comrades' indicated that 'friendly relations' with the viceroy were at an end.[2] The viceroy's reply of 31 December, which Crerar drafted, expressed willingness to see Gandhi but not to discuss the ordinances. It made clear that Gandhi was expected to repudiate the activities of his lieutenants in the U.P. and the N.W.F.P. Gandhi cabled back, seeking a meeting without conditions and intimating that the C.W.C. had accepted his advice and resolved upon a plan of civil disobedience. If an interview were granted the resolution would be suspended. Gandhi informed Sapru that as far as he was concerned the 'door [was] still open for negotiation under self-respecting conditions'.[3] However, 'I hope you don't still think that I can see the Viceroy if he makes no response to my wire. . . . My conscience is quite clear. The Government here simply don't want to see me unless I approach them with the straw in the mouth.'[4] On 2 January the government replied that the viceroy could not see Gandhi 'under the threat of resumption of civil disobedience', and that Gandhi and the Congress would be held responsible for all the consequences that may flow from such a resumption.[5] Nor could the government accept that its ordinance policy could be dependent upon Gandhi's approval. On 4 January Gandhi was arrested and placed in Yervada 'during the pleasure of Government'. Within a week leading Congressmen all over India were in gaol.

Gandhi was the victim of the government's draconian policy on the one hand and Nehru's intransigence on the other. He was forced to choose between following Nehru to gaol or

[1] Sec. of S. to viceroy, 7 December 1931 (t/g), T.C.
[2] Gandhi to viceroy, 29 December 1931, in *India in 1931–32*, p. 231.
[3] Gandhi to Sapru, 1 January 1932, S.C. 2, M. 120.
[4] Gandhi to Sapru, 2 January 1932, S.C. 1, G. 15.
[5] P.S.V. to Gandhi, 2 January 1932, in *India in 1931–32*, p. 238.

repudiating him. 'How nicely the Pandit has forced Gandhi's hand', wrote an astute observer.[1] In Sapru's words, Gandhi had 'succumbed to the influence of the extreme wing among the Congressmen, who had already prepared the stage for him by starting the no-rent campaign in the U.P.'[2] Willingdon confessed to feeling like 'a sort of Mussolini in India'.[3] He, too, felt that Gandhi was the victim of his own left wing and that 'Government had no option in the matter'.[4] Nehru's strength within the Congress had grown remarkably. Though he had been unable to prevent the truce in March, with Gandhi absent from India he contrived to destroy it beyond repair.

[1] Sir N. N. Sircar to Sapru, 1 January 1932, S.C. 2, S. 77.
[2] Sapru to Bikaner, 4 January 1932, S.C. 2, S. 270.
[3] Willingdon to Hoare, 20 December 1931, T.C.L.B.
[4] Willingdon to Jayakar, 31 December 1931, J.C. 455.

CHAPTER 6

The Resurgence of Reaction: January 1932—January 1933

The new procedure is an illustration of the Conservative view that we Indians must not be allowed to treat with the British on terms of equality.

Sir Tej Bahadur Sapru, 3 July 1932

In my view . . . it is in no way necessary to secure the co-operation of the Congress in order that the new constitution may be properly launched. . . .

H. G. Haig, 28 December 1932

I. THE RELUCTANCE TO CONFER

Gandhi's arrest on Monday 4 January 1932 marks a turning-point in relations between the Raj and Indian nationalism. Never before, not in 1920–2 nor in 1930–1, had the government refused even to talk with Gandhi unless he first disavowed civil disobedience. Never before had satyagraha suffered such relentless repression. The Government of India resorted to the assumption of powers that had always seemed incompatible with Montagu's declaration of purpose. Gandhi's arrest was accompanied by the battery of carefully prepared ordinances: the Emergency Powers Ordinance conferring special powers against the press and prospective breaches of law and order; the Unlawful Instigation Ordinance to deal with no-tax campaigns; the Prevention of Molestation and Boycott Ordinance against picketing and the intimidation of government servants; the Unlawful Association Ordinance enabling the Congress to be suppressed. Many Congress organizations were banned and their offices and funds were seized. In January 14,803 arrests were made in connection with civil disobedience; in February, a further 17,818, and in March, 6,909. In consequence, the movement failed to approach the dimensions of the 1930 campaign. The pre-emptive strike was a brilliant success. The only form of protest now available to Gandhi was personal self-suffering, which the rigidity of officialdom in 1932 would make difficult for him to employ in the service of freedom or unity.

At the outset, the British Government endorsed the repressive policy readily. It sated the Tory longing for strong government. On 8 January Hoare assured Willingdon that 'the big body of public opinion' was behind him: 'It seems to me that we have entered the contest upon very strong ground. The all-important thing is now to maintain it and not to lose the moral support that is behind us.'[1] Three months later Hoare was still writing that 'the great body of public opinion will back you to the full in maintaining such Ordinances as are necessary for the emergency of the time'.[2] However, repression played different roles in the strategies favoured by Whitehall and New Delhi. The home government accepted it as a temporary necessity, whereas the Government of India assigned it a continuing validity. The contrast appeared over policy towards Bengal. When the Indian authorities proposed a permanent Bengal Criminal Law Amendment Bill, MacDonald objected that the temporary emergency did not justify it.

At the end of March MacDonald expressed concern at what should follow the ordinance regime: 'Will a point come when Mr. Gandhi will be allowed to enter into political conversations for the purpose of reaching an agreement; or must we go on keeping him in prison, whilst a policy of smashing Congress is being pursued by Ordinance methods?'[3] Haig, now Home Member of the viceroy's executive, enunciated the government's policy. Congress must be beaten in order to demonstrate that they could not secure their ends by force. The problem of reaching any agreement with Congress was their preoccupation with their own prestige:

They will always try to twist round any agreement so as to convince people that they have been the victors. This was demonstrated by the Pact.... What we require is a constitution as early as possible that will give free scope to Congress activities, and into which Congress

---

[1] Hoare to Willingdon, 8 January 1932, T.C.L.B.
[2] Hoare to Willingdon, 22 April 1932, T.C.L.B.
[3] P.M. to viceroy, 31 March 1932, quoted in Miéville to Haig, 10 April 1932, Haig Coll. 1.

will come gradually, but not by a formal compact. We can't afford to do anything that will increase the prestige of the Congress.[1]

The policy was to prove that India could be governed without yielding to Congress. Its negative aspect was repression. Its positive side was the early introduction of a constitution that would attract sufficient Indian support to induce Congress to co-operate.

Willingdon urged upon Hoare repeatedly the need for early changes in the central government. In January 1932 he insisted that his three English councillors endorsed his view 'that it is essential at this juncture to show our *bona fides* by strengthening Indian representation on my Council'.[2] He wanted to appoint an Indian as Commerce member when Rainy retired. Only when Hoare resolved to seek Cabinet support for his opposition did Willingdon relent. But he reverted at once to the case for conferring responsibility at the British Indian centre if, as seemed likely, the princes resiled. Hoare declared that this was 'not practical politics': neither the Cabinet nor parliament would concede central responsibility until an all-India federation was established.[3]

By early 1932 the respective decisions of Whitehall and New Delhi had narrowed Britain's policy options appreciably. By refusing to negotiate with Congress the Government of India was limiting consultation to the remaining parties in the hope that Congress would eventually come to heel. By refusing to contemplate British Indian responsibility despite the recoil of the princes the Cabinet was consigning British India to bureaucratic rule pending the pleasure of their highnesses. Britain had committed herself to pursuing constitutional progress by securing the co-operation of the princes and the collaboration of sectional interests, the Muslims, the Hindu Liberals, moderates and communalists, the minor minorities, and the landed, commercial, and industrial magnates.

Consistently with MacDonald's closing declaration at the second Round Table Conference, a consultative committee of the conference was set up under the viceroy's chairmanship and three expert committees were dispatched to India. The

[1] Note by Haig, n.d. [probably June 1932], ibid.
[2] Willingdon to Hoare, 23 January 1932 (secret t/g), T.C.
[3] Hoare to Willingdon, 19 February 1932, T.C.L.B.

members of the Consultative Committee were Sapru, C. P. R. Aiyer, Jayakar, Patro, Ambedkar, Thakurdas, Joshi, Zafrullah Khan, Ghaznavi, Shafi, Shafa'at Ahmad Khan, Ujjal Singh, Benthall (for the non-official Europeans), Hydari, Mirza Ismail, Manubhai Mehta (for Bikaner), Liaquat Hyat Khan (for the confederationists), and Krishnamachari (for the maritime states). The expert committees went to India early in 1932 and reported in the middle of the year. They were the Federal Finance Committee, with J. C. C. Davidson as chairman and Haksar and Hydari among the members; the Indian States Inquiry Committee, chaired by Lord Eustace Percy; and the Franchise Committee with Lothian in the chair. The expert committees provided Hoare with the information that he and the officials at the India Office required for the preparation of the heads of the India bill. In addition, Hoare was aided by a Cabinet Committee on India, which operated as the co-ordinating authority on Indian constitutional development. It contained the prime minister, the lord chancellor (Sankey), the foreign secretary (Simon), the war secretary (Lord Hailsham), the president of the board of trade (W. Runciman), and Hoare himself. Irwin joined the group in July, when he accepted a minor Cabinet post, and Davidson was added to it after he returned from India.

Despite the hostility of the Hindu moderates, Hoare continued to favour constitutional advance by two stages. On 15 April he resurrected the scheme in a 'Note on Programme for Reform', for which he claimed the general approval of MacDonald and Baldwin.[1] He argued that whereas a provincial autonomy bill could be introduced in the coming October or November, the princes could not be brought to so early an agreement upon the terms of their entry to an all-India federation. He advocated the official determination of the communal issue in the provinces and the preparation of a provincial bill, with a preamble promising a federal bill in due course. He assured Willingdon that the latter would follow 'as soon as the data are ready, but with the best will in the world the settlement of these details will take time'.[2] Willingdon resisted blandishment: the Hindus would be suspicious and only the Muslims would be compliant.

[1] Enclosure to Hoare to Willingdon, 15 April 1932, T.C.L.B.
[2] Hoare to Willingdon, 28 April 1932, T.C.L.B.

Hindu moderates were adamant that the two-phase scheme would destroy the prospect of Indian unity. In his correspondence with Sapru, Haksar agreed that the 'danger inherent in the present situation [was] the emergence of Provincial Autonomy, to the destruction, possibly for all time, of the prospect of a united India'.[1] Sastri spelled out the implications of the scheme in a long letter to MacDonald:

It would be a mistake to rely much on such an expedient as a declaration in the statute that central responsibility will follow when arrangements have been completed. Those that do not desire central responsibility will find or create a dozen reasons for not completing the necessary arrangements, and those who wish to implement the declaration will find it hard to surmount the active opposition of provincial leaders on whom autonomy has just been conferred.... I am convinced that to bring one part of the scheme into operation in advance of the other is to endanger the whole. The followers of the Congress, who cannot be kept out of action indefinitely, will be strong enough to obstruct effectively the working of provincial autonomy; and if the Government of His Majesty is to be carried on it will have to be through the nearly exclusive agency of those minor communities whose claims are fully conceded. Expressions like Anglo–Muslim Raj were heard even while we were in England, and they seem now to be louder here.... You will be a sad man when you discover that your lifelong labours for the welfare of India have ended in the setting up of class against class and an application on a colossal scale of the principle of Divide and Rule.[2]

Sastri had a horrific vision: 'Imagine what will happen if provincial autonomy is granted and four provinces under Muslim rule oppose central responsibility (or stipulate impossible conditions) while seven Hindu provinces wish to go ahead.'[3] So had Jayakar:

If Congress runs the first Government in the Provinces... there are elements in its ranks which will be only too glad to create difficulties in the way of the Princes coming in. They will insist, for instance, on the regulation of their internal affairs so as to bring them on a par with British Indian Provinces and similar conditions will be imposed which may frighten the Princes away. Similarly in Mussalman Provinces the communalist element, frightened of the majority at the

---

[1] Haksar to Sapru, 19 January 1932, S.C. 2, H. 50.
[2] Sastri to MacDonald, 15 April 1932, in *Sastri's Letters*, pp. 224–7.
[3] Sastri to P. Kodanda Rao, 2 July 1932, ibid., pp. 231–2.

Centre, will create troubles, and these two elements, under Gandhi's guidance, may even combine for the limited purpose of putting obstacles in the way of the Princes coming in.[1]

Sapru believed that a hiatus between two instalments of reform would 'virtually amount to the postponement of the Federation to the Greek Kalends, as a single province, by withholding its consent, may make it impossible for the Federation to come into existence'.[2]

In May Hoare yielded to pressure from the Government of India and dropped the scheme for two bills. However, within the Cabinet there was a group headed by Lord Hailsham, leader of the House of Lords, that favoured a hiatus in excess of the four or five months required for the creation of autonomous provinces and their election of federal representatives. On 15 June the Cabinet approved advance by a single bill, which, Hoare stressed, assumed the practicability of all-India federation and the accession of sufficient of the princes. Hailsham warned of trouble in the Lords, especially over the adequacy of safeguards. The hiatus was left undefined, which depressed Sapru profoundly: 'What is the good of a single Bill if the single Bill provides only for conditions on which Federation may come into existence some time?'[3] Britain had left 'the actual materialization of the Federation in uncertainty so far as time is concerned'.[4]

Sapru protested that the government was taking fundamental decisions on the constitution without consulting Indian opinion. In fact, Hoare preferred this procedure. In April he confided to Willingdon that during the second conference the government had decided 'that another meeting of the whole Round Table Conference would be terribly cumbrous and expensive, and that so big a body would only serve to bring out differences of opinion and to give partisans opportunities for making set speeches'.[5] He claimed that British opinion had turned against the Round Table Conference procedure:

[1] Jayakar to Polak, 3 June 1932, J.C. 407.
[2] Sapru to Jayakar, 27 May 1932, J.C. 449.
[3] Sapru to Jayakar, 1 July 1932, J.C. 449.
[4] Sapru to viceroy, 6 July 1932 (resignation from Consultative Committee), encl. to Sapru to Jayakar, 4 July 1932, J.C. 449.
[5] Hoare to Willingdon, 8 April 1932, T.C.L.B.

I go so far as to say that another meeting of the Federal Structure Committee or of the Round Table Conference on the scale and in the manner of the last two autumns, would destroy any chance that I may have of getting a constitutional Bill through the House of Commons.

Parliament cannot bear the appearance of a constituent assembly sitting close to it in London, and nobody knows what a difficulty I had last year in preventing both Houses going off the deep end on the subject. It is my considered view that they will not stand a repetition of this next year.[1]

The purpose of future meetings with Indians in Britain should not be to decide 'whether such and such a provision should be made in the Bill, but rather whether the Indians have a better way to suggest of carrying out the Government's decision'.[2]

Hoare secured the support of MacDonald, Sankey, Lothian, and Davidson for jettisoning the conference. On 15 June the Cabinet approved his proposed procedure.[3] The Indian delegations would still be heard through the Consultative Committee, which was an 'epitome' of the conference. Then Indian experts would be brought to London for detailed informal discussions on safeguards, federal structure, and the accession of the states. Finally, a joint parliamentary committee on the India bill would hear Indian political opinion.

Hoare's plans were again upset by Sapru and Jayakar. No sooner had Willingdon's government accepted them (a surrender of its preference for reconvening the conference in autumn) than they were leaked to Jayakar by B. Rama Rau of the Government of India secretariat. Jayakar conveyed the news to Sapru, who confirmed its authenticity with Sir B. L. Mitter, a member of the viceroy's council. Jayakar and Sapru were particularly alarmed at the British assumption that the Consultative Committee gave Indians a sufficient forum, for the Committee contained no princes. They construed the new procedure as a stratagem of Hoare's to prevent federation and to cut off their access to influential Englishmen.

On 17 June Sapru and Jayakar waited on the viceroy at

---

[1] Hoare to Willingdon, 5 and 12 May 1932, T.C.L.B.
[2] Hoare to Willingdon, 12 May 1932, T.C.L.B.
[3] Cabinet Conclusions, 15 June 1932, I. O., L/PO/247.

Simla. They threatened to resign from the Consultative Committee if the conference procedure was abandoned. Willingdon was taken aback by the leakage of the new plans and shaken by the moderates' protest. His council agreed to press Hoare to attempt conciliation. However, Willingdon seems not to have understood the moderates' objection. He wrote of the draft of a statement on procedure that Hoare was to deliver in parliament on 27 June: 'It should fulfil all our requirements over here, and I can't conceive that Sapru and Jayakar can stand out when they see its contents.'[1] Yet the only concessions in the statement were the provisions for Indian experts to attend informal meetings in London and for the bill to be referred to the joint committee, before which Indians would appear as 'assessors', prior to the second reading. This reversal of the normal parliamentary sequence (from second reading to joint committee) was, of course, a device to improve the reception of the bill in parliament rather than to appease the Indians.

In a series of letters and cables to leading British statesmen and Indian colleagues during June and July, Sapru marshalled arguments for another conference session. He cabled to MacDonald that the proposed change was 'tantamount [to a] complete reorientation [of] procedure'.[2] It was a departure from the Irwin–Benn–MacDonald plan of proceeding by agreement with Indians and not merely by consultation. The essence of the conference procedure was that Britain was obliged to seek agreement with Indians participating as equals and expressing their views freely on all matters. The Indian witnesses before a joint committee would be on quite a different footing. The Consultative Committee was no substitute for a conference, because the third party required for a tripartite agreement, the princes, were not members of it. 'Without such agreement constitution passed by Parliament is not agreed constitution and makes future developments difficult.'[3]

Sapru quoted Irwin's statement of 9 July 1930 on the status of the conference: '... not a mere meeting for discussion and debate, but a joint assembly of representatives of both countries, on whose agreement the precise proposals to Parliament may

[1] Willingdon to Hoare, 27 June 1932, T.C.L.B.
[2] Sapru and Jayakar to MacDonald, 18 June 1932 (t/g), S.C. 1, M. 15.
[3] Ibid.

be founded'.[1] Hoare's plan violated the promise made by the prime minister in parliament on 2 December 1931:

> ... the Cabinet must carry on these negotiations, the Government must carry on these negotiations, until a point is reached when a proposed agreement is initialled—a very well-known stage in the negotiation of treaties. When the parties to the negotiation initial it, then, at that point, the House of Commons is asked whether it agrees or whether it disagrees....

The new plan did not require Indian agreement before the bill went before parliament. Sapru wrote bitterly to Haksar that the change reflected the Conservatives' abiding sense of racial superiority.[2] The joint committee procedure had originally been regarded as the stage that should follow the completion of the Simon Commission's work, and it carried the same insulting implications as the Commission's all-white membership. On 6 July Sapru and Jayakar resigned from the Consultative Committee. The return to Simonism had brought the return of the boycott.

The new procedure was but one of several disquieting features of the Indian situation around the middle of the year. On 27 June, when Hoare announced it in parliament, he also told of the government's decision soon to issue a communal award to prepare the way for provincial autonomy. In June, too, the Cabinet approved the consolidation of the repressive ordinances (which were due to expire on 3 July) into a Special Powers Ordinance, and its extension for a further six months.[3]

The deteriorating communal situation was a further cause of gloom among the Hindus. Outrageous riots in Bombay during May led Sapru to despair: 'Facts have proved too strong for me to permit me to continue to believe in the abstract theory of nationalism. I think the utmost ... we can do ... is to minimize the causes of friction and not to be misled by the will-o-the-wisp of nationalism. We must leave that to our children.'[4] Narendra Nath desponded: 'The situation is very critical and the outlook very gloomy.... What should we do? Are we not at the end of our tether?'[5] Birla reflected: 'Sometimes I sincerely

---

[1] Sapru to Willingdon, 6 July 1932, S.C. 1, W. 36.
[2] Sapru to Haksar, 3 July 1932, S.C. 1, H. 75.
[3] Cabinet Conclusions, 15 June 1932, loc. cit.
[4] Sapru to Haksar, 20 May 1932, S.C. 1, H. 65.
[5] Narendra Nath to Thakurdas, 24 June 1932, P.T.C. 107.

pray that we may not get any constitutional advance just now. Frankly speaking we are not ready for it. The communal trouble, though inspired, still exists and so long as we cannot make up our differences I do not know how we can work any constitution.'[1]
Sastri, expert at seeing two sides to every question, saw danger even in resigning from the Consultative Committee:

I am afraid we should have few nationally minded Muslims with us if we decided on abstention. The moment this position is reached, the Hindu Sabhas will take the boycott course. Surely then ... the two communities will stand face to face as proclaimed political enemies for a long time. Fearful prospect! In my opinion one of the sins of the Congress is the utter alienation of the Minorities and their consolidation. Shall we, by any course that we adopt, vindicate the Muslims and the Minorities in their anti-national policy?[2]

However, Sastri associated himself with the threat to boycott the new procedure.

Willingdon took fright at the disaffection of Sapru, Jayakar, Setalvad, Sastri, and Mudaliyar. The abstention of the Hindus from the Consultative Committee, together with the non-participation of the princes, could be fatal to all-India federation: '... my colleagues and I are in entire agreement that, if Federation is to have any chance whatever, the occasion must be made by means of conference ... to bring the representatives of the States and British India together with a view to bringing them to some sort of agreement on [the] outstanding federal issues.'[3] There was a growing cleavage of opinion between the states and British India, largely in consequence of the reports of the Federal Finance and States Inquiry (Financial) Committees. Both reports dealt generously with the states and alienated British Indian opinion. It seemed essential to settle the contentious issues at a tripartite conference. Moreover, the princes would scarcely treat seriously a federation that lacked the support of British Indian Hindus: 'There is reason to fear that Princes will not do business so long as Hindus are out.'[4]

Ever watchful of Conservative opinion, Hoare at first refused to budge: 'If it appears that we have wobbled in face of what

[1] Birla to Thakurdas, 30 June 1932, P.T.C. 107.
[2] Sastri to Sapru, 5 July 1932, S.C. 2, S. 108.
[3] Viceroy to Sec. of S., 27 July 1932(t/g), T.C.
[4] Viceroy to Sec. of S., 18 August 1932 (t/g), T.C.

everybody here regards as a petulant and perverse attitude adopted by the Hindu Liberals, we shall lose the support of the great majority of both Houses of Parliament.'[1] He insisted that Sapru was wrong in regarding the conference procedure as a treaty-making process and parliament as a rubber stamp. Parliament's sovereignty could not be limited by a conference agreement. Here Hoare was exaggerating Sapru's argument in order to demolish it.

On 9 August Sapru, Jayakar, Sastri, Joshi, Chintamani, Sethna, and others issued a manifesto against the new procedure: '... it does away with ideas of equality during discussion between British and Indian delegates and agreement between them on basis of proposals to be laid before Parliament.'[2] Now Willingdon warned Hoare that 'without such a Conference it does not seem possible to make progress in determining a workable Federal scheme, ... and without such a Conference the responsibility for failure to evolve a workable scheme ... will fall solely on His Majesty's Government'.[3]

At last Hoare conceded the need to attract Hindu support. The government agreed to hold a small London conference with states' and British Indian representatives. They would 'endeavour to reach agreement consistently with their declared policy with Indian delegates on as many points as possible'.[4] They would frame their proposals in the light of the agreements and try to defend them before the joint committee and in parliament. However, the agenda for the conference would be fixed by the government and the meetings would be held in camera. On 28 August Willingdon sounded Sapru on this proposal. Sapru had decided that he would not agree to anything 'which does not in substance restore us to the old basis of work, namely, equality of status and negotiation between Government and Indians on the basis of which the Bill should be introduced'.[5] He accepted Hoare's concession as consistent with these principles. Sastri thought that the old conference was now at an end, broken on the British side by the exclusion of non-government

[1] Hoare to Willingdon, 5 August 1932, T.C.L.B.
[2] Cited in viceroy to Sec. of S., 18 August 1932 (t/g), T.C.
[3] Ibid.
[4] Sec. of S. to viceroy, 24 August 1932 (t/g), T.C.
[5] Sapru to Haksar, 26 August 1932, S.C. 1, H. 92.

delegations, broken on the Indian side by the reduced membership, denied publicity and the freedom to frame its own agenda. However, he accepted the compromise. The National Liberal Federation welcomed it with relief but called for freedom of discussion. Of the Hindu communalists, Jayakar, Moonje, and Kelkar favoured co-operation, and the Mahasabha was not disposed to boycott the new style of conference.

Willingdon's government had secured a significant concession and retained the vital co-operation of the Hindu moderates. Despite the resurgence of reaction in the Indian Government's treatment of Congress and in the British Government's handling of constitutional reforms, the Round Table Conference experiment flickered back to life.

II. THE PLAY FOR SECTIONAL SUPPORT

Concern for the allegiance and co-operation of the Muslims was a leading motif of British policies from 1931. The policy of repression was argued from the need to reassure Muslim collaborators of the supremacy of the Raj and to prevent their desertion to the Congress as the presumed successor authority. At the second conference session Hoare argued the two-phase scheme from the need to give early satisfaction to Muslim claims for provincial autonomy. The prime minister's statement of 1 December and private intimations to Muslim delegates were intended to confirm that Sind and the N.W.F.P. would become full provinces and that Hindu opposition would not bar the settlement of the communal problem. As repression bit hard and Hindu moderates became antagonistic, Willingdon and Hoare fretted anxiously over Muslim discontents. Though Gandhi and the Mahasabhites had opposed the official determination of the communal issue, policy-makers were persuaded to issue an award in order to win Muslim co-operation with the Consultative Committee and the three expert committees.

The All-Parties Moslem Conference Working Committee met towards the end of January 1932. It shrank from supporting or opposing the new committees until the government had settled the Muslim claim to safeguards. Willingdon wrote of 'considerable feeling against co-operation with constitutional committees. ...Muslim position is unstable...and until representation in Punjab and Bengal has been settled, Muslims cannot tell whether their position will be safeguarded or not.'¹ The Aga Khan was agitating for a quick final settlement of the Sind question. Shaukat Ali was impatient for change in the Frontier Province in order to wrest it from the control of the Congress. On 22 February the Muslim members of the Consultative Committee refused to consider any question related to central responsibility until a communal decision was issued. The Committee was therefore adjourned for five months. On 6 March the Moslem Conference Working Committee advised all Muslim members of the Round Table Conference and its committees to withdraw their services until the demands of 1 January 1929 and 5 April 1931 were met. The previous evening Zafrullah, Shaukat, Shafa'at, Ghaznavi, and Sir Muhammad Khan had conveyed to Willingdon the acute disappointment of Muslims that despite their attendance at two Round Table Conferences their demands on Bengal and the Punjab remained unsatisfied. Willingdon was worried: 'The Muhammadans are the people who have mainly supported us through all these troubles, and I don't want to lose them if I can possibly avoid it.'² The full Moslem Conference was to meet at Lahore on 20 March. Willingdon persuaded Hoare to declare, on the eve of the Conference, that His Majesty's Government would issue an award. Somewhat reassured, the Moslem Conference deferred the question of boycotting the Federal Finance and Franchise Committees.

Hoare and Willingdon were concerned to appease the Muslims by the communal award of 16 August 1932. It was agreed very early that separate electorates should not be withdrawn without the consent of the community concerned and that Muslim weightage in the Hindu provinces should be preserved. For Bengal and the Punjab Hoare followed the principle of the Government of India's reforms dispatch of 20 September 1930: separate electorates should remain but they should not be capable of yielding Muslim majorities, which should depend upon the Muslims winning some of the special constituency seats, namely, those for the universities, landholders, commerce, and labour. In the Punjab, Hoare would give the Sikhs 18 per cent of the seats, and so arrange the remainder that the Muslims might reasonably expect to secure 51 per cent of the total. In Bengal,

---

[1] Viceroy to Sec. of S., 28 January 1932, Reforms 62/32.
[2] Willingdon to Hoare, 6 March 1932, T.C.L.B.

he would allocate the special interest seats and then divide the Hindu and Muslim seats on a population basis. Thereby the Muslims would enjoy more seats than the Hindus but the resident European community would hold the balance of power.

In the Punjab case there was no real difference between the views of Hoare, Willingdon, and the local government. The governor (de Montmorency) suggested that in a house of 175 seats the Muslim should get 86 (49 per cent). In addition they could expect to win three landholders' seats and one labour seat, bringing their total to 90 (51·4 per cent). The Hindus would secure about 27·42 per cent and the Sikhs 18·85 per cent of the seats. The viceroy endorsed the scheme and it passed into the award.

In the Bengal case a sharp controversy arose. Hoare's scheme provided for 250 seats, of which the Europeans would get 25 (eleven separate electorate and fourteen commercial), and the other special interests 26. The Muslims would have about 111 seats and the Hindus some 88. As the Muslims could not expect to win any of the special interest seats they would have only 44·4 per cent of the seats, though they accounted for 55 per cent of the population. The Hindus would probably get 42·8 per cent of the seats, which almost corresponded to their proportion of the population. Hoare's proposal coincided with the recommendations that the governor of Bengal (Sir Francis Jackson) had sent to Willingdon in January. Willingdon nevertheless considered it unfair to the Muslims and bound to be unpopular. He would give ten of the Hindus' seats (including two of their expected labour seats) to the Muslims. Thereby the Muslims would have 121 seats (48·4 per cent) and the Hindus 78 (39·2 per cent). Willingdon argued that Bengal was an all-India and not a merely local question. He had therefore taken the precaution of obtaining Fazl-i-Husain's assurance that the Muslims would accept his scheme. Anything less than he proposed would 'alienate us from Muslim support not merely in Bengal but throughout India':[1]

The Muslims attach the greatest importance to the Punjab and Bengal. These are the two matters that interest them profoundly. If they are seriously disappointed in either, I fear that their temper is such that

[1] Viceroy to Sec. of S., 9 July 1932 (t/g), T.C.

they will be swept into opposition.... We are dealing with people emotional, suspicious, apprehensive of their future and apt to be hasty in opinion and violent in action. If the Muslims are now carried away into opposition we shall be faced with a situation in this country which almost certainly will demand measures more drastic than any we have yet taken.[1]

Both Congress and the Hindu moderates were non-co-operating and 'if you give [the Muslims] less than . . . *I* propose for Bengal *I am quite certain* they will non-co-operate too'.[2] Willingdon issued a veiled threat: '. . . if owing to your decision I lost their support as well, I should probably have to ask you to send out someone else here to take up the role of Akbar which I have hitherto so inefficiently filled'.[3] Later in July Willingdon lost his head completely when the new governor of Bengal, Sir John Anderson (1932–7), lost his nerve. He backed Anderson's last-minute plea for a 51 per cent Muslim majority in Bengal for ten years, only to yield when Hoare argued that this would surely alienate the Hindus. The award gave the Muslims 48·6 per cent of the seats.

Sapru, Sastri, and Setalvad accepted the award as reasonable, realistic, and necessary. However, the Sikhs and the Punjab Hindus were dismayed. The Sikhs and Narendra Nath resigned from the constitutional committees. Jayakar and Kelkar expressed the Mahasabha's complaint that the award conceded communal representation unreservedly. However, Jayakar had no intention of not co-operating in the making of a constitution: 'Non-co-operation in an atmosphere like India's will never succeed. It is a double-edged political weapon, and our past experience of Congress activities proves that in most cases it is ineffectual.'[4] He refused the presidentship of the Mahasabha in order to leave it free to determine its attitude towards non-co-operation. Though the Mahasabha ultimately decided to boycott the award and the third conference, Jayakar and Moonje refused to let the Hindu case go by default, and both agreed to attend the third conference if invited.

The communal award consolidated Muslim loyalty to the

[1] Viceroy to Sec. of S., 10 July 1932 (t/g), T.C.
[2] Willingdon to Hoare, 10 July 1932, T.C.L.B.
[3] Ibid.
[4] Jayakar to Narendra Nath, 5 September 1932, J.C. 438.

Raj without alienating the co-operation of the Hindu Liberals, moderates, and leading communalists.

The government gave some solace to Sikh and Hindu dissidents by providing for the variation of the award if the communities themselves presented agreed alternative arrangements. In the last quarter of the year the Mahasabha, some Nationalist Muslims, and some members of the Moslem Conference tried desperately to reach agreement. Though a Unity Conference was held at Allahabad in November, the more representative Hindu and Muslim delegates soon absented themselves and the eventual agreement was repudiated by both sides. The government did not help matters by its determination that the conference should receive no credit for solving to the Muslims' advantage any question that it could solve itself. In order that the separation of Sind might not be presented as the bounty of Hindu generosity, it dropped a hint to the Aga Khan that the decision to create the new province would soon be announced.

In only one respect was the award varied by agreement between the interested parties: the novel concession of separate untouchable electorates was negotiated away. Gandhi had told the second Round Table Conference that he would resist this innovation with his life. In March 1932 he intimated to Hoare that he would fast unto death against separate untouchable electorates, which would 'vivisect and disrupt' Hinduism.[1] On 18 August he advised the prime minister that his fast would begin on 20 September. The Government of India prepared to move him from Yervada to a private residence for the duration of the fast, but he insisted upon remaining in gaol. He was given facilities for negotiations with Hindu leaders and the untouchables. After several days he concluded the Poona pact, which the government embodied in the award. Provisions for the reservation of seats to the untouchables replaced those for separate electorates.

In the light of the difficulties that he was suffering, Gandhi's negotiation of the Poona pact appears as an extraordinary achievement. The fast was a successful experiment in satyagraha for the sake of Indian unity. It was an epitome of his method and crucial to his objective. Separate electorates for the untouchables struck at the heart of Indian nationalism, the Hindu

[1] Gandhi to Hoare, 11 March 1932, Haig Coll. 1.

community. Yet even Nehru failed at first to see the wisdom of this fast unto death: '. . . I felt annoyed with him for choosing a side-issue for his final sacrifice—just a question of electorate. What would be the result on our freedom movement?'[1] Only after long reflection did Nehru realize the disastrous implications of separate untouchable electorates for Indian unity.

The resolution of the untouchable electorate problem offered momentary hope of a wider agreement between government and Congress. The home government was delighted at Gandhi's implicit acceptance of the official provision that the award could be modified only by agreement between the interested parties. Gandhi had worked the proposed machinery of modification by agreement, and the government construed this as a capitulation. Under pressure from Liberal Britons, Hoare began sounding Willingdon on 'negotiations with a view to abandonment of civil disobedience by agreement, with general release of prisoners'.[2] The appeal echoed an approach that Hoare had made in June, when the Archbishop of York had denounced the government's denying Gandhi any opportunity to sue for peace. Willingdon had then replied that Gandhi was free to express his views to the government; if he declined to do so 'on grounds of personal prestige, it merely shows that he is only prepared to negotiate with Government on equal terms'.[3] Negotiation would enhance Gandhi's prestige and unsettle the government's supporters. Now, in October, despite the prime minister's anxiety to improve relations with Gandhi, if necessary by releasing him, Willingdon remained implacably unconciliatory. He was following Haig's strategy: 'We must either stand firm or give away our whole position.'[4] He would not even set Gandhi free to campaign against the social evil of untouchability. The social reformer was indistinguishable from the rebel. His release would be hailed as a Congress victory, which would demoralize the government's supporters. The benefits of nine months' strong government would be lost. The prerequisite of peace was the repudiation of civil disobedience. When Sankey put this to

---

[1] J. Nehru, *Autobiography*, pp. 370–1.
[2] Sec. of S. to viceroy, 29 September 1932 (t/g), T.C.
[3] Viceroy to Sec. of S., 24 June 1932, Haig Coll. 1.
[4] Haig's notes and viceroy to Sec. of S., 1 October 1932, Haig Coll. 1.

Gandhi by cable, the reply was a bitter excoriation of government policy since December 1931:

... I returned here [to] promote peace as my speeches, private letters, talks in London and during return voyage will show. I had actually planned tour to that end. Sought interview with Viceroy and received highly discourteous reply attaching impossible conditions to grant of request for interview. Reply and scarcely veiled preparation pending arrest left me no course open but drawing up for Congress tentative programme of Civil Disobedience. Sequence of events shows that complete preparation including draft Ordinances while I was [in] London were made for execution of whole plan that followed. Conclusion irresistible that Indian Government representatives force crisis by provoking Congress to action any event.... Unnatural relations of conquerors and conquered must keep two peoples apart even as prisoners and their keepers are in reality apart though they are physically placed near one another. Through Civil Disobedience and kindred methods I am seeking might and main to bring two together by destroying unnatural relations.... Now therefore only honourable gesture I can make or is open to me is to drink cups of suffering to dregs.[1]

Britain had goaded Indians to break laws intended to humiliate them.

By late 1932 the disposition of forces between government and Congress had reverted to the alignment of early 1931. The Hindu Liberals and moderates and the Mahasabha leaders were co-operating, though with less enthusiasm, and the Muslims were more pro-government than ever. The commercial classes were also drawn towards negotiation.

Upon the revival of civil disobedience Schuster had argued the vital role of the commercial community and the legitimacy of its discontent: 'On the last occasion, without the adherence to Congress of the commercial community—especially in Bombay and Ahmedabad—the movement might have achieved little significance.'[2] In 1930 the community had joined Congress to oppose British fiscal and monetary policies. The tariff changes in 1931 had removed the substance of the cotton duties grievance but the currency complaint remained.

[1] In Bombay Spcl t/g to Home Dept. of Govt. of India, 15 November 1932, Haig Coll. 1.
[2] Schuster's note of January 1932, encl. to Willingdon to Hoare, 14 March 1932, T.C.L.B.

Since Britain had taken sterling and the rupee off the gold standard their gold value had fallen sharply. At the old gold standard value of sterling the rupee was now worth 1s. 1d. In effect sterling and the rupee had depreciated by some 30 per cent, which greatly enhanced the rupee earnings of India's agricultural exports. However, the improvement was insufficient to alleviate distress and it seemed quite likely to be short-lived. Suspicion was rife that Britain had manipulated the rupee in order to snatch the vast private hordes of Indian gold. In the first six months of floating the pound and the rupee, Britain shipped home £34m. in gold, bought from Indians taking quick rupee profits. The monetary experts on the India Council of the secretary of state, Sir Henry Strakosch and Sir Reginald Mant, reported in February 1932: '[Britain] has been able to use the gold for the discharge of its foreign obligations and to that extent to avoid impairment of its exchange with gold standard countries.'[1] In effect, India's gold stabilized sterling, thereby limiting the fall in the value of the rupee and the rise in the agriculturalists' rupee earnings. By March 1932 Indians were apprehensive of a recovery in sterling's gold value, and financiers, not unreasonably, were clamouring to be consulted about the empire's monetary policy.

Hoare was confident that imperial economic policies would bear the scrutiny of fair-minded Indian experts. The fiscal autonomy convention was an undeniable reality and there was 'not a shred of foundation for the belief that Indian financial policy is influenced by the interests of the City of London'.[2] Though the Federation of Indian Chambers of Commerce and Industry, adhering to its pro-Congress line, refused to co-operate with the Consultative Committee, Hoare denied that any conflict of interests made the mercantile community natural opponents of imperial policies. While early in 1932 he opposed a further Round Table Conference, he welcomed the Federation's demand for a committee of experts, British and Indian, to consider commerce and finance. In addition, he regarded the coming imperial conference at Ottawa as an opportunity for experts to concert mutually beneficial trade policies, which would prepare the way for a political *rapprochement*.

[1] H. Strakosch and R. A. Mant, 'The effect on India of the fall in prices and of British monetary policy', 8 February 1932, T.C.L.B.
[2] Hoare to Willingdon, 5 February 1932, T.C.L.B.

Hoare's assessment of the political predilections of Indian businessmen was shrewd. The steady growth of Nehru's socialist influence within the Congress posed a dilemma for nationalists who were committed to private enterprise. Birla, all of whose loyalty lay with Gandhi, believed that Nehru was 'losing faith in Gandhiji's methods and ideals', that 'Gandhiji's Swaraj no longer attracts him'.[1] Nehru seemed dedicated to the overthrow not only of the empire but also of vested interests within India. Birla and Thakurdas, to say nothing of less nationalistic entrepreneurs, saw advantage in co-operation. They might achieve not only trading concessions but also a say in monetary policy, from which might flow an exchange agreement favourable to agricultural exports. Nehru's success in mobilizing peasant opposition to the social and economic order owed much to low commodity prices. In May 1932 Birla and Thakurdas corresponded gloomily about the effect of the rate of exchange upon agriculture. Birla wrote of rural conditions deteriorating and Thakurdas feared an economic upheaval. Strakosch and Mant endorsed the mercantile community's reading of the economic situation and its consequences. They reported that during the two years ending in September 1931, the average fall in the price of India's main exports was 46 per cent. In most parts of India the peasant had begun to 'crack under the strain', and the popularity of Congress in the villages had increased accordingly.[2] Certainly the provincial authorities had made remissions, but the reduction of rents on the scale desirable would alienate landlords and cripple the local exchequers. An imperial monetary policy that would enhance commodity prices was essential.

The commercial community co-operated in developing an imperial tariff policy and its representatives attended the third Round Table Conference. This was contrary to the expectations of Willingdon, whose grasp of commercial opinion was limited. In June and July 1932 a strong contingent of Indian experts and British advisers attended the Imperial Economic Conference at Ottawa. Monetary as well as tariff policies were discussed. In September Strakosch and Schuster reported confidentially on the need for a monetary policy that would raise agricultural prices. The British Government accepted their arguments but

[1] Birla to Thakurdas, 28 June 1932, P.T.C. 107.
[2] Loc. cit.

left them for consideration in the context of financial safeguards at the third Round Table Conferece. While Birla's loyalty to Gandhi prevented his attending the conference, Thakurdas accepted the invitation that Hoare prodded Willingdon to extend. Willingdon's assumption that Thakurdas would be loth to co-operate had made him unwilling to risk a rebuff. He also misjudged Indian reaction to the Ottawa agreement, which conferred reciprocal trading benefits upon Britain and India through a scheme of imperial preferences. Contrary to his dismal forecasts, the central legislature ratified the agreement, much to the relief of Hoare, who predicted that its failure to do so might provoke Britain into postponing constitutional reforms.

The essentially Conservative government gave little away by agreeing to the third Round Table Conference. Yet it achieved impressive sectional support: from the commercial community, the Liberals, the Muslims, the Hindu moderates, the untouchables, and the leading Mahasabhites. Congress was effectively isolated from the other British Indian parties.

III. THE DIPLOMACY OF DRIFT

Congress was not the only absentee from the third conference. None of the princes, save Sarila, attended. This was a crucial failure of British diplomacy.

Ultimately, the princes' attitudes towards all-India federation were determined by their instinct for self-preservation. Hyderabad calculated that organic federation with a strong Crown element, plus the maintenance of paramountcy, were necessary to the survival of the dynasty as against British Indian encroachments; Bikaner, Bhopal, and the dominant Chamber group reasoned that, given substantial states' weightage in a federal legislature, organic federation minus paramountcy would enhance the princes' internal autonomy and external influence; Patiala, Dholpur, and many smaller states believed that a confederation as against British India was safer than organic federation. If Britain were ever to bring all-India federation into being her primary task was to convince a sufficient number of princes that their best chance of survival lay in their accession. This was no easy task when the princes differed fundamentally over constitutional structure. Their disagreements became sharper with each passing year. In 1932 the incompatibilities were palpable. A strategy of synthesis or syncretism became unrealistic. The situation called for a decision as to the demand that it was most politic to accommodate, followed by a campaign to ensure the accession of the princes who had pressed it. By the time of the third conference the Government of India had evidence sufficient for such a decision. Had they taken it and dispatched an authoritative states' delegation to the conference, then the putative federal structure could have been put to the touch. But the Government of India devised no strategy and allowed a low-powered states' delegation to foregather in London for discussions that brought accession no nearer.

On 20 and 21 February a gathering at Rajkot of some fifty rulers of Kathiawar, in western India, endorsed a draft presented by the Jam Sahib, Ranjitsinghji of Nawanagar. The draft opposed organic federation with British India as dangerous to the states, and proposed instead a Simonesque scheme for co-operative union of the states with British India for joint control of matters of common concern. It was largely the work of Professor L. F. Rushbrook Williams, once a joint secretary of the Standing Committee, now the adviser of the Jam Sahib. Williams explained the Rajkot initiative as the result of a growing distrust, among the generality of rulers, of the scheme for organic federation, together with a growing suspicion of commitments being made over their heads by a small Chamber clique:

At the time of the first Round Table Conference, federation seemed to show a way of escape from the unfettered and unrestricted exercise of those powers of Paramountcy which Sir Harcourt Butler and his colleagues declared to lie in the Crown's discretion. But now, the Princes have come to see that the cure may be worse than the disease: and that an alliance with British Indian politicians, though it may break Paramountcy, may break the States as well.

[The rank and file] did not clearly understand what was happening: they only saw that the dominant Bhopal–Bikaner groups were in the hands of advisers whose sympathies and connections with British India were obvious.[1]

The Jam Sahib planned an appeal to the Crown to safeguard the position of the states against British India within a limited

[1] Williams to Hoare, 3 March and 1 April 1932, I. O., L/PO/58.

Indian union. He believed his position to be similar to Hyderabad's and he called upon Keyes for an alliance:

> I think that ... you will see how nearly our ideas coincide. We both believe in the continued existence of monarchy: we both believe in the survival of the States. ... We both believe—and here we differ from British India—in the retention by the Crown and by the ... Crown's representative, the Viceroy, of complete and unfettered control over the Army, Foreign Affairs, and the Financial essentials upon which this control also depends.[1]

However, the Jam Sahib's advocacy of 'two Indias' alienated Keyes, who still believed that the Crown would be unable to prevent a discrete British India from overpowering the states.

The dominant Chamber group, led by Bikaner and Bhopal, could not be other than disturbed by the growing dissent from the federal formula. The smaller states' fears of the 'octopus embrace'[2] of British India in an organic federation were amply evidenced by the support that the Patiala–Dholpur and Rajkot schemes had attracted. The Bikaner–Bhopal group had to come to terms with the dissidents. On 11 March a number of princes and ministers met at Delhi and set up a committee of ministers 'for the purpose of reconciliation, as far as possible, in the different schemes for associating the States with the proposals for all-India constitutional reforms'.[3] The result of the deliberations of the committee and, subsequently, of the Chamber of Princes, was the healing of the federation–confederation breach and the unanimous acceptance of the principle of all-India federation subject to certain safeguards. The agreement was aided by a judicious arrangement of honours. Bikaner and Patiala accepted that neither they nor their immediate followers should be Chancellor in the current year, though Patiala was to hold that office in 1933–4. The importance of the Jam Sahib's recent initiative was recognized by his elevation to the chancellorship for 1932–3.

On 1 April the healing resolution was proposed by Bhopal and seconded by Patiala:

> This Chamber declares that the States will join an all-India Federation

---

[1] Jam Sahib to Keyes, 21 March 1932, K.C. 31.
[2] Williams to Hoare, 3 March 1932, loc. cit.
[3] Chamber of Princes' circular regarding the 'Delhi Pact', cited in U. Phadnis, *Towards the Integration of the Indian States, 1919–47*, London, 1968, p. 65.

The Resurgence of Reaction

on the assumption that the Crown will accept responsibility for securing to them the following guarantees:
(a) that the necessary safeguards will be embodied in the constitution;
(b) that under the constitution their rights arising from Treaties, or Sanads or Engagements, remain inviolate and inviolable;
(c) that the sovereignty and internal independence of the States remain intact and are preserved and fully respected and that the obligations of the Crown to the States remain unaltered.[1]

The states should be able to enter the federation singly or in confederal groups.

The Jam Sahib and Patiala, the spokesmen for those rulers who had opposed organic federation because of their fear of British Indian infringements of their sovereignty, had agreed to federation provided that the Crown guaranteed their internal autonomy. Bikaner and Bhopal had conceded the chancellorship to them for the next two years but won approval for organic federation and the embodiment in the constitution of their treaty rights as against the paramount power. Whereas the former group emphasized the need for protection by the Crown, the latter stressed security against Crown interference. The Chamber authorized Krishnamachari (diwan of Baroda), Manubhai Mehta (diwan of Bikaner), Liaquat Hyat Khan (prime minister of Patiala), and Haksar to carry on negotiations with a view to federation. The princes' pact was really a victory for the Bhopal–Bikaner federationists. Haksar and Sapru congratulated themselves upon the rout of the wreckers of federation.

The Political Department regarded the resolution of 1 April as a substantial step towards federation. Willingdon communicated his advisers' views to Hoare. The princes were 'unanimously committed to federation'.[2] They had advanced beyond their stand at the Round Table Conferences. '... the Princes as a whole now feel that Federation, in some form, is inevitable, and that, if a reasonable scheme emerges, it must be accepted, even if they are not altogether satisfied with the details.'[3] It remained to produce a detailed scheme of representation, for on that question the states were deeply divided. Willingdon urged the importance of making the scheme attractive to the large states.

---
[1] Progs of Chamber of Princes, 1 April 1932, Reforms 249/32.
[2] Willingdon to Hoare, 13 April 1932, T.C.L.B.
[3] Viceroy to Sec. of S., 3 May 1932 (t/g), T.C.

The Political Department set to work in May. However, other aspects of the states problem assumed priority.

When Willingdon suggested to the Jam Sahib that the princes should come to grips with federation in some detail, the new Chancellor responded by summoning them to a meeting at Bombay on 6 May. The Jam Sahib's draft agenda stressed the need for the states as a whole to consider federal questions, and especially to define their attitude towards the safeguards and guarantees that were essential to their safety in a federation. He expressed concern that few states other than those represented on the Standing Committee or at the Round Table Conference were familiar with the problems in federation. Here was an appeal beyond the Standing Committee, emphasizing the difficulties in federation. Haksar saw it as backsliding from the Delhi resolution, as 'a subtle yet transparent attempt to arouse the apprehensions of the Princes to the end of causing hesitation in their minds for entering the Federation'.[1] At the Bombay meeting the leading members of the Standing Committee—Bikaner, Bhopal, and Patiala—rehabilitated the Delhi resolution, though a list of *sine qua nons* was agreed.

During the next few months the Jam Sahib stressed that the value of the safeguards of the states' integrity would depend upon the Crown's observance and enforcement of the agreement in which they were to be embodied. In the past the Crown had violated agreements with the states by reference to the false doctrine of paramountcy. The doctrine of paramountcy was therefore as relevant to the interpretation of safeguards in a future all-India federal constitution as it had been to the interpretation of treaties in the past. Unless the princes could obtain satisfaction over the false doctrine of paramountcy by the Crown's acceptance of a Scott type of interpretation of treaties, the princes' safeguards in the new constitution would be worthless. On 5 July the Jam Sahib addressed the other princes of the Standing Committee: '... we ought to inform the authorities in England tactfully but firmly that we can agree to no understanding concerning our entry into federation until and unless our views regarding the false doctrine of paramountcy are effectively met.'[2] Disputes concerning the states' sovereignty

[1] Haksar to Sapru, 4 May 1932, S.C. 1, H. 61.
[2] Jam Sahib to Standing Committee, 5 July 1932, I. O., L/PO/92.

should be referred to impartial tribunals, whose findings would be enforceable by the Crown. As Hoare was advised by the India Office: '[The Jam Sahib is] out to block *all* progress until [the princes] get a decision on paramountcy under which Government would bind itself to implement, possibly by the use of its armed forces, decisions on political matters by an independent tribunal, for which Government had no responsibility and which it might regard as wrong and dangerous.'[1] The Jam Sahib pressed Bikaner, Bhopal, and Patiala again and again to endorse the position that he had assumed. On their behalf, Haksar answered his fourth letter on the question: 'It is not our position that we decline to discuss further the Federation scheme, although it is our position that we shall not enter Federation unless Government settles the Paramountcy question to our satisfaction.'[2] Their emphasis was upon obtaining an assurance that the Crown would not itself infringe the states' sovereignty; the Jam Sahib's was upon binding the Crown to enforce safeguards of internal sovereignty. The distinction underlines the continuing contrast between the medium-sized states' fears of Crown encroachments and the small states' apprehension of British India's 'octopus embrace'. The Jam Sahib's April compromise with the Standing Committee over all-India federation, to which he was in reality opposed, had produced his curious distortion of the Chamber's basic grievance: paramountcy. Paradoxically, the Jam Sahib's preoccupation with 'the false doctrine of paramountcy' in mid-1932 is indicative of the small states' realization that their survival depended upon the continuing authority of the Crown.

Hyderabad, which was no less preoccupied with the protection of its sovereignty by the Crown, approached the question of paramountcy in another way. Hyderabad referred to the London solicitors, Chance, Coward and Co., for the opinion of Counsel, a treaty of accession that Manubhai Mehta had drafted. Stafford Cripps was asked for advice upon the protection that the treaty would afford to Hyderabad's sovereignty. Hitherto, Hyderabad had assumed that the Crown would have power to maintain the states' sovereignty within the federation. In the field of federal jurisdiction it had assumed that treaties with the

[1] F. Stewart to Hoare, 15 August 1932, ibid.
[2] Cited in Haksar to Sapru, 4 September 1932, S.C. 1, H. 95.

Crown would take precedence over decisions of the federal legislature. Chance, Coward and Co. believed that once the states yielded powers over certain matters to the federal authority their sovereignty over them would disappear: 'Sovereignty connotes the fact of supremacy, and once the fact of supremacy ceases to be, Sovereignty must disappear.'[1] In the federal field there must be a loss of sovereignty. However, as Hyderabad had always insisted upon limiting the number of federal subjects severely, the loss might well have seemed tolerable.

Cripps's opinion pointed out a more alarming consequence of accession: the dual nature of the Crown under a federal constitution. The Nizam had assumed that outside the federal field his treaties would remain in force. He would be able to call upon the Crown's representative, the viceroy, to enforce his treaty rights, including protection against external aggression or internal usurpation. Cripps shook such complacency by revealing the multiple personality of the Crown. Under the *status quo* the Crown was the Crown advised by responsible ministers in the United Kingdom, and so it would remain in respect of reserved subjects: defence and foreign affairs. However, in respect of subjects transferred to a responsible federal government, the Crown would become the Crown as advised by responsible Indian ministers. The F.S.C. envisaged that in due course, after a suitable period of transition, India would become a fully self-governing dominion, without reserved subjects. At that stage all material power in India would fall to the Crown as advised by the federal government. The princes' treaties would still be treaties with the Crown in England, and the Crown's relations with the states might still be conducted by the viceroy as the Crown's representative. But the viceroy would not possess the material power to protect the princes.

Cripps's opinion led the Nizam to insist that the Crown in India must, as far as the states were concerned, remain the Crown in the United Kingdom, with power to discharge its responsibilities to the states. On 1 August he told the viceroy that he refused to contemplate any end to the period of transition after which the army was to be transferred to Indian control.

---

[1] Cited in Keyes to Glancy, 16 September 1932, K.C. 31. Also Coward, Chance and Co. to Hydari, 22 and 29 July, and Opinion of S. Cripps and A. P. Fachini, 29 July 1932, K.C. 30.

In September Willingdon called together at Simla thirteen princes and the ministers of as many others. His agenda for the meetings, which were held from the 20th to the 22nd, comprised the major outstanding federal questions: representation, finance, paramountcy, and the sovereignty of the states under federation. However, it became patently clear that progress with federal finance and representation must await a conference with British Indian delegates. The Percy and Davidson committee reports had aroused strong feelings in British India as well as the states over the vexed question of the states' contribution to the federal budget. Legislative representation involved the knotty problem of communal as well as states' weightage. Willingdon postponed these items for determination by the India Committee of Cabinet and the Round Table Conference. The Simla conference concentrated upon paramountcy and the related question of the states' sovereignty.

It was obvious that federation would affect the operation of paramountcy in subjects over which the princes ceded powers to the new all-India authorities. The Government of India held that paramountcy would lapse in such cases. Treaties relating to them would be redrawn accordingly. However, the Jam Sahib regarded treaties as 'inviolate and inviolable'. He held that even in federal subjects the states might question policies that violated a treaty in the letter or in spirit, and enjoy the right of appeal to an impartial tribunal whose decisions should be binding on the Crown. Akbar Hydari, evincing a similar concern to protect the states' sovereignty, argued for the persistence of paramountcy over federal subjects. Such views were extreme. Virtually all princes accepted the need for a revision of treaties and the sole jurisdiction of the new authority over federal subjects, though the creation of a federal court to hear disputes was assumed.

The relationship between paramountcy and non-federal subjects is less obvious. In theory, paramountcy in the non-federal field was not affected by federation, and the Government of India therefore saw no cause to define it. In practice, a federal authority with a strong British Indian element was likely to weaken the Crown's capacity or inclination to safeguard the states. For this reason the Jam Sahib again demanded a definition of paramountcy that would make alleged breaches of treaty

278   *The Resurgence of Reaction*

obligations referable to impartial tribunals whose decisions the Crown was bound to enforce. He was alone in refusing to negotiate about federation until he won this point. However, Hydari and others shared his concern for the Crown's protection of the states, though it led them to the contrary conclusion: that paramountcy must remain undefined.

The main significance of the Simla conference is that it emphasized the cleavage between the states that followed Hydari in upholding the Crown's discretionary right to interfere in non-federal matters, and those that supported the Bikaner–Bhopal–Standing Committee demand for the limitation of the right of interference as a prerequisite of the princes' accession to federation. The former group 'realized that an abdication by the Crown might in the long run be fatal to their future existence as separate political entities'.[1] The latter continued to argue as it had done since the first Round Table Conference. Willingdon commented:

Generally the conference showed the wide cleavage between the Bikaner–Bhopal group on the one hand and the majority of important states and a large number of smaller states on the other.

It seems to me that there is a great deal of feeling among the greater number of Princes owing to the fact that the Standing Committee of the Chamber of Princes has for long years been a very close corporation, largely controlled by Bikaner, Bhopal and Patiala. This was certainly shown at our Conference, for the Standing Committee were there as an executive body of the Chamber, and there was no doubt during the discussions of the feeling against them among the Princes and their representatives as a whole.[2]

Haksar was contemptuous of Hydari. From the surprised tone of his observations it seems that he now realized for the first time the true nature of Hyderabad's stand: '[Hydari's] position is not so much that the British, by virtue of their Treaties, are entitled to protect the States, but that Hyderabad has the right to insist that they should remain here practically in their present position, in order to prevent that State from being swallowed up

---

[1] Secretary For. and Pol. Dept. of Govt. of India to Sec. Pol. Dept. at I. O., 14 November 1932, Reforms 248/32.
[2] Viceroy to Sec. of S., 28 September 1932 (t/g), Reforms 248/32; Willingdon to Hoare, 26 September 1932, T.C.L.B.

... by the monster of British India.'[1] It became clear that the Standing Committee's attempt to restrict paramountcy did not command the support of a majority of the delegates at Simla.[2] But it was equally clear that the Committee was unlikely to yield what it had always represented as the cardinal condition of all-India federation.

The Standing Committee left Simla defeated. The Conference agreed to the Crown retaining discretionary powers over misgovernment within a state, disputed successions, and minority administrations. The viceroy should be free to deal with disputes between states, between states and provinces, and between states and the federal authority over non-federal matters. The conflict between the Standing Committee and the Government of India over paramountcy was reduced appreciably; it now concerned only that class of disputes between a state and the Crown which was deemed 'justiciable'. The latter term had never been defined precisely but now it connoted disputes in the non-federal field in which the Crown was both judge and party. The Standing Committee maintained that such disputes should not be subject to viceregal decision but should be referred to *ad hoc* tribunals whose decisions should bind the state and the Crown. Finally, agreement was reached that justiciable issues should be referred to tribunals but that the findings should not fetter the viceroy. However, soon after the conference the viceroy received intimations from some states that they disapproved of his being obliged to refer issues to tribunals. The home government ruled that no dispute in the non-federal field should be subject to compulsory arbitration. The point remained at issue between the Standing Committee and the British Government.

At the end of September the viceroy-in-council decided the means of selecting the states' representatives for the third Round Table Conference. Willingdon and Hoare had agreed upon an Indian delegation of thirty-six members, twelve of them from the states. The unpopularity of the Standing Committee at Simla meant that it could not again be accorded the preponderance that it had enjoyed at the earlier conferences. The Government of India chose twelve states that seemed to reflect the spectrum of attitudes towards federation and invited their rulers to attend

[1] Haksar to Sapru, 5 October 1932, S.C. 1, H. 99.
[2] Sec. F. and P.D. to Sec. P.D.I.O., 14 November 1932, loc. cit.

the conference themselves or to nominate ministerial delegates. Haksar was mortally offended by the procedure, which prevented his attending the Conference. A more serious effect was that none of the princes save Sarila chose to attend in person, though the Jam Sahib was to be in London during the Conference. In September Bikaner, Bhopal, and Patiala had decided to send ministerial delegates but to go to London to advise them behind the scenes. However, when the Resident of Patiala counselled restraining him from leaving India in view of his financial difficulties, the maharaja persuaded Bikaner and Bhopal to stay behind too. Surprisingly, for he had earlier stressed the need for joint deliberations between the states and British India over finance and representation, Willingdon advised Hoare of his satisfaction with the states' delegation. The ministers of Hyderabad, Mysore, Travancore, and Baroda would enjoy plenipotentiary status. As the rulers of Kashmir, Kolhapur, Jaipur, Jodhpur, and Udaipur had been unwilling to go to London, their nomination of ministers was the most that could have been achieved. As for Bikaner and Bhopal, they were so committed to federation that their absence would be of little account; it would, indeed, ensure that the paramountcy question was not pressed. In October Willingdon was extraordinarily over-confident: '[The Princes] are committed to Federation to such an extent that it should not be difficult to show them that it is not to their advantage to withdraw now.'[1]

The Jam Sahib saw Hoare in October and argued that the princes' abstention would be fatal to the conference. As the ministers were powerless to take decisions binding on their states no agreement of substance seemed possible. At Hoare's behest Willingdon now scrambled to send Bikaner, Bhopal, Dholpur, Kashmir, and Rewa to London; but only Rewa went. Willingdon explained that the princes shrank from attending because they wished to avoid pressure for promises to accede to federation. Yet he believed that Hyderabad, Mysore, Travancore, and Baroda would be bound to join any reasonable federation by dint of pressure from their subjects, while the other princes would not find their advantage served by resilement. In the event, the princes' absence prevented the conference from achieving agreement upon federal finance and representation.

[1] Viceroy to Sec. of S., 28 October 1932, For. and Pol. Reforms 137/32.

The Resurgence of Reaction

During November, on the eve of the conference, Hoare and the India Committee of Cabinet considered the extent to which the creation of federation should depend upon the agreement of the states. Hoare interpreted the federal formula to mean that there should be no central responsibility until a prescribed number or proportion of princes had acceded. Neither of the previous sessions of the conference had discussed the quantification of the prerequisite, though Hydari had voiced the common assumption that one half of the states' people should be covered by the accessions. Hoare now argued that as the eight largest states accounted for one half of the princes' subjects some regard may need to be taken of the number of states. In April Bikaner had told the Bombay gathering of states that 'if you are going to have federation of the States ... we must really have a majority of the States entering'.[1] Hoare expressed the requisite accessions in terms of 'States with an aggregate of over fifty per cent of [the] total States' population, provided that they include not less than half of [the] States individually represented in the Upper [Federal] Chamber'.[2] The membership of the latter had, of course, still to be decided.

In early December Hoare discerned a serious weakness in his formulation: on the one hand it would expose federation to the risk of being torpedoed by the Standing Committee, which might non-co-operate over paramountcy or representation, and which would probably command a majority among the states in the upper house; on the other hand, federation might be defeated by a few large states comprising the majority of the population. He now put an either/or formulation to Willingdon: the accession should be required of states either representing one half of the population or commanding a majority of the seats in the upper house. The Government of India demurred, apprehending that a federation pursuant to the latter proviso might be an alliance of the British Indian politicians and the Standing Committee and its adherents. As the Standing Committee group was open to influence and infiltration from British India, the princes' accession might well fail to provide the federation with the desired element of stability: 'In our opinion the adherence of a sufficient number of the *important* states is necessary for Federation

[1] Bikaner's speech to Chamber of Princes, 1 April 1932, Reforms 249/32.
[2] Sec. of S. to viceroy, 21 November 1932 (t/g), ibid.

to be launched successfully and your original formula appears to express this position. If important States come in smaller units must ultimately adhere.'¹ Hoare dropped his revised proposal. He thereby detonated, somewhat perfunctorily, a torpedo that could explode the whole structure of all-India federation. For in view of the general expectation about the membership of the upper house, his original formula tied federation to the whim of the Standing Committee group. It was assumed by the F.S.C. and the Lothian committee that the upper chamber should be a states' house, providing individual representation to as many states of rank as possible. The assumption might be controverted and representation in the upper house might be related to population. Alternatively, the states' house might be made a small chamber in which only the leading princes enjoyed individual representation. The decisions upon the form and size of the upper house would now be of strategic importance to the emergence of an all-India federation. The diplomatic significance that attached to them transcended their constitutional function. Unfortunately, Willingdon and the Political Department were far from consummate diplomatists.

The Government of India's treatment of the states question during 1932 is open to criticism in several respects. Early in the year Hoare commented: 'Almost everyone who visits me from India and talks to me about our relations with the States says that the Political Department wants a stronger personnel at the top.'² J. C. C. Davidson's letters home to Baldwin were scornful of the Political Service and the government's handling of federation:

I have been most deeply impressed by the exceedingly low standard of the Indian political service. The Residents at Hyderabad and Mysore and the A.G.G.³ here [Travancore] are completely worked out and largely passengers waiting to disembark at the earliest possible moment.

Federation is not the policy of the Government of India, and they dislike it.

If the Viceroy had only grasped what in fact was the policy of His

---

[1] Viceroy to Sec. of S., 9 December 1932 (t/g), ibid.
[2] Hoare to Willingdon, 22 April 1932, T.C.L.B.
[3] A.G.G. = Agent to the governor-general.

Majesty's Government and if the political officers from the A.G.G.'s downwards had been given instructions as to the policy they were to preach, the situation would have been very different. Directly I get home I hope that Sam [Hoare] and the India Committee of the Cabinet will decide what policies are to be preached in India and make the A.G.G.'s and political officers go full steam ahead to prepare the ground on the lines of the policy which will then have been decided.[1]

Willingdon's correspondence with Hoare reveals clearly that the Political Department failed to develop an effective policy and impress it upon him. The Political Secretary, Sir Charles Watson, had probably not changed his original opinion that the federation of British India and the princely states was 'impracticable'. After the recoil of the princes at the second Round Table Conference the Government of India had criticized the policy of yoking progress in British India to the whims of the princes. On the eve of the third conference it lacked the will to develop a diplomacy to deal with the princes.

Willingdon himself failed to steer a steady course, vacillating between unthinking pessimism and exuberant optimism. After the second conference he observed that the princes' attachment to federation had weakened appreciably. A few months later he remarked that the princes were too deeply committed to federation to resile. At the close of the second conference he opposed granting them a virtual veto on British India's advance to central responsibility; yet on the eve of the third he rejected Hoare's either/or formula, which seemed likely to keep the veto out of the control of the Standing Committee. His rejection therefore enhanced the Standing Committee's ability to demand the definition of paramountcy as a condition of accession; yet he had resisted the demand vigorously. He stressed the need for a London conference that would confront the states and British India with the outstanding problems of federation, principally, finance and representation; yet he weakly acquiesced in the abstention from the Round Table Conference of the princes, without whom no negotiations could be concluded. He took refuge in the comfortable assumption that the pressure of public opinion would drive the great princes into federation and that

---

[1] Davidson to Baldwin, 13 February, 28 March and 5 April 1932, in R. R. James, *Memoirs of a Conservative: J. C. C. Davidson's Memoirs and Papers, 1910–37*, London, 1969, pp. 390, 391; and Middlemas and Barnes, *Baldwin*, p. 704.

the lesser potentates would have to follow them; yet the large states looked to the Crown for protection against the hostility of their subjects. A federal structure attractive to the princes was essential if Willingdon's assumption about the princes' probable accession was to prove tenable; yet on the eve of the third conference Willingdon's government failed to send home any guidance on the relative attractiveness of the possible forms and sizes of the upper house.

The fruits of Willingdon's diplomacy of drift began to be reaped at the third session of the Round Table Conference.

IV. THE VESTIGIAL CONFERENCE

The third Round Table Conference opened on 17 November and closed on Christmas Eve. It was attended by the eight members of the India Committee of Cabinet, except that R. A. Butler, Hoare's under-secretary, replaced Runciman, and by four party representatives, Reading and Lothian, and Peel and Winterton. Hoare offered representation to the Labour party, with the provisos that the delegates must be members of parliament and that the government would decide the agenda. However, at its annual conference in October the party resolved to abstain, reserving its comment until the joint committee stage. Ten states' ministers attended but Sarila was the only prince. The Aga Khan, Ghaznavi, Iqbal, Begum Shah Nawaz, Shafa'at Ahmad Khan, and Zafrullah Khan represented the Muslims; Jayakar, Kelkar, and Nanak Chand (from the Punjab) the Hindu communalists; and Tara Singh the Sikhs. Sapru was present, but of the Liberals only Sir Cowasji Jehangir was invited. The minor minorities were again represented: the untouchables (by Ambedkar), the non-Brahmans (by Patro and Mudaliyar), the European community (by Carr), and the Anglo-Indians (by Gidney). Thakurdas attended for the mercantile community, Joshi for labour, and the landholders were represented. All told, there were 46 delegates, as against some 112 at the previous session. The conference was much more tightly controlled than its predecessors. Sankey had already prepared a bill embodying 'Proposals for a Federal Constitution' (d. 30 July) that Hoare and the Cabinet Committee had scrutinized during October. Hoare knew exactly what he wanted from the conference and he imposed his own agenda upon it.

At the outset the states' ministers told Hoare that they had 'explicit instructions not to commit their rulers too far'.[1] Hydari carried a precise brief from the Nizam, stating, in particular, that 'nothing should be done to impair in India in any way the Supremacy of the Crown in the United Kingdom, since any invasion of that Supremacy will inevitably react on its ability to protect my Dynasty and my Dominions'.[2] The Crown must not be advised by Indian ministers in the reserved sphere, while outside the federal sphere it must be held to its existing obligations, retaining power to secure the states' treaty rights. Hyderabad favoured the immediate creation of a federal council to advise the viceroy on matters that would become federal, and they should be limited to the subjects so defined by the F.S.C. The federal legislature must be stable and should reflect the size, population, and revenue of the various states. The upper house should have no more than 200 seats and the lower no more than 300. The Nizam also required assurance of the financial viability of federation and demanded the separation of Berar from the C.P. and its constitution as a federal unit.

Hydari played a leading part at the conference, marshalling the support of the ministers of the large states for small federal chambers. On 10 December he told Hoare that Hyderabad, Mysore, and Baroda, and probably Jodhpur and Udaipur, wanted the upper house to be less than 200 strong, with half of the seats going to the states. They opposed equal representation as between states in the upper house, which should reflect the size and importance of each state. This principle could well mean a house of far fewer than 200 seats, with the great preponderance of states being denied individual representation. Mirza Ismail favoured a house of only sixty members. Hoare himself had 'always preferred Hydari's idea of a small Chamber or Chambers', which would operate as expert bodies dealing effectively with specific administrative problems, rather than as political assemblies.[3]

The Standing Committee group favoured Bikaner's scheme for an upper house of 250 seats, with about half of them falling to the states in much the same way that the 120 seats in the

[1] Hoare to Willingdon, 18 November 1932, T.C.L.B.
[2] Nizam's firman to Hyderabad delegation, 24 October 1932, Reforms 205/32.
[3] Hoare to Willingdon, 1 April 1932, T.C.L.B.

Chamber of Princes were distributed. The 108 princes with individual seats in the Chamber would be similarly represented in the upper house. As Sir Reginald Glancy had observed in June: 'Failure to secure direct representation is regarded by most of the medium and smaller States as the first step on the road to their extinction. . . .'[1] Of course the very small states had no hope of individual representation. Many of them favoured a small upper house, in which their interests were less likely to be prejudiced by the solidarity of the medium-sized Chamber states.

Nor could the states agree over the proportion of federal seats that they wished to claim as against British India. In private discussions some ministers accepted less than parity, but none would do so publicly.

Towards the end of the conference Sapru wrote to Haksar 'full of apprehensions and fears':

I cannot say that the Princes have played the game as I expected them to do. The result will be further estrangement between British India and the States in future. Meanwhile, they seem to be justifying the official view, that they are speaking with double voices. With one to us and with the other to the Government. The whole thing is a sickening business.[2]

Similarly, Reading wrote of the princes: 'One cannot but feel some apprehension in view of the contradictory statements that keep recurring.'[3] Sir Maurice Gwyer, the official solicitor whose drafting skill was brought to bear on the India bill, noted that the 'States seem to have receded from the position which they had taken up earlier, . . . and the links which will bind them to the Federation are becoming a little tenuous'.[4]

Sapru was alarmed at the possibility of the states' failure to accede delaying federation indefinitely. His remedy was to write an accession deadline into the bill. If sufficient princes had not joined within one year a British Indian federation should be set up. The suggestion was no more acceptable to the government than had been Willingdon's proposal for central responsibility

---

[1] Glancy's note on 'Representation of States in the Upper House of the Federal Legislature', [June] 1932, I. O., L/PO/58.
[2] Sapru to Haksar, 9 December 1932, S.C. 1, H. 105.
[3] Reading to Hailey, 6 February 1933, R.C. 56 k.
[4] Gwyer to Keyes, 16 December 1932, K.C. 31.

in British India. Hoare shrank from confronting the princes with anything resembling an ultimatum. He argued disingenuously that the nomination of a deadline might delay the earlier creation of a federation. However, he was aghast at the prospect of princely intransigence undoing the years of work that had gone into the making of the India bill.

There was every reason for worry. Three Round Table Conferences and many less formal gatherings had failed to produce a federal structure with attractions sufficient to ensure the princely accessions that were required for India's safe and steady advance to central responsibility. At the close of the third session Hoare was backing away from the Lothian committee's scheme for an upper house of 250 members and a lower house of 450, towards the earlier F.S.C. plan for 200- and 300-member chambers. Bikaner and his friends would simply have to pocket their preferences. With the process of consultation at an end Hoare was still groping for acceptable solutions to vital problems.

The states question apart, the third conference was concerned mainly with the distribution of powers between the centre and the provinces, and between the governor-general and responsible Indian ministers. The Hindu–Muslim dispute over residuary powers was not resolved. As for reserve powers, the government insisted upon defence and external relations remaining with officials appointed by the governor-general, who was ultimately responsible to the home government. Hoare noted privately that external relations could not be transferred 'within any measurable time'.[1] Sapru and Jayakar pressed in vain for the defence minister to be an Indian. With regard to finance, in September Hoare and the India Committee of Cabinet had favoured reservation. The world financial situation seemed too precarious to permit control to pass into Indian hands. Hailey contested this proposition vigorously and successfully, arguing that unless finance were transferred there could be no effective responsibility in any department of state. However, he accepted that the establishment of a reserve bank to control India's currency and exchange should be a precondition of financial responsibility; and that the governor-general, with a financial adviser, should have a special responsibility for the financial stability and credit of India. Sapru, Jayakar, and Thakurdas questioned these

[1] Hoare to Willingdon, 18 November 1932, T.C.L.B.

arrangements. Hoare sent them off for discussions with Montagu Norman, governor of the Bank of England, and other City gentlemen. They eventually accepted the need for a reserve bank, insisting only that delay in setting it up should not be allowed to retard federation. The other special responsibilities assigned to the governor-general (and the governors) were for peace and tranquillity, the protection of the minorities and the rights of the states and the services, and the prevention of commercial discrimination. The governor-general was to intervene in only the law-and-order field of provincial administration, and then only to counter menaces to India's internal security.

The conference achieved little by way of agreed solutions to the outstanding constitutional problems. After its closure Jayakar and Sapru submitted for publication with the proceedings a memorandum listing the demands to which they had been unable to obtain official agreement.[1] However, the government might now feel reasonably confident that its proposals would be accepted, if grudgingly, by British Indian moderates.

The conference cleared the way for the measured series of stages necessary to parliamentary legislation. The government would prepare a white paper embodying its proposals. The paper would be presented to parliament. A joint committee of both houses would, after hearing witnesses, report back to parliament on the proposed legislation. Finally, a bill would be prepared and presented for parliament's approval.

V. UNREPENTANT REPRESSION

As far as the Government of India's policy towards the Congress was concerned the year 1932 ended as it began. In his final speech at the third conference Hoare promised that full consideration would be given to an appeal that Sapru had made for the release of Gandhi and the civil disobedience prisoners. In a private cable to Willingdon he urged that upon their return Sapru and Jayakar should be allowed to meet Gandhi in order to acquaint him of the results of the conference. In the Home Department Haig took stock. The local governments and the viceroy's executive were consulted. Officialdom closed its ranks. The supremacy of the bureaucracy over Congress was asserted

[1] Sapru and Jayakar to R. A. Carter, 26 December 1931, S.C. 2, C. 13.

as vigorously in India as the supremacy of the government over the conference delegates had been in England.

Haig advised the viceroy's private secretary of his immediate response: 'I am seriously disturbed with Secretary of State's speech and general atmosphere which appears to prevail in England of trying to seek agreement with Congress.'[1] He at once penned a note on Gandhi and the Congress for circulation to his colleagues. He averred that an agreement with Congress was not only unnecessary for the launching of the new constitution, but would set up 'conditions ... which might in certain Provinces wreck the constitution at the outset'.[2] At the first elections in some provinces Congress would overwhelm the moderate parties and destroy the constitution. On the other hand, if Congress were ignored for the moment a right-wing faction would emerge and coalesce with the moderates, providing strong parties willing to work the constitution.

Haig elaborated on a theme that had become familiar:

If the opponents of Congress are once thoroughly disheartened, as they will be if Government again saves the battered reputation of Congress, they will never recover and Congress will be established in unchallenged supremacy.... If Congress prestige is restored, I should imagine they would try to build up their position by the methods used successfully in 1931 after the Pact.... Any idea ... that it would be possible to reach a 'gentlemen's agreement' with the Congress I regard as fantastic.

If Gandhi were freed, so must be 17,000 of his followers, with dire results for the U.P., where the 'fanatical' Jawaharlal would soon be at work, and for the N.W.F.P., given the influence of Abdul Ghaffar. Even 1930-style gaol *pourparlers* would damage government credit and suggest official weakness. The repetition of the methods of 1930–1 would replicate their results:

My general conclusion is that we should not now be afraid of our own policy just as it appears to be succeeding. We can, in my view, do without the goodwill of Congress, and in fact I do not believe for a moment that we shall ever have it, but we cannot afford to do without the confidence of those who have supported us in the long struggle against the Congress.

[1] Haig to P.S.V., 27 December 1932, Home Pol. 31/97/32 (secret).
[2] Haig's note for circulation to Council, 28 December 1932, ibid.

Willingdon, who had remarked in November that India was quieter than at any time during his viceroyalty, 'entirely agreed with the views expressed in Haig's note'.[1] The governors were of the same general disposition. It would be foolish to convey the impression that Congress was in any position to negotiate, thereby undermining the strength that government had striven to establish. Nothing should be done to suggest that any Round Table Conference delegate was acting as an 'Envoy Extraordinary from the Secretary of State to a "rival power" '.[2] Gandhi must not be 'resurrected as a rival authority to the Government of India'. Interviews between Jayakar and Sapru and Gandhi, 'now half-forgotten', would dishearten the services, the loyalists, and the co-operators.[3] Not a single governor favoured negotiations. They might have taken as their text an observation that was made by the secretary of the Home Department, Sir Maurice Hallett: 'It is curious how history repeats itself and one can learn a good many lessons from examining a previous history.'[4]

Strengthened by the unanimous support of governors and councillors, Willingdon advised Hoare of the folly of recurring to the policies of 1930. Though Gandhi himself might prove reasonable at first, he would soon, as in 1930, succumb to pressure from Nehru and other extreme lieutenants. Hoare accepted that there could be no question of negotiating a bargain with Gandhi, though he was less convinced of the wisdom of preventing Sapru and Jayakar from meeting him.

On 4 January 1933 MacDonald wrote to Sapru: 'If the Congress will not abandon the method of civil disobedience, it is a question for the Government to decide when it can act with the certainty that its action will not be mistaken for weakness and will not lead to consequences which would be as much opposed to the interests of the community as a whole as to those of the Government itself.'[5] The date marked the first anniversary of the inauguration of the policy of repression. MacDonald was signifying, in fact, that the old Labour–Irwin policy of

---

[1] P.S.V. to Haig, 30 December 1932, ibid.
[2] Governor of Bengal to viceroy, 29 December 1932, ibid.
[3] Governor of Bihar and Orissa to viceroy, 31 December 1932, ibid.
[4] Hallett's note of 2 January 1933, ibid.
[5] MacDonald to Sapru, 4 January 1933, S.C. 1, M. 22.

co-operation and conciliation towards the Congress was utterly discredited. The spirit of the Round Table Conference was dead. Congress was crushed. Repression and reaction had triumphed.

CHAPTER 7

The Problem of Freedom with Unity: January 1933—March 1940

This quarrel is not old; this quarrel is coeval with this acute shame. I dare to say it is coeval with the British advent, and immediately this relationship, the unfortunate, artificial, unnatural relationship between Great Britain and India is transformed into a natural relationship, ... a voluntary partnership ... to be dissolved at the will of either party, ... you will find that Hindus, Mussulmans, Sikhs, Europeans, Anglo-Indians, Christians, Untouchables, will all live together as one man.

M. K. GANDHI, 30 November 1931

If I can achieve this unity, believe me, half the battle of the country's freedom is won.... So long as Hindus and Muslims are not united ... we shall both remain slaves of foreign domination.

M. A. JINNAH, 18 February 1935

I. THE FAILURE OF CIVIL DISOBEDIENCE

CIVIL disobedience was crushed so effectively in the first months of 1932 that the government could soon release prisoners with impunity. Their number fell from a peak of 32,500 in April 1932 to *c.* 14,000 in January 1933, when Willingdon could write of India enjoying a 'sense of confidence, security and general restfulness from all worries of agitation'.[1] In April 1931 the early success of civil disobedience had raised Congress to virtually coequal status with a conciliatory government. Two years later, it was apparent that civil disobedience could never wring freedom from a government bent on maintaining its supremacy. It was Gandhi's tragedy that satyagraha, the means he had chosen to unite India and prise her free of imperial control, neutralized the Congress as a party of opposition. Yet throughout 1933 and well into 1934 Gandhi shrank from abandoning his experiment. To co-operate with Britain's consti-

[1] Willingdon to Hoare, 29 January 1933, T.C.L.B.

tutional experiment meant that Congress would become merely one of the competing parties while the Raj kept the ring. Gandhi's insight into the inherent divisiveness of the parliamentary game among a subject people goes far to explain the tortuous turnings of his subtle genius that preceded his withdrawal from politics in October 1934.

After the Poona pact Gandhi devoted himself increasingly to his 'Harijan'[1] work, the logical extension of his campaign to bring the untouchables within general electorates. Under his inspiration Anti-Untouchability and Temple Entry bills were prepared for presentation to the legislative assembly in January 1933, and the journal *Harijan* began to appear in February. Orthodox Hindu opinion reacted sharply. In Bengal caste Hindus attacked the Poona pact. Hindu politicians stifled the Temple Entry legislation. The Mahasabha abandoned civil disobedience as prejudicial to Hindu interests. Many moderate Congressmen were concerned at the apparent diversion of the freedom struggle into a mere movement for social reform. Distressed and frustrated, on 8 May 1933 Gandhi embarked upon a three-week anti-untouchability fast. The same day the government released him, 'in view of the nature and objects of the fast and the attitude of mind it discloses'.[2]

However, Gandhi had not forsaken politics for social reform. At once he advised the acting Congress president to suspend civil disobedience for six weeks and appealed to government to release the remaining civil resisters in preparation for the restoration of peace. The complete withdrawal of civil disobedience must await the general amnesty. The official response was stiff: Gandhi's release was not connected with civil disobedience; negotiation for the withdrawal of the movement was impossible. Gandhi's initiative thus failed to re-establish his status in relation to the government. As for his authority over Congress, overt dissension emerged, between moderates who favoured the replacement of civil disobedience by council entry and parliamentary agitation, and extremists who wanted to intensify the movement and criticized its suspension. During a further six-week suspension Congress provincial leaders gathered at Poona from 12 to 14 July in order to compose their differences.

[1] Harijans = children of God = untouchables.
[2] Government communiqué, cited in *India in 1932–33*, Delhi, 1934, p. 24.

Gandhi successfully opposed an initiative to call off the movement unconditionally and carried through a resolution that he should seek a viceregal interview in the hope of achieving peace. This, his second, overture to government was no more successful than his first. Willingdon made an interview conditional upon the withdrawal of civil disobedience. Despite further entreaty he stood firm.

Next, Gandhi suspended civil disobedience as a mass movement organized and directed by Congress, replacing it with individual resistance. In effect, he was arguing that the machinery had failed, but not the method. As Congress had been unable to communicate the essence of satyagraha to the masses by precept it must now be conveyed to them by the example of individuals acting in a true 'spirit of resistance'. The shift recalls the intention that Gandhi had confided to Jawaharlal soon after the Lahore Congress: to separate his own experiment in satyagraha, or that of a few followers, from the Congress movement for freedom. Now he would make a controlled experiment in anarchism. He dissolved his ashram at Sabarmati and laid plans reminiscent of those for the epic trek to Dandi. He would march with some followers from Sabarmati to Ras, on the way exhorting villagers to begin individual civil disobedience. This initiative failed too. On 1 August he was arrested. When he declared his intention to defy an order of restraint he was sentenced to a year's imprisonment. His activities during three months at liberty had neither regenerated the movement nor secured peace with dignity. By the end of August only 4,500 civil resisters were in gaol. On 16 August he began another fast on the untouchability issue. A week later he became ill and was released yet again. On 16 September he decided to refrain from individual civil disobedience until 3 August 1934, the term of his sentence.

During the next year Congressmen cast about for fresh strategies. When Jawaharlal was released in September 1933 he expounded a socialist interpretation of the Indian situation. He identified imperialist and vested Indian interests as the objects of attack. If India were to enjoy freedom not only the Raj but also the princes, the landlords, and the commercial classes must be removed by direct action. He denounced Indian capitalists and communalists, whether Hindu or Muslim, as essentially self-interested. He gave offence to many Congressmen and to many former sympathizers. In February 1934 he was sentenced to two years in gaol for sedition. Three months later, young Congressmen who shared his doctrines formed the Congress Socialist Party. In contrast, constitutionalists within the Congress were turning from direct action to form swaraj parties. On 30 March and 1 April 1934 an informal meeting of Congressmen at Delhi resolved to revive the All-India Swaraj Party. It would contest the coming elections for the legislative assembly in order to secure the repeal of repressive laws and to oppose the government's scheme of reforms. Gandhi gave the resolutions his blessing but reaffirmed his conviction that council entry would not produce freedom.

At the same time (on 7 April), Gandhi announced the suspension of 'civil resistance for swaraj'. He had decided upon this step before the Delhi meeting began. He explained that satyagraha had been adulterated in transmission to the masses. If it were ever to achieve purna swaraj he must now bear sole responsibility for its practice:

... I must advise all Congressmen to suspend civil resistance for swaraj as distinguished from the specific grievances. They should leave it to me alone.... Henceforth ... those who have been impelled to civil resistance for swaraj under my advice ... will please desist from civil resistance. I am quite convinced that this is the best course in the interests of India's fight for freedom.[1]

On 16 April the government made it clear that no obstacle would be raised to a meeting of Congress 'for the purpose of ratifying a statement of policy recently made by Mr. Gandhi calling off civil disobedience'.[2]

The A.I.C.C. met at Patna on 17 and 18 May. The Congress was in danger of splitting into factions over civil disobedience, council entry, and the communal award. Gandhi controlled the proceedings masterfully and unity was preserved. The A.I.C.C. accepted his advice on the restriction of civil disobedience to him alone. The Swaraj party was contained within the Congress by the A.I.C.C.'s endorsement of its parliamentary programme. A parliamentary board was set up to select Congress candidates for the elections and to control Congressmen in the legislature.

[1] *Mahatma*, III. 319.
[2] *India in 1933–34*, Delhi, 1935, p. 14.

In effect, the limitation and suspension of civil disobedience had been agreed, but not its abandonment, and Congressmen disenchanted with the method could divert their energies to parliamentary activity. On 6 June the government lifted the ban on the Congress and most of its organizations, though the Red Shirts were still proscribed and Abdul Ghaffar Khan, Jawaharlal, and Vallabhbhai remained in gaol. From the middle of 1934 Congress resumed lawful political activity as one of the competing parties. On 17 September Gandhi announced that he would retire from the Congress after its session at Bombay in October, the first since the Karachi Congress in 1931. Under Gandhi's guidance the session confirmed the general policy that had been agreed at Patna.

The Bombay Congress represents a major achievement for Gandhi, as well as bringing him to another parting of the ways. Organizational unity was secured, but only by the condonation of a method that he could not espouse for himself. He could not believe that freedom could flow from parliamentary activity and he hoped that some Congressmen would abstain from council entry. He continued to argue that satyagraha was the way to freedom, if only it could be conveyed to the masses. If only it could be practised in the true spirit of non-violence, it must convince government of India's right to freedom. He left the Congress on 28 October, with the words: 'What I am aiming at is the development of the capacity for civil disobedience. Disobedience that is wholly civil should never provoke retaliation.'[1] He was denying that a great experiment in civil disobedience had failed: true civil disobedience had never been tried.

II. THE FAILURE OF THE ROUND TABLE CONFERENCE

The Round Table Conference experiment in constitutional method came to an end in December 1932, though its original spirit had lapsed a year earlier. The third session was a bridge between the Irwin–Benn–MacDonald conception of a self-determining conference preparing an agreed constitution for submission to parliament; and the return to the Simonesque procedure for the preparation of an official scheme, its embodiment in a state document, and its consideration by a joint

[1] *Mahatma*, III. 373.

committee, assisted by witnesses or assessors, prior to its presentation to parliament. The white paper of 18 March 1933 contained the substance of the proposal that the government had adumbrated at the third conference. It was accepted in essence by the joint committee, which sat from April 1933 until October 1934, and finally incorporated into the India Act of August 1935.

The experiment's great achievement was the federal formula, which enabled a majority of the Conservative party to accept the principle of central responsibility with safeguards. With the end of the experiment and the formula's appearance in the white paper, dissident Tories flexed their muscles for combat within the party and in parliament. The principle of central responsibility in an all-India federation was challenged at every stage. The opposition to the Cabinet policy was led by Churchill and Salisbury in the parliamentary party. It gained substantial support from the party's constituency associations, through the National Union of Conservative Associations, the Central Council of the party, and the annual conference. Its main propagandists were the *Daily Mail*, the *Daily Express*, and the *Morning Post*. At times the battle was fought without scruple, as when Churchill impeached Hoare for allegedly tampering with the evidence to be given by Lancashire witnesses to the joint committee. The majority of Conservatives in favour of central responsibility was sometimes exceedingly slim. At the party's annual conference on 4 October 1934 it was only twenty-three (543 *v*. 520), though two months later the Central Council of the Conservative Party voted 3:1 in favour (1,020 *v*. 390). The effect of the sustained opposition was to delay the passing of the act for two years beyond Hoare's target date.

A sufficient section of the Conservative party remained hostile to the goal of 'Dominion Status' to prevent the government's using the term prior to the passing of the bill. In August 1933, when Willingdon employed the expression with approval to describe British policy Hoare administered a rebuke. The government decided against a preamble to the 1935 act, for unless it merely repeated that of 1919 it could 'possibly prejudice the whole passage of the Bill'.[1] Willingdon was astounded that Hoare proposed simply to say at the second reading stage that

[1] Sec. of S. to viceroy, 17 February 1935 (t/g), T.C.

India would 'ultimately attain self-government within the Empire'.[1] His counsel was responsible for Hoare stating in debate that India would 'ultimately . . . take her place among the fully self-governing members of the British Commonwealth of Nations'.[2]

From the close of the Round Table Conference to the passing of the bill Hoare was ever anxious about the most vulnerable aspect of the federal scheme: the princes' reluctance to commit themselves to accession. Salisbury told him that 'probably his main difficulty' with the government's policy was 'due to doubts about the real attitude of Princes to Federation'.[3] Hoare was challenged repeatedly by Conservative dissidents on the 'sham Federation',[4] an expression immortalized in Churchill's savage description of the bill as 'a monstrous monument of sham built by the pygmies'.[5] In order to silence Conservative opposition, and because princely accessions were essential to the scheme of federation, Hoare hectored Willingdon continuously to secure assurances from their highnesses. He laboured strenuously to make the princes' role in the federation attractive to them and reassuring to his party. As the princes' intransigence was responsible for the eventual failure of the federal scheme it is necessary to follow their tergiversations closely.

In January 1933 Hoare asked Willingdon to secure some indication from the princes of their general willingness to federate. Willingdon quipped that it was 'almost hopeless' to do so.[6] If they were approached individually they adopted bargaining positions, seeking satisfaction of specific demands of various kinds. As a body they would be loth to commit themselves until the details of representation and federal finance were decided: 'If you can proceed with the Bill and deal with your Party under existing conditions, that is to say without more definite assurances of adhesion but also without definite resolutions condemning Federation as set out in the White Paper, I hope and believe that the passage of the Bill will make entry of most of the important states practically inevitable.'[7] Hoare pressed

---

[1] Viceroy to Sec. of S., 31 January 1935 (t/g), T.C.
[2] *Hansard*, 6 February 1935.
[3] Sec. of S. to viceroy, 16 June 1933 (t/g), T.C.
[4] Hoare to Willingdon, 17 February 1933, T.C.L.B.
[5] Quoted in N. Mansergh, *The Commonwealth Experience*, London, 1969, p. 267 n.
[6] Viceroy to Sec. of S., 26 January 1933 (t/g), T.C.
[7] Viceroy to Sec. of S., 9 February 1933 (t/g), T.C.

for instructing political officers to expound and commend the federal scheme to the states: 'to secure from as many as possible provisional assurances of their intention to federate subject to satisfactory settlement of points which concern them individually'.¹ After meeting a large number of the princes who gathered at Delhi during March to consider the white paper, Willingdon concluded: 'We can't possibly get any assurance from any of them until the Bill is an Act, and they see exactly what their position is going to be. This really is reasonable, and I don't see any other way out of it.'²

The princes' reactions to the white paper were indeed disturbing. Between 20 and 23 March the confederationists met and demanded that provision for representation through confederation be made in the statute. On 25 March at a Chamber meeting the outgoing Chancellor, the Jam Sahib, denounced federation as dangerous to the states and the British connection. The viceroy had to call him to order. The Chamber resolved that accession to the federation would depend upon the inclusion in the statute of essential safeguards of the princes' sovereignty and internal autonomy. It elected as Chancellor and Pro-Chancellor for the coming year Patiala and Dholpur, the authors of the confederation scheme. Dholpur had never wavered in his opposition to federation since the first Round Table Conference, chiefly because he feared the domination of the 'independence wallahs' of British India. The Chamber was also averse to a scheme of princely representation that Willingdon, briefed by Hoare, had sketched tentatively. The white paper provided for an upper house of 260, of which the states should have two-fifths, but made no detailed allocation to the individual states. The tentative scheme of allotment offered plural representation to the larger states, thereby denying seats to many of the Chamber princes. It produced a cleavage between the larger potentates and the Chamber group.

Willingdon summed up the results of ten days of discussions in the Chamber and outside as 'rather disappointing and deplorable'.³ He averted the outright rejection of federation only by conceding that the Chamber might continue to press for safeguards, the statutory recognition of confederation, and amend-

¹ Sec. of S. to viceroy, 16 February 1933 (t/g), T.C.
² Willingdon to Hoare, 26 March 1933, T.C.L.B.   ³ Ibid.

ments to the tentative allotment scheme. Patiala soon took up these matters in a letter to Hoare: '... unless these omissions are made good at the Joint Select Committee stage, and the necessary safeguards are incorporated, we do not see light.'[1] Willingdon offered Hoare a crumb of comfort with comments on the weakness and unrepresentativeness of the Chamber. Besides the large states that had never attended the Chamber, now Kashmir, Bhopal, Udaipur, Jaipur, and Jodhpur had turned their backs on it. The Chamber as a 'representative body of princely opinion is moribund'.[2] Willingdon believed that the existing safeguards would be 'thoroughly satisfactory' and that 'the great number of Princes are quite clear that Paramountcy as it exists ... must generally be maintained'.[3] The real problem was to find a satisfactory system for allotting the states' seats.

The white paper incorporated Hoare's original formula that the inauguration of federation should await the accession of princes who accounted for one half of the states' peoples and one half of the states' seats in the upper house. In view of Willingdon's inability to obtain the princes' general approval of the paper, on 1 May Hoare asked for his suggestions upon the allocation of the states' seats, a major desideratum in princely calculations. Hoare was prepared to reduce the upper chamber if the prospects of federation would be improved thereby. Certainly, the larger states favoured chambers in which they would not be swamped by hordes of lesser rulers. The Conservative dissidents preferred small houses because they offered greater promise of stability than large ones. A further advantage was that the energies of the Political Department might be directed at negotiations with a manageable number of princes. Surprisingly, Willingdon opposed small chambers. He appreciated that if the large states acceded then the lesser ones would follow; and he had suffered vexation in dealing with the Chamber group. Yet he thought it a decisive disadvantage that most princes, and in particular those with seats in the Chamber, would oppose a small upper house.

Willingdon and his government allotted the white paper's 104 states' seats on the basis of traditional status and importance.

[1] Patiala to Hoare, 20 April 1933, I. O., L/PO/58.
[2] Viceroy to Sec. of S., 26 March 1933 (t/g), T.C.
[3] Willingdon to Hoare, 30 April 1933, I. O., L/PO/58.

The political officers were instructed to acquaint the princes of the allotment and to ascertain their intentions towards accession. In November Willingdon produced an extraordinary computation: excluding eight seats provided for states under the titular administration of minors, he had assurances of accession from states accounting for 65 of the 96 seats and 33m. of the 70m. states' peoples. The important states, notably Hyderabad, Mysore, Travancore, Udaipur and Bhopal were standing out, but he believed that the great southern states would fall into line eventually. Willingdon was convinced that the necessary accessions would be obtained. Now that he seemed to have assured support for the white paper's upper house, he refused adamantly to contemplate any smaller alternative, despite formidable pressure from Hoare and the joint committee.

In December Hoare advanced a plan for small houses. The joint committee considered that they would be stabler, cheaper, and of better quality than those of the white paper's size. The plan provided for an upper house of 100 seats (60 British India: 40 states), and a lower house of 300 (200 British India: 100 states). The former would provide individual representation to the eighteen or twenty largest states, with three seats to Hyderabad and two to each of the next four in order of size. The remaining 15 seats would be filled through a system of regional representation. Hoare believed that the plan would attract the large and medium-sized princes. (Bikaner, Bhopal, and Patiala would enjoy individual representation.) Willingdon replied that the plan would dash the hopes of federation. Hoare was sceptical. He criticized the failure of Willingdon's scheme to appeal to Hyderabad and Mysore, which between them accounted for 25 per cent of the states' peoples. The states individually represented in the house of 100 would account for 50m. of the states' population. He could hardly agree that the larger house was more likely to attract the princes.

Willingdon replied:

> It might be possible by manipulating the allocation in favour of States representing the majority of the population and neglecting the remainder to secure acceptances sufficient to place beyond all doubt the fulfilment of [the accession requirements].... But States not so favoured could never be induced to regard this proposition as fair, after the hopes that have been held out to them. Result would be

large congeries of States interwoven with various parts of British India refusing to federate, and I still hold to my opinion that such abstentions would render practical federation more unworkable than if large self-contained areas like Hyderabad elected to hold aloof.[1]

The argument gave priority to short-term administrative convenience over the achievement of the major British policy objective: bringing the paper federation to life. It revealed a crucial shortcoming in the viceroy's judgement. Surely a federation in operation could employ leverage of many kinds to draw in recalcitrant princes. When active diplomacy was needed Willingdon was supine and foolishly sanguine:

> In order that Select Committee might be given assurance of probable adherences, we consulted Princes on allocation proposed on basis of Upper and Lower Houses of size suggested in White Paper. By representing that allocation as final recommendation of the Government of India, we have succeeded in securing acceptances from about 66 per cent of the Princes, which is, I think, to be regarded as a general[ly] satisfactory result.[2]

What Willingdon had really discovered was that most princes preferred large houses; not, as he supposed, that they would accede to a federation that embraced them.

The princes' stubborn aversion to federation was manifested after the publication of the bill. A committee of states' ministers met at Delhi from 19 to 21 February 1935 under Hydari's chairmanship and called for several amendments. On 25 February a meeting of princes and ministers at Bombay resolved that the bill and the draft instrument of accession were unacceptable and required fundamental modification. The objections related mainly to the long-standing grievances over paramountcy and internal sovereignty. On 27 February Bikaner, Bhopal, and Patiala wrote to the viceroy: 'The Chamber of Princes have from the very outset urged a satisfactory settlement of the claims of paramountcy to be a condition precedent to the accession of the States to any Federation.'[3] The princes objected to the instrument of accession as derogatory to their status and insisted upon its replacement by treaties of accession, bilateral agree-

---

[1] Viceroy to Sec. of S., 26 January 1934 (t/g), T.C.
[2] Viceroy to Sec. of S., 22 April 1934 (t/g), T.C.
[3] *Views of the Indian States on the Bill*, Cd. 4843, P.P. 1934–5, XVI.

ments imposing upon Britain an obligation 'to preserve and safeguard the whole of their sovereignty and internal autonomy ... from any encroachment in future'.[1] They recurred to the demand, enunciated clearly in 1933, for the bill to incorporate safeguards of their sovereignty. They also resented the bill's extension to the viceroy of power to infringe their internal autonomy if events in a state appeared to menace the peace of India. In effect, they were not prepared to allow the diminution of their sovereignty that was implied by the exercise of federal jurisdiction in their states—either by the agents of the federal executive, or by the governor-general in discharge of his responsibility for peace and tranquillity.

Hoare was taken aback by the princes' intractability. For three years he had harassed Willingdon with his anxieties over the princes' compliance, only to be rebuffed with suave intimations that the princes were too far committed to resile. Willingdon's government was primarily responsible for the adoption of the double-edged accession precondition of federation and the rejection of Hoare's either/or formulation. It also insisted upon the white paper's upper house, misleading Hoare with its computation of probable accessions at a stage when a small house strategy would have won Tory converts and enhanced the likelihood of support from the larger princes.

It is scarcely surprising that in his retirement, long after the failure of federation to materialize, Hoare should have written lamentingly that the indifference and laxity of the Government of India, together with the diehards' delaying tactics, frustrated the federal scheme. He extended his strictures beyond the period during which the bill was in the making to the interval between its enactment and the outbreak of the war, when the paper federation was suspended. He is more convincing as a critic of Willingdon's government, which, had it approached the federation problem more constructively, might well have defined realistic conditions for the achievement of princely accessions, than as a guide to the shortcomings of its successor, which was encumbered by the virtually unworkable federal provisions of the statute.[2]

[1] Ibid., cited in R. Coupland, *Indian Politics, 1936–40*, London, 1943, p. 3.
[2] For an analysis of Hoare's argument see my 'The Making of India's Paper Federation, 1927–35' and 'British Policy and the Indian Problem, 1936–40', in

Perhaps, then, the juggernaut of all-India federation might best have been set in motion by Britain entering into a compact with the great states and framing the statute accordingly. In 1936, the viceroy, Lord Linlithgow (18 April 1936—20 October 1943), sent three emissaries to the states to represent the federal scheme. They reported that many of the smaller rulers were awaiting the lead of the prominent princes and that federation had most to fear from its 'professed friends', such as Bikaner, Bhopal, Patiala, and Dholpur.[1] A. C. Lothian, the emissary who visited Hyderabad, Travancore, Cochin, and Central India, believed that if one or two of the big states could be persuaded 'even at the sacrifice of principle, financial or otherwise' to join the federation, others would 'tumble over each other to follow'.[2] Some half-dozen of the leading states, say, Hyderabad, Mysore, Baroda, Bhopal, and Gwalior, should be accorded unusual consideration. A second of the emissaries, Francis Wylie, has written that 'only about six of [the states] had any claim to serious consideration at all as potential federal units'.[3] Furthermore, in the absence of force 'there was never the slightest chance of getting rulers representing fifty per cent of the population of the princely states to sign instruments of accession' during the pre-war years. Apparently there had been good reason to design a structure that took account of the few great states rather than the multitude of minor ones, most of which must eventually suffer mediatization.

The weakness of the argument for a bargain between British imperialism and Indian autocracy in the 1930s is the assumption of its compatibility with responsible government in the provinces. As early as March 1930 Watson had minuted in the Political Department that without 'the grant of constitutional government to the States' subjects' a 'true Federal Scheme with British India seems impracticable'.[4] Neither Gandhi's conception of Indian unity nor Jawaharlal's understanding of freedom could be con-

---

C. H. Philips and M. D. Wainwright (eds.), *The Partition of India*, London, 1970, pp. 54–94.

[1] Letters of H.E. the viceroy's special representative commenting on his federal discussions with the Indian States, F. and P.D. 20/41 (secret), cited in Phadnis, *Towards the Integration of the Indian States*, p. 104.   [2] Ibid.

[3] Sir F. Wylie, 'Federal Negotiations in India, 1935–39, and After', in Philips and Wainwright, op. cit., p. 521.

[4] Watson's minute, 28 March 1930, F. and P.D. Spcl 22/30.

tained within British India. In order to explain the princes' failure to accede to the all-India federation it is unnecessary, in the final analysis, to look beyond the policies that the Congress developed towards the states.

III. CONGRESS UNITARIANISM

In September 1934 the Congress Working Committee reaffirmed that the goal of Congress was purna swaraj or complete independence, including 'unfettered national control over the army and other defence forces, external affairs, fiscal and commercial matters, and financial and economic policy'.[1] At the November 1934 legislative assembly elections the Congress won 44 of the 88 elected seats, Malaviya's Congress Nationalist Party (which differed from the Congress parliamentary board in rejecting the communal award) 11, the Independents 22, and the Europeans 11. Such rapid mobilization of electoral support was remarkable after Congress's four and a half years of non-constitutional activity. In December the C.W.C.'s decisions reflected the immediate electoral success as well as the eventual goal of purna swaraj: the joint committee's proposals were rejected but the even less satisfactory existing constitution was to be worked. In February 1935 the leader of the Congress in the legislative assembly proposed that as the new constitution had been 'conceived in a spirit of Imperialist domination' and would transfer 'no real power to the people of India' it should not be introduced.[2] Congress rejected the 1935 act root and branch, and proposed the formation of a swaraj constitution by an assembly elected on adult suffrage.

In 1936 the Lucknow Congress, with Jawaharlal presiding, decided to contest the forthcoming elections to the new provincial councils. Jawaharlal urged that Congress should then refuse ministerial office. As the point was disputed fiercely the A.I.C.C. postponed its settlement until after the elections, though it affirmed that Congressmen should enter the legislatures, 'not to co-operate in any way with the Act, but to combat it and seek the end of it'.[3] The elections were a Congress triumph.

[1] Wardha Congress resolution, cited in *India in 1933–34*, p. 28.
[2] Bhulabhai Desai's amendment of 7 February 1935, cited in *India in 1934–35*, p. 97.
[3] A.I.C.C. election manifesto, in Coupland, op. cit., p. 12.

Some 54 per cent of the qualified electors voted and Congress won 711 out of the total 1,585 seats. Congress had majorities in five of the eleven provinces and could form governments in a further two. The victory was the fruit of the civil disobedience movement, in which the Congress had identified itself with the interests of large segments of the new electorate, four-fifths (some 28m.) of whom were voting for the first time.

On 18 March 1937 the A.I.C.C. drew the following conclusion from the election results:

> The electorate has, in overwhelming measure, set its seal on ... [the Congress policy of opposing the 1935 act, which] stands condemned and utterly rejected by the people through the self-same democratic process which had been evoked by the British Government, and the people have further declared that they desire to frame their own constitution, based on national independence, through the medium of a Constituent Assembly elected by adult franchise. This Committee therefore demands, on behalf of the people of India, that the new Constitution be withdrawn.[1]

Of course there was no possibility of the constitution being withdrawn. The government directed its efforts to persuading Congress to accept office without conceding its demand that the provincial governors' special safeguard powers be waived. Eventually, Congress took office, but with disastrous consequences for all-India federation.

The nub of the 1935 scheme was the division of the monolithic Raj into quasi-autonomous units. Co-ordinate provincial authority, similar to the internal sovereignty of the states, was to be substituted for subordination to the central government. This was essential to the Muslims', as to the princes', acquiescence in federation.

However, the Congress chose to operate the provincial governments through a unitary party structure. It had long claimed to be the one authentic voice of India, a truly national movement. Gandhi's agitational strategy was directed at achieving unity: at framing the substance of independence in a form to which rich and poor could subscribe, as in the eleven points; at reaching Hindu–Muslim accord through fighting for a common cause; at preserving the unity of the Hindu community, as in his

---

[1] A.I.C.C. resolution of 18 March 1937, cited in ibid., p. 16.

Harijan fasts. He had constituted the Congress with care so that it could contain diversity: a Swaraj party, a socialist movement, a spinning movement, a Nationalist Muslim group, Malaviya's Nationalist party, the Mahasabhites. The Congress was to be a microcosm of India. At the second Round Table Conference Gandhi expounded unequivocally his doctrine that the Congress represented 'the whole of India', 'even the Princes'. All other parties stood for 'sectional interests'; only Congress could claim to represent 'all interests'.[1] However, he had never conceived of Congress as primarily a parliamentary party. Indeed, he saw clearly that for Congress to operate within a constitutional context framed by Britain was tantamount to its accepting the status of one among a number of competing Indian parties. There had long existed in Gandhi's mind a sharp distinction between the Congress as a fully national, extra-constitutional 'parallel government' to that of the Raj, and the Congress as a constitutional party, with other parties, under the Raj. In 1934 the parliamentary board was set up as an autonomous body, under the direction of the A.I.C.C., which was not itself involved in parliamentary work. In March 1937, the month following the elections, the board was reconstituted as the parliamentary sub-committee of the C.W.C. In consequence, the constitutional party was now regarded in the same perspective as the agitational movement: as the one authentic voice of India. The parallelism of the nationalist movement had been constitutionalized. Instead of the Congress ministries operating as autonomous provincial governments within a federal structure they accepted the C.W.C. as the legitimate directorate of a unitary government. The monolithic Congress stood in the place that the unitary Raj had vacated. The new provincial system had been incorporated within the old Congress system.

The constitutionalization of Congress 'unitarianism'[2] alarmed the princes, who might reasonably have expected the provincialization of British India to check the exercise of authority by a centralized democratic party. In terms of the metaphor that Montagu and Chelmsford had used to express the implications of nationalism in British India for the princes, the 1937 election triumph was the fire that caused Congress agitation to 'overleap

[1] *Progs of R.T.C.* 2, 30 November 1931, pp. 390–1.
[2] Coupland, op. cit., pp. 93–108.

frontier lines like sparks across a street'.[1] The Congress had always refrained from interfering in the states, largely in deference to Gandhi's view that the princes held power in trust for their people. From 1937 it was working within a constitutional framework that was intended to embrace the states, and it soon began to pronounce upon their peoples' rights. In October 1937, when Mysore took action against a Congress agitator, the A.I.C.C. called upon 'the people of the Indian States and British India to give all support and encouragement to the people of Mysore in their struggle against the State for the right of self-determination'.[2] In February 1938 the Congress resolved:

> The *Purna Swaraj* or complete Independence, which is the objective of the Congress, is for the whole of India, inclusive of the States, for the integrity and unity of India must be maintained in freedom as it has been maintained in subjection. The only kind of federation that can be acceptable to the Congress is one in which the States participate as free units, enjoying the same measure of democratic freedom as the rest of India.[3]

The old Congress respect for the princes' authority was gone for ever, and though the Congress as a body refrained from direct interference, its individual members were encouraged to support the states' peoples' freedom struggles. During 1938 there were popular movements, aided by Congress volunteers from neighbouring provinces, in a number of the larger states. In some cases the concessions that were extracted gave the princes' subjects a say in the selection of federal representatives. In December Gandhi warned the princes to 'cultivate friendly relations with an organization which bids fair in the future, not very distant, *to replace the Paramount Power*'.[4] In 1939 C.W.C. members entered two selected states and inaugurated civil disobedience. The same year the Arya Samaj and the Mahasabha launched campaigns against Hyderabad from the encircling Hindu provinces.

The Congress assaults upon the states from 1937 violated the spirit of the federal constitution, with its emphasis upon autonomous units. In 1938 the ministers of Hyderabad, Gwalior,

[1] *Montford Report*, para. 157.
[2] A.I.C.C. resolution of October 1937, cited in Coupland, op. cit., p. 171.
[3] Congress resolution of February 1938, in ibid., p. 172.
[4] *Harijan*, 3 December 1938, in ibid., p. 173.

The Problem of Freedom with Unity

Baroda, Kolhapur, and Travancore concerted their views in a memorandum to the Political Department. The growing agitation was started by Congress 'against the Indian States in furtherance of their programme to capture power in the forthcoming Federation'.[1] The princes would stand for no interference in their states. Federation was envisaged as 'the coming together for certain purposes of Indian States and Provinces for joint action on matters of common interest', and if they had imagined that constitutional changes in their states were to precede its accomplishment then 'the idea of federation would never have emerged into the realm of practical politics'. The memorandum sought the British Government's assurance that constitutional reform in the states was irrelevant to federation, and support to suppress agitation. The under-secretary of state declared in parliament that the rulers were free to decide their own forms of government, and that the paramount power would protect them against violence and disorder, while assisting them to redress the legitimate grievances of their subjects.

Congress operated the new constitution until soon after the outbreak of war, when, failing to obtain its demand for a constituent assembly, the C.W.C. called upon its provincial ministries to resign. However, it operated in a spirit inimical to the spirit of the constitution, whether in relation to the provinces or the states. If Gandhi contended that true civil disobedience had never been tried, Britain might make a similar claim for the products of the Round Table Conference experiment: provincial autonomy and all-India federation had not failed, but failed to get a fair trial. Yet the inability to implement the products was surely evidence of the failure of the process. The experiment was doomed to failure by dint of the abstention of the Congress. One prerequisite to the working of an all-India federation was an accommodation between Congress and the princes, which, alas, was never even approached at the Round Table Conference.

Another was an accommodation between the Congress and the Muslims.

IV. MUSLIM SEPARATISM

The communal award, the federal constitution, and provincial autonomy gave the Muslims much that they wanted.

[1] Princes' memo. quoted in Phadnis, op. cit., pp. 121–2.

Fazl-i-Husain's son and biographer rejoiced at the result of his father's efforts:

The Muslim position under the new constitution was adequately safeguarded, and the demands first put forward in the Delhi Resolution (1929) were to a large extent secured. The N.W.F.P. became a Governor's Province. Sind was separated from Bombay and declared to be a Governor's Province. The Muslim share in the public services was fixed at 25% of all Imperial appointments. With regard to residuary powers, it is true that the Muslim demand that they should be vested in the provinces was not accepted, but as desired by Muslims they were not vested in the Centre, but were to be exercised by the Governor-General in his discretion. The demand for $33\frac{1}{3}$% representation in the Cabinet, Central and Provincial, was not met in the Act, but provision for giving effect to it was made in the Instrument of Instructions issued to the Governor-General and the Governors. Muslims were to be represented by separate electorates without prejudice to the weightages obtained by the Muslim minorities under the Lucknow Pact; Muslims in the Punjab were given a statutory majority. The only demand in this respect which was not conceded was in the case of Bengal, because of the necessity for providing representation for Europeans. . . . All this put the Muslim mind at rest and it also concluded the labours of Fazl-i-Husain for five years in the Government of India.[1]

In effect the Muslim position in Bengal was strong. In their four majority provinces the Muslims enjoyed supremacy and exercised authority co-ordinate with, rather than subordinate to, the Government of India. In their minority provinces they enjoyed separate electorates and weightage. At the federal level they would have weightage which, combined with the princes' weightage, should make Congress rule impossible.

Jinnah's emergence from self-exile in 1934 as a critic of the new constitution gives a misleading impression of Muslim opinion. Muslim politics were now, in fact, subdued. In 1934 Jinnah was unusual in his disposition to seek accommodation with the Congress. He was prepared to join the opposition to the federal safeguards and reserves and the terms conceded to the princes, if only the Hindus would approve the communal award. His overtures failed because of Malaviya's virulent opposition to the award. Jinnah had little Muslim support in the mid-thirties.

---

[1] Azim Husain, op. cit., p. 265.

Willingdon explained his presidentship of the League in 1934 as a stratagem of the Aga Khan's, 'the idea being that [his dangerous tendencies] would be neutralized by the organization committee of the League'.[1] The League became moribund and its denunciation of the 1935 Act is of little significance. Whereas in 1936 Jinnah was still an advocate of Hindu–Muslim unity, the leaders of the Muslim provinces were well content with the *status quo*. The League parliamentary board that he organized to contest the provincial elections was a disappointment. The League won only 109 of the 482 Muslim seats: one out of 84 in the Punjab; 39 out of 117 in Bengal; 3 out of 33 in Sind, and none out of 36 in the N.W.F.P. It fared better in the minority provinces, gaining 20 of the 29 Muslim seats in Bombay, 10 out of 28 in Madras, 27 out of 64 in the U.P., and 9 out of 34 in Assam.

From the time of the Congress election triumph and the formation of the provincial ministries, the ambassador of Hindu–Muslim unity and the Muslim League became steadily more separatist in outlook. The grievances of the Muslim minorities against the Congress governments were innumerable. They began from resentment at the refusal of Congress to enter into coalitions in provinces where it was the largest but not the majority party, as in the U.P. They developed through alleged discrimination against Muslims in public preferment, through assaults on Muslim culture and religion and the Urdu language. They culminated in fears that the Congress 'High Command' would obtain dominance at the federal level, thereby neutralizing the balance between Muslim and Hindu provinces. Alarm at the strength of the centralized Congress machine and of Congress unitarianism converted the League into a Muslim separatist organization.

By the end of 1938 the League executive could discern the implication of the Congress campaign against the princes for the Muslims' position in an all-India federation: '[The Congress's] main objective in championing the cause of the States' people is only to secure the establishment in the Indian States of an elective system enabling their representatives to be returned to the Federal Legislature, irrespective of anything else, in the hope

---

[1] Viceroy to Sec. of S., 8 April 1934 (t/g), T.C.

that it might get a majority.'[1] As the Aga Khan reflected in 1940: '... the sugar had all come off the [federation] pill the moment the States' representatives were to be elected by the States' peoples rather than nominated by the Rulers, for under such an arrangement the Muslims would not get from the States in the Central Legislature the support they required to balance the Congress votes.'[2] If the federation was to be controlled by a Congress-dominated legislature then Indian Muslims would have nothing to do with it. From 1938 the Muslims began to demand a constitutional review *de novo*. Schemes that would weld the Muslim provinces into something very like separate nations began to appear. They culminated in the League's 'Pakistan resolution' at Lahore in March 1940:

... it is the considered view of this session of the All-India Muslim League that no constitutional plan would be workable in this country or acceptable to the Muslims unless it is designed on the following basic principle, viz., that geographically contiguous units are demarcated into regions which should be so constituted with such territorial readjustments as may be necessary that the areas in which the Muslims are numerically in a majority, as in the north-western and eastern zones of India, should be grouped to constitute 'independent States' in which the constituent units shall be autonomous and sovereign....[3]

The very creation of autonomous Muslim provinces under the 1935 Act encouraged and validated the demand for separate nationhood. The Muslim League's achievement was to convert the process of provincialization into the process of separation. Defeated by the Congress in the politics of Indian unity, Muslims sought refuge through the politics of Partition.

V. EXPERIMENT, DEVOLUTION, AND PARTITION

The Round Table Conference experiment was a major departure in the devolution of imperial power. As King–Emperor George V said at the ceremonial opening of the conference:

More than once the Sovereign has summoned historic assemblies on the soil of India, but never before have British and Indian Statesmen

[1] All-India Muslim League Executive Council resolution, December 1938, in Coupland, op. cit., p. 197.
[2] Linlithgow to Zetland, 27 February 1940, Zetland Collection.
[3] Muslim League resolution at Lahore, 24 March 1940, Philips, *Documents*, pp. 354–5.

and Rulers of Indian States met, as you now meet, in one place and round one table, to discuss the future system of government for India and seek agreement for the guidance of My Parliament as to the foundations upon which it must stand.[1]

The Round Table Conference marked a change from the paternalism of 'tutorial Commissions'.[2] Indian participation in a free conference formed the natural accompaniment to the promise of Irwin and the Labour government that India should enjoy full partnership in the Commonwealth. It was to be an experiment with freedom, though the interests and responsibilities of the Raj meant that complete freedom could not be granted at a stroke. It was also to be an experiment in unity. The work of the conference was to devise a constitution that would devolve an agreed measure of freedom while retaining the imperial principle of unity.

The first major step from Raj to Swaraj, the Montagu–Chelmsford constitution, had exacerbated strains within the unitary empire, and the spectroscope afforded by the appointment of the Simon Commission had revealed them clearly. The problem of advancing towards national freedom and unity was clearly one of accommodating dualities within a common constitution. The first duality was between the Raj and its aspirant successor, the parallel government of the Indian National Congress. The Congress claimed to represent all India and sought parity of status with the Raj. The accommodation of this duality meant finding a constitution that conceded the essence of the Congress claim whilst the necessary degree of British authority remained. The second duality was between Hindu India and Muslim India, which were geographically separate to a major extent. In this case the accommodation must preserve the separate interests and identity of the Muslim communities within a nation that was bound to be predominantly Hindu. The third duality was between British India and the Indian states. Here the necessary accommodation must establish a central authority common to the two Indias yet guarantee the substantial sovereignty of the princes.

The first fruits of the Round Table Conference initiative were disappointing. Gandhi refused to participate in the conference

[1] *Progs. of R.T.C. 1*, 12 November 1930, p. 15.
[2] Benn's phrase, *Progs. of R.T.C. 2*, 30 November 1931, p. 293.

experiment at the outset because it afforded insufficient prospect of resolving either of the two dualities with which he was primarily concerned. First, Irwin was unable to guarantee that the work of the conference would be to frame a Dominion constitution. In the absence of such a guarantee, Gandhi considered that the claim of the Congress to parity of status had not been met. Secondly, the Hindu–Muslim question divided India, and the duality might be exploited at the conference table in order to reinforce and justify India's subjection. If either dualism had been resolved then Gandhi might have attended the first conference. But without a guarantee of the substance of freedom or of unity in British India he considered the experiment to be futile and possibly dangerous.

However, the results of the first Round Table Conference were heartening. MacDonald was able to close the conference with a conditional promise: Dominion Status with safeguards provided that an all-India federal structure was actually established. The formula was vague and could mean much or little. But it was as close as Britain came to solving the problem of freedom with unity.

The civil disobedience experiment that Gandhi launched in 1930 was an alternative approach to the problem. It was an explicit attempt to achieve unity through agitation and to secure Britain's recognition of the representative character of the Congress. The experiment produced an impressive show of national solidarity, and by negotiating a pact direct with the viceroy Gandhi won the status of a plenipotentiary. His success owed much to the forbearance of the Government of India and to Irwin's concern to constitutionalize a legitimate demand for national freedom. In the aftermath of the pact Gandhi sought without success to assume for Congress the role of a parallel authority charged with administering the pact, the role of an intermediary between the Raj and the people. Despite his inability to give effective form in administrative action to the status that he had enjoyed in negotiation, Gandhi still chose to attend the second Round Table Conference. In view of the Willingdon government's predilection for upholding the dignity of the Raj, even at the cost of ruthless repression, Gandhi's new preference for negotiation above agitation was wise. Furthermore, as the civil disobedience experiment had not solved the

Hindu–Muslim problem, there was little to be said for a further agitation.

The second conference was unable to accommodate any of the dualities of the Indian problem. Gandhi's claim for the Congress as the epitome of India was denied by the delegates of the British parties, the Muslims, the minor minorities, and the states. Moreover, with an essentially Conservative government now in office, and with the effects of the slump being widely felt, Britain was disposed to concede less freedom and retain more safeguards than she had been at the first conference. Parity between Congress and the Raj was now much further away than at any time since the Irwin declaration. In addition, the Muslims and the princes had used the interval between the first two conferences to clarify the terms of their acceptance of an all-India federation. The Hindu delegates considered the Muslim demands to violate the basic principles of Indian national unity. The princes were unlikely to countenance the subtraction from their sovereignty that was involved in the cession of powers to an all-India federation. On the British side there was little will to make the second conference an experiment in freedom. On the Indian side there seemed to be no hope of the experiment yielding unity.

During the closing stages of the second conference the British Government was already veering from the way of experimenting with partnership towards the old imperial ways of paternalism, collaboration, and repression. The direction was confirmed in the following years. The days of negotiating with Gandhi were brought to an abrupt end in January 1932 when civil disobedience was revived and rapidly crushed. There would be no talks with Gandhi unless and until he repudiated his experiment. There would still be devolution but the timing and the method would be officially determined. There would still be consultation with co-operative Indians, for they could appear as witnesses before a joint parliamentary committee, as they had at the time of the Montagu–Chelmsford reforms, but the days of free conferences were over. There was indeed a third Round Table Conference, but it was a poor semblance of the earlier sessions, incomplete for want of Congress, princely, and British Labour delegates, a sop to the Hindu Liberal and moderate collaborators, meeting to assess official proposals.

From 1930 until 1932 the Round Table Conference and civil disobedience experiments dominated Indian and imperial politics. After their demise the future lay with their progeny: the enactment of the federal formula and the constitutionalization of the Congress as a mass party. British policy was to grant freedom with safeguards upon the creation of unity through the federation of autonomous provinces and principalities. The objective was freedom with unity, but on terms dictated by Britain. Between 1937 and 1939 the design was frustrated by the success of the Congress in the provinces and its subsequent attempt to resolve the dualities of the Indian problem by direct confrontation with the Muslims and the princes. The Congress purpose was to create a *de facto* unitary government and proclaim its freedom. The process of devolution defeated both the British objective and the Congress purpose.

There can be no doubt that after the second conference the method and timing of the devolutionary process exacerbated divisions within India. Britain's no freedom without unity principle placed freedom beyond early reach. The enlistment of Muslim collaborators through the concession of autonomous communal provinces enabled Muslims to entrench themselves in their majority provinces. After 1937, when Congress sought to achieve its national mandate by mass contact, the political geography created by the 1935 act made Partition a strong possibility. The extension to the princes of a veto on Indian constitutional progress gave them little incentive to emulate in the states the liberality of a formerly autocratic Raj in the provinces. When Congress sought to awaken national feeling in the states' peoples and clamoured at the princes' gates for reforms, the princes were encouraged by the 1935 act to believe that they could keep British India at arm's length.

The devolution of power by stages was bound to involve the attachment to the Raj of individuals or communities whose interests were served by collaboration. Attaching in order to devolve is not necessarily the same thing as dividing in order to rule. However, the devolution of power by stages did contribute substantially to the eventual partition of India. This was largely because the Congress refused to co-operate with the Raj unless it was accorded plenipotentiary status, yet failed to secure a mandate from the Muslims.

Between 1917 and 1940 India advanced steadily towards freedom and, it seems, inexorably towards division. The process of devolution generated the crisis of Indian unity. The Round Table Conference and civil disobedience experiments were attempts to arrest the logic that the British principle of devolution by stages and the Congress doctrine of parallel government imposed upon Indian history. They stand as noble attempts to escape authoritarianism on the one side and violent rebellion on the other. However, they failed to solve the problem of freedom with unity.

Bibliography

A. PRIVATE PAPERS

1. *India Office Library (I.O.L.), London*
   Brown Collection, MSS. Eur. D712.
   Haig Collection, MSS. Eur. F115, no. 1.
   Hailey Collection, MSS. Eur. E220, esp. nos. 30–4.
   Halifax Collection (I.C.), MSS. Eur. C152, esp. letters and telegrams.
   'Indian Round Table Conference, 1931', Album by Kelen, nos. X254, X255.
   Keyes Collection (K.C.), MSS. Eur. F131, esp. files 28–31.
   Reading Collection (R.C.), MSS. Eur. E238, esp. files 56 a–k, 57.
   Sapru Collection (S.C.), ser. 1–2, microfilm reels 2189–99.
   Simon Commission Collection (S.C.C.), MSS. Eur. F77, Box 34.
   Templewood Collection (T.C.), MSS. Eur. E240, esp. letter books, secret and ordinary telegrams, and files (indexed in file I.O.L. no. 51). Note Templewood's numbering sequence revised by I.O.L., so that T.C. 1 etc. = I.O.L. 52 etc.
   Zetland Collection, MSS. Eur. D609, esp. letter books and no. 26.

2. *National Archives of India, New Delhi*
   Jayakar Collection (J.C.), files. Diaries for 1930–4 consulted on microfilm.
   Sastri Collection, consulted on microfilm.

3. *Indian National Library, Calcutta*
   Moonje Collection, diaries, esp. for 1928–32.
   Sapru Collection, series subsequent to series 1–2, now consolidated as series 3. Consulted chiefly on microfilm.

4. *Gandhi Smarak Nidhi, Delhi*
   Gandhi Collection, correspondence.

5. *Nehru Memorial Library, New Delhi*
   All-India Congress Committee (A.I.C.C.) files, esp. 1929–32.
   Nehru Collection, Jawaharlal's corr., Motilal's corr., and Jawaharlal–Motilal corr.
   Sethna Collection, extracts from letters.
   Thakurdas Collection (P.T.C.), files.

Bibliography 319

6. *Jamia College Central Library, Jamia Millia Islamia, New Delhi*
   Ali Brothers Collection.
   Ansari Collection.

B. OFFICIAL PAPERS

1. *Public Record Office, London*
   Cabinet Conclusions and Memoranda.

2. *India Office Library, London*
   Private Office Papers, series numbered L/PO/1 etc.

3. *National Archives of India, New Delhi*
   Foreign and Political Dept. (F. and P.D.) files, esp. 1929–35.
   Home Dept., Political Branch Progs., esp. 1929–32.
   Reforms Office, Reforms Branch, files and notes, 1930–2.

C. OFFICIAL PRINTED SOURCES

Government of India, *The Indian States*, Simla, 1923.
Government of India, *The Civil Disobedience Movement, 1930–34: A note on the general measures taken to deal with the movement*, New Delhi, 1936.
Report on Indian Constitutional Reforms, 1918 (Montagu-Chelmsford), Cd. 9109, 1918.
Report of the Sedition Committee, 1918 (Rowlatt), Cd. 9190, 1918.
Government of India, *India in 1920*, to *India in 1934–35*, reports prepared annually for presentation to parliament, pub. from Calcutta for 1920 to 1931–2, thereafter from Delhi.
Government of India, *Reports of Currency Committees, 1893–1926*, Calcutta, 1931.
Report of the Indian States Committee, 1928–29 (Butler), Cd. 3302, 1929 (March).
Report of the Indian Statutory Commission (Simon), Cd. 3568–9, 1930 (May).
Government of India Despatch on Proposals for Constitutional Reforms, 20 September 1930, Cd. 3700, 1930 (November).
Indian Round Table Conference, 12 November 1930—19 January 1931, Proceedings, Cd. 3778, 1931.
Indian Round Table Conference, 7 September—1 December 1931, Proceedings, Cd. 3997, 1932.
Indian Round Table Conference, 17 November—24 December 1932, Reports and Secretary of State's Closing Speech, Cd. 4238, 1933.
Indian Round Table Conference: Proceedings of Sub-Committees (12 November 1930—19 January 1931, and 7 September 1931—1 December 1931), H.M.S.O., 1931–2.

Proposals for Indian Constitutional Reform (White Paper), Cd. 4268, 1933 (March).

Other Parliamentary Papers

1929–30	xxiii	Indian Press Ordinance, 1930.
1930–1	xxiv	Statement by Jayakar and Sapru on conversations with Congress leaders, July–September 1930.
1931–2	i	Indian Pay (Temporary Abatement) Act.
	viii	Reports of Indian Franchise, Federal Finance, and States Inquiry Committees.
1931–2	xviii	Communal award.
		Emergency measures to deal with civil disobedience.
1932–3	vi-ix ⎫	Report and proceedings of joint committees on constitutional reform.
1933–4	vi-viii ⎭	
1934–5	i-ii, xvi	Government of India Bill.
	xvi	Views of Indian states on the Bill.

D. PRINTED BOOKS
(SELECTIVE)

AHMAD, AZIZ, *Islamic Modernism in India and Pakistan, 1857–1964*, London, 1967.
BIRKENHEAD, LORD, *Birkenhead*, 2 vols., London, 1933–5.
—— *Halifax*, London, 1965.
BOLITHO, H., *Jinnah, Creator of Pakistan*, London, 1954.
BOLTON, G., *Peasant and Prince*, London, 1931.
BOSE, S. C., *The Indian Struggle 1920–42*, London, 1964.
BROOMFIELD, J. H., *Elite Conflict in a Plural Society: Twentieth Century Bengal*, California, 1968.
BUTLER, J. R. M., *Lord Lothian, 1882–1940*, London, 1960.
CHAMBER OF PRINCES, DIRECTORATE OF SPEICAL ORGANIZATION OF, *The British Crown and the Indian States*, London, 1929.
CHINTAMANI, C. Y., *Indian Politics Since the Mutiny*, London, 1940.
J. COATMAN, *Years of Destiny: India 1926–32*, London, 1932.
COEN, T. C., *The Indian Political Service, A Study in Indirect Rule*, London, 1971.
COUPLAND, R., *The Indian Problem, 1833–1935*, Pt. I of Report on the Constitutional Problem in India [1942], Oxford, 1968.
—— *Indian Politics, 1936–40* (Pt. II of preceding), London, 1943.
DE MONTMORENCY, G., *The Indian States and Indian Federation*, Cambridge, 1942.
FISCHER, G., *Le Parti travailliste et la décolonization de l'Inde*, Paris, 1966.
FITZE, K., *Twilight of the Maharajas*, London, 1956.

Bibliography

GANDHI, M. K., *An Autobiography: The Story of My Experiments with Truth*, London, 1949.
GLENDEVON, J., *The Viceroy at Bay: Lord Linlithgow in India, 1936–43*, London, 1971.
GOPAL, S., *The Viceroyalty of Lord Irwin, 1926–31*, Oxford, 1957.
GWYER, M., and APPADORAI, A. (eds.), *Speeches and Documents on the Indian Constitution, 1922–47*, 2 vols., Oxford, 1957.
HALIFAX, LORD, *Fulness of Days*, London, 1957.
HAMID, ABDUL, *Muslim Separatism in India, 1858–1947*, Karachi, 1967.
HARDY, P., *Partners in Freedom—and True Muslims: The political thought of some Muslim scholars in British India, 1912–47*, Scandinavian Inst. of Asian Studies, 1971.
HUSAIN, A., *Fazl-i-Husain: A Political Biography*, Bombay, 1946.
HYDE, H. M., *Lord Reading*, London, 1967.
IRSCHICK, E., *Politics and Social Conflict in South India: The Non-Brahman Movement and Tamil Separatism, 1916–29*, California, 1969.
ISMAIL, MIRZA, *My Public Life*, London, 1954.
JAGADISAN, T. N. (ed.), *Letters of the Right Hon'ble V. S. Srinivasa Sastri*, 2nd ed., London, 1963.
—— *V. S. Srinivasa Sastri*, New Delhi, 1969.
KHALIQUZZAMAN, C., *Pathway to Pakistan*, Lahore, 1961.
KUMAR, R. (ed.), *Essays on Gandhian Politics: The Rowlatt Satyagraha of 1919*, Oxford, 1971.
LOTHIAN, A. C., *Kingdoms of Yesterday*, London, 1951.
LOW, D. A. (ed.), *Soundings in Modern South Asian History*, London, 1968.
—— ILTIS, J. C., and WAINWRIGHT, M. D. (eds.), *Government Archives in South Asia*, Cambridge, 1969.
MANKEKAR, D. R., *Homi Mody*, Bombay, 1968.
MEHROTRA, S. R., *India and the Commonwealth, 1885–1929*, London, 1965.
MIDDLEMAS, J. K., and BARNES, A. J. L., *Baldwin, A Biography*, London, 1969.
MORAES, F., *Sir Purshotamdas Thakurdas*, Bombay, 1957.
NANDA, B. R., *Mahatma Gandhi*, London [1958], 1965 ed.
NEHRU, J., *An Autobiography*, London, 1936.
—— (ed.), *A Bunch of Old Letters*, Bombay, 1958.
OHDEDAR, O. K., *The Sapru Correspondence*, Calcutta, 1961.
PANIKKAR, K. M., *British Government and the Indian States*, London, 1929.
—— *His Highness the Maharaja of Bikaner*, London, 1937.
—— *Autobiography*, 2 vols., Trichur [1953 and 1964], 1967 ed. in Malayalam.
PATEL, G. I., *Vithalbhai Patel: Life and Times*, 2 vols., Bombay, 1951.
PATIALA, MAHARAJA OF, *Federation and the Indian States*, n.d. [1931].

PHADNIS, U., *Towards the Integration of the Indian States, 1919–47*, London, 1968.
PHILIPS, C. H. (ed.), *The Evolution of India and Pakistan, 1858–1947: Select Documents*, London, 1962.
—— and WAINWRIGHT, M. D. (eds.), *The Partition of India: Policies and Perspectives, 1935–47*, London, 1970.
PRAKASH, INDRA, *Hindu Mahasabha, Its Contribution to Indian Politics*, New Delhi, 1966.
READING, MARQUESS OF, *Rufus Isaacs, First Marquess of Reading: 1914–35*, London, 1945.
ROTHERMUND, D., *Die politische Willensbildung in Indien, 1900–60*, Wiesbaden, 1965.
RUDOLPH, L. I. and S. H., *The Modernity of Tradition*, Chicago, 1967.
SAIYID, M. H., *Muhammad Ali Jinnah, A Political Study*, Lahore, 1962.
SAYEED, KHALID BIN, *Pakistan: The Formative Phase*, 2nd ed., London, 1968.
SETALVAD, C. H., *Recollections and Reflections: An Autobiography*, Bombay, n.d.
SIMON, VISCOUNT, *Retrospect*, London, 1952.
TEMPLEWOOD, LORD, *Nine Troubled Years*, London, 1954.
TENDULKAR, D. G., *Mahatma*, 8 vols., Bombay, 1951–4.
'TRENCH, VICTOR' (pseud.), *Lord Willingdon in India*, Bombay, 1934.
WILSON, F. W., *The Indian Chaos*, London, 1932.
WINTERTON, EARL OF, *Orders of the Day*, London, 1953.
WRENCH, J. E., *Geoffrey Dawson and Our Times*, London, 1955.
ZETLAND, MARQUESS OF, *'Essayez'*, London, 1956.

E. ARTICLES

BAGCHI, A. K., 'European and Indian Entrepreneurship in India, 1900–30', in S. N. Mukherjee and E. Leach (eds.), *Elites in South Asia*, Cambridge, 1970.
DALTON, D. G., 'Mahatma Gandhi: The Shaping of Satyagraha', *South Asian Review*, ii (1969), 105–14.
DANZIG, R., 'The Announcement of August 20th, 1917', *Journal of Asian Studies (J.A.S.)*, xxviii (1968), 19–37.
—— 'The Many-Layered Cake: A Case Study in the Reform of the Indian Empire', *Modern Asian Studies*, iii (1969), 57–74.
GHOSH, S. C., 'Decision-making and Power in the British Conservative Party: A Case Study of the Indian Problem, 1929–34', *Political Studies*, xii (1965), 198–212.
HAITHCOX, J. P., 'Left Wing Unity and the Indian Nationalist Movement', *Modern Asian Studies*, iii (1969), 17–56.

HOLDSWORTH, W. S., 'The Indian States and India', *Law Quarterly Review*, xlvi (1930), 407–46.
JONES, K. W., 'Communalism in the Punjab', *J.A.S.* xxviii (1968), 39–54.
KRISHNA, Gopal, 'The Development of the Indian National Congress as a Mass Organization, 1918–1923', *J.A.S.* xxv (1965–6), 413–30.
—— 'The Khilafat Movement in India: the First Phase', *Journal of Royal Asiatic Society*, xix (1968), 37–53.
LOW, D. A., 'The Government of India and the First Non-Co-operation Movement, 1920–1922', *J.A.S.* xxv (1965–6), 241–59.
MEHROTRA, S. R., 'The Early Organization of the Indian National Congress, 1885–1920', *India Quarterly*, xx (1966), 329–52.
ROTHERMUND, D., 'Constitutional Reforms versus National Agitation in India, 1900–1950', *J.A.S.* xxi (1961–2), 505–22.
Modern Asian Studies, Gandhi Centenary Number, October 1969.

Glossary

A.G.G.	Agent to the Governor-General. Indian political officer responsible for Crown relations with major groups of states (agencies).
ARYA SAMAJ	Militant Hindu missionary movement founded in Punjab in late nineteenth century.
ASHRAM	Hermitage, spiritual retreat.
BRAHMAN	A man of the first rank or priestly caste of Hindus.
CHAUTH	Claim made by Marathas on revenue of country that they overran.
COLLECTOR	Chief British administrator of a district.
COMMISSIONER	British official controlling several districts.
CONGRESS, THE INDIAN NATIONAL	Political movement founded in 1885.
DEPRESSED CLASSES	Castes or communities regarded as impure by orthodox Hindus. Also 'Untouchables' or 'Harijans'.
DISTRICT	Administrative unit of British India.
DIWAN	A minister or chief officer of a state.
FARMAN	A mandate, order.
HARIJANS (People of God)	See Depressed Classes.
HARTAL	Closure of shops or strike (a traditional form of protest).
IZZAT	Honour or reputation.
KHALIFA (Successor)	The religious and temporal head of Islam, as acknowledged by Sunnis.
KHILAFAT	Office of Khalifa, to protect which from destruction after World War I Indian Muslims formed an organized movement.
KHUDAI KHIDMATGARS (Servants of God)	A Pathan political organization. Also 'Red Shirts'.

KISAN	Peasant.
MAHASABHA (Great Assembly)	The All-India Hindu Mahasabha was a communalist party founded in 1915.
MAHATMA (Great Soul)	Title given to Gandhi (and others).
MOPLAHS	Muslims on the Malabar coast.
MUSLIM LEAGUE, THE ALL-INDIA	Founded in 1906 to protect Muslims' interests.
MUS(S)ALMAN	Muslim.
NAWAB	Muslim title of high rank.
NIZAM	Administrator of the Deccan, a title of the rulers of Hyderabad.
PANDIT	A learned Brahman.
PARSIS	Zoroastrians from Persia settled chiefly in Bombay city and Gujarat.
PURNA SWARAJ	Complete independence.
RAJ	A rule, sovereignty. When used with the definite article in the British period, British rule is implied.
RAJA	A king or prince.
RESIDENT	Representative of the Crown in an important Indian state.
RYOT	A peasant.
SABHA	An assembly, association.
SANAD	A grant, charter.
SATYAGRAHA (Truth-force, soul-force)	Coined by Gandhi to embrace forms of non-violent moral pressure, e.g. civil disobedience.
SATYAGRAHI	One who practises satyagraha.
SWARAJ	Self-rule.
TALUQ	Administrative unit within a district.

Index

Abdul Ghaffar Khan, 172, 203, 243-7, 289, 295
Aga Khan, the, 38, 262, 265, 284, 311; at 1st R.T.C., 121, 126, 144, 158-63; at 2nd R.T.C., 219, 237; on all-India federation, 312
Ahmed, Sir Sayed Sultan, 150
Aiyer, Sir C. P. Ramaswami, 12, 122, 129, 150, 253
Aiyer, Sir P. S. Sivaswamy, 12, 96, 146
Ali, Waris Ameer, 160
Ali Imam, Sir Saiyid, 51, 52, 193
Allahabad District Congress Committee, 242
All-India Congress Committee (A.I.C.C.), 14-15, 295, 305-8
All-India Hindu Mahasabha, 18, 23, 25, 30, 105-6, 193, 204, 267, 270, 293, 307-8; and All-Parties Conference Report, 34-7, 39, 101; at 1st R.T.C., 122, 124-6, 158-61, 163; at 2nd R.T.C., 222; and communal award, 261, 264-5
All-India Moderates' Conference, 12
All-India Moslem Conference. See All-Parties Moslem Conference.
All-India Muslim League, 19-24, 34-9, 103-4, 311-12
All-India Nationalist Muslim Party, 39, 169, 188, 189, 190, 193
All-India States' Peoples Conference, 33
All-India Swaraj Party (Congress-Khilafat Swaraj Party), 4, 16-19, 23, 30, 34, 45, 53, 56, 295, 307
All-Parties Conference, 33, 35-7, 43, 129. See also Nehru Report
All-Parties Moslem Conference, 38, 121, 158, 163, 172, 189-91, 193, 261-2, 265
Alwar, Maharaja of, 130, 142, 144
Ambedkar, Dr. B. R., 122, 124, 126, 233, 237, 253, 284
Amery, L. S., 67
Amritsar massacre, 4, 13, 100
Anderson, Sir John, 264
Andrews, C. F., 210
Aney, M. S., 18

Anglo-Indians, 35, 105, 107, 122, 220, 222, 284, 292
Ansari, Dr. M. A., 35, 95, 101, 165, 169, 183, 189-90, 192, 203
Arya Samaj, 18, 22, 308
Ataturk, 22
Attlee, Clement, 50, 51
Azad, Abul Kalam, 101, 165

Bahawalpur, 229
Baldwin, Stanley, 10, 217, 253, 282; and Irwin declaration, 51, 61, 66-94, 97-8; and Irwin's July 1930 statement, 109-13; and R.T.C. delegation, 114, 118; and all-India federation, 155-6, 208-9
Balfour, A. J., 93
Baluchistan, 24, 34-7, 104, 193
Banerjea, Surendranath, 11, 12
Bardoli taluq, 15, 185, 194-5, 203
Baroda, 28, 32, 128, 136, 231, 280, 282, 304, 309
Barton, Sir William, 133
Beaverbrook, Lord, 81-3
Bengal Criminal Law Amendment Bill, 251
'Bengal Pact', 23
Bengal Province, 36-7, 104, 123-4, 126, 159, 161-2, 191, 193, 219-21, 235, 239, 311; under Montford reforms, 5, 11-12, 15-17, 20, 22-3, 25, 34; repression in, 242, 244-8, 251; and communal award, 261-4, 310
Benn, Wedgwood, 159, 160, 162, 163, 202, 208-9, 213, 233, 236; and Irwin declaration, 59-94; 98; and Irwin's July 1930 statement, 108-10; and R.T.C., 114, 118-20, 125, 137, 142; and all-India federation, 150, 152-4, 157; and civil disobedience, 172, 181, 206-7
Benthall, E. C., 253
Berar, 29-31, 132-3, 137, 231, 285
Besant, Mrs. Annie, 4, 15, 95
Bhavnagar, 228, 229
Bhopal, 28, 301, 304
Bhopal, Nawab of, 126, 130, 150, 158, 160, 190, 219, 280, 300; and

328 Index

Chamber group on federation and paramountcy, 225–7, 275, 278, 301–4; and confederationists, 229–31, 270–4
Bhore, Sir Joseph W., 173
Bikaner, 28
Bikaner, Maharaja of, 175, 226, 239; note to Reading, 29; on Butler Report, 128; on Simon Report, 130–1; at 1st R.T.C., 127, 141–3, 150, 154, 157; at 2nd R.T.C., 217; and confederation, 228–32; and Chamber group on federation, 270–5, 278, 287, 301–2, 304; and 3rd R.T.C., 280–1, 285
Birkenhead, Lord, 10, 31, 33, 35, 41–4, 46; and Irwin declaration, 66, 68, 71–4, 76, 80–3, 85–7, 91–4
Birla, G. D., 165, 173, 179, 204, 258–9, 269–70
Bombay Commercial Associations, Committee of, 216
Bombay, Millowners' Association of, 180
Bombay City, civil disobedience in, 168, 173–4, 180, 183, 216, 267
Bombay Province, 3, 12, 19–20, 22, 24, 34, 171–2, 311
Bose, Subhas Chandra, 95
Bray, Sir Denys, 133, 137
Burnham, Viscount, 50, 65, 74, 86, 114, 115
Butler (Indian States) Committee (1928–9), 32–3, 44, 60, 127–33, 137, 227, 229, 271
Butler, Sir (Spencer) Harcourt. See Butler (Indian States) Committee
Butler, R. A., 284

Cadogan, E. C. G., 50, 74
Campbell-Bannerman, Sir Henry, 152
Carr, Sir Hubert, 122, 284
Cawnpore riots (March 1931), 188, 210
Central Provinces, 16, 18, 20, 29, 30, 35, 137
Chamber of Princes, 28–9, 128–9, 132–5, 138, 141–2, 157, 225–9, 270–3, 299–300, 302–3; Standing Committee of, 33, 127, 275, 278–9, 281–3, 285–6; Special Organization of, 32, 106, 137
Chamberlain, Austen, 1, 3, 6, 118; and Irwin declaration, 66, 83, 91; and Irwin's July 1930 statement, 109–13

Chamberlain, Neville, 82, 90, 155
Chand, Nanak, 284
Chauri Chaura incident, 16
Chelmsford, Lord, 1, 5, 8. See also Montagu–Chelmsford Reforms
Chintamani, C. Y., 12, 18, 33, 106, 122, 260; and all-India federation, 145–6
Chittari, Nawab of, 121
Christians, Indian, 24, 35, 105, 122, 220, 222, 292
Churchill, Winston S., 6; and Irwin declaration, 66, 83, 86, 89; and all-India federation, 155–7, 208, 238 n.3, 297–8
Coatman, John, 24–5, 101, 119–22, 140, 143–4, 152, 156, 160
Cochin, 28, 32, 127, 138, 139, 304
Communal Award (1932), 162–3, 232–3, 235, 237–9, 253, 258, 261–6, 295, 305, 309–10
Congress Nationalist Party, 305
Congress Socialist Party, 295
Congress Working Committee (C.W.C.), 14, 96, 97, 176–7, 181–4, 187, 193, 204, 206, 207, 246–8, 305, 307–9
Conservative Party, Business Committee (Shadow Cabinet) of, 66–8, 72, 74, 80, 155–7; Central Council of, 297; delegation at R.T.C., 113–14, 118–20, 149–50, 154–7, 208–9; India Committee of, 118, 209, 284
Consultative Committee (of Round Table Conference), 235, 238, 252–3, 256–62, 268
Corbett, Sir Geoffrey, 221–2, 233–4, 237
Cotton duties, 211–15, 267
Council of Greater India, 130–1, 136–7
Council of Indian Chambers of Commerce in Great Britain, 216
Coupland, Sir Reginald, 234
Craddock, Sir Reginald, 5
Crawford and Balcarres, Earl of, 90
Crerar, Sir James, 61, 192, 248
Crewe, Lord, 85, 91–2, 94 n.3, 110–11
Criminal Law Amendment Act (1908), 5, 194, 197, 206
Criminal Procedure Code, 244
Cripps, Stafford, 275–6
Cunningham, Sir George, 134
Curzon, Lord, 2, 6

Daily Express, 82, 297

Index

Daily Herald, 175, 236
Daily Mail, 297; attack on Baldwin, 80–6
Daily Telegraph, 73, 159
Das, C. R., 5, 15–17, 23
Datta, S. K., 234
Daudi, Muhammad Shafi, 190, 193
Davidson, J. C. C., 76, 81–2, 84, 87–8, 253, 256, 282–3
Dawson, Geoffrey, 114, 138, 156; and Irwin declaration, 41, 47–51, 55, 58, 73, 82–4
Delhi Pact (March 1930), 189, 205, 206, 207; negotiated, 183–6; operation of, 193–204, 240, 243, 246, 251; breakdown of, 247, 249
de Montmorency, Sir Geoffrey, 59, 61, 121, 189, 206, 210, 263
Delhi Manifesto (November 1929), 95–8, 103, 105, 167
Depressed Classes, 34–5, 107, 122, 125, 270, 284, 292; and Minorities Committee of R.T.C., 220–3; and Poona pact, 265–6; legislation for, 293
Dholpur, 28
Dholpur, Maharaj Rana of, 130; and confederation, 228–31, 270–1, 299, 304
Dinshaw, F. E., 180
Dominion Status declaration (1929). See Irwin, Lord, declaration of
Dyarchy, 2–4, 6, 20–1, 23, 33, 115–16, 149
Dyer, General Reginald, 4, 13

Emergency Powers Ordinance (1931–2), 206–7, 245–7, 250
Emerson, H. W., 182, 197–8, 200, 203, 241, 243
Empire Economic Union, 81

Fazl-i-Husain, Mian, 20, 21, 23, 25, 121–4, 158, 160 and n., 189–93, 219, 220, 225, 263, 309
Fazlul Huq, A. K., 20–1, 23, 121, 162
Federal Finance Committee (1932), 235, 253, 259, 262, 277
Federal Structure Committee (of Round Table Conference), 150–1, 157, 192–3, 210–11, 218, 224, 228–30, 232, 256, 276, 282, 285, 287
Federation of Indian Chambers of Commerce and Industry, 174, 179, 268

Fiscal Autonomy Convention, 7, 155–6, 168, 174, 180, 212, 218, 267–9
Fisher, H. A. L., 6, 90, 131
Fitze, Kenneth, 134
Foot, Isaac, 119, 152, 161
Fox, Colonel George Lane, 48, 50, 81, 114, 154
Franchise Committee (1932), 235, 253, 262

Gandhi, Devadas, 243
Gandhi, Mohandas Karamchand, 17, 39, 40, 46, 48, 122, 208, 216, 226, 255, 261, 269; and non-co-operation (1920–2), 5–6, 13–16, 22; and Irwin declaration, 95–105, 109; and civil disobedience, 106–8, 165–82; and Delhi Pact, 183–5; in truce period, 187–202, 210; and second settlement, 203–7; at 2nd R.T.C., 219–23, 231, 233–6; and end of truce, 239–49; repression of, 250–1, 267, 288–90; and Poona Pact, 265–6; and individual satyagraha, 293–6; and problem of freedom with unity, 292, 304–9, 314–15
George, D. Lloyd, 8, 10, 13, 109–13; and Irwin declaration, 66, 68–72, 73, 80–4, 86–8; and Liberal delegation at R.T.C., 118, 119, 153
Ghaznavi, A. H., 38, 121, 161, 253, 262, 284
Gidney, Lieutenant-Colonel H. A. J., 122, 284
Gladstone, W. E., 152
Glancy, Sir Reginald, 231, 286
Goschen, Lord, 61, 82, 84, 94
Gour, H. S., 129
Government of India Act (1919), 2–4, 6, 12, 17, 33; and Dominion Status and Irwin declaration, 56–7, 69–71, 73–5, 85, 88–9, 92, 297
Government of India Act (1935), 297–9, 302–6, 311
Government of India Reforms Dispatch (September 1930), 124, 131, 148, 262,
Gujarat, 171–2, 185, 194–203, 207, 210
Gwalior, 106, 136–7, 304, 308
Gwyer, Sir Maurice, 286
Gwynn, J. T., 148–9

Haig, H. G., 288–90; at 1st R.T.C.,

120, 145, 147, 152, 156, 160; and civil disobedience, 170, 250, 251, 266, 288–90
Hailey, Sir Malcolm, and Irwin declaration, 42, 45, 49, 50, 56–61, 89, 94, 98; at 1st R.T.C., 143–5, 147–9, 156, 159–63; and U.P. rent agitation, 199, 201; and finance, 287
Hailsham, Lord, 67, 155, 243, 255
Haksar, Colonel Kailas Narain, 32, 106, 129–31, 137, 226, 254, 258, 280, 286; at 1st R.T.C., 127, 135, 140–51, 154; and Jam Sahib on federation 273–5; on Hydari, 278–9
Halifax, 1st Earl of. See Irwin, Lord
Hallett, Sir Maurice, 290
Hamilton, Sir Robert, 119, 152
Hammond, Sir Laurie, 51
Harijan, 293
Harijans. See Depressed Classes
Hartshorn, V., 50, 51, 79
Hoare, Sir Samuel, 202, 208–18, 227, 252; and Irwin declaration, 68, 72, 82, 87, 92; and Irwin's July 1930 statement, 114; and Conservatives at 1st R.T.C., 118–19, 125, 149–50, 154–6; at 2nd R.T.C., 232–8; and repression, 245, 247, 251, 290; and reaction, 253, 255, 257–70; and the princes, 272, 275, 279–83; and 3rd R.T.C., 284–8; and 1935 Act, 297–303
Home Rule League, 4, 12
House of Commons, 48, 76–7, 80, 85–8, 109–10, 210, 238, 256, 258, 260
House of Lords, 66, 80, 85, 92, 210, 238, 255, 260
Hunter Committee Report (1920), 13, 100
Hydari, Nawab Sir Muhammad Akbar, 130, 253, 281, 302; at 1st R.T.C., 127, 135, 138–45, 147, 150–1, 154, 157; and F.S.C. scheme, 219, 224–6, 229; and paramountcy, 277–8; at 3rd R.T.C., 285
Hyderabad, 28, 32, 127, 132–8, 141, 224–6, 231, 270, 272, 276, 278, 280, 282, 285, 301–2, 304, 308
Hyderabad External Relations Committee, 128
Hyderabad, Nizam of, 231; and paramountcy, 29–32, 275–6, 278; and federation, 132-9, 285

Imperial Conference (1926), 93
Imperial Economic Conference (Ottawa, 1932), 268–70
Independence for India League, 96
Independence Youth League, 40, 95
Independent Congress Party, 19, 34, 35
Independent Party, 17, 23, 38
India Committee of Cabinet, 253, 277, 281, 283–4, 287
India Office, 1, 54, 215, 219, 223, 253, 275
Indian Army, Indianization of, 8–9, 11, 70
Indian Central Committee, 42, 89
Indian Civil Service, Indianization of, 7–11, 70
Indian Daily Mail, 226
Indian Empire Society, 119
Indian Political Service, 9–10, 282–3
Indian States (Butler) Committee (1928–9), 32–3, 44, 60, 127–33, 137, 227, 229, 271
Indian States Inquiry Committee (1932), 235, 253, 259, 277
Indian Trade Union Congress, 96
Indore, 137
Indore, Maharaja of, 228, 229
Iqbal, Dr. Muhammad, 190, 193, 284
Irish Treaty of Settlement (1921), 10, 118, 211
Irwin, Lord, 125, 151, 160, 162–3, 189, 191, 194, 204, 210, 253; and princes, 32, 128, 157; declaration of (1929), 41–103, 165, 169, 313–15; statement of in July 1930, 107–14, 257; and Simon Report, 115–17, 123, 148; and 1st R.T.C., 118–20; and federation, 131–2, 138, 143–4; and Keyes, 133–4; and civil disobedience, 172–6, 247; and Delhi Pact, 181–6; on Hoare, 208–9; on Lancashire, 213
Ismail, Sir Mirza, 127, 130, 138–44, 150, 158, 225, 253, 285
Iyengar, Rangaswami, 165

Jackson, Sir Francis, 263
Jaipur, 28, 231, 280, 300
Jam Sahib, See Nawanagar, Maharaja of
Jamal Muhammad, 204, 216
Jayakar, M. R., 15, 18–19, 25, 34, 48, 95, 105–6, 192, 201, 230, 239, 264; and Nehru Report, 37, 101; at 1st R.T.C.,

Index

122, 124, 126, 150, 152, 158, 161; as intermediary, 175–85, 290; and British reaction, 253–61; at 3rd R.T.C., 284, 287–8
Jehangir, Sir Cowasji, 12, 122, 284
Jinnah, Muhammad Ali, 17, 20, 23–5, 107, 175, 219, 237, 292; and All-Parties Conference, 34–7; and Irwin declaration, 48, 58, 99–101; and 14 points, 38–9, 103–5, 189, 241; at 1st R.T.C., 121, 124, 126, 144, 150, 158–63; and 1935 Act, 310–11
Jodhpur, 28, 280, 282, 300
Jones, T. F. Gavin, 150
Joshi, N. M., 123, 253, 260, 284
Junagadh, 32
Justice Party, 2, 12, 15, 17, 34, 35, 105, 122, 125, 284

Kashmir, 22, 300
Kashmir, Maharaja of, 130, 137 n., 280
Kathiawar States, 32, 228, 271
Kelkar, N. C., 16, 18, 19, 33, 105, 106, 165, 261, 264, 284
Kesari, 16
Keyes, Lieutenant-Colonel Terence H., and all-India federation, 132–43, 152–4, 224–9, 272
Khaliquzzaman, Chaudhri, 169, 190
Khan Saheb, Dr., 244
Khilafat movement, 4, 6, 13, 15, 20, 22, 35, 38–9
Khudai Khidmatgars (Red Shirts), 172, 243–4, 295
Kidwai, R. A., 169
Kolhapur, 280, 309
Krishnamachari, V. T., 142, 253, 272

Lahore Resolution (1929), 102, 165, 167, 177, 186
Lajpat Rai, Lala, 5, 18, 19, 25
Lancashire interests, 210–12, 215
Laski, Harold, 115
Lawrence, Sir Walter, 143
Leader (Allahabad), 106
League of Nations, 7, 222
Liaquat Hyat Khan, 253, 272
Liberal Party delegation, at R.T.C., 113–14, 119–20, 149–50, 152–3
Lindsay, A. D., 234
Linlithgow, Lord, 304
Lloyd, Sir George, 3, 6
Lothian, A. C., 304

Lothian, Lord, 210, 253, 256, 284; at 1st R.T.C., 119, 125, 138, 150, 152; at 2nd R.T.C., 233–4, 236
Lucknow Pact, 19–21, 25, 310
Lytton, Lord, 82, 88

MacDonald, Malcolm, 234
MacDonald, Ramsay, 10, 214; and Irwin declaration, 51, 58–67, 75–8, 85, 88, 91, 96–8, 103; and Irwin's July 1930 statement, 109–14; at 1st R.T.C., 117, 150–1, 161–3, 181, 190, 314; at 2nd R.T.C., 233, 236, 237; and repression, 251–3, 290; and reaction, 254, 256–7
Madras Province, 3–5, 12, 15, 17, 20, 22, 34, 311
Mahmud, Dr. Syed, 169
Mahmudabad, Raja of, 193
Mahratta, 16
Malaviya, Madan Mohan, 6, 15, 18–19, 25, 34, 105–6, 204, 220, 234; and Irwin declaration, 48, 51–3, 95, 101, 165; and civil disobedience, 173, 183, 213, 217; and communal award, 305, 307, 310
Manchester Guardian, 148–9, 152, 191
Mant, Sir Reginald, 268–9
Mears, Sir Grimwood, 51–5, 62, 95, 98, 106
Mehta, Sir Manubhai, 129, 142, 145, 253, 272, 275
Melchett, Lord, 81–2
Miéville, Sir Eric, 241–3
Minorities Committee (of Round Table Conference), 220–2
Minto, Lord, 10, 26
Mitter, Sir B. L., 256
Mody, Sir H. P., 123, 180–1
Mohani, Hasrat, 22
Montagu–Chelmsford report and reforms, 3–4, 8, 10–12, 16, 20–1, 25–6, 29, 33, 35–6, 92, 98, 116, 307, 313, 315
Montagu declaration (1917), 1–11, 19, 26, 33, 41, 64, 68–73, 78, 92, 108, 250
Montagu, Edwin S., 1–3, 6, 8, 10–11, 26, 155, 307. See also Montagu declaration, and Montagu–Chelmsford report and reforms
Moonje, Dr. B. S., 18–19, 34, 37, 95, 101, 105–6, 173, 179, 261; at 1st

R.T.C., 122, 124–6, 158, 160–2; on 2nd R.T.C., 238–9
Moplah rebellion, 22
Morley-Minto reforms, 2, 4
Morning Post, 208, 297
Mudaliyar, Ramaswami, 122, 150, 259, 284
Muhammad Ali, 15, 22, 24, 38, 95, 129, 169, 191; and 1st R.T.C., 121, 124
Muhammad Khan, Sir, 262
Muhammad Yakub, 36
Mysore, 28, 32, 127-9, 136, 138–9, 231, 280, 282, 301, 304, 308

Naidu, Mrs. Sarojini, 95, 10Ւ, 179, 190, 204
Naranji, Lalji, 168, 175
Narendra Nath, Raja, 18, 122, 158, 161–3, 258, 264
'National Demand', 17, 23, 39, 56
National Liberal Federation of India, 3, 12, 15, 21, 192, 230; and Simon boycott, 34–5, 39, 41; favours R.T.C. scheme, 45, 48, 94, 103–7; at 1st R.T.C., 122, 125–6, 144–7, 149, 151–2, 158–9, 161–3, 224; and civil disobedience, 166–7; as intermediaries, 179, 182, 185; at 2nd R.T.C., 223, 233–4, 236; and British reaction, 252, 260–1, 265, 267, 270; at 3rd R.T.C., 284, 315
National Liberal League, 11, 35
National Union of Conservative Associations, 297
Nawanagar, 28, 231
Nawanagar, Maharaja of (the Jam Sahib, Ranjitsinghji), and all-India federation and paramountcy, 271–80, 299
Nawaz, Begum Shah, 123, 284
Nehru, Jawaharlal, 40, 51, 105, 190, 226, 266, 269, 289 90, 291–5, 304–5; and Irwin declaration, 95–9, 102, 105; and civil disobedience, 165, 167, 171, 176–80, 182–4, 186, 194–205; and end of Delhi Pact, 240–9
Nehru, Motilal, 5, 16–17, 35, 39–40, 129, 183; and Irwin declaration, 46, 48, 51–5, 95, 97–100, 103; and civil disobedience, 167, 170, 175–81
Nehru (All-Parties Conference Committee) Report (1928), 35–40, 57, 101, 189, 227

Neogy, K. C., 142
Non-cooperation movement (1920–2), 4–6, 11–13, 15–18, 20–3, 29, 34, 39
Noon, Feroz Khan, 191
Norman, Montagu, 288
North West Frontier Province, status of, 23–4, 34–8, 104, 123–4, 126, 191, 193, 219, 222, 235, 238–9, 310–11; civil disobedience in, 172, 188, 206, 242–9, 261–2, 289

O'Dwyer, Sir Michael, 3, 125, 126, 158, 159
Oliver, F. S., 137, 138

Pakistan resolution (Lahore 1940), 312
Panikkar, K. M., 32, 127, 131, 140–1, 145, 151, 154, 228
Panna, 229
Pant, Govind Ballabh, 240
Paramountcy, 40; Reading's clarification of, 27–33, 70–1; Nehru Report and, 36; Butler Report and, 127–8; Princes' concern over, 130–3, 143–4, 157–8, 226–30, 270–81, 300, 302
Paris Peace Conference, 7
Parmoor, Lord, 85, 86
Parsis, 12, 107
Partition of India, 191, 219, 312, 316
Passfield, Lord, 86
Patel, Vallabhbhai, 98, 165, 170, 179, 185, 194, 199–200, 203, 240–3, 295
Patel, Vithalbhai J., 16, 46–7, 55, 95, 98–9, 165, 173, 213, 217
Patiala, 28
Patiala, Maharaja of, 137 n.; and 1st R.T.C., 127–30, 143–4; and confederation, 228–31, 270; and Jam Sahib's initiative, 272–5; and paramountcy and 1935 Act, 278, 280, 299–304
Patro, Sir A. P., 122, 124, 253, 284
Pattani, Sir Prabhashankar, 142, 175, 228
Paul, K. T., 122
Peel, Lord, 46, 209, 284; and Irwin declaration, 66, 68, 71–4, 80, 86, 91–3; at 1st R.T.C., 118, 120, 150, 154–5, 161
Pentland, Lord, 3
Percy, Lord Eustace, 253
Pioneer, 54
Polak, H. S., 210, 234

Index   333

Poona Pact (1932), 265–6, 293
Press Act (1910) and Ordinance (1930), 173
Prevention of Molestation and Boycott Ordinance (1932), 245, 247, 250
Pudakottai, 139
Punjab Province, 36–7, 104, 123–4, 126, 159, 161–3, 191, 193, 219, 220–2, 235, 239, 311; and Montford constitution, 3, 5, 15, 18, 20–5, 34; and communal award, 261–4, 310

Rahim, Sir Abdur, 24
Rahimtoolah, Ibrahim, 38
Rainy, Sir George, 218, 252
Rampur, 32, 229
Rangachariar, Diwan Bahadur, 56
Rau, B. Rama, 256
Rawlinson, Lord, 9
Reading, Lord, 117, 236, 248, 286; as viceroy, 5–11, 15, 22, 29–32, 132; and Irwin declaration, 56, 61, 65–6, 68–74, 76, 80–92; and Irwin's July 1930 statement, 109–15; at 1st R.T.C., 119–20, 125, 142, 149–54, 156, 158, 160–1
Red Shirt movement (Khudai Khidmatgars), 172, 243–4, 295
Responsive Co-operation movement, 12, 18–19, 23, 30, 34–5, 102, 105–6, 122, 173
Rewa, Maharaja of, 127, 130, 280
Rothermere, Lord, 81, 82, 83, 108
Rowlatt Bills (1919), 4
Runciman, W., 253, 284
Rupee-sterling exchange rate, 7, 155–6, 167–8, 173–4, 181, 213–18, 267–9, 287–8
Russell, Lord, 107

Sahai, Sitla, 196
Salisbury, Lord, 68, 74, 86, 92, 118, 238, 297, 298
Salt Satyagraha, 168–72, 177–8, 184–5
Samuel, Herbert, 110, 111
Sangli, Raja of, 127, 130, 229
Sankey, Lord, 209–11, 253, 256, 266, 284; at 1st R.T.C., 118, 150, 163; at 2nd R.T.C., 232–7. See also Federal Structure Committee
Sapru, Sir Tej Bahadur, 12, 35, 190, 192, 226, 230, 248–9, 250, 264, 290; and Irwin declaration, 46, 51–5, 95–100; for counterpoise to C.D., 103–8, 166; at 1st R.T.C., 122, 124–6, 129, 132, 137, 140, 142, 145–7, 150–2, 154–5, 158–63; as intermediary, 176–9, 181–5; at 2nd R.T.C., 221, 233–9; and British reaction, 253–60; at 3rd R.T.C., 284, 286–8
Sarila, Raja of, 270, 280, 284
Sastri, V. S. Srinivasa, 12, 182–3, 210, 234, 264; and Irwin declaration, 95–7; at 1st R.T.C., 122, 141, 145–6, 150, 161, 166; and British reaction, 254, 259–60
Schuster, Sir George, at 1st R.T.C., 120, 138–9, 142, 144, 147, 152; and fiscal and currency policies, 212–14, 216, 218, 237, 267, 269
Scott, Sir Leslie, 32, 33, 133, 143, 226
Second settlement (August 1931), 203–5, 240, 247
Seditious Meetings Act (1907), 5
Setalvad, Sir Chimanlal, 12, 107, 175, 259, 264; and Irwin declaration, 41–2, 46–7, 55, 62, 95–6; at 1st R.T.C., 122, 126, 161
Sethna, Sir Pheroze, 107, 122, 175, 260
Sèvres, Treaty of, 6, 11, 12, 22
Shafa'at Ahmad Khan, Dr., 38, 121, 124, 160, 193, 218–19, 253, 262, 284
Shafi, Sir Muhammad, 24, 34, 38, 189, 190, 219, 237, 253; at 1st R.T.C., 121, 126, 129, 144, 150, 152, 158, 160–2
Shaukat Ali, 15, 22, 24, 36, 169, 189–90 262
Sherwani, T. A., 39, 169, 190
Shradhanand, Swami, 24
Sikhs, 21, 35, 107, 122, 158, 161, 163, 190, 220–3, 262–5, 284, 292
Simon, Sir John, 106, 108, 118, 132, 141, 146, 148, 154–5, 209, 233, 236–7, 253; and Statutory Commission and Irwin declaration, 42–96, 107; and Irwin's July 1930 statement, 110–14; and his Report, 115–17
Simon (Statutory) Commission, 258; appointment and boycott of, 33–4, 39, 41–2, 313; and Irwin declaration, 43–55, 60–80, 83–8, 91, 96; report of, 108, 110–19, 123–4, 130–2, 135–8, 148, 154–5, 157, 208, 229, 233, 239
Sind, separation of, from Bombay, 22, 24, 34–8, 104, 123–4, 126, 191,

193, 219, 235, 238–9, 261–2, 265, 310–11
Singh, Bhagat, 187, 188, 210
Singh, Sampuran, 122
Singh, Tara, 284
Singh, Ujjal, 122, 126, 150, 158, 163, 253
Skeen (Indian Sandhurst) Committee (1926), 9
Slocombe, George, 175–7
Smith, H. B. Lees, 150, 233, 236
Snowden, Philip, and Irwin declaration, 67, 74–9, 83
Special Powers Ordinance (1932), 258
Stanley, Oliver, 118, 154, 155, 161
Statutory Commission. See Simon Commission
Strakosch, Sir Henry, 268–9
Stopford, R. J., 118
Strathcona, Lord, 50
Sykes, Sir Frederick, 186

Tambe, S. B., 18, 122
Thakurdas, Sir Purshotamdas, 95, 217, 253, 269–70 284, 287–8; and civil disobedience, 173–5, 179–81, 183
Times, The, 41, 72, 73
Trade Unions, All-India Federation of, 99
Travancore, 28, 32, 127, 129, 138, 280, 282, 301, 304, 309

Udaipur, 28, 280, 282, 300, 301
Unionist Party (Punjab), 21, 121
United Provinces, 221, 311; and Montford constitution, 3, 5, 12, 15–16, 19, 22, 34; and rent agitation, 194–204, 206, 210, 240–9, 289

Unlawful Association Ordinance (1931–2), 207, 245–7, 250
Unlawful Instigation Ordinances (May 1930 and 1931–2), 197, 245, 246, 250
Untouchables. See Depressed Classes

Vincent, Sir William, 5

Watson, Sir Charles, 129, 134, 283, 304
Williams, Professor L. F. Rushbrook, 32, 127, 271
Willingdon, Lady, 205 n.
Willingdon, Lord, 3, 192, 255, 286, 311; and second settlement, 201–4, 238–41, 243; and fiscal and currency policies, 215, 217, 269–70; and paramountcy, 226–7, 277–9; and all-India federation, 232, 237–8, 252, 273–4; and repression, 246–9, 251–2, 266, 288, 290, 292, 294, 314; and British reaction, 253, 257, 259–61; and communal award, 262–4; poor diplomacy of, 279–84, 298–303; and Dominion Status, 297–8
Wilson, F. W., 54, 226
Wilson, Sir Leslie, 194
Winterton, Lord, 118, 284; and Irwin declaration, 68, 74, 82, 87, 91, 93
Worthington-Evans, Sir L., 6, 81, 83, 86
Wylie, Francis, 304

York, Archbishop of, 266
Young India, 97, 202

Zafrullah Khan, Chaudhuri, 121, 193, 219, 253, 262, 284
Zetland, Marquess of, 118, 149, 154